Hands-On Ensemble Learning with R

A beginner's guide to combining the power of machine learning algorithms using ensemble techniques

Prabhanjan Narayanachar Tattar

Lead Statistician and Manager
Ford Motor Company

BIRMINGHAM - MUMBAI

Hands-On Ensemble Learning with R

Commissioning Editor: Sunith Shetty
Acquisition Editor: Tushar Gupta
Content Development Editor: Aaryaman Singh
Technical Editor: Dinesh Chaudhary
Copy Editors: Safis Editing
Project Coordinator: Manthan Patel
Proofreader: Safis Editing
Indexer: Mariammal Chettiyar
Graphics: Jisha Chirayil
Production Coordinator: Nilesh Mohite

First published: July 2018

Production reference: 1250718

Published by Packt Publishing Ltd.
Livery Place
35 Livery Street
Birmingham B3 2PB, UK.

ISBN 978-1-78862-414-5

www.packtpub.com

On the personal front, I continue to benefit from the support of my family: my daughter, Pranathi; my wife, Chandrika; and my parents, Lakshmi and Narayanachar. The difference in their support from acknowledgement in earlier books is that now I am in Chennai and they support me from Bengaluru. It involves a lot of sacrifice to allow a writer his private time with writing. I also thank my managers, K. Sridharan, Anirban Singha, and Madhu Rao, at Ford Motor Company for their support. Anirban had gone through some of the draft chapters and expressed confidence in the treatment of topics in the book.

My association with Packt is now six years and four books! This is the third title I have done with Tushar Gupta and it is needless to say that I enjoy working with him. Menka Bohra and Aaryaman Singh have put a lot of faith in my work and strived to accommodate the delays, so special thanks to both of them. Manthan Patel and Snehal Kolte have also extended their support. Finally, it is a great pleasure to thank Storm Mann for improving the language of the book. If you still come across a few mistakes, the blame is completely mine.

It is a pleasure to dedicate this book to them for all their support.

`mapt.io`

Mapt is an online digital library that gives you full access to over 5,000 books and videos, as well as industry leading tools to help you plan your personal development and advance your career. For more information, please visit our website.

Why subscribe?

- Spend less time learning and more time coding with practical eBooks and Videos from over 4,000 industry professionals

- Learn better with Skill Plans built especially for you

- Get a free eBook or video every month

- Mapt is fully searchable

- Copy and paste, print, and bookmark content

PacktPub.com

Did you know that Packt offers eBook versions of every book published, with PDF and ePub files available? You can upgrade to the eBook version at `www.PacktPub.com` and as a print book customer, you are entitled to a discount on the eBook copy. Get in touch with us at `service@packtpub.com` for more details.

At `www.PacktPub.com`, you can also read a collection of free technical articles, sign up for a range of free newsletters, and receive exclusive discounts and offers on Packt books and eBooks.

Contributors

About the author

Prabhanjan Narayanachar Tattar is a lead statistician and manager at the Global Data Insights & Analytics division of Ford Motor Company, Chennai. He received the IBS(IR)-GK Shukla Young Biometrician Award (2005) and Dr. U.S. Nair Award for Young Statistician (2007). He held SRF of CSIR-UGC during his PhD. He has authored books such as *Statistical Application Development with R and Python, 2nd Edition*, Packt; *Practical Data Science Cookbook, 2nd Edition*, Packt; and *A Course in Statistics with R*, Wiley. He has created many R packages.

> The statistics and machine learning community, powered by software engineers, is striving to make the world a better, safer, and more efficient place. I would like to thank these societies on behalf of the reader.

About the reviewer

Antonio L. Amadeu is a data science consultant and is passionate about artificial intelligence and neural networks. He uses machine learning and deep learning algorithms in his daily challenges, solving all types of issues in any business field. He has worked for Unilever, Lloyds Bank, TE Connectivity, Microsoft, and Samsung. As an aspiring astrophysicist, he does some research with the Virtual Observatory group at São Paulo University in Brazil, a member of the International Virtual Observatory Alliance – IVOA.

Packt is Searching for Authors Like You

If you're interested in becoming an author for Packt, please visit `authors.packtpub.com` and apply today. We have worked with thousands of developers and tech professionals, just like you, to help them share their insight with the global tech community. You can make a general application, apply for a specific hot topic that we are recruiting an author for, or submit your own idea.

Table of Contents

Preface

Ensemble learning! This specialized topic of machine learning broadly deals with putting together multiple models with the aim of providing higher accuracy and stable model performance. The ensemble methodology is based on sound theory and its usage has seen successful applications in complex data science scenarios. This book grabs the opportunity of dealing with this important topic.

Moderately sized datasets are used throughout the book. All the concepts—well, most of them—have been illustrated using the software, and R packages have been liberally used to drive home the point. While care has been taken to ensure that all the codes are error free, please feel free to write us with any bugs or errors in the codes. The approach has been mildly validated through two mini-courses based on earlier drafts. The material was well received by my colleagues and that gave me enough confidence to complete the book.

The Packt editorial team has helped a lot with the technical review, and the manuscript reaches you after a lot of refinement. The bugs and shortcomings belong to the author.

Who this book is for

This book is for anyone who wants to master machine learning by building ensemble models with the power of R. Basic knowledge of machine learning techniques and programming knowledge of R are expected in order to get the most out of the book.

What this book covers

Chapter 1, *Introduction to Ensemble Techniques*, will give an exposition to the need for ensemble learning, important datasets, essential statistical and machine learning models, and important statistical tests. This chapter displays the spirit of the book.

Chapter 2, Bootstrapping, will introduce the two important concepts of jackknife and bootstrap. The chapter will help you carry out statistical inference related to unknown complex parameters. Bootstrapping of essential statistical models, such as linear regression, survival, and time series, is illustrated through R programs. More importantly, it lays the basis for resampling techniques that forms the core of ensemble methods.

Chapter 3, Bagging, will propose the first ensemble method of using a decision tree as a base model. Bagging is a combination of the words *bootstrap aggregation*. Pruning of decision trees is illustrated, and it will lay down the required foundation for later chapters. Bagging of decision trees and k-NN classifiers are illustrated in this chapter.

Chapter 4, Random Forests, will discuss the important ensemble extension of decision trees. Variable importance and proximity plots are two important components of random forests, and we carry out the related computations about them. The nuances of random forests are explained in depth. Comparison with the bagging method, missing data imputation, and clustering with random forests are also dealt with in this chapter.

Chapter 5, The Bare-Bones Boosting Algorithms, will first state the boosting algorithm. Using toy data, the chapter will then explain the detailed computations of the adaptive boosting algorithm. Gradient boosting algorithm is then illustrated for the regression problem. The use of the gbm and adabag packages shows implementations of other boosting algorithms. The chapter concludes with a comparison of the bagging, random forest, and boosting methods.

Chapter 6, Boosting Refinements, will begin with an explanation of the working of the boosting technique. The gradient boosting algorithm is then extended to count and survival datasets. The extreme gradient boosting implementation of the popular gradient boosting algorithm details are exhibited with clear programs. The chapter concludes with an outline of the important h2o package.

Chapter 7, The General Ensemble Technique, will study the probabilistic reasons for the success of the ensemble technique. The success of the ensemble is explained for classification and regression problems.

Chapter 8, Ensemble Diagnostics, will examine the conditions for the diversity of an ensemble. Pairwise comparisons of classifiers and overall interrater agreement measures are illustrated here.

Chapter 9, Ensembling Regression Models, will discuss in detail the use of ensemble methods in regression problems. A complex housing dataset from kaggle is used here. The regression data is modeled with multiple base learners. Bagging, random forest, boosting, and stacking are all illustrated for the regression data.

Chapter 10, Ensembling Survival Models, is where survival data is taken up. Survival analysis concepts are developed in considerable detail, and the traditional techniques are illustrated. The machine learning method of a survival tree is introduced, and then we build the ensemble method of random survival forests for this data structure.

Chapter 11, Ensembling Time Series Models, deals with another specialized data structure in which observations are dependent on each other. The core concepts of time series and the essential related models are developed. Bagging of a specialized time series model is presented, and we conclude the chapter with an ensemble of heterogeneous time series models.

Chapter 12, What's Next?, will discuss some of the unresolved topics in ensemble learning and the scope for future work.

To get the most out of this book

1. The official website of R is the **Comprehensive R Archive Network (CRAN)** at www.cran.r-project.org. At the time of writing this book, the most recent version of R is 3.5.1. This software is available for three platforms: Linux, macOS, and Windows. The reader can also download a nice frontend, such as RStudio.

2. Every chapter has a header section titled *Technical requirements*. It gives a list of R packages required to run the code in that chapter. For example, the requirements for *Chapter 3, Bagging,* are as follows:

    *   class
    *   FNN
    *   ipred
    *   mlbench
    *   rpart

The reader then needs to install all of these packages by running the following lines in the R console:

```
install.packages("class")
install.packages("mlbench")
install.packages("FNN")
install.packages("rpart")
install.packages("ipred")
```

Download the example code files

You can download the example code files for this book from your account at `http://www.packtpub.com`. If you purchased this book elsewhere, you can visit `http://www.packtpub.com/support` and register to have the files emailed directly to you.

You can download the code files by following these steps:

1. Log in or register at `http://www.packtpub.com`.
2. Select the **SUPPORT** tab.
3. Click on **Code Downloads & Errata**.
4. Enter the name of the book in the **Search** box and follow the on-screen instructions.

Once the file is downloaded, please make sure that you unzip or extract the folder using the latest version of:

- WinRAR / 7-Zip for Windows
- Zipeg / iZip / UnRarX for Mac
- 7-Zip / PeaZip for Linux

The code bundle for the book is also hosted on GitHub at `https://github.com/PacktPublishing/Hands-On-Ensemble-Learning-with-R`. In case there's an update to the code, it will be updated on the existing GitHub repository.

We also have other code bundles from our rich catalog of books and videos available at `https://github.com/PacktPublishing/`. Check them out!

Download the color images

We also provide a PDF file that has color images of the screenshots/diagrams used in this book. You can download it here: `http://www.packtpub.com/sites/default/files/downloads/HandsOnEnsembleLearningwithR_ColorImages.pdf`.

Conventions used

There are a number of text conventions used throughout this book.

`CodeInText`: Indicates code words in text, database table names, folder names, filenames, file extensions, pathnames, dummy URLs, user input, and Twitter handles. For example; "The computation of the values of the density functions using the `dexp` function."

A block of code is set as follows:

```
> Events_Prob <- apply(Elements_Prob,1,prod)
> Majority_Events <- (rowSums(APC)>NT/2)
> sum(Events_Prob*Majority_Events)
[1] 0.9112646
```

Bold: Indicates a new term, an important word, or words that you see on the screen, for example, in menus or dialog boxes, also appear in the text like this. For example: "Select **System info** from the **Administration** panel."

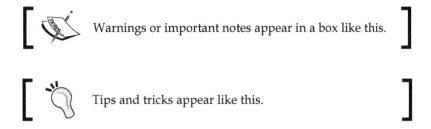

Warnings or important notes appear in a box like this.

Tips and tricks appear like this.

Get in touch

Feedback from our readers is always welcome.

General feedback: Email feedback@packtpub.com, and mention the book's title in the subject of your message. If you have questions about any aspect of this book, please email us at questions@packtpub.com.

Errata: Although we have taken every care to ensure the accuracy of our content, mistakes do happen. If you have found a mistake in this book we would be grateful if you would report this to us. Please visit, http://www.packtpub.com/submit-errata, selecting your book, clicking on the Errata Submission Form link, and entering the details.

Piracy: If you come across any illegal copies of our works in any form on the Internet, we would be grateful if you would provide us with the location address or website name. Please contact us at copyright@packtpub.com with a link to the material.

If you are interested in becoming an author: If there is a topic that you have expertise in and you are interested in either writing or contributing to a book, please visit http://authors.packtpub.com.

Reviews

Please leave a review. Once you have read and used this book, why not leave a review on the site that you purchased it from? Potential readers can then see and use your unbiased opinion to make purchase decisions, we at Packt can understand what you think about our products, and our authors can see your feedback on their book. Thank you!

For more information about Packt, please visit `packtpub.com`.

1
Introduction to Ensemble Techniques

Ensemble techniques are model output aggregating techniques that have evolved over the past decade and a half in the area of statistical and machine learning. This forms the central theme of this book. Any user of statistical models and machine learning tools will be familiar with the problem of building a model and the vital decision of choosing among potential candidate models. A model's accuracy is certainly not the only relevant criterion; we are also concerned with its complexity, as well as whether or not the overall model makes practical sense.

Common modeling problems include the decision to choose a model, and various methodologies exist to aid this task. In statistics, we resort to measures such as **Akaike Information Criteria (AIC)** and **Bayesian Information Criteria (BIC)**, and on other fronts, the p-value associated with the variable in the fitted model helps with the decision. This is a process generally known as **model selection**. Ridge penalty, Lasso, and other statistics also help with this task. For machine learning models such as neural networks, decision trees, and so on, a k-fold cross-validation is useful when the model is built using a part of the data referred to as training data, and then accuracy is looked for in the untrained area or validation data. If the model is sensitive to its complexity, the exercise could be futile.

The process of obtaining the *best* model means that we create a host of other models, which are themselves nearly as efficient as the best model. Moreover, the best model accurately covers the majority of samples, and other models might accurately assess the variable space region where it is inaccurate. Consequently, we can see that the final shortlisted model has few advantages over the runner up. The next models in line are not so poor as to merit outright rejection. This makes it necessary to find a way of taking most of the results already obtained from the models and combining them in a meaningful way. The search for a method for putting together various models is the main objective of ensemble learning. Alternatively, one can say that ensemble learning transforms competing models into collaborating models. In fact, ensemble techniques are not the end of the modeling exercise, as they will also be extended to the unsupervised learning problems. We will demonstrate an example that justifies the need for this.

The implementation of ensemble methods would have been impossible without the invention of modern computational power. Statistical methods foresaw techniques that required immense computations. Methods such as permutation tests and jackknife are evidence of the effectiveness of computational power. We will undertake an exercise to learn these later in the chapter, and we will revisit them later on in the book.

From a machine learning perspective, *supervised* and *unsupervised* are the two main types of learning technique. **Supervised learning** is the arm of machine learning, the process in which a certain variable is known, and the purpose is to understand this variable through various other variables. Here, we have a target variable. Since learning takes place with respect to the output variable, supervised learning is sometimes referred to as learning with a teacher. All target variables are not alike, and they often fall under one of the following four types. If the goal is to classify observations into one of k types of class (for example, Yes/No, Satisfied/Dissatisfied), then we have a classification problem. Such a variable is referred to as a *categorical variable* in statistics. It is possible that the variable of interest might be a continuous variable, which is numeric from a software perspective. This may include car mileage per liter, a person's income, or a person's age. For such scenarios, the purpose of the machine learning problem is to learn the variables in terms of other associated variables, and then predict it for unknown cases in which only the values of associated variables are available. We will broadly refer to this class of problem as a **regression problem**.

In clinical trials, the time to event is often of interest. When an illness is diagnosed, we would ask whether the proposed drug is an improvement on the existing one. While the variable in question here is the length of time between diagnosis and death, clinical trial data poses several other problems. The analysis cannot wait until all the patients have died, and/or some of the patients may have moved away from the study, making it no longer possible to know their status. Consequently, we have censored data. As part of the study observations, complete information is not available. Survival analysis largely deals with such problems, and we will undertake the problem of creating ensemble models here.

With classification, regression, and survival data, it may be assumed that that the instances/observations are independent of each other. This is a very reasonable assumption in that there is a valid reason to believe that patients will respond to a drug independently of other patients, a customer will churn or pay the loan independently of other customers, and so forth. In yet another important class of problems, this assumption is not met, and we are left with observations depending on each other via time series data. An example of time series data is the closure stock exchange points of a company. Clearly, the performance of a company's stock can't be independent each day, and thus we need to factor in dependency.

In many practical problems, the goal is to understand patterns or find groups of observations, and we don't have a specific variable of interest with regard to which algorithm needs to be trained. Finding groups or clusters is referred to as unsupervised learning or learning without a teacher. Two main practical problems that arise in finding clusters is that (i) it is generally not known in advance how many clusters are in the population, and (ii) different choices of initial cluster centers lead to different solutions. Thus, we need a solution that is free from, or at least indifferent to, initialization and takes the positives of each useful solution into consideration. This will lead us toward unsupervised ensemble techniques.

The search for the best models, supervised or unsupervised, is often hindered by the presence of outliers. The presence of a single outlier is known to heavily influence the overall fit of linear models, and it is also known to significantly impact even nonlinear models. Outlier detection is a challenge in itself, and a huge body of statistical methods help in identifying outliers. A host of machine learning methods also help in identifying outliers. Of course, ensembles will help here, and we will develop R programs that will help solve the problem of identifying outliers. This method will be referred to as outlier ensembles.

At the outset, it is important that the reader becomes familiar with the datasets used in this book. All major datasets will be introduced in the first section. We begin the chapter with a brief introduction to the core statistical/machine learning models and put them into action immediately afterward. It will quickly become apparent that there is not a single class of model that would perform better than any other model. If any such solution existed, we wouldn't need the ensemble technique.

In this chapter, we will cover:

- **Datasets**: The core datasets that will be used throughout the book
- **Statistical/machine learning models**: Important classification models will be explained here
- **The right model dilemma**: The absence of a *dominating* model
- **An ensemble purview**: The need for ensembles
- **Complementary statistical tests**: Important statistical tests that will be useful for model comparisons will be discussed here

The following R packages will be required for this chapter:

- ACSWR
- caret
- e1071
- factoextra
- mlbench
- NeuralNetTools
- perm
- pROC
- RSADBE
- Rpart
- survival
- nnet

Datasets

Data is undoubtedly the most important component of machine learning. If there was no data, we wouldn't have a common purpose. In most cases, the purpose for which the data is collected defines the problem itself. As we know that the variable might be of several types, the way it is stored and organized is also very important.

Lee and Elder (1997) considered a series of datasets and introduced the need for ensemble models. We will begin by looking at the details of the datasets considered in their paper, and we will then refer to other important datasets later on in the book.

Hypothyroid

The hypothyroid dataset `Hypothyroid.csv` is available in the book's code bundle packet, located at `/.../Chapter01/Data`. While we have 26 variables in the dataset, we will only be using seven of these variables. Here, the number of observations is n = 3163. The dataset is downloaded from `http://archive.ics.uci.edu/ml/datasets/thyroid+disease` and the filename is `hypothyroid.data` (`http://archive.ics.uci.edu/ml/machine-learning-databases/thyroid-disease/hypothyroid.data`). After some tweaks to the order of relabeling certain values, the CSV file is made available in the book's code bundle. The purpose of the study is to classify a patient with a thyroid problem based on the information provided by other variables. There are multiple variants of the dataset and the reader can delve into details at the following web page: `http://archive.ics.uci.edu/ml/machine-learning-databases/thyroid-disease/HELLO`. Here, the column representing the variable of interest is named `Hypothyroid`, which shows that we have 151 patients with thyroid problems. The remaining 3012 tested negative for it. Clearly, this dataset is an example of *unbalanced data*, which means that one of the two cases is outnumbered by a huge number; for each thyroid case, we have about 20 negative cases. Such problems need to be handled differently, and we need to get into the subtleties of the algorithms to build meaningful models. The additional variables or covariates that we will use while building the predictive models include `Age`, `Gender`, `TSH`, `T3`, `TT4`, `T4U`, and `FTI`. The data is first imported into an R session and is subset according to the variables of interest as follows:

```
> HT <- read.csv("../Data/Hypothyroid.csv",header =
TRUE,stringsAsFactors = F)
> HT$Hypothyroid <- as.factor(HT$Hypothyroid)
> HT2 <- HT[,c("Hypothyroid","Age","Gender","TSH","T3","TT4","T4U","F
TI")]
```

The first line of code imports the data from the `Hypothyroid.csv` file using the `read.csv` function. The dataset now has a lot of missing data in the variables, as seen here:

```
> sapply(HT2,function(x) sum(is.na(x)))
Hypothyroid         Age        Gender         TSH          T3
TT4
          0         446            73         468         695
249
        T4U         FTI
        248         247
```

Consequently, we remove all the rows that have a missing value, and then split the data into training and testing datasets. We will also create a formula for the classification problem:

```
> HT2 <- na.omit(HT2)
> set.seed(12345)
> Train_Test <- sample(c("Train","Test"),nrow(HT2),replace=TRUE,
prob=c(0.7,0.3))
> head(Train_Test)
[1] "Test"  "Test"  "Test"  "Test"  "Train" "Train"
> HT2_Train <- HT2[Train_Test=="Train",]
> HT2_TestX <- within(HT2[Train_Test=="Test",],rm(Hypothyroid))
> HT2_TestY <- HT2[Train_Test=="Test",c("Hypothyroid")]
> HT2_Formula <- as.formula("Hypothyroid~.")
```

The `set.seed` function ensures that the results are reproducible each time we run the program. After removing the missing observations with the `na.omit` function, we split the hypothyroid data into training and testing parts. The former is used to build the model and the latter is used to validate it, using data that has not been used to build the model. Quinlan – the inventor of the popular tree algorithm C4.5 – used this dataset extensively.

Waveform

This dataset is an example of a simulation study. Here, we have twenty-one variables as input or independent variables, and a class variable referred to as `classes`. The data is generated using the `mlbench.waveform` function from the `mlbench` R package. For more details, refer to the following link: `ftp://ftp.ics.uci.edu/pub/machine-learning-databases`. We will simulate 5,000 observations for this dataset. As mentioned earlier, the `set.seed` function guarantees reproducibility. Since we are solving binary classification problems, we will reduce the three classes generated by the waveform function to two, and then partition the data into training and testing parts for model building and testing purposes:

```
> library(mlbench)
> set.seed(123)
> Waveform <- mlbench.waveform(5000)
> table(Waveform$classes)

   1    2    3
1687 1718 1595
> Waveform$classes <- ifelse(Waveform$classes!=3,1,2)
> Waveform_DF <- data.frame(cbind(Waveform$x,Waveform$classes)) # Data
Frame
> names(Waveform_DF) <- c(paste0("X",".",1:21),"Classes")
```

```
> Waveform_DF$Classes <- as.factor(Waveform_DF$Classes)
> table(Waveform_DF$Classes)
   1    2
3405 1595
```

The R function `mlbench.waveform` creates a new object of the `mlbench` class. Since it consists of two sub-parts in x and classes, we will convert it into `data.frame` following some further manipulations. The `cbind` function binds the two objects x (a matrix) and classes (a numeric vector) into a single matrix. The `data.frame` function converts the matrix object into a data frame, which is the class desired for the rest of the program.

After partitioning the data, we will create the required `formula` for the waveform dataset:

```
> set.seed(12345)
> Train_Test <- sample(c("Train","Test"),nrow(Waveform_DF),replace =
TRUE,
+ prob = c(0.7,0.3))
> head(Train_Test)
[1] "Test"  "Test"  "Test"  "Test"  "Train" "Train"
> Waveform_DF_Train <- Waveform_DF[Train_Test=="Train",]
> Waveform_DF_TestX <- within(Waveform_DF[Train_
Test=="Test",],rm(Classes))
> Waveform_DF_TestY <- Waveform_DF[Train_Test=="Test","Classes"]
> Waveform_DF_Formula <- as.formula("Classes~.")
```

German Credit

Loans are not always repaid in full, and there are defaulters. In this case, it becomes important for the bank to identify potential defaulters based on the available information. Here, we adapt the GC dataset from the RSADBE package to properly reflect the labels of the factor variable. The transformed dataset is available as `GC2.RData` in the data folder. The GC dataset itself is mainly an adaptation of the version available at `https://archive.ics.uci.edu/ml/datasets/statlog+(german+credit+data)`. Here, we have 1,000 observations, and 20 covariate/independent variables such as the status of existing checking account, duration, and so forth. The final status of whether the loan was completely paid or not is available in the `good_bad` column. We will partition the data into training and testing parts, and create the formula too:

```
> library(RSADBE)
> load("../Data/GC2.RData")
> table(GC2$good_bad)
 bad good
```

```
  300   700
> set.seed(12345)
> Train_Test <- sample(c("Train","Test"),nrow(GC2),replace =
TRUE,prob=c(0.7,0.3))
> head(Train_Test)
[1] "Test"  "Test"  "Test"  "Test"  "Train" "Train"
> GC2_Train <- GC2[Train_Test=="Train",]
> GC2_TestX <- within(GC2[Train_Test=="Test",],rm(good_bad))
> GC2_TestY <- GC2[Train_Test=="Test","good_bad"]
> GC2_Formula <- as.formula("good_bad~.")
```

Iris

Iris is probably the most famous classification dataset. The great statistician Sir R. A. Fisher popularized the dataset, which he used for classifying the three types of iris plants based on length and width measurements of their petals and sepals. Fisher used this dataset to pioneer the invention of the statistical classifier linear discriminant analysis. Since there are three species of iris, we converted this into a binary classification problem, separated the dataset, and created a formula as seen here:

```
> data("iris")
> ir2 <- iris
> ir2$Species <- ifelse(ir2$Species=="setosa","S","NS")
> ir2$Species <- as.factor(ir2$Species)
> set.seed(12345)
> Train_Test <- sample(c("Train","Test"),nrow(ir2),replace =
TRUE,prob=c(0.7,0.3))
> head(Train_Test)
[1] "Test"  "Test"  "Test"  "Test"  "Train" "Train"
> ir2_Train <- ir2[Train_Test=="Train",]
> ir2_TestX <- within(ir2[Train_Test=="Test",],rm(Species))
> ir2_TestY <- ir2[Train_Test=="Test","Species"]
> ir2_Formula <- as.formula("Species~.")
```

Pima Indians Diabetes

Diabetes is a health hazard, which is mostly incurable, and patients who are diagnosed with it have to adjust their lifestyles in order to cater to this condition. Based on variables such as pregnant, glucose, pressure, triceps, insulin, mass, pedigree, and age, the problem here is to classify the person as diabetic or not. Here, we have 768 observations. This dataset is drawn from the mlbench package:

```
> data("PimaIndiansDiabetes")
> set.seed(12345)
> Train_Test <- sample(c("Train","Test"),nrow(PimaIndiansDiabetes),re
place = TRUE,
```

```
+ prob = c(0.7,0.3))
> head(Train_Test)
[1] "Test"  "Test"  "Test"  "Test"  "Train" "Train"
> PimaIndiansDiabetes_Train <- PimaIndiansDiabetes[Train_
Test=="Train",]
> PimaIndiansDiabetes_TestX <- within(PimaIndiansDiabetes[Train_
Test=="Test",],
+                                       rm(diabetes))
> PimaIndiansDiabetes_TestY <- PimaIndiansDiabetes[Train_
Test=="Test","diabetes"]
> PID_Formula <- as.formula("diabetes~.")
```

The five datasets described up to this point are classification problems. We look at one example each for regression, time series, survival, clustering, and outlier detection problems.

US Crime

A study of the crime rate per million of the population among the 47 different states of the US is undertaken here, and an attempt is made to find its dependency on 13 variables. These include age distribution, indicator of southern states, average number of schooling years, and so on. As with the earlier datasets, we will also partition this one into the following chunks of R program:

```
> library(ACSWR)
Warning message:
package 'ACSWR' was built under R version 3.4.1
> data(usc)
> str(usc)
'data.frame':    47 obs. of  14 variables:
 $ R  : num  79.1 163.5 57.8 196.9 123.4 ...
 $ Age: int  151 143 142 136 141 121 127 131 157 140 ...
 $ S  : int  1 0 1 0 0 0 1 1 1 0 ...
 $ Ed : int  91 113 89 121 121 110 111 109 90 118 ...
 $ Ex0: int  58 103 45 149 109 118 82 115 65 71 ...
 $ Ex1: int  56 95 44 141 101 115 79 109 62 68 ...
 $ LF : int  510 583 533 577 591 547 519 542 553 632 ...
 $ M  : int  950 1012 969 994 985 964 982 969 955 1029 ...
 $ N  : int  33 13 18 157 18 25 4 50 39 7 ...
 $ NW : int  301 102 219 80 30 44 139 179 286 15 ...
 $ U1 : int  108 96 94 102 91 84 97 79 81 100 ...
 $ U2 : int  41 36 33 39 20 29 38 35 28 24 ...
 $ W  : int  394 557 318 673 578 689 620 472 421 526 ...
 $ X  : int  261 194 250 167 174 126 168 206 239 174 ...
```

```
> set.seed(12345)
> Train_Test <- sample(c("Train","Test"),nrow(usc),replace =
TRUE,prob=c(0.7,0.3))
> head(Train_Test)
[1] "Test"  "Test"  "Test"  "Test"  "Train" "Train"
> usc_Train <- usc[Train_Test=="Train",]
> usc_TestX <- within(usc[Train_Test=="Test",],rm(R))
> usc_TestY <- usc[Train_Test=="Test","R"]
> usc_Formula <- as.formula("R~.")
```

In each example discussed in this section thus far, we had a reason to believe that the observations are independent of each other. This assumption simply means that the regressands and regressors of one observation have no relationship with other observations' regressands and regressors. This is a simple and reasonable assumption. We have another class of observations/datasets where such assumptions are not practical. For example, the maximum temperature of a day is not completely independent of the previous day's temperature. If that were to be the case, we could have a scorchingly hot day, followed by winter, followed by another hot day, which in turn is followed by a very heavy rainy day. However, weather does not happen in this way as on successive days, the weather is dependent on previous days. In the next example, we consider the number of overseas visitors to New Zealand.

Overseas visitors

The New Zealand overseas dataset is dealt with in detail in Chapter 10 of Tattar, et al. (2017). Here, the number of overseas visitors is captured on a monthly basis from January 1977 to December 1995. We have visitors' data available for over 228 months. The osvisit.dat file is available at multiple web links, including https://www.stat.auckland.ac.nz/~ihaka/courses/726-/osvisit.dat and https://github.com/AtefOuni/ts/blob/master/Data/osvisit.dat. It is also available in the book's code bundle. We will import the data in R, convert it into a time series object, and visualize it:

```
> osvisit <- read.csv("../Data/osvisit.dat", header= FALSE)
> osv <- ts(osvisit$V1, start = 1977, frequency = 12)
> class(osv)
[1] "ts"
> plot.ts(osv)
```

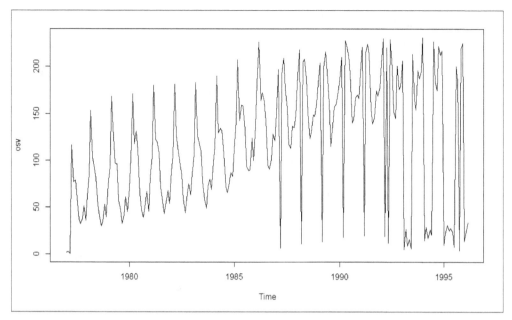

Figure 1: New Zealand overseas visitors

Here, the dataset is not partitioned! Time series data can't be arbitrarily partitioned into training and testing parts. The reason is quite simple: if we have five observations in a time sequential order $y1$, $y2$, $y3$, $y4$, $y5$, and we believe that the order of impact is $y1{\to}y2{\to}y3{\to}y4{\to}y5$, an arbitrary partition of $y1$, $y2$, $y5$, will have different behavior. It won't have the same information as three consecutive observations. Consequently, the time series partitioning has to preserve the dependency structure; we keep the most recent part of the time as the test data. For the five observations example, we choose a sample of $y1$, $y2$, $y3$, as the test data. The partitioning is simple, and we will cover this in *Chapter 11, Ensembling Time Series Models*.

Live testing experiments rarely yield complete observations. In reliability analysis, as well as survival analysis/clinical trials, the units/patients are observed up to a predefined time and a note is made regarding whether a specific event occurs, which is usually failure or death. A considerable fraction of observations would not have failed by the pre-decided time, and the analysis cannot wait for all units to fail. A reason to curtail the study might be that the time by which all units would have failed would be very large, and it would be expensive to continue the study until such a time. Consequently, we are left with incomplete observations; we only know that the lifetime of the units lasts for at least the predefined time before the study was called off, and the event of interest may occur sometime in the future. Consequently, some observations are censored and the data is referred to as censored data. Special statistical methods are required for the analysis of such datasets. We will give an example of these types of datasets next, and analyze them later, in *Chapter 10, Ensembling Survival Models*.

Primary Biliary Cirrhosis

The pbc dataset from the survival package is a benchmark dataset in the domain of clinical trials. Mayo Clinic collected the data, which is concerned with the primary biliary cirrhosis (PBC) of the liver. The study was conducted between 1974 and 1984. More details can be found by running pbc, followed by library(survival) on the R terminal. Here, the main time to the event of interest is the number of days between registration and either death, transplantation, or study analysis in July 1986, and this is captured in the time variable. Similarly to a survival study, the events might be censored and the indicator is in the column status. The time to event needs to be understood, factoring in variables such as trt, age, sex, ascites, hepato, spiders, edema, bili, chol, albumin, copper, alk.phos, ast, trig, platelet, protime, and stage.

The eight datasets discussed up until this point have a target variable, or a regressand/dependent variable, and are examples of the supervised learning problem. On the other hand, there are practical cases in which we simply attempt to understand the data and find useful patterns and groups/clusters in it. Of course, it is important to note that the purpose of clustering is to find an identical group and give it a sensible label. For instance, if we are trying to group cars based on their characteristics such as length, width, horsepower, engine cubic capacity, and so on, we may find groups that might be labeled as hatch, sedan, and saloon classes, while another clustering solutions might result in labels of basic, premium, and sports variant groups. The two main problems posed in clustering are the choice of the number of groups and the formation of robust clusters. We consider a simple dataset from the factoextra R package.

Multishapes

The multishapes dataset from the factoextra package consists of three variables: x, y, and shape. It consists of different shapes, with each shape forming a cluster. Here, we have two concurrent circle shapes, two parallel rectangles/beds, and one cluster of points at the bottom-right. Outliers are also added across scatterplots. Some brief R code gives a useful display:

```
> library(factoextra)
> data("multishapes")
> names(multishapes)
[1] "x"      "y"      "shape"
> table(multishapes$shape)
  1    2    3    4    5    6
400  400  100  100   50   50
> plot(multishapes[,1],multishapes[,2],col=multishapes[,3])
```

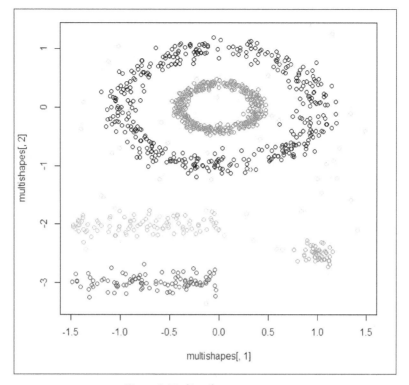

Figure 2: Finding shapes or groups

This dataset includes a column named shape, as it is a hypothetical dataset. In true clustering problems, we will have neither a cluster group indicator nor the visualization luxury of only two variables. Later in this book, we will see how ensemble clustering techniques help overcome the problems of deciding the number of clusters and the consistency of cluster membership.

Although it doesn't happen that often, frustrations can arise when fine-tuning different parameters, fitting different models, and other tricks all fail to find a useful working model. The culprit of this is often the outlier. A single outlier is known to wreak havoc on an otherwise potentially useful model, and their detection is of paramount importance. Hitherto this, the parametric and nonparametric outlier detections would be a matter of deep expertise. In complex scenarios, the identification would be an insurmountable task. A consensus on an observation being an outlier can be achieved using the ensemble outlier framework. To consider this, the board stiffness dataset will be considered. We will see how an outlier is pinned down in the conclusion of this book.

Board Stiffness

The board stiffness dataset is available in the ACSWR package through the stiff data. frame stiff. The dataset consists of four measures of stiffness for 30 boards. The first measure of stiffness is obtained by sending a shock wave down the board, the second measure is obtained by vibrating the board, and the remaining two are obtained from static tests. A quick method of identifying the outliers in a multivariate dataset is by using the Mahalanobis distance function. The further the distance an observation is from the center, the more likely it is that the observation will be an outlier:

```
> data(stiff)
> sort(mahalanobis(stiff,colMeans(stiff),cov(stiff)),decreasing =
TRUE)
 [1]  16.8474070168  12.2647549939   9.8980384087   7.6166439053
 [5]   6.2837628235   5.4770195915   5.2076098038   5.0557446013
 [9]   4.9883497928   4.5767867224   3.9900602512   3.5018290410
[13]   3.3979804418   2.9951752177   2.6959023813   2.5838186338
[17]   2.5385575365   2.3816049840   2.2191408683   1.9307771418
[21]   1.4876569689   1.4649908273   1.3980776252   1.3632123553
[25]   1.0792484215   0.7962095966   0.7665399704   0.6000128595
[29]   0.4635158597   0.1295713581
```

Statistical/machine learning models

The previous section introduced a host of problems through real datasets, and we will now discuss some standard model variants that are useful for dealing with such problems. First, we set up the required mathematical framework.

Suppose that we have n independent pairs of observations, $(Y_i, \mathbf{x}_i), i = 1, \ldots, n$, where Y_i denotes the random variable of interest, also known as the *dependent variable*, regress and, endogenous variable, and so on. $\mathbf{x}_i$ is the associated vector of explanatory variables, or independent/exogenous variables. The explanatory vector will consist of k elements, that is, $\mathbf{x}_i = (x_1, x_2, \ldots, x_k)$. The data realized is of the form $(y_i, \mathbf{x}_i), i = 1, \ldots, n$, where y_i is the realized value (data) of random variable Y_i. A convention will be adapted throughout the book that $x_{i1} = 1, \forall i$, and this will take care of the intercept term. We assume that the observations are from the true distribution F, which is not completely known. The general regression model, including the classification model as well as the regression model, is specified by:

$$Y_i = f(\mathbf{x}_i, \boldsymbol{\beta}) + \epsilon_i$$

Here, the function *f* is an unknown function and β is the regression parameter, which captures the influence of $\mathbf{x}_i$ on Y_i. The error $\in_i$ is the associated unobservable error term. Diverse methods can be applied to model the relationship between the Ys and the xes. The statistical regression model focused on the complete specification of the error distribution $\in$, and in general the functional form would be linear as in $f(\mathbf{x}_i, \beta) = g(\mathbf{x}_i^T \beta)$. The function $g(\mathbf{x}_i^T \beta)$ is the link function in the class of generalized linear models. Nonparametric and semiparametric regression models are more flexible, as we don't place a restriction on the error's probability distribution. Flexibility would come with a price though, and here we need a much higher number of observations to make a valid inference, although that number is unspecified and is often subjective.

The machine learning paradigm includes some *black box* methods, and we have a healthy overlap between this paradigm and non- and semi-parametric models. The reader is also cautioned that black box does not mean unscientific in any sense. The methods have a firm mathematical foundation and are reproducible every time. Next, we quickly review some of the most important statistical and machine learning models, and illustrate them through the datasets discussed earlier.

Logistic regression model

The logistic regression model is a binary classification model, and it is a member of the exponential family which belongs to the class of generalized linear models. Now, let Y_i denote the binary label:

$$Y_i = \begin{cases} 1 & \text{if observation denotes success,} \\ 0, & \text{if observation denotes failure.} \end{cases}$$

Using the information contained in the explanatory vector $\mathbf{x}_i = (x_1, x_2, \ldots, x_k)$ we are trying to build a model that will help in this task. The logistic regression model is the following:

$$\pi(\mathbf{x}) = P(Y = 1) = \frac{e^{x^T \beta}}{1 + e^{x^T \beta'}}$$

Here, $\beta = (\beta_1, \beta_2, \ldots, \beta_k)$ is the vector of regression coefficients. Note that the logit function $\ln\left(\frac{\pi(x)}{1 - \pi(x)}\right) = \mathbf{x}^T \beta$ is linear in the regression coefficients and hence the name for the model is a logistic regression model. A logistic regression model can be equivalently written as follows:

$$y = \pi(\mathbf{x}) + \in$$

Here, $\in$ is the binary error term that follows a Bernoulli distribution. For more information, refer to Chapter 17 of Tattar, et al. (2016). The estimation of the parameters of the logistic regression requires the **iterative reweighted least squares (IRLS)** algorithm, and we would use the `glm` R function to get this task done. We will use the Hypothyroid dataset in this section. In the previous section, the training and test datasets and formulas were already created, and we will carry on from that point.

Logistic regression for hypothyroid classification

For the `hypothyroid` dataset, we had `HT2_Train` as the training dataset. The test dataset is split as the covariate matrix in `HT2_TestX` and the outputs of the test dataset in `HT2_TestY`, while the formula for the logistic regression model is available in `HT2_Formula`. First, the logistic regression model is fitted to the training dataset using the `glm` function and the fitted model is christened `LR_fit`, and then we inspect it for model fit summaries using `summary(LR_fit)`. The fitted model is then applied to the covariate data in the test part using the `predict` function to create `LR_Predict`. The predicted probabilities are then labeled in `LR_Predict_Bin`, and these labels are compared with the actual `testY_numeric` and overall accuracy is obtained:

```
> ntr <- nrow(HT2_Train) # Training size
> nte <- nrow(HT2_TestX) # Test size
> p <- ncol(HT2_TestX)
> testY_numeric <- as.numeric(HT2_TestY)
> LR_fit <- glm(HT2_Formula,data=HT2_Train,family = binomial())
Warning message:
glm.fit: fitted probabilities numerically 0 or 1 occurred
> summary(LR_fit)
Call:
glm(formula = HT2_Formula, family = binomial(), data = HT2_Train)
Deviance Residuals:
    Min       1Q   Median       3Q      Max
-3.6390   0.0076   0.0409   0.1068   3.5127
Coefficients:
             Estimate Std. Error z value Pr(>|z|)
(Intercept) -8.302025   2.365804  -3.509 0.000449 ***
Age         -0.024422   0.012145  -2.011 0.044334 *
GenderMALE  -0.195656   0.464353  -0.421 0.673498
TSH         -0.008457   0.007530  -1.123 0.261384
T3           0.480986   0.347525   1.384 0.166348
TT4         -0.089122   0.028401  -3.138 0.001701 **
T4U          3.932253   1.801588   2.183 0.029061 *
FTI          0.197196   0.035123   5.614 1.97e-08 ***
---
```

```
Signif. codes:  0 '***' 0.001 '**' 0.01 '*' 0.05 '.' 0.1 ' ' 1

(Dispersion parameter for binomial family taken to be 1)

    Null deviance: 609.00  on 1363  degrees of freedom
Residual deviance: 181.42  on 1356  degrees of freedom
AIC: 197.42
Number of Fisher Scoring iterations: 9
> LR_Predict <- predict(LR_fit,newdata=HT2_TestX,type="response")
> LR_Predict_Bin <- ifelse(LR_Predict>0.5,2,1)
> LR_Accuracy <- sum(LR_Predict_Bin==testY_numeric)/nte
> LR_Accuracy
[1] 0.9732704
```

It can be seen from the summary of the fitted GLM (the output following the line
`summary(LR_fit)`) that we are having four significant variables in `Age`, `TT4`, `T4U`,
and `FTI`. Using the `predict` function, we apply the fitted model on unknown test
cases in `HT2_TestX`, compare it with the actuals, and find the accuracy to be 97.33%.
Consequently, logistic regression is easily deployed in the R software.

Neural networks

Logistic regression might appear restricted as it allows only a linear impact of the
covariates through the link function. The linearity assumption might not hold, and
in most practical cases, we don't have enough information to specify the functional
form of the nonlinear relationship. Thus, all we know is that there is most likely an
unknown nonlinear relationship. Neural networks are the nonlinear generalization
of logistic regression, and this involves two important components: hidden neurons
and learning rate. We will revise the structure of neural networks first.

In a neural network, the input variables are considered the first layer of neurons
and the output the final and concluding layer of neurons. The structure of a neural
network model can be visualized using the R package `NeuralNetTools`. Suppose
that we have three input variables and two hidden layers, and each contains two
hidden neurons. Here, we have a neural network with four layers. The next code
segment gives a visualization of a neural network's structure with three input
variables, two hidden neurons in two hidden layers, and one output variable:

```
> library(NeuralNetTools)
> plotnet(rep(0,17),struct=c(3,2,2,1))
> title("A Neural Network with Two Hidden Layers")
```

We find the R package `NeuralNetTools` very useful in visualizing the structure of a neural network. Neural networks built using the core R package `nnet` can also be visualized using the `NeuralNetTools::plotnet` function. The `plotnet` function sets up a neural network whose structure consists of three neurons in the first layer, two neurons in each of the second and third layers, and one in the final output layer, through the `struct` option. The weights along the arcs are set at zero in `rep(0,17)`:

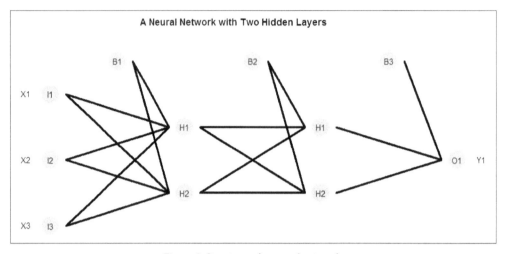

Figure 3: Structure of a neural network

In the previous diagram, we have four layers of the neural network. The first layer consists of **B1** (the bias), **I1 (X1)**, **I2 (X2)**, and **I3 (X3)**. The second layer consists of three neurons in **B2** (the bias of the first hidden layer), **H1**, and **H2**. Note that the bias **B2** does not receive any input from the first hidden layer. Next, each neuron receives an overall input from each of the neurons of the previous layer, which are **B1**, **X1**, **X2**, and **X3** here. However, **H1** and **H2** of the first hidden layer will receive different aggregated input from **B1**, **X1**, **X2**, and **X3**. Appropriate weights are in action on each of the arcs of the network and it is the weights that form the parameters of the neural networks; that is, the arrival of **H1** (of the first layer) would be like $B_1 + w_1^1 X_1 + w_2^1 X_2 + w_3^1 X_3$ and the effective arrival is through a *transfer function*. A transfer function might be an identity function, sigmoidal function, and so on. Similarly, the arrival at the second neuron of the first layer is $B_1 + w_1^2 X_1 + w_2^2 X_2 + w_3^2 X_3$. By extension, **B2**, **H1**, and **H2** (of the first layer) will be the input for the second hidden layer, and **B3**, **H1**, and **H2** will be the input for the final output. At each stage of the neural network, we have weights. The weights need to be determined in such a manner that the difference between predicted output **O1** and the true **Y1** is as small as possible. Note that the logistic regression is a particular case of the neural network as can be seen by directly removing all hidden layers and input layer leads in the output one. The neural network will be fitted for the hypothyroid problem.

Neural network for hypothyroid classification

We use the nnet function from the package of the same name to set up the neural network for the hypothyroid classification problem. The formula, training, and test datasets continue as before. The accuracy calculation follows along similar lines to the segment in logistic regression. The fitted neural network is visualized using the plotnet graphical function from the NeuralNetTools package:

```
> set.seed(12345)
> NN_fit <- nnet(HT2_Formula,data = HT2_Train,size=p,trace=FALSE)
> NN_Predict <- predict(NN_fit,newdata=HT2_TestX,type="class")
> NN_Accuracy <- sum(NN_Predict==HT2_TestY)/nte
> NN_Accuracy
[1] 0.9827044025
> plotnet(NN_fit)
> title("Neural Network for Hypothyroid Classification")
```

Here, the accuracy is 98.27%, which is an improvement on the logistic regression model. The visual display of the fitted model is given in the following diagram. We have fixed the seed for the random initialization of the neural network parameters at 12345, using set.seed(12345), so that the results are reproducible at the reader's end. This is an interesting case for ensemble modeling. Different initial seeds – which the reader can toy around with – will lead to different accuracies. Sometimes, you will get an accuracy lower than any of the models considered in this section, and at other times you will get the highest accuracy. The choice of seed as arbitrary leads to the important question of which solution is useful. Since the seeds are arbitrary, the question of a good seed or a bad seed does not arise. In this case, if a model is giving you a higher accuracy, it does not necessarily mean anything:

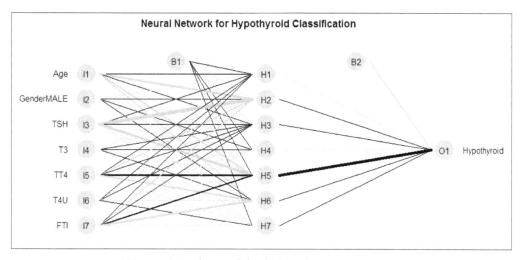

Figure 4: Neural network for the hypothyroid classification

Naïve Bayes classifier

The naïve Bayes classifier is a simplistic implementation based on the Bayes formula. It is based on simple empirical and conditional probabilities, as evidenced in the actual data. Beyond the simplest assumption of observation independence, we don't have any restrictions in using this model.

Naïve Bayes for hypothyroid classification

A naïve Bayes classifier is fit using the `naiveBayes` function from the `e1071` R package. The prediction and accuracy assessment is carried out using two functions, `predict` and `sum`:

```
> NB_fit <- naiveBayes(HT2_Formula,data=HT2_Train)
> NB_predict <- predict(NB_fit,newdata=HT2_TestX)
Warning message:
In data.matrix(newdata) : NAs introduced by coercion
> NB_Accuracy <- sum(NB_predict==HT2_TestY)/nte
> NB_Accuracy
[1] 0.9732704403
```

The accuracy of the naïve Bayes classifier is 97.33%, which is the same as the logistic regression model and less than the one provided by the neural network. We remark here that it is only a coincidence that the accuracy of this method and logistic regression is the same.

Decision tree

Breiman and Quinlan mainly developed decision trees, which have evolved a lot since the 1980s. If the dependent variable is continuous, the decision tree will be a regression tree and if it is categorical variable, it will be a classification tree. Of course, we can have a survival tree as well. Decision trees will be the main model that will be the beneficiary of the ensemble technique, as will be seen throughout the book.

Consider the regression tree given in the following diagram. We can see that there are three input variables, which are X_1, X_2, X_3, and the output variable is Y. Strictly speaking, a decision tree will not display all the variables used to build the tree. In this tree structure, a decision tree is conventionally displayed upside down. We have four terminal nodes. If the condition $X_1 < 25$ is satisfied, we move to the right side of the tree and conclude that the average Y value is 40. If the condition is not satisfied, we move to the left, and check whether $X_2 > 2500$. If this condition is not satisfied, we move to the left side of the tree and conclude that the average Y value is 100. Upon the satisfactory meeting of this condition, we move to the right side and then if the categorical variable $X_3 = 'Good'$, the average Y value would be 250, or 10 otherwise. This decision tree can be captured in the form of an equation too, as follows:

$$Y = 40 I_{\{X_1 < 25\}} + 100 I_{\{X_1 > 25, X_2 \leq 2500\}} + 10 I_{\{X_1 > 25, X_2 > 2500, X_3 = 'Good'\}}$$

$$+ 250 I_{\{X_1 > 25, X_2 > 2500, X_3 \neq 'Good'\}}$$

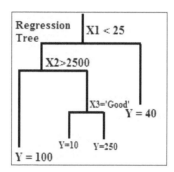

Figure 5: Regression tree

The statistician Terry Therneau developed the `rpart` R package.

Decision tree for hypothyroid classification

Using the `rpart` function from the `rpart` package, we build a classification tree for the same formula as the earlier partitioned data. The constructed tree can be visualized using the plot function, and the variable name is embossed on the tree with the text function. The equation of the fitted classification tree (see Figure *Classification Tree for Hypothyroid*) is the following:

$$Y = 'negative' I_{\{FTI < 63.5\}} + 'negative' I_{\{FTI \geq 63.5, TSH \geq 5.95\}} + 'Hypothyroid' I_{\{FTI \geq 63.5, TSH < 5.95\}}$$

Prediction and accuracy is carried out in a similar way as mentioned earlier:

```
> CT_fit <- rpart(HT2_Formula,data=HT2_Train)
> plot(CT_fit,uniform=TRUE)
> text(CT_fit)
> CT_predict <- predict(CT_fit,newdata=HT2_TestX,type="class")
> CT_Accuracy <- sum(CT_predict==HT2_TestY)/nte
> CT_Accuracy
[1] 0.9874213836
```

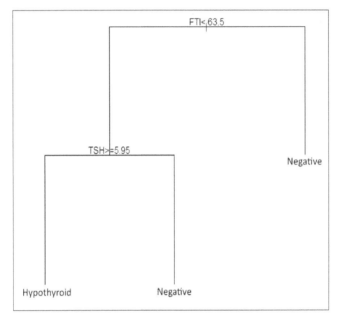

Figure 6: Classification tree for Hypothyroid

Consequently, the classification tree gives an accuracy of 98.74%, which is the best of the four models considered thus far. Next, we will consider the final model, support vector machines.

Support vector machines

Support vector machines, abbreviated popularly as **SVM**, are an important class of machine learning techniques. Theoretically, SVM can take an infinite number of features/covariates and build the appropriate classification or regression SVMs.

SVM for hypothyroid classification

The svm function from the e1071 package will be useful for building an SVM classifier on the Hypothyroid dataset. Following the usual practice, we have the following output in the R session:

```
> SVM_fit <- svm(HT2_Formula,data=HT2_Train)
> SVM_predict <- predict(SVM_fit,newdata=HT2_TestX,type="class")
> SVM_Accuracy <- sum(SVM_predict==HT2_TestY)/nte
> SVM_Accuracy
[1] 0.9842767296
```

The SVM technique gives us an accuracy of 98.43%, which is the second best of the models set up thus far.

In the next section, we will run each of the five classification models for the Waveform, German Credit, Iris, and Pima Indians Diabetes problem datasets.

The right model dilemma!

In the previous section, we ran five classification models for the Hypothyroid dataset. Here, the task is to repeat the exercise for four other datasets. It would be a very laborious task to change the code in the appropriate places and repeat the exercise four times over. Thus, to circumvent this problem, we will create a new function referred to as Multiple_Model_Fit. This function will take four arguments: formula, train, testX, and testY. The four arguments have already been set up for each of the five datasets. The function is then set up in a way that generalizes the steps of the previous section for each of the five models.

The function proceeds to create a matrix whose first column consists of the model name, while the second column consists of the accuracy. This matrix is returned as the output of this function:

```
> Multiple_Model_Fit <- function(formula,train,testX,testY){
+    ntr <- nrow(train) # Training size
+    nte <- nrow(testX) # Test size
+    p <- ncol(testX)
+    testY_numeric <- as.numeric(testY)
+
+    # Neural Network
+    set.seed(12345)
+    NN_fit <- nnet(formula,data = train,size=p,trace=FALSE)
+    NN_Predict <- predict(NN_fit,newdata=testX,type="class")
+    NN_Accuracy <- sum(NN_Predict==testY)/nte
+
```

```
+    # Logistic Regressiona
+    LR_fit <- glm(formula,data=train,family = binomial())
+    LR_Predict <- predict(LR_fit,newdata=testX,type="response")
+    LR_Predict_Bin <- ifelse(LR_Predict>0.5,2,1)
+    LR_Accuracy <- sum(LR_Predict_Bin==testY_numeric)/nte
+
+    # Naive Bayes
+    NB_fit <- naiveBayes(formula,data=train)
+    NB_predict <- predict(NB_fit,newdata=testX)
+    NB_Accuracy <- sum(NB_predict==testY)/nte
+
+    # Decision Tree
+    CT_fit <- rpart(formula,data=train)
+    CT_predict <- predict(CT_fit,newdata=testX,type="class")
+    CT_Accuracy <- sum(CT_predict==testY)/nte
+
+    # Support Vector Machine
+    svm_fit <- svm(formula,data=train)
+    svm_predict <- predict(svm_fit,newdata=testX,type="class")
+    svm_Accuracy <- sum(svm_predict==testY)/nte
+
+    Accu_Mat <- matrix(nrow=5,ncol=2)
+    Accu_Mat[,1] <- c("Neural Network","Logistic Regression","Naive
Bayes",
+               "Decision Tree","Support Vector Machine")
+    Accu_Mat[,2] <- round(c(NN_Accuracy,LR_Accuracy,NB_Accuracy,
+               CT_Accuracy,svm_Accuracy),4)
+    return(Accu_Mat)
+
+ }
```

`Multiple_Model_Fit` is now applied to the `Hypothyroid` dataset, and the results can be seen to be in agreement with the previous section:

```
> Multiple_Model_Fit(formula=HT2_Formula,train=HT2_Train,
+                     testX=HT2_TestX,
+                     testY=HT2_TestY)
     [,1]                       [,2]
[1,] "Neural Network"           "0.989"
[2,] "Logistic Regression"      "0.9733"
[3,] "Naive Bayes"              "0.9733"
[4,] "Decision Tree"            "0.9874"
[5,] "Support Vector Machine"   "0.9843"
```

The `Multiple_Model_Fit` function is then applied to the other four classification datasets:

```
> Multiple_Model_Fit(formula=Waveform_DF_Formula,train=Waveform_DF_
Train,
+                       testX=Waveform_DF_TestX,
+                       testY=Waveform_DF_TestY)
     [,1]                     [,2]
[1,] "Neural Network"          "0.884"
[2,] "Logistic Regression"     "0.8873"
[3,] "Naive Bayes"             "0.8601"
[4,] "Decision Tree"           "0.8435"
[5,] "Support Vector Machine" "0.9171"
> Multiple_Model_Fit(formula=GC2_Formula,train=GC2_Train,
+                       testX=GC2_TestX,
+                       testY =GC2_TestY )
     [,1]                     [,2]
[1,] "Neural Network"          "0.7252"
[2,] "Logistic Regression"     "0.7572"
[3,] "Naive Bayes"             "0.8083"
[4,] "Decision Tree"           "0.7061"
[5,] "Support Vector Machine" "0.754"
> Multiple_Model_Fit(formula=ir2_Formula,train=ir2_Train,
+                       testX=ir2_TestX,
+                       testY=ir2_TestY)
     [,1]                     [,2]
[1,] "Neural Network"          "1"
[2,] "Logistic Regression"     "1"
[3,] "Naive Bayes"             "1"
[4,] "Decision Tree"           "1"
[5,] "Support Vector Machine" "1"
> Multiple_Model_Fit(formula=PID_Formula,train=PimaIndiansDiabetes_
Train,
+                       testX=PimaIndiansDiabetes_TestX,
+                       testY=PimaIndiansDiabetes_TestY)
     [,1]                     [,2]
[1,] "Neural Network"          "0.6732"
[2,] "Logistic Regression"     "0.751"
[3,] "Naive Bayes"             "0.7821"
[4,] "Decision Tree"           "0.7588"
[5,] "Support Vector Machine" "0.7665"
```

The results for each of the datasets are summarized in the following table:

Dataset/ Model	Hypothyroid	Waveform	German	Iris	Pima Indian Diabetes
Neural Network	98.27%	88.40%	72.52%	100.00%	67.32%
Logistic Regression	97.33%	88.73%	75.72%	100.00%	75.10%
Naïve Bayes	97.33%	86.01%	80.83%	100.00%	78.21%
Decision Tree	98.74%	84.35%	70.61%	100.00%	75.88%
SVM	98.43%	91.71%	75.40%	100.00%	76.65%

Table 1: Accuracy of five models for five datasets

The iris dataset is a straightforward and simplistic problem, and therefore each of the five models gives us 100% accuracy on the test data. This dataset will not be pursued any further.

For each dataset, we highlight the highest accuracy cell in grey, and highlight the next highest in yellow.

Here is the modeling dilemma. The naïve Bayes method turns out the best for the German and Pima Indian Diabetes datasets. The decision tree gives the highest accuracy for the Hypothyroid dataset, while SVM gives the best results for Waveform. The runner-up place is secured twice by logistic regression and twice by SVM. However, we also know that, depending on the initial seeds and maybe the number of hidden neurons, the neural networks are also expected to perform the best for some datasets. We then also have to consider whether the results will turn out differently for different partitions.

It is in such practical scenarios we would prefer to have a single approach that ensures reasonable properties. With the Hypothyroid dataset, the accuracy for each of the models is 97% or higher, and one might not go wrong with any of the models. However, in the German and Pima Indian Diabetes problems, the maximum accuracy is 80% and 78%, respectively. It would then be better if we can make good use of all the models and build a single unified one with increased accuracy.

An ensemble purview

The caret R package is core to ensemble machine learning methods. It provides a large framework and we can also put different statistical and machine learning models together to create an ensemble. For the recent version of the package on the author's laptop, the caret package provides access to the following models:

```
> library(caret)
> names(getModelInfo())
   [1] "ada"              "AdaBag"         "AdaBoost.M1"
   [4] "adaboost"         "amdai"          "ANFIS"
```

[7] "avNNet"	"awnb"	"awtan"

[229] "vbmpRadial"	"vglmAdjCat"	"vglmContRatio
[232] "vglmCumulative"	"widekernelpls"	"WM"
[235] "wsrf"	"xgbLinear"	"xgbTree"
[238] "xyf"		

Depending on your requirements, you can choose any combination of these 238 models. The authors of the package keep on updating this list. It is to be noted that not all models will be available in the `caret` package, and that it is a platform that facilitates the ensembling of these methods. Consequently, if you choose a model such as `ANFIS`, and the R package `frbs` contains this function, which is not available on your machine, then caret will display a message on the terminal as indicated in the following snippet:

```
1 package is needed for this model and is not installed. (frbs). Would you like to
try to install it now?
1: yes
2: no

Selection: |
```

Figure 7: Caret providing a message to install the required R package

You need to key in the number `1` and continue. The package will be installed and loaded, and the program will continue. It is good to know the host of options for ensemble methods. A brief method for stack ensembling analytical models is provided here, and the details will unfold later in the book.

For the `Hypothyroid` dataset, we had a high accuracy of an average of 98% between the five models. The `Waveform` dataset saw an average accuracy of approximately 88%, while the average for `German` Credit data is 75%. We will try to increase the accuracy for this dataset. The accuracy improvement will be attempted using three models: naïve Bayes, logistic regression, and classification tree. First, we need to partition the data into three parts: train, test, and stack:

```
> load("../Data/GC2.RData")
> set.seed(12345)
> Train_Test_Stack <- sample(c("Train","Test","Stack"),nrow(GC2),repla
ce = TRUE,prob = c(0.5,0.25,0.25))
> GC2_Train <- GC2[Train_Test_Stack=="Train",]
> GC2_Test <- GC2[Train_Test_Stack=="Test",]
> GC2_Stack <- GC2[Train_Test_Stack=="Stack",]
The dependent and independent variables will be marked next in
character vectors for programming convenient.

> # set label name and Exhogenous
> Endogenous <- 'good_bad'
> Exhogenous <- names(GC2_Train)[names(GC2_Train) != Endogenous]
```

The model will be built on the training data first and accuracy will be assessed using the metric of Area Under Curve, the curve being the ROC. The control parameters will be set up first and the three models, naïve Bayes, classification tree, and logistic regression, will be created using the training dataset:

```
> # Creating a caret control object for the number of
> # cross-validations to be performed
> myControl <- trainControl(method='cv', number=3,
returnResamp='none')
> # train all the ensemble models with GC2_Train
> model_NB <- train(GC2_Train[,Exhogenous], GC2_Train[,Endogenous],
+                 method='naive_bayes', trControl=myControl)
> model_rpart <- train(GC2_Train[,Exhogenous], GC2_Train[,Endogenous],
+                 method='rpart', trControl=myControl)
> model_glm <- train(GC2_Train[,Exhogenous], GC2_Train[,Endogenous],
+                 method='glm', trControl=myControl)
```

Predictions for the test and stack blocks are carried out next. We store the predicted probabilities along the test and stack data frames:

```
> # get predictions for each ensemble model for two last datasets
> # and add them back to themselves
> GC2_Test$NB_PROB <- predict(object=model_NB, GC2_Test[,Exhogenous],
+                             type="prob")[,1]
> GC2_Test$rf_PROB <- predict(object=model_rpart, GC2_
Test[,Exhogenous],
+                             type="prob")[,1]
> GC2_Test$glm_PROB <- predict(object=model_glm, GC2_
Test[,Exhogenous],
+                               type="prob")[,1]
> GC2_Stack$NB_PROB <- predict(object=model_NB, GC2_
Stack[,Exhogenous],
+                               type="prob")[,1]
> GC2_Stack$rf_PROB <- predict(object=model_rpart, GC2_
Stack[,Exhogenous],
+                             type="prob")[,1]
> GC2_Stack$glm_PROB <- predict(object=model_glm, GC2_
Stack[,Exhogenous],
+                                 type="prob")[,1]
```

The ROC is an important measure for model assessments. The higher the area under the ROC, the better the model would be. Note that these measures, or any other measure, will not be the same as the models fitted earlier since the data has changed:

```
> # see how each individual model performed on its own
> AUC_NB <- roc(GC2_Test[,Endogenous], GC2_Test$NB_PROB )
> AUC_NB$auc
Area under the curve: 0.7543
> AUC_rf <- roc(GC2_Test[,Endogenous], GC2_Test$rf_PROB )
> AUC_rf$auc
Area under the curve: 0.6777
> AUC_glm <- roc(GC2_Test[,Endogenous], GC2_Test$glm_PROB )
> AUC_glm$auc
Area under the curve: 0.7446
```

For the `test` dataset, we can see that the area under curve for the naïve Bayes, classification tree, and logistic regression are respectively `0.7543`, `0.6777`, and `0.7446`. If we put the predicted values together in some format, and that leads to an increase in the accuracy, the purpose of the ensemble technique has been accomplished. As such, we consider the new predicted probabilities under the three models and append them to the stacked data frame. These three columns will now be treated as new input vectors. We then build a naïve Bayes model, an arbitrary choice, and you can try any other model (not necessarily restricted to one of these) for the stacked data frame. The AUC can then be predicted and calculated:

```
> # Stacking it together
> Exhogenous2 <- names(GC2_Stack)[names(GC2_Stack) != Endogenous]
> Stack_Model <- train(GC2_Stack[,Exhogenous2], GC2_
Stack[,Endogenous],
+                       method='naive_bayes', trControl=myControl)
> Stack_Prediction <- predict(object=Stack_Model,GC2_
Test[,Exhogenous2],type="prob")[,1]
> Stack_AUC <- roc(GC2_Test[,Endogenous],Stack_Prediction)
> Stack_AUC$auc
Area under the curve: 0.7631
```

The AUC for the stacked data observations is higher than any of the earlier models, which is an improvement.

A host of questions should arise for the critical thinker. Why should this technique work? Will it lead to improvisations under all possible cases? If yes, will simply adding new model predictions lead to further improvements? If no, how does one pick the base models so that we can be reasonably assured of improvisations? What are the restrictions on the choice of models? We will provide solutions to most of these questions throughout this book. In the next section, we will quickly look at some useful statistical tests that will aid the assessment of model performance.

Complementary statistical tests

Here, a model is selected over another plausible one. The accuracy of one model seems higher than the other. The **area under curve (AUC)** of the ROC of a model is greater than that of another. However, it is not appropriate to base the conclusion on pure numbers only. It is important to conclude whether the numbers hold significance from the point of view of statistical inference. In the analytical world, it is pivotal that we make use of statistical tests whenever they are available to validate claims/hypotheses. A reason for using statistical tests is that probability can be highly counterintuitive, and what appears on the surface might not be the case upon closer inspection, after incorporating the chance variation. For instance, if a fair coin is tossed 100 times, it is imprudent to think that the number of heads must be exactly 50. Hence, if a fair coin shows up 45 heads, we need to incorporate the chance variation that the number of heads can be less than 50 too. Caution must be exerted all the while when we are dealing with uncertain data. A few examples are in order here. Two variables might appear to be independent of each other, and the correlation might also be nearly equal to zero. However, applying the correlation test might result in the conclusion that the correlation is not significantly zero. Since we will be sampling and resampling a lot in this text, we will look at related tests.

Permutation test

Suppose that we have two processes, A and B, and the variances of these two processes are known to be equal, though unknown. Three independent observations from process A result in yields of 18, 20, and 22, while three independent observations from process B gives yields of 24, 26, and 28. Under the assumption that the yield follows a normal distribution, we would like to test whether the means of processes A and B are the same. This is a suitable case for applying the t-test, since the number of observations is smaller. An application of the `t.test` function shows that the two means are different to each other, and this intuitively appears to be the case.

Now, the assumption under the null hypothesis is that the means are equal, and that the variance is unknown and assumed to be equal under the two processes. Consequently, we have a genuine reason to believe that the observations from process A might well have occurred in process B too, and vice versa. We can therefore swap one observation in process B with process A, and recompute the t-test. The process can be repeated for all possible permutations of the two samples. In general, if we have m samples from population 1 and n samples from population 2, we can have $\binom{m+n}{m}$ different samples and as many tests. An overall test can be based on such permutation samples and such tests are called **permutation tests**.

For process A and B observations, we will first apply the t-test and then the permutation test. The t.test is available in the core stats package and the permutation t-test is taken from the perm package:

```
> library(perm)
> x <- c(18,20,22); y <- c(24,26,28)
> t.test(x,y,var.equal = TRUE)
Two Sample t-test
data:  x and y
t = -3.6742346, df = 4, p-value = 0.02131164
alternative hypothesis: true difference in means is not equal to 0
95 percent confidence interval:
 -10.533915871  -1.466084129
sample estimates:
mean of x mean of y
        20        26
```

The smaller p-value suggests that the means of processes A and B are not equal. Consequently, we now apply the permutation test permTS from the perm package:

```
> permTS(x,y)
Exact Permutation Test (network algorithm)
data:  x and y
p-value = 0.1
alternative hypothesis: true mean x - mean y is not equal to 0
sample estimates:
mean x - mean y
             -6
```

The p-value is now at 0.1, which means that the permutation test concludes that the means of the processes are equal. Does this mean that the permutation test will always lead to this conclusion, contradicting the t-test? The answer is given in the next code segment:

```
> x2 <- c(16,18,20,22); y2 <- c(24,26,28,30)
> t.test(x2,y2,var.equal = TRUE)
Two Sample t-test
data:  x2 and y2
t = -4.3817805, df = 6, p-value = 0.004659215
alternative hypothesis: true difference in means is not equal to 0
95 percent confidence interval:
 -12.46742939  -3.53257061
sample estimates:
mean of x mean of y
        19        27
```

```
> permTS(x2,y2)
Exact Permutation Test (network algorithm)
data:  x2 and y2
p-value = 0.02857143
alternative hypothesis: true mean x2 - mean y2 is not equal to 0
sample estimates:
mean x2 - mean y2
              -8
```

Chi-square and McNemar test

We had five models for the hypothyroid test. We then calculated the accuracy and were satisfied with the numbers. Let's first look at the number of errors that the fitted model makes. We have 636 observations in the test partition and 42 of them test positive for the hypothyroid problem. Note that if we mark all the patients as negative, we would be getting an accuracy of *1-42/636 = 0.934*, or about 93.4%. Using the table function, we pit the actuals against the predicted values and see how often the fitted model goes wrong. We remark here that identifying the hypothyroid cases as the same and the negative cases as negative is the correct prediction, while marking the hypothyroid case as negative and vice versa leads to errors. For each model, we look at the misclassification errors:

```
> table(LR_Predict_Bin,testY_numeric)
              testY_numeric
LR_Predict_Bin    1    2
             1   32    7
             2   10  587
> table(NN_Predict,HT2_TestY)
              HT2_TestY
NN_Predict     hypothyroid negative
  hypothyroid           41       22
  negative               1      572
> table(NB_predict,HT2_TestY)
              HT2_TestY
NB_predict     hypothyroid negative
  hypothyroid           33        8
  negative               9      586
> table(CT_predict,HT2_TestY)
              HT2_TestY
CT_predict     hypothyroid negative
  hypothyroid           38        4
  negative               4      590
> table(SVM_predict,HT2_TestY)
              HT2_TestY
SVM_predict    hypothyroid negative
  hypothyroid           34        2
  negative               8      592
```

From the misclassification table, we can see that the neural network identifies 41 out of the 42 cases of hypothyroid correctly, but it identifies way more cases of hypothyroid incorrectly too. The question that arises is whether the correct predictions of the fitted models only occur by chance, or whether they depend on truth and can be explained. To test this, in the hypotheses framework we would like to test whether the actuals and predicted values of the actuals are independent of or dependent on each other. Technically, the null hypothesis is that the prediction is independent of the actual, and if a model explains the truth, the null hypothesis must be rejected. We should conclude that the fitted model predictions depend on the truth. We deploy two solutions here, the chi-square test and the McNemar test:

```
> chisq.test(table(LR_Predict_Bin,testY_numeric))
Pearson's Chi-squared test with Yates' continuity correction
data:  table(LR_Predict_Bin, testY_numeric)
X-squared = 370.53501, df = 1, p-value < 0.00000000000000022204
> chisq.test(table(NN_Predict,HT2_TestY))
Pearson's Chi-squared test with Yates' continuity correction
data:  table(NN_Predict, HT2_TestY)
X-squared = 377.22569, df = 1, p-value < 0.00000000000000022204
> chisq.test(table(NB_predict,HT2_TestY))
Pearson's Chi-squared test with Yates' continuity correction
data:  table(NB_predict, HT2_TestY)
X-squared = 375.18659, df = 1, p-value < 0.00000000000000022204
> chisq.test(table(CT_predict,HT2_TestY))
Pearson's Chi-squared test with Yates' continuity correction
data:  table(CT_predict, HT2_TestY)
X-squared = 498.44791, df = 1, p-value < 0.00000000000000022204
> chisq.test(table(SVM_predict,HT2_TestY))
Pearson's Chi-squared test with Yates' continuity correction
data:  table(SVM_predict, HT2_TestY)
X-squared = 462.41803, df = 1, p-value < 0.00000000000000022204
> mcnemar.test(table(LR_Predict_Bin,testY_numeric))
McNemar's Chi-squared test with continuity correction
data:  table(LR_Predict_Bin, testY_numeric)
McNemar's chi-squared = 0.23529412, df = 1, p-value = 0.6276258
> mcnemar.test(table(NN_Predict,HT2_TestY))
McNemar's Chi-squared test with continuity correction
data:  table(NN_Predict, HT2_TestY)
McNemar's chi-squared = 17.391304, df = 1, p-value = 0.00003042146
> mcnemar.test(table(NB_predict,HT2_TestY))
McNemar's Chi-squared test with continuity correction
data:  table(NB_predict, HT2_TestY)
McNemar's chi-squared = 0, df = 1, p-value = 1
> mcnemar.test(table(CT_predict,HT2_TestY))
McNemar's Chi-squared test
data:  table(CT_predict, HT2_TestY)
```

```
McNemar's chi-squared = 0, df = 1, p-value = 1
> mcnemar.test(table(SVM_predict,HT2_TestY))
McNemar's Chi-squared test with continuity correction
data:  table(SVM_predict, HT2_TestY)
McNemar's chi-squared = 2.5, df = 1, p-value = 0.1138463
```

The answer provided by the chi-square tests clearly shows that the predictions of each fitted model is not down to chance. It also shows that the prediction of hypothyroid cases, as well as the negative cases, is expected of the fitted models. The interpretation of and conclusions from the McNemar's test is left to the reader. The final important measure in classification problems is the ROC curve, which is considered next.

ROC test

The ROC curve is an important improvement on the false positive and true negative measures of model performance. For a detailed explanation, refer to Chapter 9 of Tattar et al. (2017). The ROC curve basically plots the true positive rate against the false positive rate, and we measure the AUC for the fitted model.

The main goal that the ROC test attempts to achieve is the following. Suppose that Model 1 gives an AUC of 0.89 and Model 2 gives 0.91. Using the simple AUC criteria, we outright conclude that Model 2 is better than Model 1. However, an important question that arises is whether 0.91 is significantly higher than 0.89. The roc.test, from the pROC R package, provides the answer here. For the neural network and classification tree, the following R segment gives the required answer:

```
> library(pROC)
> HT_NN_Prob <- predict(NN_fit,newdata=HT2_TestX,type="raw")
> HT_NN_roc <- roc(HT2_TestY,c(HT_NN_Prob))
> HT_NN_roc$auc
Area under the curve: 0.9723826
> HT_CT_Prob <- predict(CT_fit,newdata=HT2_TestX,type="prob")[,2]
> HT_CT_roc <- roc(HT2_TestY,HT_CT_Prob)
> HT_CT_roc$auc
Area under the curve: 0.9598765
> roc.test(HT_NN_roc,HT_CT_roc)
    DeLong's test for two correlated ROC curves
data:  HT_NN_roc and HT_CT_roc
Z = 0.72452214, p-value = 0.4687452
alternative hypothesis: true difference in AUC is not equal to 0
sample estimates:
 AUC of roc1  AUC of roc2
0.9723825557 0.9598765432
```

Since the p-value is very large, we conclude that the AUC for the two models is not significantly different.

Statistical tests are vital and we recommend that they be used whenever suitable. The concepts highlighted in this chapter will be drawn on in more detail in the rest of the book.

Summary

The chapter began with an introduction to some of the most important datasets that will be used in the rest of the book. The datasets covered a range of analytical problems including classification, regression, time series, survival, clustering, and a dataset in which identifying an outlier is important. Important families of classification models were then introduced in the statistical/machine learning models section. Following the introduction of a variety of models, we immediately saw the shortcoming, in that we don't have a model for all seasons. Model performance varies from dataset to dataset. Depending on the initialization, the performance of certain models (such as neural networks) is affected. Consequently, there is a need to find a way to ensure that the models can be improved upon in most scenarios.

This paves the way for the ensemble method, which forms the title of this book. We will elaborate on this method in the rest of the book. This chapter closed with quick statistical tests that will help in carrying out model comparisons. Resampling forms the core of ensemble methods, and we will look at the important jackknife and bootstrap methods in the next chapter.

2
Bootstrapping

As seen in the previous chapter, statistical inference is enhanced to a very large extent with the use of computational power. We also looked at the process of permutation tests, wherein the same test is applied multiple times for the resamples of the given data under the (null) hypothesis. The rationale behind resampling methods is also similar; we believe that if the sample is truly random and the observations are generated from the same identical distribution, we have a valid reason to resample the same set of observations with replacements. This is because any observation might as well occur multiple times rather than as a single instance.

This chapter will begin with a formal definition of resampling, followed by a look at the jackknife technique. This will be applied to multiple, albeit relatively easier, problems, and we will look at the definition of the pseudovalues first. The bootstrap method, invented by Efron, is probably the most useful resampling method. We will study this concept thoroughly and vary the applications from simple cases to regression models.

In this chapter, we will cover the following:

- **The jackknife technique**: Our first resampling method that enables bias reduction
- **Bootstrap**: A statistical method and generalization of the jackknife method
- **The boot package**: The main R package for bootstrap methods
- **Bootstrap and testing hypothesis**: Using the bootstrap method for hypothesis testing
- **Bootstrapping regression models**: Applying the bootstrap method to the general regression model
- **Bootstrapping survival models**: Applying the bootstrap method for the survival data
- **Bootstrapping time series models**: The bootstrap method for the time series data – observations are dependent here

Technical requirements

We will be using the following libraries in the chapter:

- ACSWR
- boot
- car
- gee
- mvtnorm
- pseudo
- RSADBE
- survival

The jackknife technique

Quenouille (1949) invented the jackknife technique. The purpose of this was to reduce bias by looking at multiple samples of data in a methodical way. The name jackknife seems to have been coined by the well-known statistician John W. Tukey. Due mainly to the lack of computational power, the advances and utility of the jackknife method were restricted. Efron invented the bootstrap method in 1979 (see the following section for its applications) and established the connection with the jackknife method. In fact, these two methods have a lot in common and are generally put under the umbrella of *resampling methods*.

Suppose that we draw a random sample $X_1, X_2, ..., X_n$ of size n from a probability distribution F, and we denote by θ the parameter of interest. Let $\phi_n(X_1, X_2, ..., X_n)$ be an estimator of θ, and here we don't have the probability distribution of $\phi_n(X_1, X_2, ..., X_n)$ for a given θ. Resampling methods will help in carrying out statistical inference when the probability distribution is unknown. A formal definition of the concept is in order.

Definition: *Resampling methods* are ways of estimating the bias and variance of the estimator $\phi_n(X_1, X_2, ..., X_n)$ that uses the values of $\phi_n(\cdot)$ based on subsamples from the available observations $X_1, X_2, ..., X_n$.

The **jackknife technique** is a resampling method, and we will lay down its general procedure in the ensuing discussion. As stated previously, $\phi_n(X_1, X_2, ..., X_n)$ is an estimator of θ. For simplicity, we define the vector of the given observations by $X = (X_1, X_2, ..., X_n)$. The important quantity in setting up this procedure is the *pseudovalue*, and we will define this mathematically next.

Definition: Let $X_{[i]} = (X_1, X_2, \ldots, X_{i-1}, X_{i+1}, \ldots, X_n)$, that is, $X_{[i]}$ is the vector X without the *i-th* observation. The *i-th pseudovalue* of $\phi_n(X)$ is then defined as follows:

$$ps_i(X) = n\phi_n(X) - (n-1)\phi_{n-1}(X_{[i]})$$

It can be mathematically demonstrated that the *pseudovalue* is equivalent to the following:

$$ps_i(X) = \phi_n(X) + (n-1)\left(\phi_n(X) - \phi_{n-1}(X_{[i]})\right)$$

Thus, the *pseudovalue* is seen as the bias-corrected version of $\phi_n(X)$. The pseudovalues defined here are also referred to as *delete-one* jackknife. The jackknife method treats the pseudovalues as independent observations with mean θ, and then applies the *central limit theorem* for carrying out the statistical inference. The mean and (sampling) variance of the pseudovalues is given as follows:

$$ps(X) = \frac{1}{n}\sum_{i=1}^{n} ps_i(X)$$

$$V_{ps}(X) = \frac{1}{n-1}\sum_{i=1}^{n}\left(ps_i(X) - ps(X)\right)^2$$

The jackknife method for mean and variance

Suppose the probability distribution is unknown, and the histogram and other visualization techniques suggest that the assumption of normal distribution is not appropriate. However, we don't have rich information either to formulate a reasonable probability model for the problem at hand. Here, we can put the jackknife technique to good use.

We define mean and variance estimators as follows:

$$\phi_n^m(X) = \frac{1}{n}\sum_{i=1}^{n} X_i$$

$$\phi_m^v(X) = \frac{1}{n-1}\sum_{i=1}^{n}\left(X_i - \bar{X}\right)^2$$

The pseudovalues associated with $\phi_n^m(X)$ and $\phi_n^v(X)$ are respectively given in the following expressions:

$$ps_i^m(X) = n\bar{X} - (n-1)\bar{X}_{[i]}$$

$$ps_i^v(X) = \frac{n}{n-2}(X_i - \bar{X})^2 - \frac{1}{(n-2)(n-2)}\sum_{i=1}^{n}(X_i - \bar{X})^2$$

The mean of $ps_i^m(X)$ will be the sample mean, and the mean of $ps_i^v(X)$ will be sampling variance. However, the application of the jackknife method lies in the details. Based on the estimated mean alone, we would not be able to infer about the population mean, and based on the sample variance, we would not be able to exact inference about the population variance. To see what is happening with these formulas of pseudovalues and how their variances will be useful, we will set up an elegant R program next.

We will simulate $n = 1000$ observations from the Weibull distribution with some scale and shape parameters. In the standard literature, we will be able to find the estimates of these two parameters. However, a practitioner is seldom interested in these parameters and would prefer to infer about the mean and variance of the lifetimes. The density function is a complex form. Furthermore, the theoretical mean and variance of a Weibull random variable in terms of the scale and shape parameter is easily found to be too complex, and the expressions involving Gamma integrals do not help the case any further. If the reader tries to search for the string *statistical inference for the mean of Weibull distribution* in a search engine, the results will not be satisfactory, and it won't be easy to proceed any further, except for individuals who are mathematically adept. In this complex scenario, we will look at how the jackknife method saves the day for us.

A note is in order before we proceed. The reader might wonder, *who cares about Weibull distribution in this era of brawny super-computational machines?* However, any reliability engineer will vouch for the usefulness of lifetime distributions, and Weibull is an important member of this class. The second point might be that the normal approximation will hold well for large samples. However, when we have moderate samples to carry out the inference, the normal approximation for a highly skewed distribution such as Weibull might lose out on the power and confidence of the tests. Besides, the question is that if we firmly believe that the underlying distribution is Weibull (without parameters) it remains a monumental mathematical task to obtain the exact distributions of the mean and variance of the Weibull distribution.

The R program will implement the jackknife technique for the mean and variance for given raw data:

```
> # Simulating observations from Weibull distribution
> set.seed(123)
> sr <- rweibull(1000,0.5,15)
> mean(sr); sd(sr); var(sr)
[1] 30.41584
[1] 69.35311
[1] 4809.854
```

As mentioned in earlier simulation scenarios, we plant the seed for the sake of reproducible results. The `rweibull` function helps to enact the task of simulating observations from the Weibull distribution. We calculate the mean, standard deviation, and variance of the sample. Next, we define the `pv_mean` function that will enable computation of `pseudovalues` of mean and variance:

```
> # Calculating the pseudovalues for the mean
> pv_mean <- NULL; n <- length(sr)
> for(i in 1:n)
+    pv_mean[i] <- sum(sr)- (n-1)*mean(sr[-i])
> head(sr,20)
 [1]  23.29756524   0.84873231  11.99112962   0.23216910   0.05650965
 [6] 143.11046494   6.11445277   0.19432310   5.31450418   9.21784734
[11]   0.02920662   9.38819985   2.27263386   4.66225355  77.54961762
[16]   0.16712791  29.48688494 150.60696742  18.64782005   0.03252283
> head(pv_mean,20)
 [1]  23.29756524   0.84873231  11.99112962   0.23216910   0.05650965
 [6] 143.11046494   6.11445277   0.19432310   5.31450418   9.21784734
[11]   0.02920662   9.38819985   2.27263386   4.66225355  77.54961762
[16]   0.16712791  29.48688494 150.60696742  18.64782005   0.03252283
> mean(pv_mean); sd(pv_mean)
[1] 30.41584
[1] 69.35311
```

Note that the values and `pseudovalues` of the mean and the value of the observation are the same for all observations. In fact, this is anticipated, as the statistic we are looking at is the mean, which is simply the average. Removing the average of other observations from that should return the value. Consequently, the mean of the `pseudovalues` and the sample mean would be the same too. However, that does not imply that the efforts are futile. We will continue with the computations for the variance term as follows:

```
> # Calculating the pseudovalues for the variance
> pv_var <- NULL
```

```
> pseudo_var <- function(x,i){
+    n = length(x)
+    psv <- (n/(n-2))*(x[i]-mean(x))^2-(1/(n-1)*(n-2))*sum(x-mean(x))^2
+    return(psv)
+ }
> pv_var <- NULL
> for(i in 1:n)
+    pv_var[i] <- pseudo_var(sr,i)
> head(pv_var)
[1]     50.77137    875.96574    340.15022    912.87970    923.53596
12725.52973
> var(sr); mean(pv_var)
[1] 4809.854
[1] 4814.673
> sd(pv_var)
[1] 35838.59
```

Now, there is no counterpart to the `pseudovalue` of the observation in the actual data. Here, the mean of the `pseudovalues` will approximately equal the sample variance. This is the standard deviation `sd(pv_var)` which will help in carrying out the inference related to the variance or standard deviation.

We have seen how the jackknife is useful in inferring the mean and variance. In the next part of this section, we will see how the `pseudovalues` can be useful in solving problems in the context of a survival regression problem.

Pseudovalues method for survival data

The primary biliary cirrhosis data, `pbc`, was introduced in *Chapter 1*, *Introduction to Ensemble Techniques*, in *Section 2*, and we made a note that the data is special in that it is survival data and the variable of interest time is subject to censoring, which complicates further analysis. Specialized methods for dealing with survival data will be dealt with in *Chapter 10*, *Ensembling Survival Models*. The specialized methods include the hazards regression, and the impact of covariates is measured on the hazard rate and not on the lifetime. It has been observed that practitioners find these concepts a tad difficult, and hence we will briefly discuss an alternative approach based on the pseudovalues.

Andersen and Klein have effectively used the notion of pseudovalues for various problems in a series of papers:

```
> library(survival)
> library(pseudo)
> library(gee)
```

```
> data(pbc)
> time_pseudo <- pseudomean(time=pbc$time,event=pbc$status==2)
> pbc_gee <- gee(time_pseudo ~ trt + age + sex + ascites + hepato +
+                spiders + edema + bili + chol + albumin + copper +
+                alk.phos + ast + trig + platelet + protime + stage,
+                id=1:nrow(pbc), family="gaussian",
+                data=pbc)
Beginning Cgee S-function, @(#) geeformula.q 4.13 98/01/27
running glm to get initial regression estimate
  (Intercept)          trt          age         sexf      ascites
hepato
5901.1046673  115.5247130  -23.6893551  233.0351191 -251.2292823
-63.1776549
      spiders        edema         bili         chol      albumin
copper
-264.2063329 -441.2298926  -67.7863015   -0.5739644  438.5953357
-2.3704801
      alk.phos          ast         trig     platelet      protime
stage
  -0.0619931   -1.1273468    0.2317984   -0.4243154 -160.6784722
-292.9838866
> summary(pbc_gee)

 GEE:  GENERALIZED LINEAR MODELS FOR DEPENDENT DATA
 gee S-function, version 4.13 modified 98/01/27 (1998)


Model:
 Link:                      Identity
 Variance to Mean Relation: Gaussian
 Correlation Structure:     Independent

Call:
gee(formula = time_pseudo ~ trt + age + sex + ascites + hepato +
    spiders + edema + bili + chol + albumin + copper + alk.phos +
    ast + trig + platelet + protime + stage, id = 1:nrow(pbc),
    data = pbc, family = "gaussian")

Summary of Residuals:
       Min         1Q      Median         3Q         Max
-3515.1303  -792.8410    112.1563   783.9519   3565.1490



Coefficients:
                Estimate   Naive S.E.    Naive z  Robust S.E.    Robust
z
```

```
(Intercept) 5901.1046673 1.524661e+03   3.8704367 1.470722e+03
4.0123856
trt           115.5247130 1.616239e+02   0.7147750 1.581686e+02
0.7303895
age           -23.6893551 8.507630e+00  -2.7844835 8.204491e+00
-2.8873643
sexf          233.0351191 2.701785e+02   0.8625227 3.215865e+02
0.7246421
ascites      -251.2292823 4.365874e+02  -0.5754387 5.133867e+02
-0.4893568
hepato        -63.1776549 1.884840e+02  -0.3351885 1.786614e+02
-0.3536166
spiders      -264.2063329 1.986929e+02  -1.3297220 2.045738e+02
-1.2914962
edema        -441.2298926 4.155360e+02  -1.0618331 4.850261e+02
-0.9097034
bili          -67.7863015 2.651543e+01  -2.5564852 2.009844e+01
-3.3727151
chol           -0.5739644 4.117889e-01  -1.3938317 3.929789e-01
-1.4605475
albumin       438.5953357 2.321347e+02   1.8894000 2.156405e+02
2.0339196
copper         -2.3704801 1.120153e+00  -2.1162114 1.102365e+00
-2.1503594
alk.phos       -0.0619931 3.932052e-02  -1.5766092 4.571919e-02
-1.3559535
ast            -1.1273468 1.640940e+00  -0.6870130 1.797116e+00
-0.6273089
trig            0.2317984 1.416552e+00   0.1636356 1.375674e+00
0.1684980
platelet       -0.4243154 9.348907e-01  -0.4538663 9.106646e-01
-0.4659403
protime      -160.6784722 9.139593e+01  -1.7580484 9.254740e+01
-1.7361749
stage        -292.9838866 1.137951e+02  -2.5746618 1.025891e+02
-2.8558966

Estimated Scale Parameter:  1675818
Number of Iterations:  1
Working Correlation
     [,1]
[1,]    1
```

Bootstrap – a statistical method

In this section, we will explore complex statistical functional. What is the statistical distribution of the correlation between two random variables? If normality assumption does not hold for the multivariate data, then what is an alternative way to obtain the standard error and confidence interval? Efron (1979) invented the *bootstrap technique*, which provides the solutions that enable statistical inference related to complex statistical functionals. In *Chapter 1, Introduction to Ensemble Techniques*, the permutation test, which repeatedly draws samples of the given sample and carries out the test for each of the resamples, was introduced. In theory, the permutation test requires $\binom{m+n}{m}$ number of resamples, where m and n are the number of observations in the two samples, though one does take their foot off the pedal after having enough resamples. The bootstrap method works in a similar way and is an important resampling method.

Let $X = (X_1, X_2, ..., X_n)$ be an independent random sample from a probability distribution F, the parameter of interest be θ, and an estimator of the parameter be denoted by $\phi_n(X_1, X_2, ..., X_n)$. If the probability distribution of $\phi_n(X_1, X_2, ..., X_n)$ for the θ parameter is either unknown or intractable, then the statistical inference about the parameter can't be carried out. Consequently, we need a generic technique that will aid in the inference.

Efron's method unfolds as follows. The estimate provided by $\phi_n(X_1, X_2, ..., X_n)$ is a single value. Given the data and based on the assumption that we have an IID sample, the bootstrap method explores the possibility that any observed value is as likely as any other observed value. Thus, a random sample of size n drawn *with replacement* is intuitively expected to carry the same information as the actual sample, and we can obtain an estimate of the θ parameter based on this sample. This step can then be repeated a large number of times, and we will produce a varied number of estimates of the parameter. Using this distribution of estimates, statistical inference can then be performed. A formal description of this method is in order.

Draw a random sample with replacement of size n from $X_1, X_2, ..., X_n$ and denote it by $X^{*1} = (X_1^{*1}, X_2^{*1}, ..., X_n^{*1})$. The sample X^{*1} is referred to as the *first bootstrap sample*. Compute the estimate ϕ_n for this sample X^{*1} and denote it by ϕ_n^{*1}. Repeat the steps a large number of times and obtain $\phi_n^{*2}, \phi_n^{*3}, ..., \phi_n^{*B}$. The inference for θ can then be based on the bootstrap estimates $\phi_n^{*1}, \phi_n^{*2}, ..., \phi_n^{*B}$. We can put this description in the form of an algorithm:

1. Given data $X = (X_1, X_2, ..., X_n)$, the parameter of interest θ, calculate the estimate $\phi_n(X)$.

2. Draw a bootstrap sample of size n with replacement from X, and denote it by $X^{*1} = (X_1^{*1}, X_2^{*1}, ..., X_n^{*1})$.

3. Calculate the statistic $\phi_n^{*1}\left(X^{*1}\right)$ for the bootstrap sample.

4. Repeat *Repeat Steps 2 and 3* 'B – 1' number of times to produce $\phi_n^{*2}\left(X^{*2}\right), \phi_n^{*3}\left(X^{*3}\right), \ldots, \phi_n^{*B}\left(X^{*B}\right)$.

5. Use $\phi_n^{*1}\left(X^{*1}\right), \phi_n^{*2}\left(X^{*2}\right), \ldots, \phi_n^{*B}\left(X^{*B}\right)$ to carry out the statistical inference related to θ.

What does *Step 5* convey here? We have each of the $\phi_n^*\left(X^*\right)$ values estimate the parameter of interest, B estimates to be precise. Since the estimate (based on the sample) is $\phi_n\left(X\right)$, we (intuitively) expect that the average of the bootstrap estimates $\phi_n^*\left(X^*\right)$ will be very close to $\phi_n\left(X\right)$, hence the variance of the bootstrap estimates also gives a 'good' measure of the variance of the estimator too. The bootstrap mean and standard deviation are then computed as the following:

$$\widehat{\theta}_B^* = \frac{\sum_{i=1}^B \phi_n^{*i}\left(X^{*i}\right)}{B}$$

$$se_B^* = \left\{ \frac{\sum_{i=1}^B \left(\phi_n^{*i}\left(X^{*i}\right) - \widehat{\theta}_B^*\right)^2}{B-1} \right\}^{1/2}$$

Using $\widehat{\theta}_B^*$ and se_B^*, we can carry out inference for θ.

It should be noted that the bootstrap method is a very generic algorithm, and the execution of this is illustrated to address occasions when faced with certain interesting problems.

The idea of sampling with replacement needs to be elucidated here. For the purpose of simplicity, assume that we have only five observations, for example X_1, X_2, X_3, X_4, X_5. Now, when we draw the first bootstrap sample with a replacement size of 5, we might get the labels 2, 4, 4, 1, 3. This means that, from the original sample, we select X_2, X_4, X_4, X_1, X_3, and consequently the observations labeled 2, 1, and 3 are selected once and 4 is selected twice. This is the same as $X_1^1 = X_2, X_2^1 = X_4, X_3^1 = X_4, X_4^1 = X_1, X_5^1 = X_3$. In the bootstrap notation, it would be $X^{*1} = \left(X_2, X_4, X_4, X_1, X_3\right)$. The second bootstrap might be $X^{*2} = \left(X_3, X_3, X_3, X_2, X_4\right)$, and the third might be $X^{*3} = \left(X_5, X_2, X_1, X_4, X_1\right)$, and so on.

Next, we will illustrate this technique and clarify its implementation. The bootstrap method will be applied to two problems:

• Standard error of correlation coefficient

• Eigenvalue of the covariance/correlation matrix

The standard error of correlation coefficient

Consider a hypothetical scenario where we are trying to study the relationship between two variables. The historical information, intuition, and scatterplot all align, showing that there is a linear relationship between the two variables, and the only problem is that the histogram of each of the two variables suggests a shape that is anything but a bell shape. In other words, the assumption of normal distribution looks very unlikely, and since it fails in the univariate cases (of each variable), the analyst is skeptical about the joint bivariate normality holding true for the two variables.

Let $(X_1,Y_1),(X_2,Y_2),....,(X_n,Y_n)$ be n pairs of observations. The sample correlation coefficient is easily calculated using the following formula:

$$\hat{\rho} = \frac{\sum_{i=1}^{n}(X_i - \bar{X})(Y_i - \bar{Y})}{\sqrt{\sum_{i=1}^{n}(X_i - \bar{X})^2 \sum_{i=1}^{n}(Y_i - \bar{Y})^2}}$$

Here we have $\phi((X_1,Y_1),(X_2,Y_2),....,(X_n,Y_n)) = \hat{\rho}$. An estimate of any parameter is no good if we can't carry out the relevant statistical inference. A confidence interval suffices with the relevant results to perform the statistical inference. We will now learn how the bootstrap method helps us to do that. We will use the vector notation to maintain consistency, and toward this define $X_i = (X_i,Y_i), i = 1,2,...,n$, that is, X_i is a vector now. The first bootstrap sample is obtained by selecting n pairs of observations randomly and with replacement, and we will denote the first bootstrap sample by $X^{*1} = (X_1^1, X_2^1,..., X_n^1)$. Now, using the bootstrap sample, we will estimate the correlation coefficient by $\hat{\rho}^{*1} = \phi(X^{*1})$. Repeating the process of obtaining the bootstrap samples $B - 1$ more times, we will compute the correlation coefficients $\hat{\rho}^{*2},...,\hat{\rho}^{*B}$.

The law school data is used here, drawn from Table 3.1 of Efron and Tibshirani (1990, p.19). In this study, fifteen schools are randomly selected from a pool of 82 law schools. Two variables measured for the schools include the average score for the class on a national law test (LSAT) and the average undergraduate grade point (GPA). We will first import the data from the CSV file, display it, and then visualize the histograms of the two variables along with the scatterplot:

```
> LS <- read.csv("../Data/Law_School.csv",header=TRUE)
> LS
   School LSAT  GPA
1       1  576 3.39
2       2  635 3.30
3       3  558 2.81

13     13  545 2.76
```

```
14        14   572 2.88
15        15   594 2.96
> windows(height=100,width=100)
> layout(matrix(c(1,2,3,3),byrow=TRUE, nrow=2))
> hist(LS$LSAT,xlab="LSAT",main="Histogram of LSAT")
> hist(LS$GPA,xlab="GPA",main="Histogram of GPA")
> plot(LS[,2:3],main="Scatter plot between LSAT and GPA")
```

We will look at the code first. The read.csv file helps in importing the dataset from the chapter's Data folder, as unzipped from the code bundle and stored in the LS object. The LS is then displayed in the console. Here, we give the first and last three observations. The windows function creates a new graphical device with specified height and weight. Note that this function will only work on the Windows OS. Next, we specify the layout for the graphical device. To confirm that it's working, running the line matrix(c(1,2,3,3),byrow=TRUE, nrow=2) in R terminal gives the following result:

```
> matrix(c(1,2,3,3),byrow=TRUE, nrow=2)
     [,1] [,2]
[1,]   1    2
[2,]   3    3
```

This means that the first graphical output, as a consequence of running any code that results in a graph, is displayed in region 1 (upper left) of the device. The second graphical output is displayed in the right upper part, while the third will be spread across the lower part. It is a convenient manipulation for visual displays. The histogram of the two variables does not suggest normal distribution, though it may be argued that the number of observations is much less; fifteen, in this case. However, the scatter plot suggests that as LSAT increases, the GPA does too. Consequently, the correlation coefficient is a meaningful measure of the linear relationship between the two variables. However, the normal distribution assumption is not suitable here, or at least we need more observations that are not available as of now, and hence it remains a challenge to carry out the statistical inference. To overcome this, we will use the bootstrap technique. Take a look at the following figure:

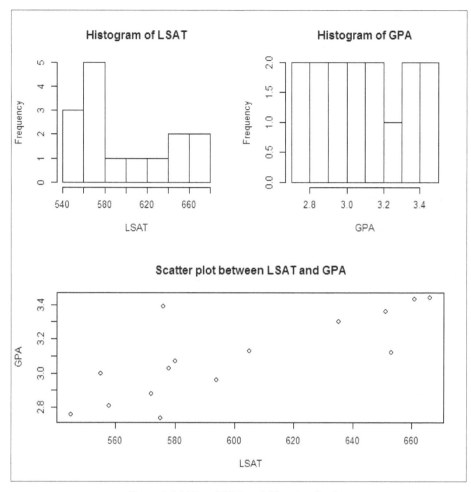

Figure 1: LSAT and GPA variables visualization

Imitating Efron and Tibshirani's illustration, we fix the number of bootstrap samples at 3200, and we will be interested when the number of bootstrap samples is at 25, 50, 100, 200, 400, 800, 1600, and 3200. The R program approach is as follows:

- After finding the number of observations, fixing the number of bootstrap samples, and bootstrap samples of interest, we will initialize the bootstrap mean and standard vector.

- For the purpose of replicating the results, we will fix the initial seed at 54321. The seed will be stepped up by an increment of 1 for obtaining the bootstrap sample, which will ensure that all the bootstrap samples are different.

- The value of the correlation coefficient is computed for each of the bootstrap samples, and thus we will have B = 3200 correlation coefficients.

- The mean and standard deviation of the correlation coefficients up to the desired number of bootstrap samples is calculated.

- For comparisons with Efron and Tibshirani (1990, p.50), the results are reported for bootstrap samples 25, 50, 100, 200, 400, 800, 1600, and 3200.

The R program along with the output is given next:

```
> n <- nrow(LS)
> B <- 3200
> TB <- c(25,50,100,200,400,800,1600,3200)
> seB <- NULL
> tcorr <- NULL
> myseed <- 54321
> for(i in 1:B){
+    myseed <- myseed+1
+    set.seed(myseed)
+    tcorr[i] <- as.numeric(cor(LS[sample(1:n,n,replace=TRUE),2:3])
[1,2])
+ }
> for(j in 1:length(TB)) seB[j] <- sd(tcorr[1:TB[j]])
> round(seB,3)
[1] 0.141 0.124 0.115 0.135 0.133 0.132 0.133 0.131
> for(j in 2:B){
+    corrB[j] <- mean(tcorr[1:j])
+    seB[j] <- sd(tcorr[1:j])
+    }
> round(corrB[TB],3)
[1] 0.775 0.787 0.793 0.777 0.782 0.773 0.771 0.772
> round(seB[TB],3)
[1] 0.141 0.124 0.115 0.135 0.133 0.132 0.133 0.131
> plot.ts(seB,xlab="Number of Bootstrap Samples",
+         ylab="Bootstrap Standard Error of Correlation")
```

The time series plot is displayed as follows:

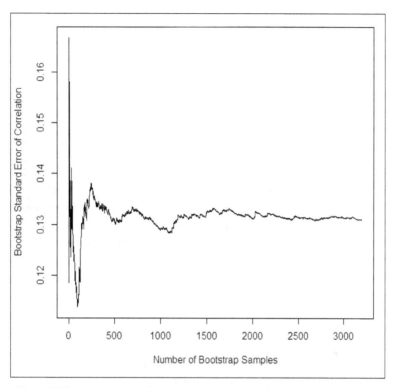

Figure 2: The nonparametric bootstrap standard error for correlation coefficient

The standard error of the correlation coefficient can be seen to stabilize at around `0.13`. Finally, to carry out the statistical inference, we can use the bootstrap confidence intervals. A `naïve` method is to simply obtain the 95% coverage of the correlation coefficient estimates in the bootstrap samples. This is easily achieved in the software. We will use the quantile function to achieve the result, as follows:

```
> for(i in 1:length(TB)) print(quantile(tcorr[1:TB[i]]
,c(0.025,0.975)))
     2.5%      97.5%
0.5225951 0.9481351
     2.5%      97.5%
0.5205679 0.9399541
     2.5%      97.5%
0.5429510 0.9513826
     2.5%      97.5%
0.4354776 0.9588759
     2.5%      97.5%
0.4662406 0.9668964
```

```
      2.5%        97.5%
 0.4787843  0.9667736
      2.5%        97.5%
 0.4614067  0.9621344
      2.5%        97.5%
 0.4609731  0.9606689
```

We have learned how to carry out statistical inference using the bootstrap technique.

One of the main reasons for carrying out the bootstrap method here is that we can't assume bivariate normal distribution for the LSAT and GPA variables. Now, if we are told that the distribution of LSAT and GPA historically follows bivariate normal distribution, then technically the probability distribution of the sample correlation coefficient ρ can be derived. However, as a practitioner, suppose that you are unable to derive the probability distribution of the sample correlation coefficient. How do you then carry out the statistical inference? Using the same technique as discussed here might seem tempting. We will continue to explore this matter in the next subsection.

The parametric bootstrap

As mentioned in the previous subsection, it might be tempting to carry out the usual *nonparametric* bootstrap method. However, nonparametric methods are traditionally known to be somewhat inefficient compared with the parametric methods. We will now look at a mixture of both of these methods.

We have seen that the bootstrap method relies heavily on the resamples. The bootstrap samples and the consequent estimates are then expected to meet the true underlying probability distributions. However, we might occasionally know more about the shape of the underlying probability distributions, except for a few parameters. The approach for mixing up these two methods will require a modification. The parametric bootstrap method is set up and run as follows:

- Let $X_1, X_2, ..., X_n$ be the IID sample from $F_\theta : \theta \in \Theta$, and let $\hat{\theta}$ denote an estimator of the parameter based on an appropriate method, say maximum likelihood estimation or method of moments, for example.

- Simulate the first bootstrap sample $X^{*1} = \left(X_1^{*1}, ... X_n^{*1} \right)$ of size n from $F_{\hat{\theta}}$, and obtain the first bootstrap estimate $\hat{\theta}^{*1}$ based on X^{*1} using the same estimation technique as used in the previous step.

- Repeat the previous step $B - 1$ number of times to obtain $\hat{\theta}^{*2}, \hat{\theta}^{*3}, ..., \hat{\theta}^{*B}$ respectively, based on the bootstrap samples $X^{*2}, X^{*3}, ..., X^{*B}$.

- Carry out the inference based on the B bootstrap estimates $\hat{\theta}^{*1}, \hat{\theta}^{*2}, ..., \hat{\theta}^{*B}$.

The parametric bootstrap technique will be illustrated using the earlier example of LSAT and GPA variables. For the bivariate normal distribution, the mean vector is an estimator of the population mean, and it enjoys statistical properties as being the unbiased estimator and MLE. Similarly, the sample variance-covariance matrix also gives an important estimate of the population variance-covariance matrix. The colMeans is applied on the data frame to obtain the vector mean and the var function to compute the sample variance-covariance matrix. The R code block easily follows:

```
> LS_mean <- colMeans(LS[,2:3])
> LS_var<- var(LS[,2:3])
> LS_mean; LS_var
        LSAT        GPA
600.266667    3.094667
              LSAT         GPA
LSAT 1746.780952 7.9015238
GPA      7.901524 0.0592981
```

Thus, we have the mean and variance-covariance matrix estimators. We now look at the parametric bootstrap computations. Now, using the rmvnorm function from the mvtnorm package, we are able to simulate observations from a multivariate (bivariate) normal distribution. With the (parametric) bootstrap sample available, the rest of the program and conclusion is similar. The complete R program with the resulting diagram is as follows:

```
> TB <- c(25,50,100,200,400,800,1600,3200)
> ptcorr <- NULL
> ptcorrB <- NULL
> pseB <- NULL
> myseed <- 54321
> for(i in 1:B){
+    myseed <- myseed+1
+    set.seed(myseed)
+    temp <- rmvnorm(n,LS_mean,LS_var)
+    ptcorr[i] <- as.numeric(cor(temp)[1,2])
+ }
> for(j in 2:B){
+    ptcorrB[j] <- mean(ptcorr[1:j])
+    pseB[j] <- sd(ptcorr[1:j])
+ }
> round(ptcorrB[TB],3)
[1] 0.760 0.782 0.772 0.761 0.766 0.763 0.762 0.766
> round(pseB[TB],3)
[1] 0.129 0.114 0.109 0.129 0.118 0.117 0.120 0.120
> windows(height=100,width=100)
> plot.ts(pseB,xlab="Number of Bootstrap Samples",
+         ylab="Parametric Bootstrap Standard Error of Correlation")
```

```
> for(i in 1:length(TB)) print(quantile(ptcorr[1:TB[i]],c(0.025,0.975
)))
      2.5%      97.5%
0.4360780 0.9048064
      2.5%      97.5%
0.5439972 0.9211768
      2.5%      97.5%
0.5346929 0.9200953
      2.5%      97.5%
0.4229031 0.9179324
      2.5%      97.5%
0.4650078 0.9194452
      2.5%      97.5%
0.4747372 0.9214653
      2.5%      97.5%
0.4650078 0.9245066
      2.5%      97.5%
0.4662502 0.9241084
```

The difference between parametric and nonparametric bootstrap can easily be seen. The confidence intervals are very short, and the standard error decreases to zero as the number of bootstrap samples increases. In spite of the advantage, we generally need bootstrap methods when the parametric methods fail. Take a look at the following figure:

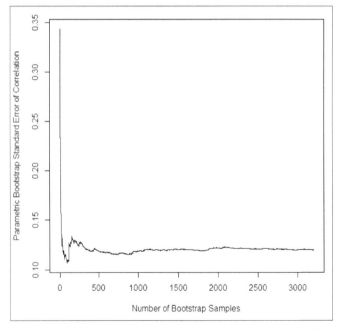

Figure 3: The parametric bootstrap standard error for correlation coefficient

Next, we will consider a slightly complex problem for the application of the bootstrap method.

Eigen values

Multivariate statistics is the arm of Statistics which deals with a vector of random variables. In the previous example, we have bivariate data, where LSAT and GPA scores are obtained for fifteen schools. Now we will consider another example, where we have more than two variables; namely we have five observations here. The description and bootstrap technique-related details are drawn from *Chapter 7, The General Ensemble Technique,* of Efron and Tibshirani (1990). The chapter discusses the score data from the classic multivariate book by Mardia, Kent, and Bibby (1979).

A quick brief of notation is as follows. We will denote the vector of random variables by $X = (X_1, X_2, ..., X_p)$, and for the *ith* observation, the vector will be $X_i = (X_{i1}, X_{i2}, ..., X_{ip}), i = 1, 2, ..., n$. Here, each component *Xi* is assumed to be a continuous random variable. Most often, and for practical and theoretical purposes, we assume that the random vector follows a multivariate normal distribution with mean vector $\mu = (\mu_1, \mu_2, ..., \mu_p)$ and variance-covariance matrix Σ. Since it is not feasible to go into the details of multivariate statistics here, the interested reader might simply consult Mardia, Kent, and Bibby (1979).

In this example, *n = 88* students' scores are noted for the five subjects of mechanics, vectors, algebra, analysis, and statistics, and a further difference in the test is that the first two subjects, mechanics and vectors, were closed-book tests while algebra, analysis, and statistics were open-book exams. We will first perform the simple preliminary task here of calculating the mean vector, the variance-covariance matrix, and the correlation matrix:

```
> OC <- read.csv("../Data/OpenClose.csv")
> pairs(OC)
> OC_xbar <- colMeans(OC)
> OC_xbar
      MC       VC       LO       NO       SO
38.95455 50.59091 50.60227 46.68182 42.30682
> OC_Cov <- cov(OC)
> OC_Cov
         MC        VC        LO        NO        SO
MC 305.7680 127.22257 101.57941 106.27273 117.40491
VC 127.2226 172.84222  85.15726  94.67294  99.01202
LO 101.5794  85.15726 112.88597 112.11338 121.87056
NO 106.2727  94.67294 112.11338 220.38036 155.53553
SO 117.4049  99.01202 121.87056 155.53553 297.75536
> OC_Cor <- cor(OC)
```

```
> OC_Cor
           MC         VC         LO         NO         SO
MC  1.0000000  0.5534052  0.5467511  0.4093920  0.3890993
VC  0.5534052  1.0000000  0.6096447  0.4850813  0.4364487
LO  0.5467511  0.6096447  1.0000000  0.7108059  0.6647357
NO  0.4093920  0.4850813  0.7108059  1.0000000  0.6071743
SO  0.3890993  0.4364487  0.6647357  0.6071743  1.0000000
```

Here, the data is imported from a .csv file, and using the colMeans, cov, and cor functions, we obtain the mean vector, variance-covariance matrix, and correlation matrix. Clearly, we can see from the output of the correlation matrix that a strong association exists between all variables. The visual depiction of the data is obtained by the pairs function, which gives us a matrix of scatter plots. This plot is as follows:

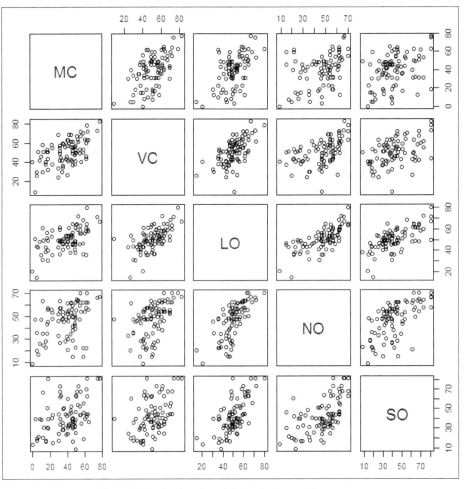

Figure 4: Matrix of scatter plots for the five subjects scores

Dimensionality reduction is one of the goals of multivariate statistics. Given a large number of variables, the intent of dimensionality reduction is to find a set of variables that will explain most of the variability in the overall data. A method of dimensionality reduction is *principal component analysis*. Here, we try to find a new random vector $\mathbf{Y} = (Y_1, Y_2, ..., Y_p)$, which is a *vector of principal components*. Each component of this new random vector is some linear combination of the original variables which will achieve two objectives: (a) the components $Y_1, Y_2, ..., Y_p$ will be ordered in the sense that the first component will have variance larger than the second, the second larger than the third, and so on, and (b) each principal component is uncorrelated with the others. The core working of the principal components is tied with the `eigen` values of the variance-covariance matrix or the correlation matrix. The `eigen` values of the variance-covariance matrix indicates the importance of the associated principal components. Consequently, if have p related random variables, and the estimated variance-covariance matrix is not singular, the normalized p `eigen` values will give us the fraction of the variation explained by the principal component. For the purpose of the data, we will explain this here:

```
> OC_eigen <- eigen(OC_Cov)
> OC_eigen$values
[1] 686.98981 202.11107 103.74731  84.63044  32.15329
> OC_eigen$vectors
             [,1]        [,2]        [,3]         [,4]         [,5]
[1,] -0.5054457  0.74874751 -0.2997888  0.296184264 -0.07939388
[2,] -0.3683486  0.20740314  0.4155900 -0.782888173 -0.18887639
[3,] -0.3456612 -0.07590813  0.1453182 -0.003236339  0.92392015
[4,] -0.4511226 -0.30088849  0.5966265  0.518139724 -0.28552169
[5,] -0.5346501 -0.54778205 -0.6002758 -0.175732020 -0.15123239
> OC_eigen$values/sum(OC_eigen$values)
[1] 0.61911504 0.18214244 0.09349705 0.07626893 0.02897653
```

The first `eigen` value is `686.9898`, the second one is `202.1111`, and so on. Now, these values divided by their cumulative sum gives the percentage of variation in the data explained by the principal component. Thus, the total variation of data explained by the first principal component is 61.91%, while 18.21% is explained by the second principal component. Here comes the important question then: how do we conduct the statistical inference related to this quantity? Naturally, we will provide the answer using the bootstrap method:

```
> thetaB <- NULL; sethetaB <- NULL
> B <- 500
> n <- nrow(OC)
> myseed <- 54321
> for(i in 1:B){
```

```
+    myseed <- myseed+1
+    set.seed(myseed)
+    OCt <- OC[sample(1:n,n,replace=TRUE),]
+    OCt_eigen <- eigen(cov(OCt))
+    thetaB[i] <- max(OCt_eigen$values)/sum(OCt_eigen$values)
+ }
> for(j in 2:B){
+    thetaB[j] <- mean(thetaB[1:j])
+    sethetaB[j] <- sd(thetaB[1:j])
+ }
> plot.ts(sethetaB,xlab="Number of Bootstrap Samples",
+         ylab="Bootstrap Standard Error for First Principal
Component")
```

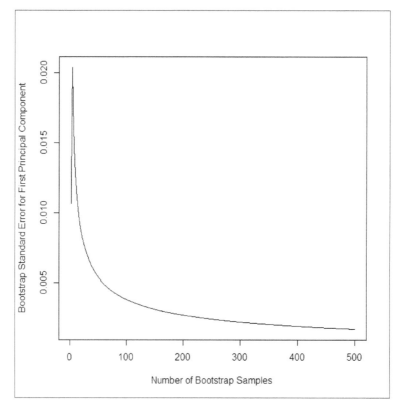

Figure 5: Bootstrap standard error of the variance explained by the first principal component

The 95% bootstrap confidence interval is obtained in the usual way:

```
> TB <- seq(50,500,50)
> for(i in 1:length(TB)) print(quantile(thetaB[1:TB[i]],c(0.025,0.975
)))
      2.5%      97.5%
0.6300403 0.6478871
      2.5%      97.5%
0.6330791 0.6424721
      2.5%      97.5%
0.6342183 0.6401195
      2.5%      97.5%
0.6348247 0.6394432
      2.5%      97.5%
0.6348774 0.6392892
      2.5%      97.5%
0.6352836 0.6391456
      2.5%      97.5%
0.6357643 0.6390937
      2.5%      97.5%
0.6360647 0.6388585
      2.5%      97.5%
0.6360818 0.6387047
      2.5%      97.5%
0.6361244 0.6386785
```

Rule of thumb

Generally, the number of B = 25 bootstrap replications is enough and one rarely requires more than 200 replications. For more information on this, see Efron and Tibshirani (1990, p.52).

Thus far we have used simulation, resampling, and loops to carry out the bootstrap inference. However, earlier in the chapter we mentioned the boot package. In the following section, we will use the package for some samples and illustrate its use.

The boot package

The boot package is one of the core R packages, and it is optimized for the implementation of bootstrap methods. In the previous examples, we mostly used loops for carrying out the resampling technique. Here, we will look at how to use the boot R package.

The main structure of the boot function is as follows:

```
boot(data, statistic, R, sim = "ordinary", stype = c("i", "f", "w"),
     strata = rep(1,n), L = NULL, m = 0, weights = NULL,
     ran.gen = function(d, p) d, mle = NULL, simple = FALSE, ...,
     parallel = c("no", "multicore", "snow"),
     ncpus = getOption("boot.ncpus", 1L), cl = NULL)
```

The central arguments of the function are data, statistic, R, and stype. The data argument is the standard one, as with most R functions. The statistic is the most important argument for the implementation of the boot function and it is this function that will be applied on the bootstrap samples obtained from the data frame. The argument R (and not the software) is used to specify the number of bootstrap samples to be drawn, and stype will indicate the second argument of statistic. For any inference to be completed using the boot function, the critical task is to define the function for the statistic. We will continue the illustration using earlier examples.

In the study of correlation between the LSAT and GPA variables, the trick is to define the function that will include the correlation coefficient function and the data with index specified in a manner that will give us the bootstrap sample. After declaring the function for the computation of the correlation coefficient for the bootstrap sample, we use the boot function, introduce the function, and specify the resampling type as well as the number of required bootstrap samples. The boot function will be in action now:

```
> corx <- function(data,i) cor(data[i,1],data[i,2])
> corboot <- boot(data=LS[,2:3],statistic=corx,R=200,stype="i")
> corboot
ORDINARY NONPARAMETRIC BOOTSTRAP
Call:
boot(data = LS[, 2:3], statistic = corx, R = 200, stype = "i")
Bootstrap Statistics :
    original      bias    std. error
t1* 0.7763745 -0.01791293  0.1357282
```

The correlation function is defined through `corx`, and the boot function is applied on it with the data frame `LS`. The number of bootstrap samples is `200` and the resampling will occur until the next iteration. From the preceding output we can obtain the value of the statistic as `0.7763745`, the bias as `-0.01791293`, and the bootstrap standard error as `0.1357282`. But what about bias? We have made almost no mention of bias in our discussion thus far. To understand what the bootstrap bias is, we will first look at the components of the fitted `corboot boot` object. The value of the statistic, correlation coefficient here, is stored as `t0`, the bootstrap sample estimates (`R` of them) in `t`, and using these two quantities we will find the bias:

```
> corboot$t0
[1]  0.7763745
> corboot$t
                [,1]
   [1,]  0.8094277
   [2,]  0.7251170
   [3,]  0.7867994
   [4,]  0.7253745
   [5,]  0.7891611

  [196,]  0.9269368
  [197,]  0.8558334
  [198,]  0.4568741
  [199,]  0.6756813
  [200,]  0.7536155
> mean(corboot$t)-corboot$t0
[1] -0.01791293
```

We can see how useful the `boot` function is for the applications. The `confint` function can be slapped on the `corboot` object to obtain the bootstrap confidence interval:

```
> confint(corboot)
Bootstrap quantiles, type =  bca
        2.5 %     97.5 %
1 0.3294379 0.9441656
```

Next, we will apply the `boot` function for the problem of obtaining the confidence interval of the variation explained by the first principal component. To that end, we first create the necessary R function that can be supplied to the boot function:

```
> Eigen_fn <- function(data,i)  {
+   eig <- eigen(cov(data[i,]))
+   val <- max(eig$values)/sum(eig$values)
```

```
+    val
+  }
> eigenboot <- boot(data=OC,statistic = Eigen_fn,R=200,stype = "i")
> eigenboot
ORDINARY NONPARAMETRIC BOOTSTRAP
Call:
boot(data = OC, statistic = Eigen_fn, R = 200, stype = "i")
Bootstrap Statistics :
     original         bias      std. error
t1* 0.619115 -0.0002657842    0.0488226
> confint(eigenboot)
Bootstrap quantiles, type =   bca
       2.5 %     97.5 %
1 0.5242984 0.7130783
```

Thus, the boot package can be effectively used without having the need to write loops. We have used the bootstrap method for the main purpose of estimating the parameters and their functions. Hypothesis testing based on bootstrap will be covered next.

Bootstrap and testing hypotheses

We begin the bootstrap hypothesis testing problems with the t-test to compare means and the F-test to compare variances. It is understood that, since we are assuming normal distribution for the two populations under comparison, the distributional properties of the test statistics are well known. To carry out the nonparametric bootstrap for the t-statistic based on the t-test, we first define the function, and then run the bootstrap function boot on the Galton dataset. The Galton dataset is available in the galton data.frame from the RSADBE package. The galton dataset consists of 928 pairs of observations, with the pair consisting of the height of the parent and the height of their child. First, we define the t2 function, load the Galton dataset, and run the boot function as the following unfolds:

```
> t2 <- function(data,i) {
+    p <- t.test(data[i,1],data[i,2],var.equal=TRUE)$statistic
+    p
+  }
> data(galton)
> gt <- boot(galton,t2,R=100)
> gt
ORDINARY NONPARAMETRIC BOOTSTRAP
Call:
boot(data = galton, statistic = t2, R = 100)
```

```
Bootstrap Statistics :
     original      bias    std. error
t1* -2.167665 0.03612774    0.6558595
> confint(gt)
Bootstrap quantiles, type =  percent
      2.5 %      97.5 %
1 -3.286426 -0.5866314
Warning message:
In confint.boot(gt) :
  BCa method fails for this problem.  Using 'perc' instead
> t.test(galton[,1],galton[,2],var.equal=TRUE)
    Two Sample t-test
data:  galton[, 1] and galton[, 2]
t = -2.1677, df = 1854, p-value = 0.03031
alternative hypothesis: true difference in means is not equal to 0
95 percent confidence interval:
 -0.41851632 -0.02092334
sample estimates:
mean of x mean of y
 68.08847  68.30819
```

The reader should compare the bootstrap confidence interval and the confidence interval given by the t-statistic.

Next, we will carry out the bootstrap hypothesis testing for the variances. The variance function is defined for the var.test function and it will then be used in the boot function:

```
> v2 <- function(data,i) {
+    v <- var.test(data[i,1],data[i,2])$statistic
+    v
+ }
> gv <- boot(galton,v2,R=100)
> gv
ORDINARY NONPARAMETRIC BOOTSTRAP
Call:
boot(data = galton, statistic = v2, R = 100)
Bootstrap Statistics :
     original        bias    std. error
t1* 1.984632 -0.002454309    0.1052697
> confint(gv)
Bootstrap quantiles, type =  percent
      2.5 %      97.5 %
1 1.773178 2.254586
Warning message:
In confint.boot(gv) :
  BCa method fails for this problem.  Using 'perc' instead
```

```
> var.test(galton[,1],galton[,2])
    F test to compare two variances
data:  galton[, 1] and galton[, 2]
F = 1.9846, num df = 927, denom df = 927, p-value < 2.2e-16
alternative hypothesis: true ratio of variances is not equal to 1
95 percent confidence interval:
 1.744743 2.257505
sample estimates:
ratio of variances
          1.984632
```

The confidence interval and the bootstrap confidence interval can be compared by the reader. The bootstrap methods have been demonstrated for different estimation and hypothesis testing scenarios. In the remaining sections, we will consider some regression models where we have additional information on the observations in terms of the explanatory variables.

Bootstrapping regression models

The US Crime dataset introduced in *Chapter 1, Introduction to Ensemble Techniques*, is an example of why the linear regression model might be a good fit. In this example, we are interested in understanding the crime rate (R) as a function of thirteen related variables such as average age, the southern state indicator, and so on. Mathematically, the linear regression model is as follows:

$$Y = \beta_0 + \beta_1 X_1 + \beta_2 X_2 + \ldots + \beta_p X_p + \in$$

Here, $X_1, X_2, \ldots, X_p$ are the p-covariates, β_0 is the intercept term, $\beta_1, \beta_2, \ldots, \beta_p$ are the regression coefficients, and $\in$ is the error term assumed to follow a normal distribution $N(0, \sigma^2)$. The covariates can be written in a vector form and the *ith* observation can be summarized as $(Y_i, \mathbf{x}_i), i = 1, 2, \ldots, n$, where $\mathbf{x}_i = (x_{i1}, x_{i2}, \ldots, x_{ip}), i = 1, 2, \ldots, n$. The n observations $(Y_i, \mathbf{x}_i), i = 1, 2, \ldots, n$, are assumed to be stochastically independent. The linear regression model has been detailed in many classical regression books; see Draper and Smith (1999), for instance. A recent book that details the implementation of the linear regression model in R is Ciaburro (2018). As the reader might have guessed, we will now fit a linear regression model to the US Crime dataset to kick off the discussion:

```
> data(usc)
> usc_Formula <- as.formula("R~.")
> usc_lm <- lm(usc_Formula,usc)
> summary(usc_lm)
Call:
lm(formula = usc_Formula, data = usc)
```

```
Residuals:
    Min      1Q  Median      3Q     Max
-34.884 -11.923  -1.135  13.495  50.560

Coefficients:
              Estimate Std. Error t value Pr(>|t|)
(Intercept) -6.918e+02  1.559e+02  -4.438 9.56e-05 ***
Age          1.040e+00  4.227e-01   2.460  0.01931 *
S           -8.308e+00  1.491e+01  -0.557  0.58117
Ed           1.802e+00  6.496e-01   2.773  0.00906 **
Ex0          1.608e+00  1.059e+00   1.519  0.13836
Ex1         -6.673e-01  1.149e+00  -0.581  0.56529
LF          -4.103e-02  1.535e-01  -0.267  0.79087
M            1.648e-01  2.099e-01   0.785  0.43806
N           -4.128e-02  1.295e-01  -0.319  0.75196
NW           7.175e-03  6.387e-02   0.112  0.91124
U1          -6.017e-01  4.372e-01  -1.376  0.17798
U2           1.792e+00  8.561e-01   2.093  0.04407 *
W            1.374e-01  1.058e-01   1.298  0.20332
X            7.929e-01  2.351e-01   3.373  0.00191 **
---
Signif. codes:  0 '***' 0.001 '**' 0.01 '*' 0.05 '.' 0.1 ' ' 1

Residual standard error: 21.94 on 33 degrees of freedom
Multiple R-squared:  0.7692,   Adjusted R-squared:  0.6783
F-statistic: 8.462 on 13 and 33 DF,  p-value: 3.686e-07
```

It can be seen from the summary output that a lot of information is displayed about the fitted linear regression model. From the output, we can find the estimated regression coefficients in Estimate. The standard error of these estimators is in Std. Error, the corresponding value of the t-statistic in t value, and the p-values in Pr(>|t|). We can further estimate the residual standard deviation σ in Residual standard error. Similarly, we can obtain the respective multiple and adjusted R-square values in Multiple R-squared and Adjusted R-squared, the overall F-statistic in F-statistic, and finally, the model p-value in p-value. Many of these statistics/quantities/summaries have clean statistical properties and as such, exact statistical inference regarding the parameters can be carried out. However, this is not the case for a few of them. For instance, if one asks for a confidence interval of the adjusted R-square value, the author is not able to recollect the corresponding statistical distribution. Hence, using the convenience of the bootstrap technique, we can obtain the bootstrap confidence interval for Adjusted R-square. The reason the confidence interval of the Adjusted R-square might be sought is that it has a very good interpretation of explaining the variance explained in the Y's by the model. Let us look at its implementation in the R software.

With complex problems there will be many solutions, and none with a proven advantage over the other. Nevertheless, we have two main ways of carrying out the bootstrap for the linear regression model: (i) bootstrapping the residuals, and (ii) bootstrapping the observations. The two methods can work for any general regression scenario too. Before we describe the two methods, let $\hat{\beta}_0, \hat{\beta}_1, \ldots, \hat{\beta}_p$ denote the least squares estimated of $\beta_0, \beta_1, \ldots, \beta_p$, and the fitted model will be as follows:

$$\hat{Y} = \hat{\beta}_0 + \hat{\beta}_1 X_1 + \hat{\beta}_2 X_2 + \ldots + \hat{\beta}_p X_p$$

Consequently, we will also have an estimate of the variance term of the error distribution and will denote it by $\hat{\sigma}^2$. Define the vector of residual by $e = Y - \hat{Y}$. The **residual bootstrapping** method is then carried out in the following steps:

1. Draw a sample of size n with replacement from e and denote it by e^*.

2. For the resampled e^*, obtain the new regressands using $Y^* = X'\beta + e^*$. That is, Y^* is the (first) bootstrap sample Y value.

3. Using Y^* and the covariate matrix X, obtain the first bootstrap estimate of the regression coefficient vector β^*.

4. Repeat the process a large number of times, say B.

Bootstrapping the observations is the usual bootstrapping method, which does not require any further explanation. However, the rank of X might be affected, especially if a covariate is a discrete variable and only one factor is chosen. Hence, for any regression problem, bootstrapping the residual is the best approach.

The regular `boot` package won't be useful, and we will instead use the `Boot` function from the `car` package to perform the bootstrap analysis on the linear regression model. The `Boot` function will also be required to be a specified function whose output will give the value of the required statistic. Consequently, we will first define a function `f`, which will return the adjusted R-square value:

```
> f <- function(obj) summary(obj)$adj.r.squared
> usc_boot <- Boot(usc_lm,f=f,R=100)
> summary(usc_boot)
     R original bootBias   bootSE bootMed
V1 100  0.67833 0.096618 0.089858 0.79162
> confint(usc_boot)
Bootstrap quantiles, type =  bca

        2.5 %     97.5 %
V1 0.5244243 0.7639986
Warning message:
In norm.inter(t, adj.alpha) : extreme order statistics used as
endpoints
```

Thus, a 95% bootstrap confidence interval for the adjusted R-square is (0.5244243, 0.7639986). Similarly, inference related to any other parameter of the linear regression model can be carried out using the bootstrap technique.

Bootstrapping survival models*

In the first section, we looked at the role of pseudovalues in carrying out inference related to survival data. The main idea behind the use of pseudovalues is to replace the incomplete observations with an appropriate (expected) value and then use the flexible framework of the generalized estimating equation. Survival analysis and the related specialized methods for it will be detailed in *Chapter 10, Ensembling Survival Models*, of the book. We will briefly introduce the notation here as required to set up the parameters. Let T denote the survival time, or the time to the event of interest, and we naturally have $T \geq 0$, which is a continuous random variable. Suppose that the lifetime cumulative distribution is F and the associated density function is f. Since the lifetimes T are incomplete for some of the observations and subject to censoring, we will not be able to properly infer about interesting parameters such as mean survival time or median survival time. Since there are additional complications because of censoring, it suffices to note here that we will be borrowing heavily from the material in *Chapter 10, Ensembling Survival Models*.

[

* Asterisked sections can be omitted on the first reading, or you can continue if you are already familiar with the related concepts and terminologies.
]

The `censboot` function from the `boot` package is developed to handle survival data. In the `pbc` dataset, the time to event of interest is the variable named `time` and the completeness of the observation is indicated by `status==2`. The package `survival` is required to create the `Surv` objects tenable to handle the survival data. The `survfit` function would then give us an estimate of the survival function, which is the complement of the cumulative distribution function 1-F. It is well known that the mean of a continuous non-negative random variable is $\int S(s)ds$, and that the median survival time is that time point u which satisfies the condition of $S(u) = 1 - F(u) = 0.5$. Since the `summary` of the `survfit` object can be used to obtain the survival probabilities at the desired time, we will use it to find the median survival time. All these arguments are built in the `Med_Surv` function, which will return the median survival time.

Using the `Med_Surv` function as the formula/statistic for the `censboot` function, we will be able to obtain the bootstrap estimates of the median survival time; subsequently, using the bootstrap estimates, we obtain the confidence interval for the median survival time. The R program and the output are as follows:

```
> Med_Surv <- function(data){
+    s2 <- survfit(Surv(time,status==2)~1,data=data)
+    s2s <- summary(s2)
+    s2median <- s2s$time[which.min(s2s$surv>0.5)]
+    s2median
+ }
> pbc2 <- pbc[,2:3]
> pbc_median_boot <- censboot(data=pbc2,statistic=Med_Surv,R=100)
> pbc_median_boot
CASE RESAMPLING BOOTSTRAP FOR CENSORED DATA
Call:
censboot(data = pbc2, statistic = Med_Surv, R = 100)

Bootstrap Statistics :
    original   bias    std. error
t1*     3395   21.36     198.2795
> pbc_median_boot$t
         [,1]
  [1,] 3282
  [2,] 3358
  [3,] 3574
  [4,] 3358
  [5,] 3244

 [96,] 3222
 [97,] 3445
 [98,] 3222
 [99,] 3282
[100,] 3222
> confint(pbc_median_boot)
Bootstrap quantiles, type =  percent
  2.5 % 97.5 %
1  3090   3853
Warning message:
In confint.boot(pbc_median_boot) :
  BCa method fails for this problem.  Using 'perc' instead
```

For the actual data, the estimated median survival time is 3395 days. The 95% bootstrap confidence interval for the median survival time is (3090, 3853).

To carry out the inference about the mean survival time, we need to use the `survmean` function from the `survival` package and appropriately extract the estimated mean survival time. The `Mean_Surv` function delivers this task. The R program and its output are given here:

```
> Mean_Surv <- function(data,time){
+     s2 <- survfit(Surv(time,status==2)~1,data=data)
+     smean <- as.numeric(
+         survival:::survmean(s2,rmean=time)[[1]]["*rmean"])
+     smean
+ }
> censboot(data=pbc2,time=2000,statistic=Mean_Surv,R=100)
CASE RESAMPLING BOOTSTRAP FOR CENSORED DATA
Call:
censboot(data = pbc2, statistic = Mean_Surv, R = 100, time = 2000)
Bootstrap Statistics :
    original    bias    std. error
t1* 1659.415 -3.582645    25.87415
```

The reader is left with the task of obtaining the bootstrap confidence interval for the mean survival time. The following section will discuss using the bootstrap method for time series data.

Bootstrapping time series models*

An example of the time series data was seen in *Chapter 1*, *Introduction to Ensemble Techniques*, in the `New Zealand Overseas` dataset. See *Chapter 10*, *Ensembling Survival Models*, of Tattar et al. (2016). Time series is distinctive in that the observations are not stochastically independent of each other. For example, the maximum temperature of the day is very unlikely to be independent of the previous day's maximum temperature. However, we are likely to believe that the maximum temperature of a block of ten previous days is mostly independent of a ten-day block six months ago. Thus, the `bootstrap` method is modified to the `block bootstrap` method. The `tsboot` function from the `boot` package is useful to bootstrap time series data. The main structure of the `tsboot` function appears as follows:

```
tsboot(tseries, statistic, R, l = NULL, sim = "model",
        endcorr = TRUE, n.sim = NROW(tseries), orig.t = TRUE,
        ran.gen, ran.args = NULL, norm = TRUE, ...,
        parallel = c("no", "multicore", "snow"),
        ncpus = getOption("boot.ncpus", 1L), cl = NULL)
```

Here, `statistic, tseries` is the time series data, which is the usual function of interest to us. `R` is the number of bootstrap replicates, and `l` is the length of the block, which we draw from the time series data. Now, we consider the problem of estimating the variance for an autoregressive (AR) time series model and we will consider a maximum order, `order.max`, of the AR model at 25. The `Var.fun` function will fit the best AR model and obtain the variance. This function will then be fed to the `tsboot` and, using the statistic calculated for each bootstrap sample, we will obtain the 95% bootstrap confidence interval:

```
> Var.fun <- function(ts) {
+    ar.fit <- ar(ts, order.max = 25)
+    ar.fit$var
+ }
> ?AirPassengers
> AP_Boot <- tsboot(AirPassengers,Var.fun,R=999,l=20,sim="fixed")
> AP_Boot
BLOCK BOOTSTRAP FOR TIME SERIES
Fixed Block Length of 20
Call:
tsboot(tseries = AirPassengers, statistic = Var.fun, R = 999,
    l = 20, sim = "fixed")
Bootstrap Statistics :
    original   bias    std. error
t1* 906.1192 2080.571    1111.977
> quantile(AP_Boot$t,c(0.025,0.975))
    2.5%     97.5%
1216.130 5357.558
```

Consequently, we have been able to apply the bootstrap methods for the time series data.

Summary

The main purpose of dealing with the bootstrap method in detail is that it lays the foundation for the resampling methods. We began the chapter with a very early resampling method: the jackknife method. This method is illustrated for the purpose of multiple scenarios, including survival data, which is inherently complex. The bootstrap method kicked off for seemingly simpler problems, and then we immediately applied it to complex problems, such as principal components and regression data. For the regression data, we also illustrated the bootstrap method for survival data and time series data. In the next chapter, we will look at the central role the bootstrap method plays in resampling decision trees, a quintessential machine learning tool.

3
Bagging

Decision trees were introduced in *Chapter 1, Introduction to Ensemble Techniques*, and then applied to five different classification problems. Here, they can be seen to work better for some databases more than others. We had almost only used the `default` settings for the `rpart` function when constructing decision trees. This chapter begins with the exploration of some options that are likely to improve the performance of the decision tree. The previous chapter introduced the `bootstrap` method, used mainly for statistical methods and models. In this chapter, we will use it for trees. The method is generally accepted as a machine learning technique. Bootstrapping decision trees is widely known as *bagging*. A similar kind of classification method is k-nearest neighborhood classification, abbreviated as *k*-NN. We will introduce this method in the third section and apply the bagging technique for this method in the concluding section of the chapter.

In this chapter, we will cover the following:

- Classification trees and related pruning/improvement methods
- Bagging the classification tree
- Introduction and application of the *k*-NN classifier
- *k*-NN bagging extension

Technical requirements

We will be using the following libraries in the chapter:

- `class`
- `FNN`
- `ipred`
- `mlbench`
- `rpar`

Classification trees and pruning

A classification tree is a particular type of decision tree, and its focus is mainly on classification problems. Breiman, et al. (1984) invented the decision tree and Quinlan (1984) independently introduced the C4.5 algorithm. Both of these had a lot in common, but we will focus on the Breiman school of decision trees. Hastie, et al. (2009) gives a comprehensive treatment of decision trees, and Zhang and Singer (2010) offer a treatise on the recursive partitioning methods. An intuitive and systematic R programmatic development of the trees can be found in *Chapter 9, Ensembling Regression Models*, of Tattar (2017).

A classification tree has many arguments that can be fine-tuned for improving performance. However, we will first simply construct the classification tree with default settings and visualize the tree. The `rpart` function from the `rpart` package can create classification, regression, as well as survival trees. The function first inspects whether the regress and is a categorical, numerical, or survival object and accordingly sets up the respective classification, regression, or survival trees as well as using the relevant split function.

The **German credit** dataset is loaded and the exercise of splitting the data into train and test parts is carried out as in earlier settings:

```
> load("../Data/GC2.RData")
> set.seed(12345)
> Train_Test <- sample(c("Train","Test"),nrow(GC2),replace = TRUE,
+     prob = c(0.7,0.3))
> GC2_Train <- GC2[Train_Test=="Train",]
> GC2_TestX <- within(GC2[Train_Test=="Test",],rm(good_bad))
> GC2_TestY <- GC2[Train_Test=="Test","good_bad"]
> nte <- nrow(GC2_TestX)
> GC2_Formula <- as.formula("good_bad~.")
```

You can refer to *Chapter 1, Introduction to Ensemble Techniques* to understand how the R code is performed. Now, using the training dataset and the chosen formula, we will create the first classification tree. The `rpart` function applied on the formula and dataset will create a classification tree. The tree is visualized using the `plot` function, and the `uniform=TRUE` option ensures that the display aligns the splits at their correct hierarchical levels. Furthermore, the text function will display the variable names at the split points and `use.n=TRUE` will give the distribution of the Ys at the node. Finally, the fitted classification tree is then used to `predict` the good/ bad loans for the test dataset, comparisons are made for the test sample, and we find the accuracy of the tree is 70.61%, which is the same as in *Chapter 1, Introduction to Ensemble Techniques*:

```
> DT_01 <- rpart(GC2_Formula,GC2_Train)
> windows(height=200,width=200)
```

```
> par(mfrow=c(1,2))
> plot(DT_01,uniform=TRUE,main="DT - 01"); text(DT_01,use.n=TRUE)
> DT_01_predict <- predict(DT_01,newdata = GC2_TestX,type="class")
> DT_01_Accuracy <- sum(DT_01_predict==GC2_TestY)/nte
> DT_01_Accuracy
[1] 0.7060703
> DT_01$variable.importance
checking duration  savings  purpose employed  history   amount
coapp
 38.5358  19.6081  15.6824  12.8583  12.5501   9.2985   8.9475
8.1326
     age  existcr property      job resident telephon  housing
depends
  7.3921   6.0250   5.5503   5.2012   2.6356   1.6327   1.3594
0.6871
 marital installp  foreign
  0.6871   0.4836   0.2045
```

The plot of the preceding code is the left tree display, DT-01, of the next diagram.
It can be seen from the display that there are way too many terminal nodes and
there also appears to be many splits, meaning that there is a chance that we are
overfitting the data. Some of the terminal nodes have as few as seven observations
while many terminal nodes have less than 20 observations. Consequently, there is
room for improvement.

In the next iteration of the decision tree, we ask the tree algorithm not to split further
if we have less than 30 observations in the node (minsplit=30), and that the
minimum bucket size (minbucket=15) must be at least 15. This change should give
us an improvisation over the tree, DT_01. For the new tree, we will again check the
change in accuracy:

```
> DT_02 <- rpart(GC2_Formula,GC2_Train,minsplit=30,minbucket=15)
> plot(DT_02,uniform=TRUE,main="DT - 02"); text(DT_02,use.n=TRUE)
> DT_02_predict <- predict(DT_02,newdata = GC2_TestX,type="class")
> DT_02_Accuracy <- sum(DT_02_predict==GC2_TestY)/nte
> DT_02_Accuracy
[1] 0.7252396
> DT_02$variable.importance
checking duration  savings  purpose  history   amount    coapp
employed
 35.2436  15.5220  15.3025  11.6655   7.8141   7.5564   7.1990
5.6960
property  existcr      age resident  foreign  depends  marital
job
```

```
   3.7257    1.7646    1.3781    1.1833    0.7883    0.6871    0.6871
0.5353
 housing installp
   0.5072    0.4581
```

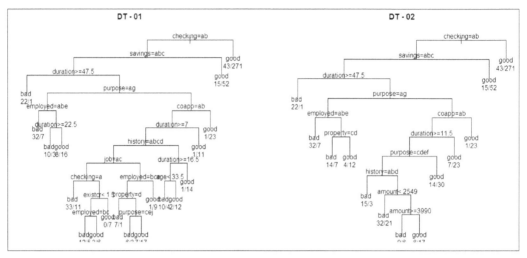

Figure 1: Classification trees for German data

The `DT-02` tree appears cleaner than `DT-01`, and each terminal node has a considerably good number of observations. Importantly, the accuracy is improved to `0.7252 - 0.7061 = 0.0191`, or about 2%, which is an improvement.

The **complexity parameter, Cp**, is an important aspect of the trees and we will now use it in improving the classification tree. Using the argument `cp=0.005` along with the `minsplit` and `minbucket`, we will try to improve the performance of the tree:

```
> DT_03 <- rpart(GC2_Formula,GC2_Train,minsplit=30,minbucket=15,
+                cp=0.005)
> plot(DT_03,uniform=TRUE,main="DT - 03"); text(DT_03,use.n=TRUE)
> DT_03_predict <- predict(DT_03,newdata = GC2_TestX,type="class")
> DT_03_Accuracy <- sum(DT_03_predict==GC2_TestY)/nte
> DT_03_Accuracy
[1] 0.7316294
> DT_03$variable.importance
checking duration  savings  purpose  history employed   amount
coapp
 35.7201  15.5220  15.3025  11.6655   7.8141   7.7610   7.5564
7.1990
property      age existcr resident  marital  foreign installp
depends
```

```
   3.7257    1.8547    1.7646    1.5010    1.0048    0.7883    0.7758
0.6871
     job  housing
   0.5353   0.5072
```

The performance has now changed from 0.7252 to 0.7316, and this is an improvement again. The tree complexity structure does not seem to have changed much in DT-03, the left-side tree of the following diagram. We now carry out two changes simultaneously. First, we change the split criteria from Gini to information, and then we add a loss matrix for misclassification.

What is a loss matrix for misclassification? If a good loan is identified or predicted by the model as a good loan in this way, we have no misclassification. Furthermore, if a bad loan is classified as a bad loan, it is also the correct decision identified by the algorithm. The consequence of misclassifying a good loan as bad is not the same as classifying the bad as good. For instance, if a bad customer is granted a loan, the loss would be a four-six digit revenue loss, while a good customer who is denied a loan might apply again in 3 months' time. If you ran matrix(c(0,200,500,0),byrow = TRUE,nrow=2), the output would be the following:

```
> matrix(c(0,200,500,0),byrow = TRUE,nrow=2)
     [,1] [,2]
[1,]    0  200
[2,]  500    0
```

This means that the penalty for misclassifying a good loan as bad is 200 while misclassifying a bad loan as good is 500. Penalties help a lot and gives weight to the classification problem. With this option and the split criteria, we set up the next classification tree:

```
> DT_04 <- rpart(GC2_Formula,GC2_Train,minsplit=30,minbucket=15,
+                parms = list(split="information",
+                            loss=matrix(c(0,200,500,0),byrow =
TRUE,nrow=2)))
> plot(DT_04,uniform=TRUE,main="DT - 04"); text(DT_04,use.n=TRUE)
> DT_04_predict <- predict(DT_04,newdata = GC2_TestX,type="class")
> DT_04_Accuracy <- sum(DT_04_predict==GC2_TestY)/nte
> DT_04_Accuracy
[1] 0.7380192
> DT_04$variable.importance
checking  savings duration  purpose employed  history   amount
existcr
 26.0182  10.4096  10.2363   5.0949   5.0434   2.1544   1.5439
 0.9943
resident       age  depends  marital property
  0.9648   0.7457   0.6432   0.6432   0.5360
```

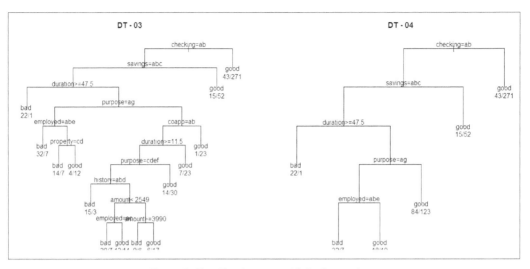

Figure 2: Classification trees with further options

Note that the decision tree DT-04 appears to have far fewer splits than DT-01-03, and does not appear to over-train the data.

Here, we can see many options that can be used to tweak the decision trees, and some of these are appropriate for the classification tree only. However, with some of the parameters tweaking might need expert knowledge, although it is nice to be aware of the options. Note how the order of the variable importance changes from one decision tree to another. Given the data and the tree structure, how reliably can we determine the variable importance of a given variable? This question will be covered in the next section. A general way of improving the performance of the decision tree will also be explored next.

Bagging

Bagging stands for **B**oostap **AGG**regat**ING**. This was invented by Breiman (1994). Bagging is an example of an *homogeneous ensemble* and this is because the base learning algorithm remains as the classification tree. Here, each bootstrap tree will be a base learner. This also means that when we bootstrapped the linear regression model in *Chapter 2, Bootstrapping*, we actually performed an ensemble there. A few remarks with regards to combining the results of multiple trees is in order here.

Ensemble methods combine the outputs from multiple models, also known as base learners, and produce a single result. A benefit of this approach is that if each of these base learners possesses a *desired property*, then the combined result will have increased stability. If a certain base learner is over-trained in a specific region of the covariate space, the other base learner will nullify such an undesired prediction. It is the increased stability that is expected from the ensemble, and bagging many times helps to improve the performance of fitted values from a given set of models. Berk (2016), Seni and Elder (2010), and Hastie, et al. (2009) may be referred to for more details.

A basic result! If N observations are drawn with replacements from N units, then 37% of the observations are left out on average.

This result is an important one. Since we will be carrying out a bootstrap method, it means that on average for each tree, we will have a holdout sample of 37%. A brief simulation program will compute the probability for us. For an N value ranging from 11 to 100, we will draw a sample with a replacement, find how many indexes are left out, and divide the number by N to obtain the empirical probability of the number of units left out of this simulation. The empirical probability is obtained via $B = 100,000$ a number of times, and that average is reported as the probability of any individual not being selected in a draw of N items drawn from N items with replacements:

```
> N <- 11:100
> B <- 1e5
> Prob_Avg <- NULL
> for(i in N){
+    set <- 1:i
+    leftout <- 0
+    for(j in 1:B){
+        s1 <- sample(set,i,replace=TRUE)
+        leftout <- leftout+(i-length(unique(s1)))/i
+    }
+    Prob_Avg[i-10] <- leftout/B
+ }
> Prob_Avg
 [1] 0.3504 0.3517 0.3534 0.3549 0.3552 0.3563 0.3571 0.3574 0.3579
0.3585
[11] 0.3585 0.3594 0.3594 0.3601 0.3604 0.3606 0.3610 0.3612 0.3613
0.3614
[21] 0.3620 0.3622 0.3625 0.3622 0.3626 0.3627 0.3627 0.3626 0.3631
0.3634
[31] 0.3635 0.3637 0.3636 0.3638 0.3639 0.3638 0.3640 0.3641 0.3641
0.3641
[41] 0.3644 0.3642 0.3645 0.3643 0.3645 0.3647 0.3645 0.3646 0.3649
0.3649
```

```
[51] 0.3648 0.3650 0.3648 0.3650 0.3651 0.3653 0.3649 0.3649 0.3653
0.3653
[61] 0.3654 0.3654 0.3654 0.3654 0.3653 0.3655 0.3654 0.3655 0.3655
0.3657
[71] 0.3657 0.3657 0.3655 0.3658 0.3658 0.3660 0.3656 0.3658 0.3658
0.3658
[81] 0.3658 0.3658 0.3660 0.3658 0.3659 0.3659 0.3662 0.3660 0.3661
0.3661
```

Consequently, we can see that in a sample of N drawn from N items with replacements, approximately 0.37 or 37% observations are not selected.

The bagging algorithm is given as follows:

- Draw a random sample of size N with replacements from the data consisting of N observations. The selected random sample is called a **bootstrap sample**.
- Construct a classification tree from the bootstrap sample.
- Assign a class to each terminal node and store the predicted class of each observation.
- Repeat steps 1-3 a large number of times, for example, B.
- Assign each observation to a final class by a majority vote over the set of trees.

The main purpose of the bagging procedure is to reduce instability, and this is mainly achieved through the `bootstrap` method. As noted earlier, and proven by a simulation program, when we draw N observations with replacements from N observations, on average, 37% observations would be excluded from the sample. The `bagging` method takes advantage of this sampling with a replacement technique and we call the unselected observations **out-of-bag** (**OOB**) observations. As with the `bootstrap` method, the resampling technique gives us multiple estimates of the different parameters and, using such a sampling distribution, it is then possible to carry out the appropriate statistical inference. For a more rigorous justification of this technique, the original Breiman (1996) paper is a good read.

A word of caution: Suppose an observation has been an out-of-bag observation for, say, 100 times out of 271 trees. In the 100th instance when the observation is marked for testing purposes, the observation might be classified as TRUE in 70 of them. It is then tempting to conclude for the observation that *P(TRUE) = 70/100 = 0.7*. Such an interpretation can be misleading since the samples in the bag are not independent.

Before we proceed to the software implementation, two important remarks from Hastie, et al. (2009) are in order. First, the bagging technique helps in reducing the variance of the estimated prediction function and it also works for high-variance, low-bias models, such as trees. Second, the core aim of bagging in aggregation is to average many noisy models that are unbiased, hence the subsequent reduction in variance. As with the bootstrap method, bagging reduces bias as it is a smoothing method. We will now illustrate the bagging method using the German credit data.

The `bagging` function from the `ipred` package will help in setting up the procedure:

```
> B <- 500
> GC2_Bagging <- bagging(GC2_Formula,data=GC2_Train,coob=FALSE,
+                         nbagg=B,keepX=TRUE)
> GC2_Margin <- predict(GC2_Bagging,newdata = GC2_TestX,
+                         aggregation="weighted",type="class")
> sum(GC2_Margin==GC2_TestY)/nte
[1] 0.7795527
```

Aggregation has helped here by significantly increasing the accuracy. Note that each run of the bagging method will result in a different answer. This is mainly because each tree is set up with different samples and the seeds generating the random samples are allowed to change dynamically. Until now, made attempts to fix the seeds at a certain number to reproduce the results. Going forward, the seeds will seldom be fixed. As an exercise to test your knowledge, work out what the `keepx` and `coob options` specified in the bagging function are. Do this by using `?bagging`.

Back to the German credit problem! We have created *B* = *500* trees and for some crazy reason we want to view all of them. Of course, Packt (the publisher of this book) would probably be a bit annoyed if the author insisted on printing all 500 trees, and besides, the trees would look ugly as they are not pruned. The program must be completed with respect to the book size constraints. With that in mind, let's kick off with the following code:

```
> pdf("../Output/GC2_Bagging_Trees.pdf")
> for(i in 1:B){
+     tt <- GC2_Bagging$mtrees[[i]]
+     plot(tt$btree)
+     text(tt$btree,use.n=TRUE)
+ }
> dev.off()
pdf
   2
```

The following steps were performed in the preceding code:

1. We will first invoke the PDF device.
2. A new file is then created in the Output folder.
3. Next, we begin a loop from 1 to B. The bagging object constitutes of B = 500 trees and in a temporary object, tt, we store the details of the i^(th) tree.
4. We then plot that tree using the plot function by extracting the tree details out of tt, and adding the relevant text associated with the nodes and splits of that tree.
5. After the loop is completed, the dev.off line is run, which will then save the GC2_Bagging_Trees.pdf file. This portable document file will consist of 500 trees.

A lot has been said about the benefits of bootstrapping and a lot has also been illustrated in the previous chapter. However, putting aside the usual advantages of bagging, which are shown in many blogs and references, we will show here how to also get reliable inference of the variable importance. It can be easily seen that the variable importance varies a lot across the trees. This is not a problem, however. When we are asked about the overall reliability of the variable importance in decision trees for each variable, we can now look at their values across the trees and carry out the inference:

```
> VI <- data.frame(matrix(0,nrow=B,ncol=ncol(GC2)-1))
> vnames <- names(GC2)[-20]
> names(VI) <- vnames
> for(i in 1:B){
+   VI[i,] <- GC2_Bagging$mtrees[[i]]$btree$variable.
importance[vnames]
+ }
> colMeans(VI)
checking duration  history  purpose    amount  savings employed
installp
  50.282   58.920   33.540   48.301   74.721   30.838   32.865
18.722
 marital    coapp resident property      age  housing  existcr
job
  17.424    8.795   18.171   20.591   51.611    9.756   11.433
14.015
 depends telephon  foreign
      NA       NA       NA
```

The preceding program needs an explanation. Recollect that `variable.importance` is displayed in descending order. If you have gone through the `GC2_Bagging_Trees.pdf` file (even a cursory look will do), it can be seen that different trees have different variables to the primary split, and consequently the order of importance for variables would be different. Thus, we first save the order of variable that we need in `vnames` object, and then order for each tree `variable.importance[vnames]` by the same order as in `vnames`. Each tree in the loop is extracted with `$mtrees` and `$btree$variable.importance` to do what is required. Thus, the `VI data.frame` object now consists of the variable importance of all 500 trees set up by the bagging procedure. The `colMeans` gives the desired aggregate of the importance across the 500 trees, and the desired statistical inference can be carried out by looking across the detailed information in the `VI` frame. Note that the last three variables have `NA` in the aggregated mean. The reason for the `NA` result is that in some classification trees, these variables provide no gains whatsoever and are not even among any surrogate split. We can quickly discover how many trees contain no information on the importance of these three variables, and then repeat the calculation of the `colMeans` using the `na.rm=TRUE` option:

```
> sapply(VI,function(x) sum(is.na(x)))
checking duration  history  purpose    amount  savings employed
installp
       0        0        0        0         0        0        0
0
 marital    coapp resident property       age  housing  existcr
job
       0        0        0        0         0        0        0
0
 depends telephon  foreign
       9       35       20
> colMeans(VI,na.rm=TRUE)
checking duration  history  purpose    amount  savings employed
installp
  50.282   58.920   33.540   48.301    74.721   30.838   32.865
18.722
 marital    coapp resident property       age  housing  existcr
job
  17.424    8.795   18.171   20.591    51.611    9.756   11.433
14.015
 depends telephon  foreign
   6.345    5.167    3.200
```

In the previous section, we explored a host of options in `minsplit`, `minbucket`, `split`, and `loss` arguments. Can bagging incorporate these metrics? Using the `control` argument for the `bagging` function, we will now improvise on the earlier results. The choice of the additional parameters is kept the same as earlier. After fitting the bagging object, we inspect the accuracy, and then write the classification trees to the `GC2_Bagging_Trees_02.pdf` file. Clearly, the trees in this file are much more readable than the counterparts in the `GC2_Bagging_Trees.pdf` file, and expectedly so. The variable information table is also obtained for the `B = 500` trees with the following code:

```
> GC2_Bagging_02 <- bagging(GC2_Formula,data=GC2_Train,coob=FALSE,
+                           nbagg=B,keepX=TRUE,
+                           control=rpart.control(minsplit=30,minbuck
et=15,
+split="information",loss=matrix(c(0,200,500,0), byrow = TRUE,
nrow=2)))
> GC2_Margin_02 <- predict(GC2_Bagging_02,newdata = GC2_TestX,
+                          aggregation="weighted",type="class")
> sum(GC2_Margin_02==GC2_TestY)/nte
[1] 0.7604
> pdf("../Output/GC2_Bagging_Trees_02.pdf")
> for(i in 1:B){
+    tt <- GC2_Bagging_02$mtrees[[i]]
+    plot(tt$btree)
+    text(tt$btree,use.n=TRUE)
+ }
> dev.off()
null device
          1
> VI_02 <- data.frame(matrix(0,nrow=B,ncol=ncol(GC2)-1))
> names(VI_02) <- vnames
> for(i in 1:B){
+    VI_02[i,] <- GC2_Bagging_02$mtrees[[i]]$btree$variable.
importance[vnames]
+ }
> colMeans(VI_02,na.rm=TRUE)
checking duration  history  purpose   amount  savings employed
installp
 38.3075  18.9377  11.6756  19.1818  18.4385  16.1309   9.6110
3.6417
```

```
  marital    coapp resident property     age  housing  existcr
job
   4.3520   4.4913   3.4810   6.5278  10.0255   3.3401   3.1011
4.5115
 depends telephon  foreign
   1.6432   2.5535   0.9193
```

The number of trees for bagging has been chosen arbitrarily at 500. There is no
particular reason for this. We will now see how the accuracy over test data changes
over the number of trees chosen. The inspection will happen over the choice of the
number of trees varying from 1 to 25 at an increment of 1, and then by incrementing
by 25 to 50, 75, …, 475, 500. The reader is left to make sense out of this plot.
Meanwhile, the following program is straightforward and does not require
further explanation:

```
> Bags <- c(1:24,seq(25,B,25))
> Bag_Acc <- NULL
> for(i in 1:length(Bags)){
+    TBAG <- bagging(GC2_Formula,data=GC2_Train,coob=FALSE,
+                         nbagg=i,keepX=TRUE,
+                         control=rpart.control(minsplit=30,minbuck
et=15,
+                                        split="information",
+
loss=matrix(c(0,200,500,0),
+                                        byrow =
TRUE,
+                                        nrow=2)))
+    GC2_Margin_TBAG <- predict(TBAG,newdata = GC2_TestX,
+                         aggregation="weighted",type="class")
+    Bag_Acc[i] <- sum(GC2_Margin_TBAG==GC2_TestY)/nte
+    print(Bags[i])
+ }
[1] 1
[1] 2
[1] 3
[1] 4
[1] 5

[1] 23
[1] 24
[1] 25
```

```
[1] 50
[1] 75

[1] 475
[1] 500
> plot(Bags,Bag_Acc,"l",ylab="Accuracy")
```

The following is the output that is generated:

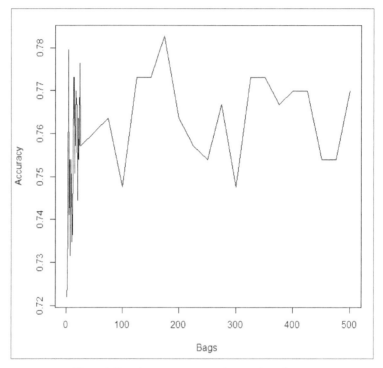

Figure 3: Bagging accuracy over the number of trees

Analytical techniques don't belong to the family of alchemies. If such a procedure is invented, we won't have to worry about modeling. The next example shows that bagging can also go wrong.

Bagging is not a guaranteed recipe!

In the first edition of his book, Berk (2016) cautions the reader not to fall prey to the proclaimed superiority of the newly invented methods. Recollect the Pima Indians Diabetes problem introduced in *Chapter 1, Introduction to Ensemble Techniques*. The accuracy table in there shows that the decision tree gives an accuracy of `0.7588`. We now apply the bagging method for the same partition and compute the accuracy as follows:

```
> data("PimaIndiansDiabetes")
> set.seed(12345)
> Train_Test <- sample(c("Train","Test"),nrow(PimaIndiansDiabetes),rep
lace = TRUE,prob = c(0.7,0.3))
> head(Train_Test)
[1] "Test"  "Test"  "Test"  "Test"  "Train" "Train"
> PimaIndiansDiabetes_Train <- PimaIndiansDiabetes[Train_
Test=="Train",]
> PimaIndiansDiabetes_TestX <- within(PimaIndiansDiabetes[Train_
Test=="Test",],
+                                      rm(diabetes))
> PimaIndiansDiabetes_TestY <- PimaIndiansDiabetes[Train_
Test=="Test","diabetes"]
> PID_Formula <- as.formula("diabetes~.")
> PID_Bagging <- bagging(PID_Formula,data=PimaIndiansDiabetes_
Train,coob=FALSE,
+                          nbagg=1000,keepX=TRUE)
> PID_Margin <- predict(PID_Bagging,newdata = PimaIndiansDiabetes_
TestX,
+                          aggregation="weighted",type="class")
> sum(PID_Margin==PimaIndiansDiabetes_TestY)/257
[1]  0.7548638
```

The overall accuracy here is `0.7548` while that of the single tree classification model was `0.7588`, which means that bagging has decreased the accuracy. This is not a worry if one understands the purpose of bagging. The purpose was always to increase the stability of the predictions, and, as such, we would rather accept that bagging would have decreased the variance term.

Bagging is a very important technique, and you need not restrict it to classification trees alone, but should rather go ahead and explore with other regression methods too, such as neural networks and support vector machines. In the next section, we will introduce the different approach of k-nearest neighbors (*k*-NN).

k-NN classifier

In *Chapter 1, Introduction to Ensemble Techniques*, we became familiar with a variety of classification models. Some readers might already be familiar with the k-NN model. The k-NN classifier is one of the most simple, intuitive, and non-assumptive models. The name of the model itself suggests how it might be working - nearest neighborhoods! And that's preceded by k! Thus, if we have N points in a study, we find the k-nearest points in neighborhood, and then make a note of the class of the k-neighbors. The majority class of the k-neighbors is then assigned to the unit. In case of regression, the average of the neighbors is assigned to the unit. The following is a visual depiction of k-NN:

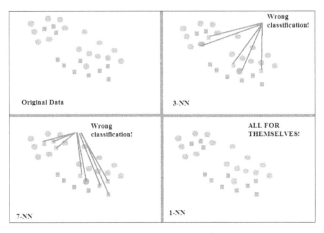

Figure 4: Visual depiction of k-NN

The top left part of the visual depiction of k-NN shows the scatterplot of 27 observations, 16 of which are circles and the remaining 11 are squares. The circles are marked in orange ⬤ while the squares are marked in blue ■. Suppose we choose to set up a classifier based on k = 3 neighbors. For every point, we then find its three neighbors and assign the majority color to it. Thus, if a circle remains orange, it has been correctly identified, and, similarly, if a square is correctly identified, its color will remain blue. However, if a circle point has two or more of its three nearest neighbors as squares, its color will change to blue and this will be denoted by ⬤ . Similarly, the color of an incorrectly classified square will change to orange ▪ . In the top-right block of the preceding diagram, we have the 3-NN predictions, while the 7-NN predictions can be found in the lower-left panel of the diagram. Note that with 3-NN, we have five misclassifications while with 7-NN, we have seven. Thus, increasing the number of the nearest neighbors does not mean that there will be an increase in the accuracy.

The bottom right panel is a 1-NN, which will always give a perfect classification. However, it is akin to a broken clock that shows the time perfectly only twice a day.

Analyzing waveform data

Next, we will perform the analyses for the waveform data. Repeat the code from *Chapter 1, Introduction to Ensemble Techniques,* to obtain the waveform data and then partition it for the train and test parts:

```
> set.seed(123)
> Waveform <- mlbench.waveform(5000)
> Waveform$classes <- ifelse(Waveform$classes!=3,1,2)
> Waveform_DF <- data.frame(cbind(Waveform$x,Waveform$classes)) # Data
Frame
> names(Waveform_DF) <- c(paste0("X",".",1:21),"Classes")
> Waveform_DF$Classes <- as.factor(Waveform_DF$Classes)
> set.seed(12345)
> Train_Test <- sample(c("Train","Test"),nrow(Waveform_DF),replace =
TRUE,
+     prob = c(0.7,0.3))
> Waveform_DF_Train <- Waveform_DF[Train_Test=="Train",]
> Waveform_DF_TestX <- within(Waveform_DF[Train_
Test=="Test",],rm(Classes))
> Waveform_DF_TestY <- Waveform_DF[Train_Test=="Test","Classes"]
> Waveform_DF_Formula <- as.formula("Classes~.")
> plot(Waveform_DF_Train$X.1,Waveform_DF_Train$X.8,col=Waveform_DF_
Train$Classes)
```

A simple scatterplot display of the two variables x.1 and x.8 by the classes is given in the following diagram. A lot of interplay of colors can be seen in the display and it does not appear that any form of logistic regression model or decision tree will help the case here. It might be that *k*-NN will be useful in this case:

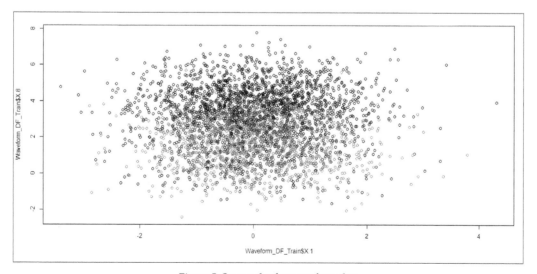

Figure 5: Scatterplot for waveform data

For k = 10, we first set up a *k*-NN model for the waveform data. The `knn` function from the `class` package is used here:

```
> WF_knn <- knn(train=Waveform_DF_Train[,-22],test=Waveform_DF_TestX,
+               cl=Waveform_DF_Train$Classes,k=10)
> sum(Waveform_DF_TestY==WF_knn)/nrow(Waveform_DF_TestX)
[1] 0.903183
```

The accuracy of 90.32% looks promising, and it is better than all the models considered in *Chapter 1, Introduction to Ensemble Techniques*, except for the support vector machine. We will expand the search grid for k over 2 to 50:

```
> k <- c(2:15,seq(20,50,5))
> knn_accuracy <- NULL
> for(i in 1:length(k)){
+    WF_temp_knn <- knn(train=Waveform_DF_Train[,-22],test=Waveform_DF_
TestX,
+                cl=Waveform_DF_Train$Classes,k=k[i])
+    knn_accuracy <- c(knn_accuracy,sum(Waveform_DF_TestY==WF_temp_
knn)/
+                      nrow(Waveform_DF_TestX))
+ }
> knn_accuracy
 [1] 0.8561 0.8919 0.8893 0.8886 0.8932 0.8985 0.8972 0.8992 0.9012
0.9025
[11] 0.9032 0.9058 0.9105 0.9019 0.8999 0.9072 0.9065 0.9098 0.9118
0.9085
[21] 0.9072
```

Note that for k = 40, we get the maximum accuracy. Why? We will put the *k*-NN in a bag in the next section.

k-NN bagging

The *k-NN* classifier introduced a classification model in the previous section. We can make this robust using the bootstrap method. The broader algorithm remains the same. As with the typical bootstrap method, we can always write a program consisting of the loop and depending on the number of required bootstrap samples, or bags, the control can be specified easily. However, here we will use a function from the FNN R package. The `ownn` function is useful for carrying out the bagging method on the *k*-NN classifier.

The owⁿn function requires all variables in the dataset to be numeric. However, we do have many variables that are factor variables. Consequently, we need to tweak the data so that we can use the `ownn` function. The covariate data from the training and test dataset are first put together using the `rbind` function. Using the `model.matrix` function with the formula `~.-1`, we convert all factor variables into numeric variables. The important question here is how does the `model.matrix` function work? To keep the explanation simple, if a factor variable has m levels, it will create m – 1 new binary variables, which will span the *m* dimensions. The reason why we combine the training and test covariates is that if any factor has less levels in any of the partition, the number of variables will be unequal and we would not be able to adopt the model built on the training dataset on the test dataset. After obtaining the covariate matrix with all numeric variables, we will split the covariates into the train and test regions again, specify the *k*-NN set up with the `ownn` function, and predict the accuracy as a consequence of using the bagging method. The program is as follows:

```
> All_Cov <- rbind(GC2_Train[,-20],GC2_TestX)
> All_CovX <- model.matrix(~.-1,All_Cov)
> GC2_Train_Cov <- All_CovX[1:nrow(GC2_Train),]
> GC2_Test_Cov <- All_CovX[(nrow(GC2_Train)+1):nrow(All_CovX),]
> k <- seq(5,50,1)
> knn_accuracy <- NULL
> for(i in 1:length(k)){
+   GC2_knn_Bagging <- ownn(train=GC2_Train_Cov, test=GC2_Test_Cov,
+                       cl=GC2_Train$good_bad,testcl=GC2_
TestY,k=k[i])
+   knn_accuracy[i] <- GC2_knn_Bagging$accuracy[3]
+ }
> knn_accuracy
 [1] 0.6198083 0.6293930 0.6357827 0.6549521 0.6549521 0.6645367
0.6869010
 [8] 0.6932907 0.7028754 0.7092652 0.7092652 0.7188498 0.7284345
0.7316294
[15] 0.7348243 0.7348243 0.7412141 0.7412141 0.7444089 0.7476038
0.7476038
[22] 0.7507987 0.7476038 0.7476038 0.7476038 0.7476038 0.7444089
0.7444089
[29] 0.7444089 0.7444089 0.7444089 0.7444089 0.7412141 0.7444089
0.7444089
[36] 0.7444089 0.7412141 0.7412141 0.7412141 0.7412141 0.7444089
0.7444089
[43] 0.7444089 0.7444089 0.7444089 0.7444089
> windows(height=100,width=100)
> plot.ts(knn_accuracy,main="k-NN Accuracy")
```

The `train`, `test`, `cl`, and `testcl` arguments are straightforward to follow; see `ownn`, and we will vary the number of neighbors on a grid of 5-50. Did we specify the number of bags or the bootstrap samples? Now, the bagging is carried out and the bagged predictions are given. It seems that there might be an approximation of the estimate as the package and the function clearly says that the predictions are based on bagging:

```
> GC2_knn_Bagging$accuracy
      knn         ownn         bnn
0.7444089 0.7444089 0.7444089
> GC2_knn_Bagging$bnnpred
  [1] good good good good good good good good good good good good good
 [14] good good good good good good good good good bad  good good good
 [27] good good good good good good good good good good bad  good good

[274] good good good good good good good good good good good good good
[287] good good good good good good good good good bad  bad  good good
[300] good good good good good good good good good good good good good
[313] good
Levels: bad good
```

The following accuracy plot shows that the model accuracy is stabilizing after about 20 neighborhoods. Thus, we have carried out the *k*-NN bagging technique:

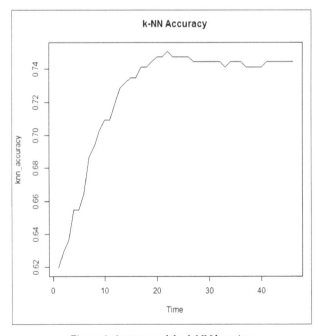

Figure 6: Accuracy of the *k*-NN bagging

Summary

Bagging is essentially an ensembling method that consists of homogeneous base learners. Bagging was introduced as a bootstrap aggregation method, and we saw some of the advantages of the bootstrap method in *Chapter 2, Bootstrapping*. The advantage of the bagging method is the stabilization of the predictions. This chapter began with modifications for the classification tree, and we saw different methods of improvising the performance of a decision tree so that the tree does not overfit the data. The bagging of the decision tress and the related tricks followed in the next section. We then introduced k-NN as an important classifier and illustrated it with a simple example. The chapter concluded with the bagging extension of the k-NN classifier.

Bagging helps in reducing the variance of the decision trees. However, the trees of the two bootstrap samples are correlated since a lot of common observations generate them. In the next chapter, we will look at innovative resampling, which will uncorrelate two decision trees.

4
Random Forests

The previous chapter introduced bagging as an ensembling technique based on homogeneous base learners, with the decision tree serving as a base learner. A slight shortcoming of the bagging method is that the bootstrap trees are correlated. Consequently, although the variance of predictions is reduced, the bias will persist. Breiman proposed randomly sampling the covariates and independent variables at each split, and this method then went on to help in decorrelating the bootstrap trees.

In the first section of this chapter, the random forest algorithm is introduced and illustrated. The notion of variable importance is crucial to decision trees and all of their variants, and a section is devoted to clearly illustrating this concept. Do the random forests perform better than bagging? An answer will be provided in the following section.

Breiman laid out the importance of proximity plots in the context of random forests, and we will delve into this soon enough. An algorithm as complex as this will have a lot of nitty-gritty details, and some of these will be illustrated through programs and real data. Missing data is almost omnipresent and we will undertake the task of imputing missing values using random forests. Although a random forest is primarily a supervised learning technique, it can also be used for clustering observations regarding the data, and this topic will be the concluding section.

The core topics of this chapter are the following:

- The Random Forest algorithm
- Variable importance for decision trees and random forests
- Comparing random forests with bagging
- Use of proximity plots
- Random forest details, nitty-gritty, and nuances
- Handling missing data by using random forests
- Clustering with random forests

Technical requirements

We will be using the following libraries in this chapter:

- `kernlab`
- `randomForest`
- `randomForestExplainer`
- `rpart`

Random Forests

Chapter 3, Bagging, generalized the decision tree using the bootstrap principle. Before we embark on a journey with random forests, we will quickly review the history of decision trees and highlight some of their advantages and drawbacks. The invention of decision trees followed through a culmination of papers, and the current form of the trees can be found in detail in Breiman, et al. (1984). Breiman's method is popularly known as **C**lassification **a**nd **R**egression **T**rees, aka **CART**. Around the late 1970s and early 1980s, Quinlan invented an algorithm called C4.5 independently of Breiman. For more information, see Quinlan (1984). To a large extent, the current form of decision trees, bagging, and random forests is owed to Breiman. A somewhat similar approach is also available in an algorithm popularly known by the abbreviation CHAID, which stands for **Chi**-square **A**utomatic **I**nteraction **D**etector. An in-depth look at CART can be found in Hastie, et al. (2009), and a statistical perspective can be found in Berk (2016). An excellent set of short notes can also be found in Seni and Elder (2010). Without any particular direction, we highlight some advantages and drawbacks of CART:

- Trees automatically address the problem of variable selection since at each split, they look for the variable that gives the best split in the regressand, and thus a tree eliminates variables that are not useful.

- Trees do not require data processing. This means that we don't have to consider transformation, rescaling, and/or weight-of-evidence preprocessing.

- Trees are computationally scalable and the time complexity is manageable.

- Trees give a metric called variable importance that is based on the contribution of the variable to error reduction across all the splits of the trees.

- Trees efficiently handle missing values and if an observation has a missing value, the tree will continue to use the available values of the observation. Handling missing data is often enabled by the notion of a surrogate split.

- Trees have fewer parameters to manage, as seen in the previous chapter.

- Trees have a simple top-down interpretation.

- Trees with great depth tend to be almost unbiased.

- The interaction effect is easily identified among the variables.

- Its drawback is that the fitted model is not continuous and it will have sharp edges. Essentially, trees are piecewise constant regression models.

- Trees can't approximate low interaction target functions.

- The greedy search approach to trees results in high variance.

The first extension of the trees was seen in the bagging algorithm discussed in the previous chapter. Suppose we have N observations. For each bootstrap sample, we draw N observations with replacement. How many observations are likely to be common between two bootstrap samples? Let's write a simple program to find it first, using the simple `sample` function:

```
> N <- seq(1e3,1e4,1e3)
> N
 [1]  1000  2000  3000  4000  5000  6000  7000  8000  9000 10000
> B <- 1e3
> Common_Prob <- NULL
>index<- 1
>for(i in N){
+    temp_prob <- NULL
+    for(j in 1:B){
+      s1 <- sample(i,size=i,replace=TRUE)
+      s2 <- sample(i,size=i,replace=TRUE)
+      temp_prob <- c(temp_prob,length(intersect(s1,s2))/i)
+    }
+    Common_Prob[index] <- mean(temp_prob)
+    index<- index + 1
+ }
> Common_Prob
 [1] 0.4011 0.4002 0.3996 0.3982 0.3998 0.3996 0.3994 0.3997 0.3996
0.3995
```

This program needs explanation. The number of *N* observations varies from 1000 to 10000 with an increment of 1000, and we run *B = 1e3 = 1000* bootstrap iterations. Now, for a fixed size of *N*, we draw two samples with replacement of size *N*, see how many observations are common between them, and divide it by *N*. The average of the *B = 1000* samples is the probability of finding a common observation between two samples. Equivalently, it gives the common observation percentage between two samples.

The bootstrap probability clearly shows that about 40% of observations will be common between any two trees. Consequently, the trees will be correlated.

In Chapter 15, Hastie, et al. (2009) points out that the bagging trees are IID trees and hence the expectation of any one tree is the same as the expectation of any other tree. Consequently, the bias of the bagged trees is the same as that of the individual trees. Thus, variance reduction is the only improvement provided by bagging. Suppose that we have B independent and identically distributed IID random variables with a variance of σ^2. The sample average has a variance of σ^2 / B. However, if we know that the variables are only identically distributed and that there is a positive pairwise correlation of ρ, then the variance of the sample average is as follows:

$$\rho\sigma^2 + \frac{1-\rho}{B}\sigma^2$$

Note that as the number of B samples increase, the second term vanishes and the first term remains. Thus, we see that the correlatedness of the bagged trees restricts the benefits of averaging. This motivated Breiman to innovate in a way that subsequent trees will not be correlated.

Breiman's solution is that before each split, select $m < p$ number of input variables at random for splitting. This lays the foundation of random forests, where we shake the data to improve the performance. Note that merely *shaking* does not guarantee improvement. This trick helps when we have highly nonlinear estimators. The formal random forest algorithm, following Hastie, et al. (2009) and Berk (2016), is given as follows:

1. Draw a random sample of size N with replacement from the data.

2. Draw a random sample without replacement of the predictors.

3. Construct the first recursive partition of the data in the usual way.

4. Repeat step 2 for each subsequent split until the tree is as large as desired. Importantly, do not prune. Compute each terminal node proportion.

5. Drop the out-of-bag (OOB) data down the tree and store the assigned class to each observation, along with each observation's predictor values.

6. Repeat steps 1-5 a large number of times, say 1000.

7. Using only the class assigned to each observation when that observation is OOB, count the number of times over the trees that the observation is classified in one category and the number of times over trees it is classified in the other category.

8. Assign each case to a category by a majority vote over the set of trees when that case is OOB.

From his practical experience, Breiman recommends randomly selecting a number of covariates at each split as $m = \sqrt{p}$ with a minimum node size of 1 for a classification problem, whereas the recommendation for a regression problem is $m = p / 3$ with a minimum node size of 5.

We will use the `randomForest` R package for software implementation. The German Credit data will be used for further analysis. If you remember, in *Chapter 1*, *Introduction to Ensemble Techniques*, the accuracy obtained by using the basic classification tree was 70%. We will set up the German credit data using the same settings as earlier, and we will build the random forest:

```
>load("../Data/GC2.RData")
>set.seed(12345)
> Train_Test <- sample(c("Train","Test"),nrow(GC2),
+ replace = TRUE,prob = c(0.7,0.3))
> GC2_Train <- GC2[Train_Test=="Train",]
> GC2_TestX <- within(GC2[Train_Test=="Test",],rm(good_bad))
> GC2_TestY <- GC2[Train_Test=="Test","good_bad"]
> GC2_Formula <- as.formula("good_bad~.")
> GC2_RF <- randomForest(GC2_Formula,data=GC2_Train,ntree=500)
> GC2_RF_Margin <- predict(GC2_RF,newdata = GC2_TestX,type="class")
>sum(GC2_RF_Margin==GC2_TestY)/313
[1] 0.7795527
```

The `randomForest` function applies over the `formula` and `data` as seen earlier. Here, we have specified the number of trees to be 500 with `ntree=500`.

If we compare this random result with the bagging result from the previous chapter, the accuracy obtained there was only `0.78`. Here, we have `p = 19` covariates, and so we will try to increase the number of covariates sampled for a split at `8`, and see how it performs:

```
> GC2_RF2 <- randomForest(GC2_Formula,data=GC2_Train,mtry=8,
+ ntree=500)
> GC2_RF_Margin <- predict(GC2_RF,newdata = GC2_TestX, type="class")
> GC2_RF2_Margin <- predict(GC2_RF2,newdata = GC2_TestX,type="class")
> sum(GC2_RF2_Margin==GC2_TestY)/313
[1] 0.7859425
```

An increase of `0.01`, or about 1%, might appear meager. However, in a banking context, this accuracy will translate into millions of dollars. We will use the usual `plot` function:

```
>plot(GC2_RF2)
> GC2_RF2.legend <- colnames(GC2_RF2$err.rate)
```

```
> legend(x=300,y=0.5,legend = GC2_RF2.legend,lty=c(1,2,3),
col=c(1,2,3))
>head(GC2_RF2$err.rate,10)
              OOB        bad        good
  [1,]  0.3206751  0.4743590  0.2452830
  [2,]  0.3218673  0.4769231  0.2490975
  [3,]  0.3222656  0.5437500  0.2215909
  [4,]  0.3006993  0.5224719  0.2005076
  [5,]  0.3262643  0.5445026  0.2274882
  [6,]  0.3125000  0.5522388  0.2027335
  [7,]  0.3068702  0.5631068  0.1893096
  [8,]  0.2951807  0.5741627  0.1670330
  [9,]  0.2976190  0.5619048  0.1774892
 [10,]  0.2955882  0.5801887  0.1666667
```

The following graph is the output of the preceding code executed using the
`plot` function:

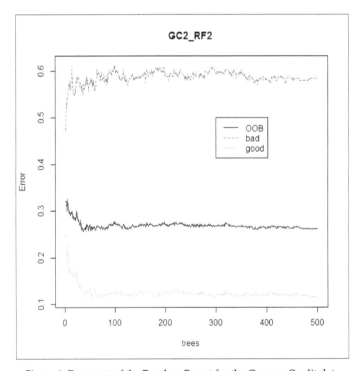

Figure 1: Error rate of the Random Forest for the German Credit data

We have three curves: the error rate for OOB, the error rate for the good class, and
the error rate for the bad class. Note that the error rate stabilizes at around 100 trees.
Using the loss matrix, it might be possible to reduce the gap between the three
curves. Ideally, the three curves should be as close as possible.

Exercise: Create random forests with the options of `split` criteria, `loss` matrix, `minsplit`, and different `mtry`. Examine the error rate curves and prepare a summary.

Visualize the random forest! Where are the trees? Apparently, we need to do a lot of exercises to extract trees out of the fitted `randomForest` object. A new function, `plot_RF`, has been defined in the `Utilities.R` file and we will display it here:

```
plot_RF <- function(RF){
  n <- RF$ntree
  for(i in 1:n){
    tt <- getTree(RF,i,labelVar = TRUE)
    dt <- to.dendrogram(tt)
    plot(dt,center=TRUE,edgePar=list(t.cex=1,p.col=NA,p.lty=0),
        yaxt='n',horiz=TRUE)
    print(i)
  }
}
```

The `plot_RF` function first obtains the number of `$ntree` trees in the forest. It will then run through a `for` loop. In each iteration of the loop, it will extract information related to that tree with the `getTree` function and create a new `dendogram` object. The `dendogram` is then visualized, and is nothing but the tree. Furthermore, the `print` command is optional and can be muted out.

Four arbitrarily chosen trees from the forest in the PDF file are displayed in the following figure, Trees of the Random Forest:

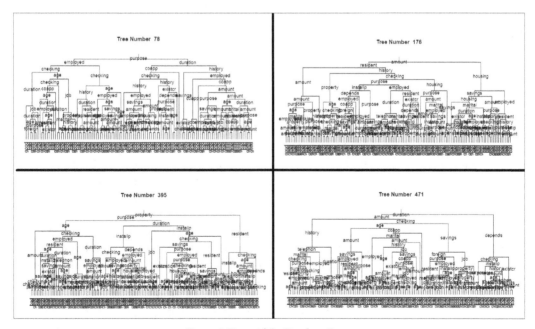

Figure 2: Trees of the Random Forest

A quick visit is paid to the Pima Indians diabetes problem. In the accuracy table of *Chapter 1, Introduction to Ensemble Techniques*, we could see that the accuracy for the decision tree was 0.7588, or 75.88%:

```
> data("PimaIndiansDiabetes")
> set.seed(12345)
> Train_Test <- sample(c("Train","Test"),nrow(PimaIndiansDiabetes),
+ replace = TRUE, prob = c(0.7,0.3))
> head(Train_Test)
[1] "Test"  "Test"  "Test"  "Test"  "Train" "Train"
> PimaIndiansDiabetes_Train <- PimaIndiansDiabetes[Train_
Test=="Train",]
> PimaIndiansDiabetes_TestX <- within(PimaIndiansDiabetes[Train_
Test=="Test",],rm(diabetes))
> PimaIndiansDiabetes_TestY <- PimaIndiansDiabetes[
+ Train_Test=="Test","diabetes"]
> PID_Formula <- as.formula("diabetes~.")
> PID_RF <- randomForest(PID_Formula,data=PimaIndiansDiabetes_
Train,coob=TRUE,
+                       ntree=500,keepX=TRUE,mtry=5,
+                       parms=list(prior=c(0.65,0.35)))
> PID_RF_Margin <- predict(PID_RF,newdata = PimaIndiansDiabetes_TestX,
type="class")
> sum(PID_RF_Margin==PimaIndiansDiabetes_TestY)/257
[1] 0.7704
```

Thus, we have an improved accuracy of 0.7704 – 0.7588 = 0.0116, or about 1.2%.

Exercise: Obtain the error rate plot of the Pima Indian Diabetes problem.

Variable importance

Statistical models, say linear regression and logistic regression, indicate which variables are significant with measures such as p-value and t-statistics. In a decision tree, a split is caused by a single variable. If the specification of the number of variables for the surrogate splits, a certain variable may appear as the split criteria more than once in the tree and some variables may never appear in the tree splits at all. During each split, we select the variable that leads to the maximum reduction in impurity, and the contribution of a variable across the tree splits would also be different. The overall improvement across each split of the tree (by the reduction in impurity for the classification tree or by the improvement in the split criterion) is referred to as the *variable importance*. In the case of ensemble methods such as bagging and random forest, the variable importance is measured for each tree in the technique. While the concept of variable importance is straightforward, its computational understanding is often unclear. This is primarily because a formula or an expression is not given in mathematical form. The idea is illustrated next through simple code.

The `kyphosis` dataset from the `rpart` package consists of four variables, and the target variable here is named `Kyphosis`, indicating the presence of the kyphosis type of deformation following an operation. The three explanatory variables are `Age`, `Number`, and `Start`. We build a classification tree with zero surrogate variables for the split criteria with the `maxsurrogate=0` option. The choice of zero surrogates ensures that we have only one variable at a split. The tree is set up and visualized as follows:

```
> data(kyphosis)
> kc<- rpart(Kyphosis~.,data=kyphosis,maxsurrogate=0)
> plot(kc);text(kc)
```

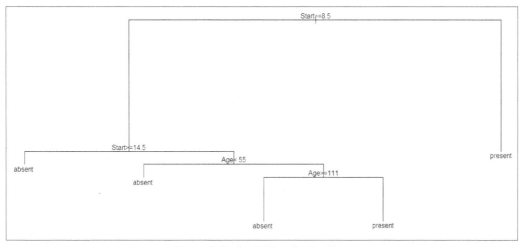

Figure 3: Kyphosis Classification Tree

In the no-surrogate tree, the first split variable is `Start`, with a terminal leaf on the right part of the split. The left side/partition further splits again with the `Start` variable, with a terminal node/leaf on the left side and a split on the later right side. In the next two split points, we use only the `Age` variable, and the `Number` variable is not used anywhere in the tree. Thus, we expect the `Number` variable to have zero importance.

Using `$variable.importance` on the fitted classification tree, we obtain the variable importance of the three explanatory variables:

```
>kc$variable.importance
Start   Age
7.783 2.961
```

As expected, the `Number` variable is not shown as having any importance. The importance of `Start` is given as `7.783` and `Age` as `2.961`. To understand how R has computed these values, run the `summary` function on the classification tree:

```
>summary(kc)
Call:
rpart(formula = Kyphosis ~ ., data = kyphosis, maxsurrogate = 0)
  n= 81
        CP nsplit rel error xerror    xstd
1 0.17647      0    1.0000      1 0.2156
2 0.01961      1    0.8235      1 0.2156
3 0.01000      4    0.7647      1 0.2156


Variable importance
Start    Age
   72     28


Node number 1: 81 observations,     complexity param=0.1765
predicted class=absent    expected loss=0.2099  P(node) =1
class counts:     64    17
probabilities: 0.790 0.210
left son=2 (62 obs) right son=3 (19 obs)
   Primary splits:
Start  < 8.5to the right, improve=6.762, (0 missing)
       Number <5.5  to the left,  improve=2.867, (0 missing)
       Age    < 39.5 to the left,  improve=2.250, (0 missing)


Node number 2: 62 observations,     complexity param=0.01961
predicted class=absent    expected loss=0.09677  P(node) =0.7654
class counts:     56     6
probabilities: 0.903 0.097
left son=4 (29 obs) right son=5 (33 obs)
   Primary splits:
Start  < 14.5to the right, improve=1.0210, (0 missing)
       Age    < 55   to the left,  improve=0.6849, (0 missing)
       Number <4.5  to the left,  improve=0.2975, (0 missing)


Node number 3: 19 observations
predicted class=present  expected loss=0.4211  P(node) =0.2346
class counts:      8    11
probabilities: 0.421 0.579


Node number 4: 29 observations
predicted class=absent    expected loss=0  P(node) =0.358
class counts:     29     0
probabilities: 1.000 0.000
```

```
Node number 5: 33 observations,    complexity param=0.01961
predicted class=absent    expected loss=0.1818  P(node) =0.4074
class counts:     27      6
probabilities: 0.818 0.182
left son=10 (12 obs) right son=11 (21 obs)
  Primary splits:
Age     < 55to the left,  improve=1.2470, (0 missing)
Start   < 12.5 to the right, improve=0.2888, (0 missing)
      Number <3.5  to the right, improve=0.1753, (0 missing)

Node number 10: 12 observations
predicted class=absent    expected loss=0  P(node) =0.1481
class counts:     12      0
probabilities: 1.000 0.000

Node number 11: 21 observations,    complexity param=0.01961
predicted class=absent    expected loss=0.2857  P(node) =0.2593
class counts:     15      6
probabilities: 0.714 0.286
left son=22 (14 obs) right son=23 (7 obs)
  Primary splits:
Age     <111   to the right, improve=1.71400, (0 missing)
Start   < 12.5 to the right, improve=0.79370, (0 missing)
      Number <3.5  to the right, improve=0.07143, (0 missing)

Node number 22: 14 observations
predicted class=absent    expected loss=0.1429  P(node) =0.1728
class counts:     12      2
probabilities: 0.857 0.143

Node number 23: 7 observations
predicted class=present   expected loss=0.4286  P(node) =0.08642
class counts:     3      4
probabilities: 0.429 0.571
```

Four lines of output have been highlighted in the summary output, and each line contains the information about the split, the best of improvement offered by each of the variables, and the variable selected at the split. Thus, for the Start variable, the first highlighted line shows the improvement at 6.762 and the second line shows 1.021. By adding these, we get 6.762 + 1.021 = 7.783, which is the same as the output given from the $variable.importance extractor. Similarly, the last two highlighted lines show the contribution of Age as 1.274 + 1.714 = 2.961. Thus, we have clearly outlined the computation of the variable importance.

Exercise: Create a new classification tree, say KC2, and allow a surrogate split. Using the summary function, verify the computations associated with the variable importance.

The VarImpPlot function from the randomForest package gives us a dot chart plot of the variable importance measure:

```
>windows(height=100,width=200)
>par(mfrow=c(1,2))
>varImpPlot(GC2_RF,main="Variable Importance plot for \n Random
+ Forest of German Data")
>varImpPlot(PID_RF,main="Variable Importance plot for \n Random Forest
of Pima Indian Diabetes")
```

A visual display is given in the following figure:

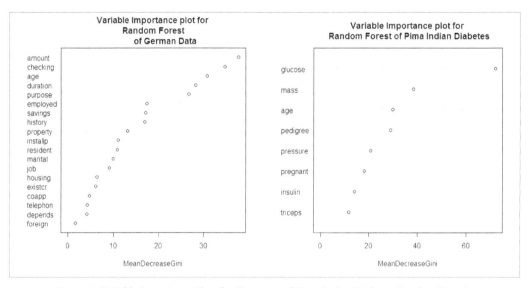

Figure 4: Variable Importance Plots for German and Pima Indian Diabetes Random Forests

Thus, the five most important variables for classifying the German credit as good or bad are amount, checking, age, duration, and purpose. For the Pima Indian Diabetes classification, the three most important variables are glucose, mass, and age.

We will look at the notion of the proximity measure next.

Proximity plots

According to Hastie, et al. (2009), *"one of the advertised outputs of a random forest is a proximity plot"* (see page 595). But what are proximity plots? If we have *n* observations in the training dataset, a proximity matrix of order $n \times n$ is created. Here, the matrix is initialized with all the values at 0. Whenever a pair of observations such as OOB occur jointly in the terminal node of a tree, the proximity count is increased by 1. The proximity matrix is visualized using the multidimensional scaling method, a concept beyond the scope of this chapter, where the proximity matrix is represented in two dimensions. The proximity plots give an indication of which points are closer to each other from the perspective of the random forest.

In the earlier creation of random forests, we had not specified the option of a proximity matrix. Thus, we will first create the random forest using the option of proximity as follows:

```
> GC2_RF3 <- randomForest(GC2_Formula,data=GC2_Train,
+                         ntree=500,proximity=TRUE,cob.prox=TRUE)
> GC2_RF3$proximity[1:10,1:10]
        5       6       7       8      11      12      14      15      16
17
5   1.0000 0.0000 0.0000 0.0133 0.0139 0.0159 0.0508 0.0645 0.0000
0.0000
6   0.0000 1.0000 0.0435 0.0308 0.0000 0.0000 0.0000 0.0000 0.0000
0.0417
7   0.0000 0.0435 1.0000 0.0000 0.0000 0.0000 0.0000 0.0000 0.0000
0.2000
8   0.0133 0.0308 0.0000 1.0000 0.0000 0.0000 0.0000 0.0000 0.0137
0.0000
11  0.0139 0.0000 0.0000 0.0000 1.0000 0.0395 0.0000 0.2034 0.0147
0.0000
12  0.0159 0.0000 0.0000 0.0000 0.0395 1.0000 0.0000 0.0323 0.0000
0.0000
14  0.0508 0.0000 0.0000 0.0000 0.0000 0.0000 1.0000 0.0167 0.0435
0.0182
15  0.0645 0.0000 0.0000 0.0000 0.2034 0.0323 0.0167 1.0000 0.0345
0.0000
16  0.0000 0.0000 0.0000 0.0137 0.0147 0.0000 0.0435 0.0345 1.0000
0.0159
17  0.0000 0.0417 0.2000 0.0000 0.0000 0.0000 0.0182 0.0000 0.0159
1.0000
>MDSplot(GC2_RF3,fac = GC2_Train$good_bad,
+         main="MDS Plot for Proximity Matrix of a RF")
```

The options `proximity=TRUE,cob.prox=TRUE` are important to obtain the
`proximity` matrix. We then simply make use of the `MDSplot` graphical function:

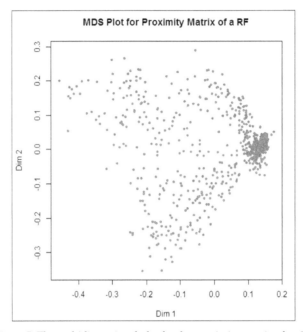

Figure 5: The multidimensional plot for the proximity matrix of an RF

It is easier to find which observation is closest to a given observation from the proximity
data perspective, and not the Euclidean distance, using the `which.max` function:

```
>which.max(GC2_RF3$proximity[1,-1])
962
657
>which.max(GC2_RF3$proximity[2,-2])
686
458
```

Thus, the observations numbered `657` in the training dataset (and `962` in the overall
dataset) are closest to the first observation. Note that the overall position is because
of the name extracted from the sample function. The `which.max` function is useful for
finding the maximum position in an array.

It turns out that most often, the graphical display using the MDSplot function results in a similar star-shape display. The proximity matrix also helps in carrying out cluster analysis, as will be seen in the concluding section of the chapter. Next, we will cover the parameters of a random forest in more detail.

Random Forest nuances

The GC_Random_Forest.pdf file consists of the 500 trees which serve as the homogeneous learners in the random forest ensemble. It is well known that a decision tree has a nice and clear interpretation. This is because it shows how one traverses the path to a terminal node. The random selection of features at each split and the bootstrap samples lead to the setting up of the random forest. Refer to the figure *Trees of the Random Forest*, which depicts trees numbered 78, 176, 395, and 471. The first split across the four trees is respectively purpose, amount, property, and duration. The second split for the first left side of these four trees is employed, resident, purpose, and amount, respectively. It is a cumbersome exercise to see which variables are meaningful over the others. We know that the earlier a variable appears, the higher its importance is. The question that then arises is, with respect to a random forest, how do we find the depth distribution of the variables? This and many other points are addressed through a powerful random forest package available as randomForestExplainer, and it is not an exaggeration that this section would not have been possible without this awesome package.

By applying the min_depth_distribution function on the random forest object, we get the depth distribution of the variables. Using plot_min_depth_distribution, we then get the plot of minimum depth distribution:

```
> GC2_RF_MDD <- min_depth_distribution(GC2_RF)
>head(GC2_RF_MDD)
tree variable minimal_depth
1    1       age            4
2    1    amount            3
3    1 checking            0
4    1     coapp            2
5    1   depends            8
6    1  duration            2
>windows(height=100,width=100)
> plot_min_depth_distribution(GC2_RF_MDD,k=nrow(GC2_TestX))
```

The result of the preceding code block is *Minimum Depth Distribution of German Random Forest*, which is as follows:

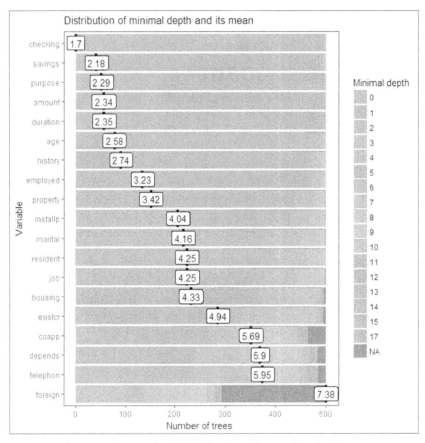

Figure 6: Minimum Depth Distribution of German Random Forest

From previous figure, it is clear that the `checking` variable appears more often as the primary split, followed by `savings`, `purpose`, `amount`, and `duration`. Consequently, we get a useful depiction through the minimum depth distribution plot. Further analyses are possible by using the `measure_importance` function, which gives us various measures of importance for the variables of the random forest:

```
> GC2_RF_VIM <- measure_importance(GC2_RF)
[1] "Warning: your forest does not contain information on local
importance so 'accuracy_decrease' measure cannot be extracted. To
add it regrow the forest with the option localImp = TRUE and run this
function again."
```

We are warned here that the random forest has not been grown with the option of `localImp = TRUE`, which is central to obtaining the measures. Thus, we create a new random forest with this option, and then run the `measure_importance` function on it:

```
> GC2_RF4<- randomForest(GC2_Formula,data=GC2_Train,
+                        ntree=500,localImp=TRUE)
> GC2_RF4_VIM <- measure_importance(GC2_RF4)
```

The output has a wider format, and hence we provide it in an image format and display the result vertically in *Analysis of Variable Importance Measure*. We can see that the `measure_importance` function gives a lot of information on the average minimum depth, number of nodes across the 500 trees that the variable appears as node, the average decrease in accuracy, the Gini decrease, and so on.

We can see from the output that if the mean minimum depth is higher, the associated p-value is also higher and hence the variable is insignificant. For example, the variables `coapp`, `depends`, `existcr`, `foreign`, and `telephon` have a higher mean minimum depth, and their p-value is also 1 in most cases. Similarly, lower values of `gini_decrease` are also associated with higher p-values, and this indicates the insignificance of the variables:

```
> GC2_RF4_VIM
    variable mean_min_depth no_of_nodes accuracy_decrease gini_decrease no_of_trees times_a_root  p_value
1        age            2.5        7750           0.00455          31.2         500           43  0.0e+00
2     amount            2.4        8512           0.00890          37.7         500           44  0.0e+00
3   checking            1.8        3347           0.03490          34.6         500          104  9.8e-01
4      coapp            5.6        1009           0.00272           4.5         456           10  1.0e+00
5     depends           5.6        1461           0.00022           4.3         486            0  1.0e+00
6    duration           2.3        6319           0.01343          28.1         500           59  0.0e+00
7    employed           3.0        4147           0.00254          16.8         500           14  2.3e-31
8     existcr           5.1        2186           0.00084           6.2         499            1  1.0e+00
9     foreign           7.8         403           0.00067           1.6         300           11  1.0e+00
10    history           2.6        3290           0.00499          17.0         500           51  1.0e+00
11    housing           4.3        1845           0.00071           6.6         496           19  1.0e+00
12   installp           4.2        3699           0.00065          11.1         500            1  2.4e-05
13        job           4.3        2612           0.00061           9.0         500            2  1.0e+00
14    marital           4.2        2847          -0.00059          10.3         499            1  1.0e+00
15   property           3.5        3401           0.00180          12.6         500           17  8.6e-01
16    purpose           2.3        4930           0.00372          27.3         500           42  4.3e-129
17   resident           4.4        3684           0.00024          10.7         500            1  6.9e-05
18     savings          2.3        2820           0.00995          17.9         500           80  1.0e+00
19    telephon          5.9        1539           0.00034           4.6         487            0  1.0e+00
```

Figure 7: Analysis of Variable Importance Measure

The importance measure object `GC2_RF_VIM` can be used for further analyses. For the `no_of_nodes` measure, we can compare the various metrics from the previous variable importance measures. For instance, we would like to see how the `times_a_root` values for the variables turns out against the mean minimum depth. Similarly, we would like to analyze other measures. By applying the `plot_multi_way_importance` graphical function on this object, we get the following output:

```
> P1 <- plot_multi_way_importance(GC2_RF4_VIM, size_measure = "no_of_
nodes",
+                                x_measure="mean_min_depth",
```

```
+                                y_measure = "times_a_root")
> P2 <- plot_multi_way_importance(GC2_RF4_VIM, size_measure = "no_of_
nodes",
+                                x_measure="mean_min_depth",
+                                y_measure = "gini_decrease")
> P3 <- plot_multi_way_importance(GC2_RF4_VIM, size_measure = "no_of_
nodes",
+                                x_measure="mean_min_depth",
+                                y_measure = "no_of_trees")
> P4 <- plot_multi_way_importance(GC2_RF4_VIM, size_measure = "no_of_
nodes",
+                                x_measure="mean_min_depth",
+                                y_measure = "p_value")
> grid.arrange(P1,P2,P3,P4, ncol=2)
```

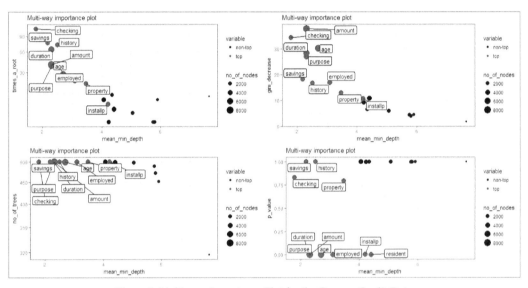

Figure 8: Multi-way Importance Plot for the German Credit Data

Here, the `times_a_root` values of the variables are plotted against the mean minimum depth, `mean_min_depth`, while keeping the number of nodes to their size. The non-top variables are black, while the top variables are blue. Similarly, we plot `gini_decrease`, `no_of_trees` and `p_value` against `mean_min_depth` in the preceding figure.

The correlation between the five measures is depicted next, using the `plot_importance_ggpairs` function:

```
> plot_importance_ggpairs(GC2_RF4_VIM)
```

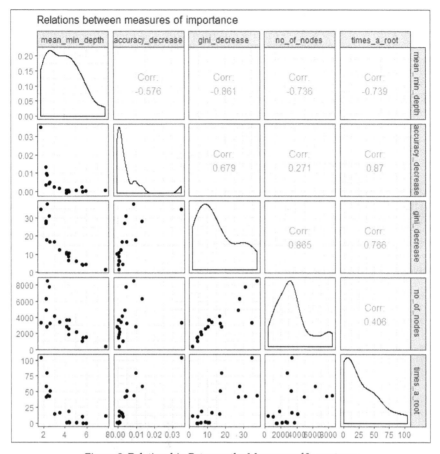

Figure 9: Relationship Between the Measures of Importance

Since the measures are strongly correlated, either positively or negatively, we need to have all five of these measures to understand random forests.

A great advantage of the tree structure is the interpretation of interaction between the variables. For instance, if the split in a parent is by one variable, and by another variable in the daughter node, we can conclude that there is interaction between these two variables. Again, the question arises for the random forests. Using the `important_variables` and `min_depth_interactions`, we can obtain the interactions among the variables of a random forest as follows:

```
> GC2_RF4_VIN <- important_variables(GC2_RF4, k = 5,
+                                    measures = c("mean_min_depth",
"no_of_trees"))
> GC2_RF4_VIN_Frame <- min_depth_interactions(GC2_RF4,GC2_RF4_VIN)
>head(GC2_RF4_VIN_Frame[order(GC2_RF4_VIN_Frame$occurrences,
decreasing = TRUE), ])
```

```
variable root_variable mean_min_depth occurrences        interaction
7    amount    checking              1.6       442    checking:amount
2       age    checking              2.0       433       checking:age
27 duration    checking              2.1       426 checking:duration
77  purpose    checking              2.0       420   checking:purpose
32 employed    checking              2.6       417 checking:employed
8    amount    duration              2.4       408    duration:amount
   uncond_mean_min_depth
7                    2.4
2                    2.5
27                   2.3
77                   2.3
32                   3.0
8                    2.4
> plot_min_depth_interactions(GC2_RF2_VIN_Frame)
```

The following is the output that will be obtained:

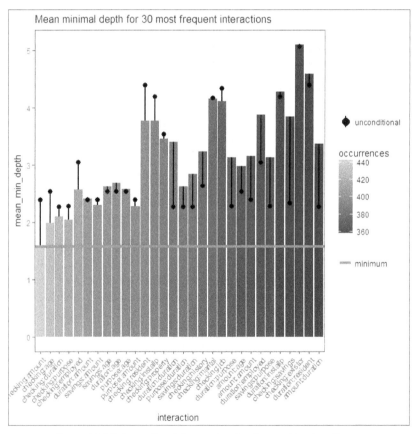

Figure 10: Minimum Depth Interaction for German Random Forest

Thus, we can easily find the interaction variables of the random forest.

The `randomForestExplainer` R package is very powerful and helps us to carry out many diagnostics after obtaining the random forests. Without post diagnostics, we cannot evaluate any fitted model. Consequently, the reader is advised to carry out most of the steps learned in this section in their implementation of random forests.

We will compare a random forest with the bagging procedure in the next section.

Exercise: Carry out the diagnostics for the random forest built for the Pima Indian Diabetes problem.

Comparisons with bagging

When comparing the random forest results with the bagging counterpart for the German credit data and Pima Indian Diabetes datasets, we did not see much improvement in the accuracy over the validated partition of the data. A potential reason might be that the variability reduction achieved by bagging is at the optimum reduced variance, and that any bias improvement will not lead to an increase in the accuracy.

We consider a dataset to be available from the R core package `kernlab`. The dataset is spam and it has a collection of 4601 emails with labels that state whether the email is spam or non-spam. The dataset has a good collection of 57 variables derived from the email contents. The task is to build a good classifier for the spam identification problem. The dataset is quickly partitioned into training and validation partitions, as with earlier problems:

```
> data("spam")
> set.seed(12345)
> Train_Test <- sample(c("Train","Test"),nrow(spam),replace = TRUE,
+ prob = c(0.7,0.3))
> head(Train_Test)
[1] "Test"  "Test"  "Test"  "Test"  "Train" "Train"
> spam_Train <- spam[Train_Test=="Train",]
> spam_TestX <- within(spam[Train_Test=="Test",],rm(type))
> spam_TestY <- spam[Train_Test=="Test","type"]
> spam_Formula <- as.formula("type~.")
```

First, we will build the simple classification tree:

```
> spam_ct <- rpart(spam_Formula,data=spam_Train)
> spam_ct_predict <- predict(spam_ct,newdata=spam_TestX,
+ type="class")
> ct_accuracy <- sum(spam_ct_predict==spam_TestY)/nrow(spam_TestX)
> ct_accuracy
[1] 0.8994
```

The classification tree gives a modest accuracy of about 90%. We will then apply randomForest and build the random forest:

```
> spam_rf <- randomForest(spam_Formula,data=spam_Train,coob=TRUE,
+                         ntree=500,keepX=TRUE,mtry=5)
> spam_rf_predict <- predict(spam_rf,newdata=spam_TestX,
+ type="class")
> rf_accuracy <- sum(spam_rf_predict==spam_TestY)/nrow(spam_TestX)
> rf_accuracy
[1] 0.9436
```

Bagging can be performed with the randomForest function. The trick is to ask the random forest to use all the variables while setting up a split. Thus, the choice of mtry=ncol(spal_TestX) will select all the variables and bagging is then easily performed:

```
> spam_bag <- randomForest(spam_Formula,data=spam_Train,coob=TRUE,
+ ntree=500,keepX=TRUE,mtry=ncol(spam_TestX))
> spam_bag_predict <- predict(spam_bag,newdata=spam_TestX,
+ type="class")
> bag_accuracy <- sum(spam_bag_predict==spam_TestY)/
+ nrow(spam_TestX)
> bag_accuracy
[1] 0.935
> windows(height=100,width=200)
> par(mfrow=c(1,2))
> plot(spam_rf,main="Random Forest for Spam Classification")
> plot(spam_bag,main="Bagging for Spam Classification")
```

The increase in accuracy is also reflected in the accuracy plots, as shown in the following figure:

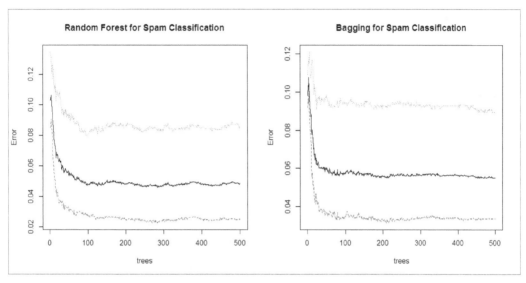

Figure 11: Random Forest and Bagging Comparisons for the Spam Classification Problem

We will look at some niche applications of random forests in the concluding two sections.

Missing data imputation

Missing data is a menace! It pops up out of nowhere and blocks analysis until it is properly taken care of. The statistical technique of the expectation-maximization algorithm, or simply the EM algorithm, needs a lot of information on the probability distributions, structural relationship, and in-depth details of statistical models. However, an approach using the EM algorithm is completely ruled out here. Random forests can be used to overcome the missing data problem.

We will use the `missForest` R package to fix the missing data problem whenever we come across it in the rest of the book. The algorithm for the `missForest` function and other details can be found at `https://academic.oup.com/bioinformatics/article/28/1/112/219101`. For any variable/column with missing data, the technique is to build a random forest for that variable and obtain the OOB prediction as the imputation error estimates. Note that the function can handle continuous as well as categorical missing values. The creators of the package have enabled the functions with parallel run capability to save time.

We will take a simple dataset from `https://openmv.net/info/travel-times`, and there are missing values in the data. The data consists of 13 variables and 205 observations. Of the 13 variables available, only the `FuelEconomy` variable has missing values. Let's explore the dataset in the R terminal:

```
> TT <- read.csv("../Data/Travel_Times.csv")
>dim(TT)
[1] 205   13
>sum(is.na(TT))
[1] 19
>sapply(TT,function(x) sum(is.na(x)))
          Date      StartTime      DayOfWeek         GoingTo
Distance
             0              0              0               0
0
       MaxSpeed       AvgSpeed AvgMovingSpeed      FuelEconomy
TotalTime
             0              0              0              19
0
     MovingTime      Take407All       Comments
             0              0              0
> TT$FuelEconomy
   [1]    NA    NA    NA    NA    NA    NA    NA    NA  8.89  8.89
 8.89  8.89
  [13]  8.89  8.89  8.89  8.89  9.08  9.08  9.08  9.08  9.08  9.08
 9.08  9.08
  [25]  9.76  9.76  9.76  9.76  9.76  9.76  9.76  9.16  9.16  9.16
NA    NA
  [37]    NA    NA    NA    NA    NA    NA  9.30  9.30  9.30  9.30
 9.30  9.30
  [49] 10.05 10.05 10.05 10.05  9.53  9.53  9.53  9.53  9.53  9.53
 9.53  9.53
  [61]  9.35  9.35  9.35  9.35  9.35  9.35  9.35  9.35  8.32  8.32
 8.32  8.32

 [181]  8.48  8.48  8.48  8.45  8.45  8.45  8.45  8.45  8.45  8.45
 8.45  8.45
 [193]  8.45  8.28  8.28  8.28  7.89  7.89  7.89  7.89  7.89  7.89
NA    NA
 [205]    NA
```

It can be seen that there are 19 observations with missing values. The `sapply` function tells us that all 19 observations have missing values for the `FuelEconomy` variable only. The `missForest` function is now deployed in action:

```
> TT_Missing <- missForest(TT[,-c(1,2,12)],
+                            maxiter = 10,ntree=500,mtry=6)
missForest iteration 1 in progress...done!
missForest iteration 2 in progress...done!
missForest iteration 3 in progress...done!
missForest iteration 4 in progress...done!
> TT_FuelEconomy <- cbind(TT_Missing$ximp[,7],TT$FuelEconomy)
> TT_FuelEconomy[is.na(TT$FuelEconomy),]
         [,1] [,2]
 [1,] 8.59   NA
 [2,] 8.91   NA
 [3,] 8.82   NA
 [4,] 8.63   NA
 [5,] 8.44   NA
 [6,] 8.63   NA
 [7,] 8.60   NA
 [8,] 8.50   NA
 [9,] 9.07   NA
[10,] 9.10   NA
[11,] 8.52   NA
[12,] 9.12   NA
[13,] 8.53   NA
[14,] 8.85   NA
[15,] 8.70   NA
[16,] 9.42   NA
[17,] 8.40   NA
[18,] 8.49   NA
[19,] 8.64   NA
```

We have now imputed the missing values. It needs to be noted that the imputed values should make sense and should not look out of place. In *Chapter 9, Ensembling Regression Models*, we will use the `missForest` function to impute a lot of missing values.

Exercise: How can the imputed values be validated? Use the `prodNA` function from the `missForest` package and puncture good values with missing data. Using the `missForest` function, get the imputed values and compare them with the original values.

The proximity matrix tells us how close the observations are from the random forest perspective. If we have information about the observations neighborhood, we can carry out a cluster analysis. As a by-product of using the proximity matrix, we can now also use random forests for unsupervised problems.

Clustering with Random Forest

Random forests can be set up without the target variable. Using this feature, we will calculate the proximity matrix and use the OOB proximity values. Since the proximity matrix gives us a measure of closeness between the observations, it can be converted into clusters using hierarchical clustering methods.

We begin with the setup of `y = NULL` in the `randomForest` function. The options of `proximity=TRUE` and `oob.prox=TRUE` are specified to ensure that we obtain the required proximity matrix:

```
>data(multishapes)
>par(mfrow=c(1,2))
>plot(multishapes[1:2],col=multishapes[,3],
+      main="Six Multishapes Data Display")
> MS_RF <- randomForest(x=multishapes[1:2],y=NULL,ntree=1000,
+ proximity=TRUE, oob.prox=TRUE,mtry = 1)
```

Next, we use the `hclust` function with the option of `ward.D2` to carry out the hierarchical cluster analysis on the proximity matrix of dissimilarities. The `cutree` function divides the `hclust` object into `k = 6` number of clusters. Finally, the `table` function and the visuals give an idea of how good the clustering has been by using the random forests:

```
> MS_hclust <- hclust(as.dist(1-MS_RF$proximity),method="ward.D2")
> MS_RF_clust <- cutree(MS_hclust,k=6)
>table(MS_RF_clust,multishapes$shape)

MS_RF_clust   1    2    3    4    5    6
          1 113    0    0    0   10    0
          2 143    0    0    0   20   50
3   57 170    0    0    3    0
4   63  55    0    0    3    0
5   24 175    0    0    2    0
          6    0    0  100  100   12    0
>plot(multishapes[1:2],col=MS_RF_clust,
+      main="Clustering with Random Forest
```

The following is a diagram illustrating clustering using random forests:

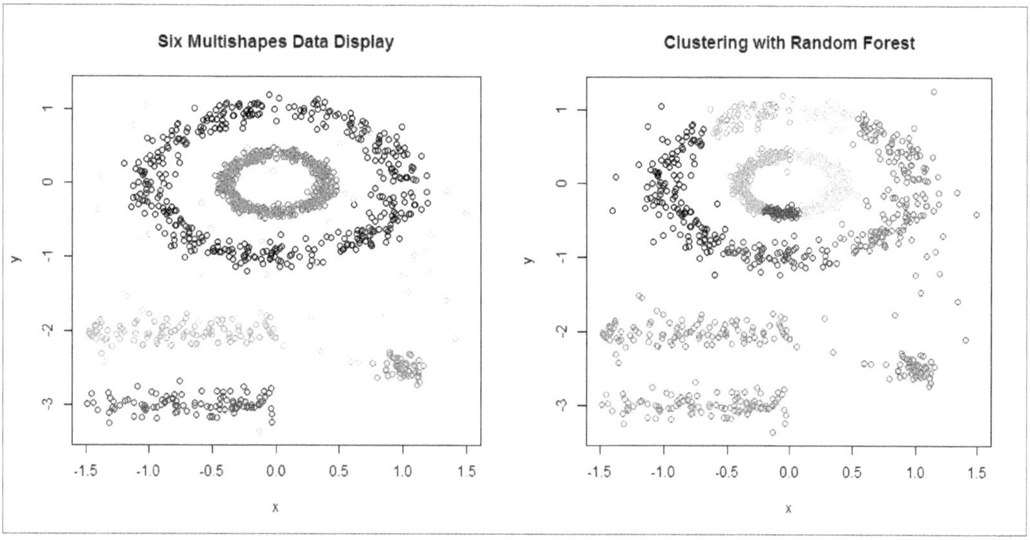

Figure 12: Clustering Using Random Forests

Although the clusters provided by the random forests do not fit the label identification problem, we will take them as a starting point. It needs to be understood that random forests can be used properly for cluster analysis.

Summary

Random forests were created as an improvement on the bagging method. As an example of the homogeneous ensemble method, we saw how the forests help in obtaining higher accuracy. Visualization and variable importance for random forests were thoroughly detailed. We also saw a lot of diagnostic methods that can be used after fitting a random forest. The method was then compared with bagging. Novel applications of random forest for missing data imputation and cluster analysis were also demonstrated.

In the next chapter, we will look at boosting, which is a very important ensemble.

5
The Bare Bones Boosting Algorithms

What do we mean by bare bones boosting algorithms? The boosting algorithm (and its variants) is arguably one of the most important algorithms in the machine learning toolbox. Any data analyst needs to know this algorithm, and eventually the push for higher accuracy invariably drives towards the need for the boosting technique. It has been reported on the `www.kaggle.org` forums that boosting algorithms for complex and voluminous data run for several weeks and that most award-winning solutions are based on this. Furthermore, the algorithms run on modern graphical device machines.

Taking its importance into account, we will study the boosting algorithm in detail here. *Bare bones* is certainly not a variant of the boosting algorithm. Since the boosting algorithm is one of the very important and vital algorithms, we will first state the algorithm and implement it in a rudimentary fashion, which will show each step of the algorithm in action.

We will begin with the adaptive boosting algorithm—popularly known and abbreviated as the **AdaBoost** algorithm—and using very simple and raw code, we will illustrate it for a classification problem. The illustration is carried over a `toy` dataset so that the steps can be clearly followed by the reader.

In the next section, we will extend the classification boosting algorithm to the regression problem. For this problem, the boosting variant is the famous **gradient boosting algorithm**. An interesting nonlinear regression problem will be improvised through a series of basic decision trees with a single split, also known as **stumps**. The gradient boosting algorithm will be illustrated for the choice of the squared-error loss function. Variable importance computation will be clarified for the boosting method. The details of the `gbm` package will be discussed in the penultimate section of the chapter. The concluding section will carry out a comparison of the bagging, random forests, and boosting methods for a spam dataset. This chapter consists of the following topics:

- The general boosting algorithm
- Adaptive boosting
- Gradient boosting
    - ° Gradient boosting based on stumps
    - ° Gradient boosting with squared-error loss
- Variable importance in the boosting technique
- Using the gbm package
- Comparison of bagging, random forests, and boosting algorithms

Technical requirements

We will be using the following libraries in the chapter:

- `rpart`
- `gbm`

The general boosting algorithm

The tree-based ensembles in the previous chapters, *Bagging* and *Random Forests*, cover an important extension of the decision trees. However, while bagging provides greater stability by averaging multiple decision trees, the bias persists. This limitation motivated Breiman to sample the covariates at each split point to generate an ensemble of "independent" trees and lay the foundation for random forests. The trees in the random forests can be developed in parallel, as is the case with bagging. The idea of averaging over multiple trees is to ensure the balance between the bias and variance trade-off. Boosting is the third most important extension of the decision trees, and probably the most effective one. It is again based on ensembling homogeneous base learners (in this case, trees), as are the bagging and random forests. The design of the boosting algorithm is completely different though. It is a *sequential* ensemble method in that the residual/misclassified point of the previous learner is improvised in the next run of the algorithm.

The general boosting technique consists of a family of algorithms that convert weak learners to provide a final strong learner. In the context of classification problems, a weak learner is a technique that is better than a random guess. That the method converts a weak learning algorithm into a better one is the reason it gets the name *boosting*. The boosting technique is designed to deliver a strong learner that is closer to the perfect classifier.

Classifier	Sub-space Ω_1	Sub-space Ω_2	Sub-space Ω_3	Sub-space Ω_4	Accuracy
h_1	☑	☑	☑	☒	0.75
h_2	☑	☑	☒	☑	0.75
h_3	☑	☒	☑	☑	0.75
h_4	☒	☑	☑	☑	0.75

Table 1 A simple classifier scenario

A broader motivation for boosting can be understood through a simple example. Suppose that the random sample of size n is drawn as IID from the sample space Ω. The distribution of the random sample is assumed to be D. Suppose we have $T=4$ classifiers in $h_i, i=1,\ldots,T$, with the classifiers being used for the truth function f.

Consider a hypothetical scenario where the sample space Ω consists of four parts in $\Omega_1, \Omega_2, \Omega_3, \Omega_4$, and the four classifiers perform as indicated in previous table. The idea behind the development of the boosting method is to improvise the classifier in a sequential manner. That is, combining the classifier is approached one after another and not all at the same time. Now, the errors of h_1 will be corrected to a new distribution D' with the errors of the classifier being given more weight for the region Ω_4. The classifier h_2 will use the distribution D' and its error zone instances in the region Ω_3 will be given more weight leading to a distribution D''. The boosting method will continue the process for the remaining classifiers and give an overall combiner/ensemble. A pseudo-boosting algorithm (see *Chapter 2* of Zhou (2012)) is summarized in the following:

1. Step 0: The initial sample distribution is D, and set D1 = D
2. Steps $t = 1, 2, \ldots, T$:
   - $h_t \sim$ Dt
   - *error rate* $\in_t = P_{\{x \sim D_t\}} \left(h_t \neq f(x) \right)$
   - Dt+1 = *Improve Distribution (Dt,* $\in_t$)
3. Final step: $H(x) = Combine\ outputs \left(h_1(x), h_2(x), \ldots, h_T(x) \right)$

The two steps of the algorithm in *Improve distribution* and *Combine outputs* clearly need implementable actions. In the next section, we will develop the adaptive boosting method with a clear numerical illustration.

Adaptive boosting

Schapire and Freund invented the adaptive boosting method. **Adaboost** is a popular abbreviation of this technique.

The generic adaptive boosting algorithm is as follows:

- Initialize the observation weights uniformly:

$$w_i = \frac{1}{n}, i = 1, \ldots, n$$

- For m, classifier hm, from 1 to m number of passes over with the data, perform the following tasks:
    - ○ Fit a classifier hm to the training data using the weights w_i
    - ○ Compute the error for each classifier as follows:

$$err_m = \frac{\sum_{i=1}^{n} w_i I\left(y_i \neq h_m\left(x_i\right)\right)}{\sum_{i=1}^{n} w_i}, m = 1, 2, \ldots, M$$

    - ○ Compute the *voting power* of the classifier hm:

$$a_m = \log\left[\frac{1 - err_m}{err_m}\right], m = 1, 2, \ldots, M$$

    - ○ Set $i = 1, \ldots, n$

$$w_i \leftarrow w_i \exp\left[a_m I\left(y_i \neq h_m\left(x_i\right)\right)\right]$$

- Output:

$$h(x) = \text{sign}\left[\sum_{m=1}^{M} a_m h_m\left(x\right)\right]$$

Simply put, the algorithm unfolds as follows:

1. Initially, we start with uniform weights w_i for all observations.
2. In the next step, we calculate the weighted error err_m for each of the classifiers under consideration.
3. A classifier (usually stumps, or decision trees with a single split) needs to be selected and the practice is to select the classifier with the maximum accuracy.

4. In *Improve distribution and Combine outputs* case of ties, any accuracy tied classifier is selected.

5. Next, the misclassified observations are given more weights and the values that are correctly classified are down-weighted. An important point needs to be recorded here:

 In the weights update step, the sum of weights correctly classified as observations will equal the sum of weights of the misclassified observations.

The steps from computing the error of the classifier to the weight updating step are repeated M number of times, and the voting power of each classifier is obtained. For any given observation, we then make the prediction by using the predictions across the M classifiers weighted by their respective voting power and using the sign function as specified in the algorithm.

As simplified as the algorithm may be, it is a useful exercise to undertake the working of the adaptive boosting method through a toy dataset. The data and computational approach is taken from the video of Jessica Noss, available at https://www.youtube.com/watch?v=gmok1h8wG-Q. The illustration of the adaptive boosting algorithm begins now.

Consider a toy data set with five triplet points: two explanatory variables and one binary output value. The variables and data can be summarized with $(x_{i1}, x_{i2}, y_i), i = 1, 2, 3, 4, 5$, and here we have the data points as $(x_{11}, x_{12}, y_i) = (1, 5, 1)$, $(x_{21}, x_{22}, y_2) = (5, 5, 1)$, $(x_{31}, x_{32}, y_3) = (3, 3, -1)$, $(x_{41}, x_{42}, y_4) = (1, 1, 1)$, and $(x_{51}, x_{52}, y_5) = (5, 1, 1)$. The data will be first entered in R and then visualized as a preliminary step:

```
> # ADAPTIVE BOOSTING with a Toy Dataset
> # https://www.youtube.com/watch?v=gmok1h8wG-Q
> # Jessica Noss
> # The Toy Data
> x1 <- c(1,5,3,1,5)
> x2 <- c(5,5,3,1,1)
> y <- c(1,1,-1,1,1)
> plot(x1,x2,pch=c("+","+","-","+","+"),cex=2,
+       xlim=c(0,6),ylim=c(0,6),
+       xlab=expression(x[1]),ylab=expression(x[2]),
+       main="The TOY Data Depiction")
> text(x1,x2,labels=names(y),pos=1)
```

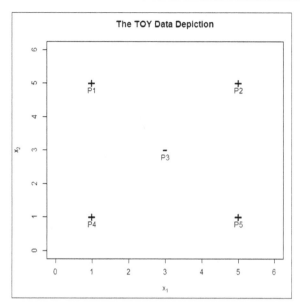

Figure 1: A simple depiction of the toy dataset

Stumps are a particular case of a decision tree that has been mentioned in the discussion. Here, we will use the stumps as the base learners. A simple look at the preceding diagram helps us to easily find stumps that have an accuracy higher than a random guess.

For example, we can put a stump at $x_1 = 2$ and mark all the observations on the left side as positives and those on the right as negatives. In the following program, the points in the green shaded region are positives as predicted by the stumps, and those in the red shaded region are negatives. Similarly, we can use additional stumps at $x_1 = 4$ and $x_1 = 6$. The predictions can be swapped for the same stumps too, thanks to symmetry(). Thus, earlier we put the green shaded region to the left of $x_1 = 2$ and predicted the values as positives, and by reversing the order the area on the right side of the stump $x_1 = 2$ will be marked as positives. A similar classification is made for the negatives. The task is repeated at stumps $x_1 = 4$ and $x_1 = 6$. Using the par, plot, text, and rect graphical functions, we present visual depictions of these base learners in the following:

```
> # Visualizing the stump models
> windows(height=200,width=300)
> par(mfrow=c(2,3))
> plot(x1,x2,pch=c("+","+","-","+","+"),cex=2,
+        xlim=c(0,6),ylim=c(0,6),
```

```
+       xlab=expression(x[1]),ylab=expression(x[2]),
+       main="Classification with Stump X1<2")
> text(x1,x2,labels=names(y),pos=1)
> plim <- par("usr")
> rect(xleft=2,ybottom = plim[3],xright = plim[2],ytop = plim[4],
+       border = "red",col="red",density=20 )
> rect(xleft=plim[1],ybottom = plim[3],xright = 2,ytop = plim[4],
+       border = "green",col="green",density=20 )
> plot(x1,x2,pch=c("+","+","-","+","+"),cex=2,
+       xlim=c(0,6),ylim=c(0,6),
+       xlab=expression(x[1]),ylab=expression(x[2]),
+       main="Classification with Stump X1<4")
> text(x1,x2,labels=names(y),pos=1)
> rect(xleft=4,ybottom = plim[3],xright = plim[2],ytop = plim[4],
+       border = "red",col="red",density=20 )
> rect(xleft=plim[1],ybottom = plim[3],xright = 4,ytop = plim[4],
+       border = "green",col="green",density=20 )
> plot(x1,x2,pch=c("+","+","-","+","+"),cex=2,
+       xlim=c(0,6),ylim=c(0,6),
+       xlab=expression(x[1]),ylab=expression(x[2]),
+       main="Classification with Stump X1<6")
> text(x1,x2,labels=names(y),pos=1)
> rect(xleft=6,ybottom = plim[3],xright = plim[2],ytop = plim[4],
+       border = "red",col="red",density=20 )
> rect(xleft=plim[1],ybottom = plim[3],xright = 6,ytop = plim[4],
+       border = "green",col="green",density=20 )
> plot(x1,x2,pch=c("+","+","-","+","+"),cex=2,
+       xlim=c(0,6),ylim=c(0,6),
+       xlab=expression(x[1]),ylab=expression(x[2]),
+       main="Classification with Stump X1>2")
> text(x1,x2,labels=names(y),pos=1)
> rect(xleft=2,ybottom = plim[3],xright = plim[2],ytop = plim[4],
+       border = "green",col="green",density=20 )
> rect(xleft=plim[1],ybottom = plim[3],xright = 2,ytop = plim[4],
+       border = "red",col="red",density=20 )
> plot(x1,x2,pch=c("+","+","-","+","+"),cex=2,
+       xlim=c(0,6),ylim=c(0,6),
+       xlab=expression(x[1]),ylab=expression(x[2]),
+       main="Classification with Stump X1>4")
> text(x1,x2,labels=names(y),pos=1)
> rect(xleft=4,ybottom = plim[3],xright = plim[2],ytop = plim[4],
+       border = "green",col="green",density=20 )
```

```
> rect(xleft=plim[1],ybottom = plim[3],xright = 4,ytop = plim[4],
+       border = "red",col="red",density=20 )
> plot(x1,x2,pch=c("+","+","-","+","+"),cex=2,
+       xlim=c(0,6),ylim=c(0,6),
+       xlab=expression(x[1]),ylab=expression(x[2]),
+       main="Classification with Stump X1>6")
> text(x1,x2,labels=names(y),pos=1)
> rect(xleft=6,ybottom = plim[3],xright = plim[2],ytop = plim[4],
+       border = "green",col="green",density=20 )
> rect(xleft=plim[1],ybottom = plim[3],xright = 6,ytop = plim[4],
+       border = "red",col="red",density=20 )
```

The result of the preceding R program is shown in the following diagram:

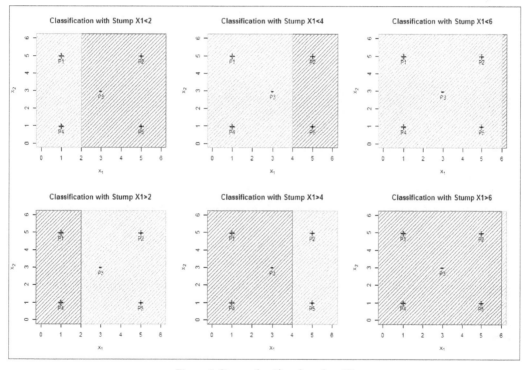

Figure 2: Stump classifiers based on X1

Note that a similar classification can be obtained for the variable x_2 at the points 2, 4, and 6. Though there is no need to give the complete R program for stumps based on x_2, we simply produce the output in the following diagram. The program is available in the code bundle. The stumps based on x_2 will be ignored in the rest of the discussion:

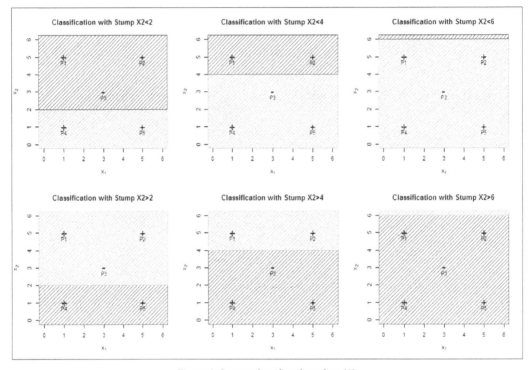

Figure 3: Stump classifiers based on X2

The choice of the stump based on $x_1 \leq 2$ leads to a few misclassifications, and we can see that the observations P1, P4, and P3 are correctly classified while P2 and P5 are misclassified. The predictions based on this stump can then be put as (1,-1,-1,1,-1). The stump based on $x_1 \leq 4$ classifies points P1 and P4 correctly, while P2, P3, and P5 are misclassified, and the prediction in vector form here is (1,-1,1,1,-1). The six models considered here will be denoted in the R program by M1, M2, ..., M6, and in terms of the algorithm specified earlier, we have $h_1 = Stump(X_1 \leq 2), h_2 = Stump(X_1 \leq 4), h_3 = Stump(X_1 \leq 6), h_4 =$. Similarly, we have $Stump(X_1 > 2), h_5 = Stump(X_1 > 4), and \, h_6 = Stump(X_1 > 6)$ predictions for the other four stumps and we enter them in R, as follows:

```
> # The Simple Stump Models
> M1 <- c(1,-1,-1,1,-1)    # M1 = X1<2 predicts 1, else -1
> M2 <- c(1,-1,1,1,-1)     # M2 = X1<4 predicts 1, else -1
```

```
> M3 <- c(1,1,1,1,1)        # M3 = X1<6 predicts 1, else -1
> M4 <- c(-1,1,1,-1,1)      # M4 = X1>2 predicts 1, else -1;M4=-1*M1
> M5 <- c(-1,1,-1,-1,1)     # M5 = X1>4 predicts 1, else -1;M5=-1*M2
> M6 <- c(-1,-1,-1,-1,-1)   # M6 = X1>6 predicts 1, else -1;M6=-1*M3
```

With the predictions given by the six models M1-M6, we can compare them with the true labels in y and see which observations are misclassified in each of these models:

```
> # Stem Model Errors
> Err_M1 <- M1!=y
> Err_M2 <- M2!=y
> Err_M3 <- M3!=y
> Err_M4 <- M4!=y
> Err_M5 <- M5!=y
> Err_M6 <- M6!=y
> # Their Misclassifications
> rbind(Err_M1,Err_M2,Err_M3,Err_M4,Err_M5,Err_M6)
          P1     P2     P3     P4     P5
Err_M1 FALSE   TRUE FALSE FALSE   TRUE
Err_M2 FALSE   TRUE  TRUE FALSE   TRUE
Err_M3 FALSE FALSE  TRUE FALSE FALSE
Err_M4  TRUE FALSE  TRUE  TRUE FALSE
Err_M5  TRUE FALSE FALSE  TRUE FALSE
Err_M6  TRUE  TRUE FALSE  TRUE  TRUE
```

Thus, the values of TRUE mean that the column named points is misclassified in the row named model. The weights $w_i = 1/n, i = 1,\ldots,n$ are initialized and the weighted errors $err_m, m = 1,2,\ldots,6$, are computed for each of the models in the following R block:

```
> # ROUND 1
> # Weighted Error Computation
> weights_R1 <- rep(1/length(y),length(y)) #Initializaing the weights
> Err_R1 <- rbind(Err_M1,Err_M2,Err_M3,Err_M4,Err_M5,Err_M6)%*%
+    weights_R1
> Err_R1 # Error rate
        [,1]
Err_M1  0.4
Err_M2  0.6
Err_M3  0.2/
Err_M4  0.6
Err_M5  0.4
Err_M6  0.8
```

Since the error corresponding to Model 3, or h_3, is the minimum, we select it first and calculate the voting power a_3 assignable to it as follows:

```
> # The best classifier error rate
> err_rate_r1 <- min(Err_R1)
> alpha_3 <- 0.5*log((1-err_rate_r1)/err_rate_r1)
> alpha_3
[1] 0.6931472
```

Consequently, the boosting algorithm steps state that $sign(a_3 \times h_3)$ gives us the required predictions:

```
> alpha_3*M3
[1] 0.6931472 0.6931472 0.6931472 0.6931472 0.6931472
> sign(alpha_3*M3)
[1] 1 1 1 1 1
```

The central observation, P3, remains misclassified and so we proceed to the next step.

Now we need to update the weights $w_i, i = 1, 2, \ldots, n$ and for the classification problem the rule in a simplified form is given using:

$$w_i \leftarrow \begin{cases} \dfrac{1}{2}\dfrac{w_i}{err_i}, if\ y_i\ is\ correctly\ classified, \\ \\ \dfrac{1}{2}\dfrac{w_i}{1-err_i}, if\ y_i\ is\ misclassified \end{cases}, i = 1, \ldots, n$$

Consequently, we need a function that will take the weight of a previous run, the error rate, and the misclassifications by the model as inputs and then return them as the updated weights that incorporated the preceding formula. We define such a function as follows:

```
> # Weights Update Formula and Function
> Weights_update <- function(weights,error,error_rate){
+    weights_new <- NULL
+    for(i in 1:length(weights)){
+        if(error[i]==FALSE) weights_new[i] <- 0.5*weights[i]/(1-error_
rate)
+        if(error[i]==TRUE) weights_new[i] <- 0.5*weights[i]/error_rate
+    }
+    return(weights_new)
+ }
```

Now, we will update the weights and calculate the error for each of the six models:

```
> # ROUND 2
> # Update the weights and redo the analyses
> weights_R2 <- Weights_update(weights=weights_R1,error=Err_M3,
+                               error_rate=err_rate_r1)
> Err_R2 <- rbind(Err_M1,Err_M2,Err_M3,Err_M4,Err_M5,Err_M6)%*%
+    weights_R2
> Err_R2 # Error rates
        [,1]
Err_M1 0.25
Err_M2 0.75
Err_M3 0.50
Err_M4 0.75
Err_M5 0.25
Err_M6 0.50
```

Here, models M1 and M5 have equal error rates with the new weights, and we simply choose Model 1, calculate its voting power, and predict based on the updated model:

```
> err_rate_r2 <- min(Err_R2)
> alpha_1 <- 0.5*log((1-err_rate_r2)/err_rate_r2)
> alpha_1
[1] 0.5493061
> alpha_3*M3+alpha_1*M1
[1] 1.242453 0.143841 0.143841 1.242453 0.143841
> sign(alpha_3*M3+alpha_1*M1)
[1] 1 1 1 1 1
```

Since the point P3 is still misclassified, we proceed with the iterations and apply the cycle once more:

```
> # ROUND 3
> # Update the weights and redo the analyses
> weights_R3 <- Weights_update(weights=weights_R2,error=Err_M1,
+                               error_rate=err_rate_r2)
> Err_R3 <- rbind(Err_M1,Err_M2,Err_M3,Err_M4,Err_M5,Err_M6)%*%
+    weights_R3
> Err_R3 # Error rates
            [,1]
Err_M1 0.5000000
Err_M2 0.8333333
Err_M3 0.3333333
```

```
Err_M4 0.5000000
Err_M5 0.1666667
Err_M6 0.6666667
> err_rate_r3 <- min(Err_R3)
> alpha_5 <- 0.5*log((1-err_rate_r3)/err_rate_r3)
> alpha_5
[1] 0.804719
> alpha_3*M3+alpha_1*M1+alpha_5*M5
[1]  0.4377344  0.9485600 -0.6608779  0.4377344  0.9485600
> sign(alpha_3*M3+alpha_1*M1+alpha_5*M5)
[1]  1  1 -1  1  1
```

Now the classification is perfect and after three iterations, we don't have any misclassifications or errors. The purpose of the programming in this section was to demonstrate the steps in the adaptive boosting algorithm in an elementary way. In the next section, we will look at the *gradient boosting* technique.

Gradient boosting

The adaptive boosting method can't be applied to the regression problem since it is constructed to address the classification problem. The gradient boosting method can be used for both the classification and regression problems with suitable loss functions. In fact, the use of gradient boosting methods goes beyond these two standard problems. The technique originated from some of Breiman's observations and developed into regression problems by Freidman (2000). We will take the rudimentary code explanation in the next section without even laying out the algorithm. After the setup is clear, we will formally state the boosting algorithm for the squared-error loss function in the following subsection and create a new function implementing the algorithm.

The following diagram is a depiction of the standard sine wave function. It is clearly a nonlinear relationship. Without explicitly using sine transformations, we will see the use of the boosting algorithm to learn this function. Of course, we need simple regression stumps and we begin with a simple function, `getNode`, that will give us the desired split:

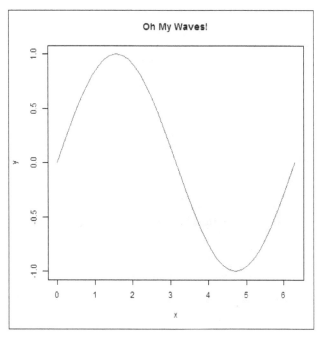

Figure 4: Can boosting work for nonlinear sine data?

Building it from scratch

In the previous section, we used simple classification stumps. In that example, a simple visual inspection sufficed to identify the stumps, and we quickly obtained 12 classification stumps. For the regression problem, we will first define a `getNode` function, which is a slight modification of the function defined in Chapter 9 of Tattar (2017). The required notation is first set up.

Suppose we have n pairs of data points $(x_1, y_1), (x_2, y_2), \ldots, (x_n, y_n)$ and we are trying to learn the relationship $y = f(x, \beta)$, where the form of f is completely unknown to us.

For the regression tree, the split criteria are rather straightforward. For data split by an x-value, we calculate the sum of mean difference squares of *y*s in each of the partitioned part and then add them up. The split criteria are chosen as that x-value. This maximizes the sum of the mean difference squares in the variable of interest. The R function, `getNode`, implements this thinking:

```
> getNode <- function(x,y)     {
+    xu <- sort(unique(x),decreasing=TRUE)
+    ss <- numeric(length(xu)-1)
+    for(i in 1:length(ss))     {
```

```
+       partR <- y[x>xu[i]]
+       partL <- y[x<=xu[i]]
+       partRSS <- sum((partR-mean(partR))^2)
+       partLSS <- sum((partL-mean(partL))^2)
+       ss[i] <- partRSS + partLSS
+     }
+     xnode <- xu[which.min(ss)]
+     minss <- min(ss)
+     pR <- mean(y[x>xnode])
+     pL <- mean(y[x<=xnode])
+     return(list(xnode=xnode,yR=pR,yL=pL))
+   }
```

The first step in the getNode function is finding the unique values of x and then sorting them in decrease(ing) order. For the unique values, we calculate the sum of squares through a for loop. The first step in the loop is to partition the data in right and left parts.

The sum of mean difference squares is calculated in each of the partitions for a specific unique value, and then summed up to get the overall residual sum of squares.

We then obtain the value of x, which leads to the least residual sum of squares. The prediction in the partitioned regions is the mean of the y-values in those regions.

The getNode function closes by returning the split value of x, and the predictions for the right and left partitions. We are now ready to create regression stumps.

The sine wave data is first easily created and we allow the x-values to range in the interval $[0, 2\pi]$. The y-value is simply the sin function applied on the x vector:

```
> # Can Boosting Learn the Sine Wave!
> x <- seq(0,2*pi,pi/20)
> y <- sin(x)
> windows(height=300,width=100)
> par(mfrow=c(3,1))
> plot(x,y,"l",col="red",main="Oh My Waves!")
```

The result of the preceding display will be *Figure 1*. We proceed to obtain the first split of data and then display the mean of the right and left partitions on the graph. The residuals will be from the sine wave and they are also put on the same display, as follows:

```
> first_split <- getNode(x,y)
> first_split
$xnode
[1] 3.141593
```

```
$yR
[1] -0.6353102
$yL
[1] 0.6050574
```

Now, our first split point occurs at x value of, π here, 3.141593. The prediction for the right side of the split point is -0.6353102 and for the left side it is 0.6050574. The predictions are plotted on the same display using the segments function:

```
> segments(x0=min(x),y0=first_split$yL,
+          x1=first_split$xnode,y1=first_split$yL)
> segments(x0=first_split$xnode,y0=first_split$yR,
+          x1=max(x),y1=first_split$yR)
```

Now, the predictions are easy to obtain here and a simple ifelse function helps in calculating them. The deviation from the sine wave is the residuals, and we calculate that the first set of residuals and summary function give the brief of the residual values:

```
> yfit1 <- ifelse(x<first_split$xnode,first_split$yL,first_split$yR)
> GBFit <- yfit1
> segments(x0=x,x1=x,y0=y,y1=yfit1)
> first_residuals <- y-yfit1
> summary(first_residuals)
    Min.  1st Qu.   Median     Mean  3rd Qu.     Max.
-0.60506 -0.25570  0.04752  0.03025  0.32629  0.63531
```

The first step in the prediction is saved in the GBFit object and the difference between the fit and predictions is found in the first_residuals vector. This completes the first iteration of the gradient boosting algorithm. The residuals of the first iteration will become the regressand/output variable for the second iteration. Using the getNode function, we carry out the second iteration, which mimics the earlier set of code:

```
> second_split <- getNode(x,first_residuals)
> plot(x,first_residuals,"l",col="red",main="The Second Wave!")
> segments(x0=min(x),y0=second_split$yL,
+          x1=second_split$xnode,y1=second_split$yL)
> segments(x0=second_split$xnode,y0=second_split$yR,
+          x1=max(x),y1=second_split$yR)
> yfit2 <- ifelse(x<second_split$xnode,second_split$yL,second_
split$yR)
> GBFit <- GBFit+yfit2
> segments(x0=x,x1=x,y0=first_residuals,y1=yfit2)
> second_residuals <- first_residuals-yfit2
> summary(second_residuals)
    Min.  1st Qu.   Median     Mean  3rd Qu.     Max.
-0.51678 -0.24187 -0.02064 -0.01264  0.25813  0.56715
```

An important difference here is that we update the prediction not by averaging but by adding. Note that we are modeling the residual of the first step and hence the remaining part of the residual explained by the next fitting needs to be added and not averaged. What is the range of residuals? The reader is advised to compare the residual values with earlier iterations. A similar extension is carried out for the third iteration:

```
> third_split <- getNode(x,second_residuals)
> plot(x,second_residuals,"l",col="red",main="The Third Wave!")
> segments(x0=min(x),y0=third_split$yL,
+          x1=third_split$xnode,y1=third_split$yL)
> segments(x0=third_split$xnode,y0=third_split$yR,
+          x1=max(x),y1=third_split$yR)
> yfit3 <- ifelse(x<third_split$xnode,third_split$yL,third_split$yR)
> GBFit <- GBFit+yfit3
> segments(x0=x,x1=x,y0=second_residuals,y1=yfit3)
> third_residuals <- second_residuals-yfit3
> summary(third_residuals)
    Min.  1st Qu.   Median     Mean  3rd Qu.     Max.
-0.47062 -0.27770 -0.03927 -0.01117  0.18196  0.61331
```

All of the visual display is shown in the following diagram:

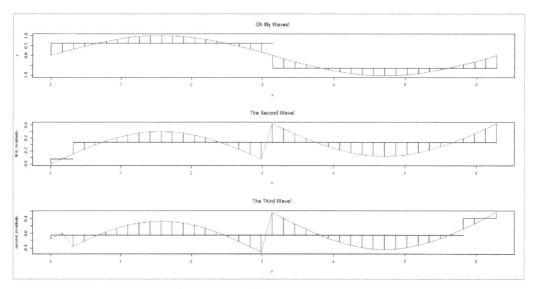

Figure 5: Three iterations of the gradient boosting algorithm

Obviously, we can't keep on carrying out the iterations in a detailed execution every time and looping is important. The code is kept in a block and 22 more iterations are performed. The output at the end of each iteration is depicted in the diagram and we put them all in an external file, `Sine_Wave_25_Iterations.pdf`:

```
> pdf("Sine_Wave_25_Iterations.pdf")
> curr_residuals <- third_residuals
> for(j in 4:25){
+     jth_split <- getNode(x,curr_residuals)
+     plot(x,curr_residuals,"l",col="red",main=paste0(c("The ", j, "th
Wave!")))
+     segments(x0=min(x),y0=jth_split$yL,
+             x1=jth_split$xnode,y1=jth_split$yL)
+     segments(x0=jth_split$xnode,y0=jth_split$yR,
+             x1=max(x),y1=jth_split$yR)
+     yfit_next <- ifelse(x<jth_split$xnode,jth_split$yL,jth_split$yR)
+     GBFit <- GBFit+yfit_next
+     segments(x0=x,x1=x,y0=curr_residuals,y1=yfit_next)
+     curr_residuals <- curr_residuals-yfit_next
+ }
> dev.off()
> summary(curr_residuals)
     Min.    1st Qu.    Median      Mean   3rd Qu.      Max.
-0.733811 -0.093432  0.008481 -0.001632  0.085192  0.350122
```

Following the 25 iterations, we have an overall fit in `GBFit` and we can plot this against the actual y values to see how well the gradient boosting algorithm has performed:

```
> plot(y,GBFit,xlab="True Y",ylab="Gradient Boosting Fit")
```

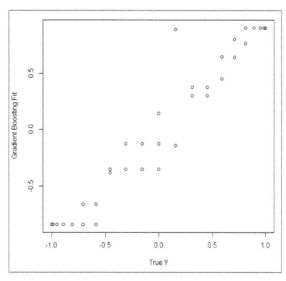

Figure 6: Gradient fit versus actual sine data

The fit is reasonably good for a nonlinear model. The approach was to get a clear understanding of the gradient boosting algorithm. A more general form of the boosting algorithm is discussed and developed in the next subsection.

Squared-error loss function

Denote the data by $\mathbf{D} = (\mathbf{y}, \mathbf{X})$, and fix the number of iterations/trees as a number B. Choose a shrinkage factor $\in$ and tree depth d. The gradient boosting algorithm based on the squared-error loss function is stated here briefly. See Algorithm 17.2 of Efron and Hastie (2016), as follows:

- Initialize residuals $\mathbf{r} = \mathbf{y}$ and the gradient boosting prediction as $\hat{G}_0 \equiv 0$
- For $b = 1, 2, \ldots, B$:
    - Fit a regression tree of depth d for the data $(\mathbf{r}, \mathbf{X})$
    - Obtain the predicted values as $\hat{g}_b$
    - Update the boosting prediction by $\hat{G}_b = \hat{G}_{b-1} + \in \hat{g}_b$
    - Update the residuals $\mathbf{r} = \mathbf{r} - \hat{g}_b$
- Return the sequence of functions $\hat{G}_b, b = 1, \ldots, B$

Now, we will define a function GB_SqEL, which will implement the gradient boosting algorithm driven by the squared-error loss function. The function must be provided with five arguments: y and x will constitute the data, depth will specify the depth of the trees (that is, the number of splits in the regression tree), iter for the number of iterations, and shrinkage is the $\in$ factor. The GB_SqEL function is set up as follows:

```
> # Gradiend Boosting Using the Squared-error Loss Function
> GB_SqEL <- function(y,X,depth,iter,shrinkage){
+    curr_res <- y
+    GB_Hat <- data.frame(matrix(0,nrow=length(y),ncol=iter))
+    fit <- y*0
+    for(i in 1:iter){
+       tdf <- cbind(curr_res,X)
+       tpart <- rpart(curr_res~.,data=tdf,maxdepth=depth)
+       gb_tilda <- predict(tpart)
+       gb_hat <- shrinkage*gb_tilda
+       fit <- fit+gb_hat
+       curr_res <- curr_res-gb_hat
+       GB_Hat[,i] <- fit
+    }
+    return(list(GB_Hat = GB_Hat))
+ }
```

The initialization takes place in specifications, and the line `fit <- y*0`. The depth argument of the algorithm is taken in the line `maxdepth=depth`, and using the `rpart` function, we create a tree of the necessary depth. The `predict` function gives the values of $\hat{g}_b$ as required at each iteration, while `fit+gb_hat` does the necessary update. Note that `GB_Hat[,i]` consists of the predicted values at the end of each iteration.

We will illustrate the algorithm with the example of Efron and Hastie (2016). The data considered is related with Lu Gerig's disease, or **amyotrophic lateral sclerosis** (**ALS**). The dataset has information on 1,822 individuals with the ALS disease. The goal is to predict the rate of progression dFRS of a functional rating score. The study has information on 369 predictors/covariates. Here, we will use the `GB_SqEL` function to fit the gradient boosting technique and analyze the mean square error as the number of iterations increases. The details and the data can be obtained from the source at `https://web.stanford.edu/~hastie/CASI/data.html`. We will now put the squared-error loss function-driven boosting method into action:

```
> als <- read.table("../Data/ALS.txt",header=TRUE)
> alst <- als[als$testset==FALSE,-1]
> temp <- GB_SqEL(y=alst$dFRS,X=alst[,-1],depth=4,
+                 iter=500,shrinkage = 0.02)
> MSE_Train <- 0
> for(i in 1:500){
+   MSE_Train[i] <- mean(temp$GB_Hat[,i]-alst$dFRS)^2
+ }
> windows(height=100,width=100)
> plot.ts(MSE_Train)
```

Using the `read.table` function, we import the data from the code bundle into the `als` object. The data is available from the source in the `.txt` format. The column `testset` indicates whether the observations were marked for training purposes or for tests. We select the training observations and also drop the first variable `testset` and store it in the object `alst`. The `GB_SqEL` function is applied on the `alst` object with appropriate specifications.

Following each iteration, we compute the mean-squared error and store it in `GB_Hat`, as explained earlier. We can see from the following diagram that as the iterations increase, the mean squared error decreases. Here, the algorithm stabilizes after nearly 200 iterations:

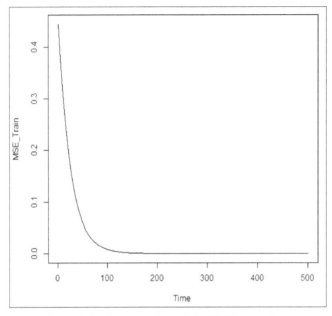

Figure 7: Gradient boosting and the MSE by iterations

In the next section, we will see the use of two powerful R packages.

Using the adabag and gbm packages

Using the boosting method as an ensemble technique is indeed very effective. The algorithm was illustrated for classification and regression problems from scratch. Once the understand the algorithm clear and transparent, we can then use R packages to deliver results going forward. A host of packages are available for implementing the boosting technique. However, we will use the two most popular packages `adabag` and `gbm` in this section. First, a look at the options of the two functions is in order. The names are obvious and `adabag` implements the adaptive boosting methods while `gbm` deals with gradient boosting methods. First, we look at the options available in these two functions in the following code:

```
> boosting
function (formula, data, boos = TRUE, mfinal = 100, coeflearn = "Breiman",
    control, ...)
> gbm
function (formula = formula(data), distribution = "bernoulli",
    data = list(), weights, var.monotone = NULL, n.trees = 100,
    interaction.depth = 1, n.minobsinnode = 10, shrinkage = 0.001,
    bag.fraction = 0.5, train.fraction = 1, cv.folds = 0, keep.data = TRUE,
    verbose = "CV", class.stratify.cv = NULL, n.cores = NULL)
```

The boosting and gbm functions

The formula is the usual argument. The argument mfinal in adabag and n.trees in gbm allows the specification of the number of trees or iterations. The boosting function gives the option of boos, which is the bootstrap sample of the training set drawn using the weights for each observation on that iteration. Gradient boosting is a more generic algorithm that is capable of handling more than the regression structure. It can be used for classification problems as well. The option of distribution in the gbm function gives those options. Similarly, one can see here that the gbm function offers a host of other options. We will neither undertake the daunting task of explaining them all nor apply them to complex datasets. The two datasets that were used to explain and elaborate adaptive and gradient boosting algorithms will be continued with the boosting and gbm functions.

The toy datasets need to be changed and we will replicate them multiple times over so that we have enough observations for running the boosting and gbm functions:

```
> # The adabag and gbm Packages
> x1 <- c(1,5,3,1,5)
> x1 <- rep(x1,times=10)
> x2 <- c(5,5,3,1,1)
> x2 <- rep(x2,times=10)
> y <- c(1,1,0,1,1)
> y <- rep(y,times=10)
> toy <- data.frame(x1=x1,x2=x2,y=y)
> toy$y <- as.factor(toy$y)
> AB1 <- boosting(y~.,data=toy,boos=TRUE,mfinal = 10,
+                 maxdepth=1,minsplit=1,minbucket=1)
> predict.boosting(AB1,newdata=toy[,1:2])$class
 [1] "1" "1" "0" "1" "1" "1" "1" "0" "1" "1" "1" "1" "0" "1" "1" "1"
"1" "0"
[19] "1" "1" "1" "1" "0" "1" "1" "1" "1" "0" "1" "1" "1" "1" "0" "1"
"1" "1"
[37] "1" "0" "1" "1" "1" "1" "0" "1" "1" "1" "1" "0" "1" "1"
```

The `maxdepth=1` function ensures that we are using only stumps as the base classifiers. It is easily seen that the boosting function works perfectly, as all the observations are correctly classified.

As with the `boosting` function, we need to have more data points. We increase this with the `seq` function and using the `distribution="gaussian"` option, we ask the `gbm` function to fit the regression boosting technique:

```
> x <- seq(0,2*pi,pi/200)
> y <- sin(x)
> sindata <- data.frame(cbind(x,y))
> sin_gbm <- gbm(y~x,distribution="gaussian",data=sindata,
+               n.trees=250,bag.fraction = 0.8,shrinkage = 0.1)
> par(mfrow=c(1,2))
> plot.ts(sin_gbm$fit, main="The gbm Sine Predictions")
> plot(y,sin_gbm$fit,main="Actual vs gbm Predict")
```

Using the plot functions, we make a comparison of the fit with the gradient boosting method. The following diagram suggests that the fit has been appropriate. However, the plots also show that something is not quite correct with the story either. The function approximation at $\frac{\pi}{2}$ and $\frac{3\pi}{2}$ by the boosting method leaves a lot to be desired, and the actual versus predicted plot suggests discontinuity/poor performance at 0. However, we will not delve too far into these issues:

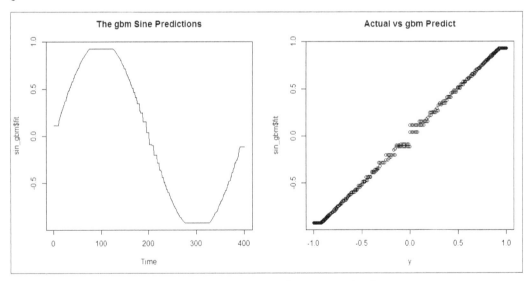

Figure 8: Sine wave approximation by using the gbm function

Next, we will discuss the concept of variable importance.

Variable importance

Boosting methods essentially use trees as base learners, and hence the idea of variable importance gets carried over here the same as with trees, bagging, and random forests. We simply add the importance of the variables across the trees as we do with bagging or random forests.

For a boosting fitted object from the `adabag` package, the variable importance is extracted as follows:

```
> AB1$importance
 x1   x2
100    0
```

This means that the boosting method has not used the x2 variable at all. For the gradient boosting objects, the importance is given by the `summary` function:

```
> summary(sin_gbm)
  var rel.inf
x   x     100
```

It is now apparent that we only have one variable and so it is important to explain the regressand and we certainly did not require some software to tell us. Of course, it is useful in complex cases. Comparisons are for different ensembling methods based on trees. Let us move on to the next section.

Comparing bagging, random forests, and boosting

We carried out comparisons between the bagging and random forest methods in the previous chapter. Using the `gbm` function, we now add boosting accuracy to the earlier analyses:

```
> data("spam")
> set.seed(12345)
> Train_Test <- sample(c("Train","Test"),nrow(spam),replace = TRUE,
+ prob = c(0.7,0.3))
> head(Train_Test)
[1] "Test"  "Test"  "Test"  "Test"  "Train" "Train"
> spam_Train <- spam[Train_Test=="Train",]
> spam_TestX <- within(spam[Train_Test=="Test",],
+                      rm(type))
> spam_TestY <- spam[Train_Test=="Test","type"]
> spam_Formula <- as.formula("type~.")
```

```
> spam_rf <- randomForest(spam_Formula,data=spam_Train,coob=TRUE,
+                         ntree=500,keepX=TRUE,mtry=5)
> spam_rf_predict <- predict(spam_rf,newdata=spam_TestX,type="class")
> rf_accuracy <- sum(spam_rf_predict==spam_TestY)/nrow(spam_TestX)
> rf_accuracy
[1] 0.9436117
> spam_bag <- randomForest(spam_Formula,data=spam_Train,coob=TRUE,
+                         ntree=500,keepX=TRUE,mtry=ncol(spam_TestX))
> spam_bag_predict <- predict(spam_bag,newdata=spam_
TestX,type="class")
> bag_accuracy <- sum(spam_bag_predict==spam_TestY)/nrow(spam_TestX)
> bag_accuracy
[1] 0.9350464
> spam_Train2 <- spam_Train
> spam_Train2$type <- ifelse(spam_Train2$type=="spam",1,0)
> spam_gbm <- gbm(spam_Formula,distribution="bernoulli",data=spam_
Train2,
+                    n.trees=500,bag.fraction = 0.8,shrinkage = 0.1)
> spam_gbm_predict <- predict(spam_gbm,newdata=spam_TestX,
+                         n.trees=500,type="response")
> spam_gbm_predict_class <- ifelse(spam_gbm_
predict>0.5,"spam","nonspam")
> gbm_accuracy <- sum(spam_gbm_predict_class==spam_TestY)/nrow(spam_
TestX)
> gbm_accuracy
[1] 0.945753
> summary(spam_gbm)
                                var       rel.inf
charExclamation    charExclamation 21.985502703
charDollar              charDollar 18.665385239
remove                     remove 11.990552362
free                         free  8.191491706
hp                             hp  7.304531600


num415                     num415  0.000000000
direct                     direct  0.000000000
cs                             cs  0.000000000
original                 original  0.000000000
table                       table  0.000000000
charHash                 charHash  0.000000000
```

The boosting accuracy of `0.9457` is higher than the random forest accuracy of `0.9436`. Further fine tuning, to be explored in the next chapter, will help in improving the accuracy. The variable importance is also easily obtained using the summary function.

Summary

Boosting is yet another ramification of decision trees. It is a sequential iteration technique where the error from a previous iteration is targeted with more impunity. We began with the important adaptive boosting algorithm and used very simple toy data to illustrate the underpinnings. The approach was then extended to the regression problem and we illustrated the gradient boosting method with two different approaches. The two packages adabag and gbm were briefly elaborated on and the concept of variable importance was emphasized yet again. For the spam dataset, we got more accuracy with boosting and hence the deliberations of the boosting algorithm are especially more useful.

The chapter considered different variants of the boosting algorithm. However, we did not discuss why it works at all. In the next chapter, these aspects will be covered in more detail.

6
Boosting Refinements

In the previous chapter, we learned about the boosting algorithm. We looked at the algorithm in its structural form, illustrated with a numerical example, and then applied the algorithm to regression and classification problems. In this brief chapter, we will cover some theoretical aspects of the boosting algorithm and its underpinnings. The boosting theory is also important here.

In this chapter, we will also look at why the boosting algorithm works from a few different perspectives. Different classes of problems require different types of loss functions in order for the boosting techniques to be effective. In the next section, we will explore the different kinds of loss functions that we can choose from. The extreme gradient boosting method is outlined in the section dedicated to working with the xgboost package. Furthermore, the h2o package will ultimately be discussed in the final section, and this might be useful for other ensemble methods too. The chapter will cover the following topics:

- Why does boosting work?
- The gbm package
- The xgboost package
- The h2o package

Technical requirements

We will be using the following R libraries in this chapter:

- adabag
- gbm
- h2o
- kernlab
- rpart
- xgboost

Why does boosting work?

The *Adaptive boosting algorithm* section in the previous chapter contained m models, classifiers $h_i, i = 1, 2, \ldots, m$, n observations and weights, and a voting power that is determined sequentially. The adaptation of the adaptive boosting method was illustrated using a toy example, and then applied using specialized functions. When compared with the bagging and random forest methods, we found that boosting provides the highest accuracy, which you may remember from the results in the aforementioned section in the previous chapter. However, the implementation of the algorithm does not tell us why it was expected to perform better.

We don't have a universally accepted answer on why boosting works, but according to subsection 6.2.2 of Berk (2016), there are three possible explanations:

- Boosting is a margin maximizer
- Boosting is a statistical optimizer
- Boosting is an interpolator

But what do these actually mean? We will now cover each of these points one by one. The margin for an observation in a boosting algorithm is calculated as follows:

$$mg = \sum_{m: y = h_m} a_m - \sum_{m: y \neq h_m} a_m$$

We can see that the margin is the difference between the sum of the passes over the correct classifications and incorrect classifications. In the preceding formula, the quantity a_m denotes the voting power. The reason why the boosting algorithm works so well, especially for the classification problem, is because it is a *margin maximizer*. In their ground-breaking paper, Schapire et al., the inventors of the boosting algorithm, claim that boosting is particularly good at finding classifiers with large margins in that it concentrates on those examples whose margins are small (or negative) and forces the base learning algorithm to generate good classifications for those examples. The bold section of this quote is what will be illustrated in the next R code block.

The spam dataset from the `kernlab` package will be used for illustrating this key idea. The `boosting` function from the `gbm` package will fit on the data to distinguish between the spam emails and the good ones. We will begin an initial model with a single iteration only, accessing the accuracy, obtaining the margins, and then producing the summary in the following code block:

```
> data("spam")
> set.seed(12345)
```

```
> Train_Test <- sample(c("Train","Test"),nrow(spam),replace =
TRUE,prob = c(0.7,0.3))
> spam_Train <- spam[Train_Test=="Train",]
> spam_Formula <- as.formula("type~.")
> spam_b0 <- boosting(spam_Formula,data=spam_Train,mfinal=1)
> sum(predict(spam_b0,newdata=spam_Train)$class==
+       spam_Train$type)/nrow(spam_Train)
[1] 0.905
> mb0 <- margins(spam_b0,newdata=spam_Train)$margins
> mb0[1:20]
 [1]  1 -1  1 -1  1  1  1  1  1  1  1  1  1  1  1  1  1  1  1  1
> summary(mb0)
   Min. 1st Qu.  Median    Mean 3rd Qu.    Max.
 -1.000   1.000   1.000   0.809   1.000   1.000
```

Next, we will increase the number of iterations to 5, 10, 20, 50, and 200. The reader should track the accuracy and the summary of the margins as they hover over the following results:

```
> spam_b1 <- boosting(spam_Formula,data=spam_Train,mfinal=5)
> sum(predict(spam_b1,newdata=spam_Train)$class==
+       spam_Train$type)/nrow(spam_Train)
[1] 0.948
> mb1 <- margins(spam_b1,newdata=spam_Train)$margins
> mb1[1:20]
 [1]  1.0000 -0.2375  0.7479 -0.2375  0.1771  0.5702  0.6069  0.7479
1.0000
[10]  0.7479  1.0000  1.0000 -0.7479  1.0000  0.7479  1.0000  0.7479
1.0000
[19] -0.0146  1.0000
> summary(mb1)
   Min. 1st Qu.  Median    Mean 3rd Qu.    Max.
 -1.000   0.631   1.000   0.783   1.000   1.000
> spam_b2 <- boosting(spam_Formula,data=spam_Train,mfinal=10)
> sum(predict(spam_b2,newdata=spam_Train)$class==
+       spam_Train$type)/nrow(spam_Train)
[1] 0.969
> mb2 <- margins(spam_b2,newdata=spam_Train)$margins
> mb2[1:20]
 [1]  0.852  0.304  0.245  0.304  0.288  0.629  0.478  0.678  0.827
0.678
[11]  1.000  1.000 -0.272  0.517  0.700  0.517  0.700  0.478  0.529
0.852
> summary(mb2)
   Min. 1st Qu.  Median    Mean 3rd Qu.    Max.
```

```
    -0.517    0.529    0.807    0.708    1.000    1.000
> spam_b3 <- boosting(spam_Formula,data=spam_Train,mfinal=20)
> sum(predict(spam_b3,newdata=spam_Train)$class==
+       spam_Train$type)/nrow(spam_Train)
[1] 0.996
> mb3 <- margins(spam_b3,newdata=spam_Train)$margins
> mb3[1:20]
 [1] 0.5702 0.3419 0.3212 0.3419 0.3612 0.6665 0.4549 0.7926 0.7687
0.6814
[11] 0.8958 0.5916 0.0729 0.6694 0.6828 0.6694 0.6828 0.6130 0.6813
0.7467
> summary(mb3)
   Min. 1st Qu.  Median   Mean 3rd Qu.    Max.
 -0.178   0.537   0.719   0.676   0.869   1.000
> spam_b4<- boosting(spam_Formula,data=spam_Train,mfinal=50)
> sum(predict(spam_b4,newdata=spam_Train)$class==
+       spam_Train$type)/nrow(spam_Train)
[1] 1
> mb4 <- margins(spam_b4,newdata=spam_Train)$margins
> mb4[1:20]
 [1] 0.407 0.333 0.386 0.333 0.379 0.518 0.486 0.536 0.579 0.647 0.695
0.544
[13] 0.261 0.586 0.426 0.586 0.426 0.488 0.572 0.677
> summary(mb4)
   Min. 1st Qu.  Median   Mean 3rd Qu.    Max.
  0.098   0.444   0.590   0.586   0.729   1.000
> spam_b5<- boosting(spam_Formula,data=spam_Train,mfinal=200)
> sum(predict(spam_b5,newdata=spam_Train)$class==
+       spam_Train$type)/nrow(spam_Train)
[1] 1
> mb5 <- margins(spam_b5,newdata=spam_Train)$margins
> mb5[1:20]
 [1] 0.386 0.400 0.362 0.368 0.355 0.396 0.368 0.462 0.489 0.491 0.700
0.486
[13] 0.317 0.426 0.393 0.426 0.393 0.385 0.624 0.581
> summary(mb5)
   Min. 1st Qu.  Median   Mean 3rd Qu.    Max.
  0.272   0.387   0.482   0.510   0.607   0.916
```

The first important difference is that the margins have moved completely away from negative numbers, and each of them is non-negative after the number of iterations reaches 50 or more. To get a clearer picture of this, we will column-bind the margins and then look at all of the observations that had a negative margin upon initialization:

```
> View(cbind(mb1,mb2,mb3,mb4,mb5)[mb1<0,])
```

The following snapshot shows the result of the preceding code:

	mb1	mb2	mb3	mb4	mb5
1	-0.2375	0.30382	0.341887	0.3332	0.400
2	-0.2375	0.30382	0.341887	0.3332	0.368
3	-0.7479	-0.27177	0.072900	0.2614	0.317
4	-0.0146	0.52949	0.681289	0.5718	0.624
5	-0.6307	-0.17281	0.105200	0.2788	0.323
6	-0.6307	-0.15168	0.030059	0.2297	0.323
7	-0.1922	0.09987	0.161135	0.4676	0.368
8	-0.6069	-0.19883	0.081071	0.2535	0.326
9	-0.2375	0.00700	0.179740	0.2616	0.338
10	-0.2009	0.30655	0.333049	0.2877	0.354
11	-0.5702	0.02514	0.169440	0.3162	0.325
12	-0.2375	0.11115	0.295751	0.3105	0.351
13	-0.6307	-0.15168	0.009839	0.2310	0.339
155	-0.3786	-0.11153	0.066041	0.2508	0.329
156	-0.1922	-0.36783	0.009775	0.2550	0.323
157	-0.3181	0.18975	0.206236	0.2970	0.347
158	-0.1922	0.18975	0.184170	0.3522	0.343
159	-0.3181	-0.03722	0.235859	0.2496	0.356
160	-0.7479	0.20146	0.169046	0.3433	0.336
161	-0.3786	0.20146	0.307440	0.3752	0.353
162	-0.3181	-0.32505	0.130531	0.2373	0.340
163	-0.2009	0.67787	0.514666	0.5280	0.424
164	-0.3181	0.12438	0.130471	0.2513	0.357
165	-0.3786	0.26382	0.060728	0.2829	0.326

Figure 1: Margins of misclassified observations over the iterations

Thus, we can clearly see that the margins increase as the number of iterations increases.

The second point to bear in mind about boosting, especially adaptive boosting, is that it is a statistical optimizer. Pages 264–5 of Berk (2016) and 25–6 of Zhou (2012) show that boosting ensembles achieves the Bayes error rate. This means that since the exponential loss is minimized, the classification error rate is also minimized.

The third point about boosting being an interpolator is straightforward. It is evident that the iterations of boosting can be seen as the weighted averaging of a random forest.

Up to this point, the boosting methods have only addressed classification and regression problems. The loss function is central for a machine learning algorithm, and the next section will discuss a variety of loss functions that will help in setting the boosting algorithm for different formats of data.

The gbm package

The R gbm package, created by Greg Ridgeway, is a very versatile package. The details of this package can be found at http://www.saedsayad.com/docs/gbm2.pdf. The document details the theoretical aspects of the gradient boosting and illustrates various other parameters of the gbm function. First, we will consider the shrinkage factor available in the gbm function.

Shrinkage parameters are very important, and also help with the problem of overfitting. Penalization is achieved through this option. For the spam dataset, we will set the shrinkage option to 0.1 (very large) and 0.0001 (very small) and also look at how the performance is affected:

```
> spam_Train2 <- spam_Train
> spam_Train2$type <- as.numeric(spam_Train2$type)-1
> spam_gbm <- gbm(spam_Formula,distribution="bernoulli",
+       data=spam_Train2, n.trees=500,bag.fraction = 0.8,
+       shrinkage = 0.1)
> plot(spam_gbm) # output suppressed
> summary(spam_gbm)
                                var       rel.inf
charExclamation     charExclamation 21.740302311
charDollar                charDollar 18.505561199
remove                        remove 11.722965305
your                            your  8.282553567
free                            free  8.142952834
hp                                hp  7.399617456


num415                        num415  0.000000000
```

```
direct                   direct   0.000000000
cs                           cs   0.000000000
original               original   0.000000000
table                     table   0.000000000
charSquarebracket charSquarebracket   0.000000000
```

The summary function also plots the relative variable importance plot. This is shown in the following screenshot:

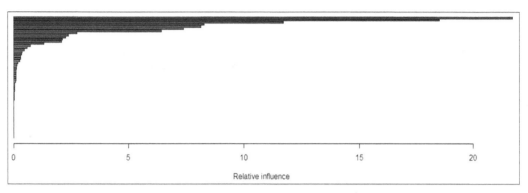

Figure 2: Relative variable influence plot

The details of the fitted object are obtained next:

```
> spam_gbm
gbm(formula = spam_Formula, distribution = "bernoulli", data = spam_
Train2,
    n.trees = 500, shrinkage = 0.1, bag.fraction = 0.8)
A gradient boosted model with bernoulli loss function.
500 iterations were performed.
There were 57 predictors, of which 43 had nonzero influence.

Here, the choice of shrinkage = 0.1 leads to 43 nonzero influential
variables. We can now reduce the shrinkage factor drastically and
observe the impact:

> spam_gbm2 <- gbm(spam_Formula,distribution="bernoulli",
+         data=spam_Train2,n.trees=500,bag.fraction = 0.8,
+         shrinkage = 0.0001)
> spam_gbm2
gbm(formula = spam_Formula, distribution = "bernoulli", data = spam_
Train2,
    n.trees = 500, shrinkage = 1e-04, bag.fraction = 0.8)
A gradient boosted model with Bernoulli loss function.
500 iterations were performed.
There were 57 predictors of which 2 had nonzero influence.
```

The shrinkage parameter is too low, and so almost none of the variables are influential. Next, we will generate a plot, as follows:

```
> windows(height=100,width=200)
> par(mfrow=c(1,2))
> gbm.perf(spam_gbm,plot.it=TRUE)
Using OOB method...
[1] 151
Warning message:
In gbm.perf(spam_gbm, plot.it = TRUE) :
  OOB generally underestimates the optimal number of iterations
although predictive performance is reasonably competitive. Using
cv.folds>0 when calling gbm usually results in improved predictive
performance.
> gbm.perf(spam_gbm2,plot.it=TRUE)
Using OOB method...
[1] 500
Warning message:
In gbm.perf(spam_gbm2, plot.it = TRUE) :
  OOB generally underestimates the optimal number of iterations
although predictive performance is reasonably competitive. Using
cv.folds>0 when calling gbm usually results in improved predictive
performance.
```

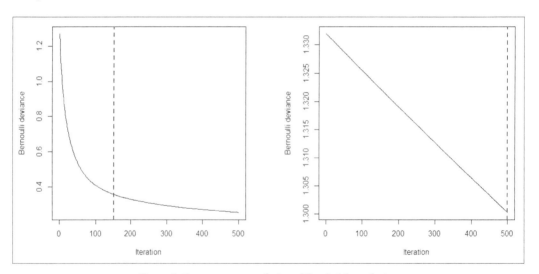

Figure 3: Convergence as a factor of the shrinkage factor

We don't have a clear convergence for the extremely small shrinkage factor.

Further details of the gbm function can be obtained from the package documentation or the source that was provided earlier. Boosting is a very versatile technique, and Ridgeway has implemented this for the varieties of data structures. The next table lists four of the most commonly occurring data structures, showing the statistical model, the deviance (related to the loss function), the initial values, the gradient, and the estimate of the terminal node output for each one:

Output type	Stat model	Deviance	Initial value	Gradient	Terminal node estimate
Numeric	Gaussian	$\dfrac{1}{\sum_{i=1}^n w_i}\sum_{i=1}^n w_i\left(y_i - f(x_i)\right)^2$	$f(x_i)=\dfrac{\sum w_i(y_i-o_i)}{\sum_{i=1}^n w_i}$	$z_i = y_i - f(x_i)$	$\dfrac{\sum w_i(y_i - f(x_i))}{\sum_{i=1}^n w_i}$
Binary	Bernoulli	$-2\dfrac{1}{\sum_{i=1}^n w_i}\sum_{i=1}^n w_i\left(y_i f(x_i)-\log\left(1+e^{f(x_i)}\right)\right)$	$f(x_i)=\log\dfrac{\sum_{i=1}^n w_i y_i}{\sum_{i=1}^n w_i(1-y_i)}$	$z_i=y_i-p_i, p_i=\dfrac{1}{1+e^{-f(x_i)}}$	$\dfrac{\sum_{i=1}^n w_i(y_i-p_i)}{\sum_{i=1}^n w_i p_i(1-p_i)}$
Count	Poisson	$-2\dfrac{1}{\sum_{i=1}^n w_i}\sum_{i=1}^n w_i\left(y_i f(x_i)-\exp(f(x_i))\right)$	$f(x_i)=\log\dfrac{\sum_{i=1}^n w_i y_i}{\sum_{i=1}^n w_i \exp(o_i)}$	$z_i = y_i - \exp(f(x_i))$	$\log\left(\dfrac{\sum_{i=1}^n w_i y_i}{\sum_{i=1}^n w_i \exp(f(x_i))}\right)$
Survival data	Cox proportional hazards model	$-2\sum_{i=1}^n w_i\left(\delta_i\left(f(x_i)-\log\left(\dfrac{R_i}{w_i}\right)\right)\right)$	$z_i=\delta_i-\sum_j \delta_j \dfrac{w_j I(t_i\geq t_j)e^{f(x_i)}}{\sum_k w_k I(t_j\geq t_k)e^{f(x_k)}}$	0	Newton–Raphson algorithm

Table 1: GBM boosting options

We will apply the gbm function for the count data and the survival data.

Boosting for count data

The number of accidents, mistakes/typographical errors, births, and so on are popular examples of count data. Here, we count the number of incidents over a particular time, place, and/or space. Poisson distribution is very popular for modeling count data. When we have additional information in the form of covariates and independent variables, the related regression problem is often of interest. The generalized linear model is a popular technique for modeling the count data.

Let's look at a simulated dataset available at `https://stats.idre.ucla.edu/r/dae/poisson-regression/`. The necessary changes are made as indicated in this source. First, we fit the Poisson regression model using the `glm` function. Next, we fit the boosting model, as follows:

```
> # Poisson regression and boosting
> # https://stats.idre.ucla.edu/r/dae/poisson-regression/
> pregnancy <- read.csv("https://stats.idre.ucla.edu/stat/data/
poisson_sim.csv")
> pregnancy <- within(pregnancy, {
+   prog <- factor(prog, levels=1:3,
+   labels=c("General", "Academic","Vocational"))
+   id <- factor(id)
+ })
> summary(pregnancy)
       id            num_awards             prog          math
 1       :  1   Min.   :0.00   General  : 45   Min.   :33.0
 2       :  1   1st Qu.:0.00   Academic :105   1st Qu.:45.0
 3       :  1   Median :0.00   Vocational: 50   Median :52.0
 4       :  1   Mean   :0.63                  Mean   :52.6
 5       :  1   3rd Qu.:1.00                  3rd Qu.:59.0
 6       :  1   Max.   :6.00                  Max.   :75.0
 (Other):194
> pregnancy_Poisson <- glm(num_awards ~ prog + math,
+                    family="poisson", data=pregnancy)
> summary(pregnancy_Poisson)

Call:
glm(formula = num_awards ~ prog + math, family = "poisson", data =
pregnancy)

Deviance Residuals:
   Min       1Q   Median       3Q      Max
-2.204   -0.844   -0.511    0.256    2.680

Coefficients:
               Estimate Std. Error z value Pr(>|z|)
(Intercept)     -5.2471     0.6585    -7.97  1.6e-15 ***
progAcademic     1.0839     0.3583     3.03   0.0025 **
progVocational   0.3698     0.4411     0.84   0.4018
math             0.0702     0.0106     6.62  3.6e-11 ***
---
```

```
Signif. codes:  0 '***' 0.001 '**' 0.01 '*' 0.05 '.' 0.1 ' ' 1

(Dispersion parameter for poisson family taken to be 1)

    Null deviance: 287.67  on 199  degrees of freedom
Residual deviance: 189.45  on 196  degrees of freedom
AIC: 373.5

Number of Fisher Scoring iterations: 6

> pregnancy_boost <- gbm(num_awards ~ prog+math,dist="poisson",
+ n.trees=100,interaction.depth = 2,shrinkage=0.1,data=pregnancy)
> cbind(pregnancy$num_awards,predict(m1,type="response"),
+        predict(pboost,n.trees=100,type="response"))
     [,1]    [,2]    [,3]
1       0 0.1352 0.1240
2       0 0.0934 0.1072
3       0 0.1669 0.3375
4       0 0.1450 0.0850
5       0 0.1260 0.0257
6       0 0.1002 0.0735

195     1 1.0469 1.4832
196     2 2.2650 2.0241
197     2 1.4683 0.4047
198     1 2.2650 2.0241
199     0 2.4296 2.0241
200     3 2.6061 2.0241
> sum((pregnancy$num_awards-predict(m1,type="response"))^2)
[1] 151
> sum((pregnancy$num_awards-predict(pboost,n.trees=100,
+    type="response"))^2)
[1] 141
> summary(pregnancy_boost)
      var rel.inf
math math    89.7
prog prog    10.3
```

This has been a very simple example with only two covariates. However, in practice, we have seen that the count data is treated as the regression problem many times. This is unfortunate, and the general regression technique is not any sort of alchemy. The data structure must be respected and the count data analysis needs to be carried out. Note that the model fitted here is nonlinear. Though the benefit is not apparent here, it is natural that as the number of variables increases, the count data framework becomes more appropriate. We will close this discussion of count data analysis with a plot of the variable importance of two trees, as well as a tabular display:

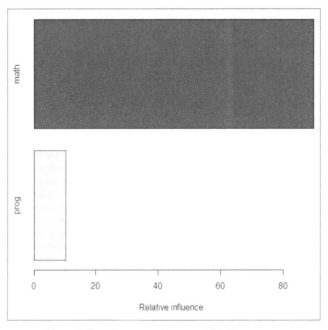

Figure 4: Boosting count data – variable importance

```
> pretty.gbm.tree(pregnancy_boost,i.tree=18)
   SplitVar SplitCodePred LeftNode RightNode MissingNode ErrorReduction
Weight
0          1        64.50000        1          5            6            10.41
100
1          1        57.50000        2          3            4             1.14
90
2         -1        -0.01146       -1         -1           -1             0.00
71
3         -1         0.02450       -1         -1           -1             0.00
19
4         -1        -0.00387       -1         -1           -1             0.00
90
5         -1         0.05485       -1         -1           -1             0.00
10
```

	SplitVar	SplitCodePred	LeftNode	RightNode	MissingNode	ErrorReduction Weight
6	-1	0.00200	-1	-1	-1	0.00
						100

	Prediction
0	0.00200
1	-0.00387
2	-0.01146
3	0.02450
4	-0.00387
5	0.05485
6	0.00200

```
> pretty.gbm.tree(pregnancy_boost,i.tree=63)
```

	SplitVar	SplitCodePred	LeftNode	RightNode	MissingNode	ErrorReduction Weight
0	1	60.50000	1	5	6	3.837
						100
1	0	20.00000	2	3	4	0.407
						79
2	-1	-0.00803	-1	-1	-1	0.000
						40
3	-1	0.05499	-1	-1	-1	0.000
						39
4	-1	0.02308	-1	-1	-1	0.000
						79
5	-1	0.02999	-1	-1	-1	0.000
						21
6	-1	0.02453	-1	-1	-1	0.000
						100

	Prediction
0	0.02453
1	0.02308
2	-0.00803
3	0.05499
4	0.02308
5	0.02999
6	0.02453

The pretty.gbm.tree function helps in extracting the hidden trees of the gbm objects. In the next section, we will deal with a gradient boosting technique for survival data.

Boosting for survival data

The pbc dataset has already been introduced in *Chapters 1, Introduction to Ensemble Techniques,* and *Chapter 2, Bootstrapping.* As seen earlier, the survival data has incomplete observations, and we need specialized techniques for this. In Table 1, we saw that the deviance function is quite complex. Thanks to Ridgeway, we don't have to worry much about such computations. Instead, we simply use the gbm function with the option of dist="coxph" and carry out the analyses as follows:

```
> # Survival data
> pbc_boost <- gbm(Surv(time,status==2)~trt + age + sex+ascites +
+                     hepato + spiders + edema + bili + chol +
+                     albumin + copper + alk.phos + ast + trig +
+                     platelet + protime + stage,
+                 n.trees=100,interaction.depth = 2,
+                 shrinkage=0.01,dist="coxph",data=pbc)
> summary(pbc_boost)
              var rel.inf
bili         bili  54.220
age           age  10.318
protime   protime   9.780
stage       stage   7.364
albumin   albumin   6.648
copper     copper   5.899
ascites   ascites   2.361
edema       edema   2.111
ast           ast   0.674
platelet platelet   0.246
alk.phos alk.phos   0.203
trig         trig   0.178
trt           trt   0.000
sex           sex   0.000
hepato     hepato   0.000
spiders   spiders   0.000
chol         chol   0.000
> pretty.gbm.tree(pbc_boost,i.tree=2)   # output suppressed
> pretty.gbm.tree(pbc_boost,i.tree=72)  # output suppressed
```

Hence, using the versatile gbm function, we can easily carry out the gradient boosting technique for a variety of data structures.

The xgboost package

The xgboost R package is an optimized, distributed implementation of the gradient boosting method. This is an engineering optimization that is known to be efficient, flexible, and portable — see https://github.com/dmlc/xgboost for more details and regular updates. This provides parallel tree boosting, and therefore has been found to be immensely useful in the data science community. This is especially the case given that a great fraction of the competition winners at www.kaggle.org use the xgboost technique. A partial list of Kaggle winners is available at https://github.com/dmlc/xgboost/tree/master/demo#machine-learning-challenge-winning-solutions.

The main advantages of the extreme gradient boosting implementation are shown in the following:

- **Parallel computing**: This package is enabled with parallel processing using OpenMP, which then uses all the cores of the computing machine

- **Regularization**: This helps in circumventing the problem of overfitting by incorporating the regularization ideas

- **Cross-validation**: No extra coding is required for carrying out cross-validation

- **Pruning**: This grows the tree up to the maximum depth and then prunes backward

- **Missing values**: Missing values are internally handled

- **Saving and reloading**: This has features that not only help in saving an existing model, but can also continue the iterations from the step where it was last stopped

- **Cross platform**: This is available for Python, Scala, and so on

We will illustrate these ideas with the spam dataset that we saw earlier in the book. The functions of the xgboost package require all the variables to be numeric, and the output should also be labelled as 0 and 1. Furthermore, the covariate matrix and the output need to be given to the xgboost R package separately. As a result, we will first load the spam dataset and then create the partitions and the formula, as follows:

```
> ## The xgboost Package
> data("spam")
> spam2 <- spam
> spam2$type <- as.numeric(spam2$type)-1
> head(data.frame(spam2$type,spam$type))
  spam2.type spam.type
1          1      spam
```

```
2              1         spam
3              1         spam
4              1         spam
5              1         spam
6              1         spam
> # 1 denotes spam, and 0 - nonspam
> set.seed(12345)
> Train_Test <- sample(c("Train","Test"),nrow(spam2),replace = TRUE,
+                       prob = c(0.7,0.3))
> spam2_Train <- spam2[Train_Test=="Train",]
> spam_Formula <- as.formula("type~.")
> spam_train <- list()
```

The xgboost package also requires the training regression data to be specified in a special dgCMatrix matrix. Thus, we can convert it using the as function:

```
> spam_train$data <- as(spam_train$data,"dgCMatrix")
> spam_train$label <- spam2_Train$type
> class(spam_train$data)
[1] "dgCMatrix"
attr(,"package")
[1] "Matrix"
```

We now have the infrastructure ready for applying the xgboost function. The option of nrounds=100 and the logistic function are chosen, and the results are obtained as follows:

```
> # Simple XGBoosting
> spam_xgb<- xgboost(data=spam_train$data,label=spam_train$label,+
nrounds = 100,objective="binary:logistic")
[1] train-error:0.064062
[2] train-error:0.063437
[3] train-error:0.053438
[4] train-error:0.050313
[5] train-error:0.047812
[6] train-error:0.045313

[95]      train-error:0.002188
[96]      train-error:0.001875
[97]      train-error:0.001875
[98]      train-error:0.001875
[99]      train-error:0.000937
[100]     train-error:0.000937
```

Using the fitted boosting model, we now apply the `predict` function and assess the accuracy:

```
> xgb_predict <- predict(spam_xgb,spam_train$data)
> sum(xgb_predict>0.5)
[1] 1226
> sum(spam_train$label)
[1] 1229
> table(spam_train$label,c(xgb_predict>0.5))

    FALSE TRUE
  0  1971    0
  1     3 1226
```

If the probability (and the response, in this case) of the observation being marked 1 is more than 0.5, then we can label the observation as 1, and 0 otherwise. The predicted label and actual label contingency table is obtained by using the table R function. Clearly, we have very good accuracy, and there are only three misclassifications.

We claimed that the `xgboost` package does not require extra coding for the cross-validation analysis. The `xgb.cv` function is useful here, and it works with the same arguments as the `xgboost` function with the cross-validation folds specified by the `nfold` option. Here, we choose `nfold=10`. Now, using the `xgb.cv` function, we carry out the analysis and assess the prediction accuracy:

```
> # XGBoosting with cross-validation
> spam_xgb_cv <- xgb.cv(data=spam_train$data,
+          label=spam_train$label,nfold=10,nrounds = 100,
+          objective="binary:logistic",prediction = TRUE)
[1] train-error:0.064410+0.001426    test-error:0.091246+0.01697
[2] train-error:0.058715+0.001862    test-error:0.082805+0.01421
[3] train-error:0.052986+0.003389    test-error:0.077186+0.01472
[4] train-error:0.049826+0.002210    test-error:0.073123+0.01544
[5] train-error:0.046910+0.001412    test-error:0.070937+0.01340
[6] train-error:0.043958+0.001841    test-error:0.066249+0.01346

[95]      train-error:0.001667+0.000340    test-
error:0.048119+0.00926
[96]      train-error:0.001528+0.000318    test-
error:0.047181+0.01008
[97]      train-error:0.001458+0.000260    test-
error:0.046868+0.00974
[98]      train-error:0.001389+0.000269    test-
error:0.047181+0.00979
[99]      train-error:0.001215+0.000233    test-
error:0.047182+0.00969
[100]     train-error:0.001111+0.000260    test-
error:0.045932+0.01115
```

```
> xgb_cv_predict <- spam_xgb_cv$pred
> sum(xgb_cv_predict>0.5)
[1] 1206
> table(spam_train$label,c(xgb_cv_predict>0.5))

    FALSE TRUE
  0  1909   62
  1    85 1144
```

The cross-validation analysis shows that the accuracy has decreased. This is an indication that we had an overfitting problem with the xgboost function. We will now look at the other features of the xgboost package. At the beginning of this section, we claimed that the technique allowed flexibility through early stoppings and also the resumption of earlier fitted model objects.

However, an important question is *when do you need to stop the iterations early?* We don't have any underlying theory with regards to the number of iterations that are required as a function of the number of variables and the number of observations. Consequently, we will kick off the proceedings with a specified number of iterations. If the convergence of error reduction does not fall below the threshold level, then we will continue with more iterations, and this task will be taken up next. However, if the specified number of iterations is way too high and the performance of the boosting method is getting worse, then we will have to stop the iterations. This is achieved by specifying the early_stopping_rounds option, which we will put into action in the following code:

```
> # Stop early
> spam_xgb_cv2 <- xgb.cv(data=spam_train$data,label=
+                spam_train$label, early_stopping_rounds = 5,
+                nfold=10,nrounds = 100,objective="binary:logistic",
+                prediction = TRUE)
[1] train-error:0.064271+0.002371    test-error:0.090294+0.02304
Multiple eval metrics are present. Will use test_error for early
stopping.
Will train until test_error hasn't improved in 5 rounds.

[2] train-error:0.059028+0.003370    test-error:0.085614+0.01808
[3] train-error:0.052048+0.002049    test-error:0.075930+0.01388
[4] train-error:0.049236+0.002544    test-error:0.072811+0.01333
[5] train-error:0.046007+0.002775    test-error:0.070622+0.01419
[6] train-error:0.042882+0.003065    test-error:0.066559+0.01670

[38]     train-error:0.010382+0.001237    test-
error:0.048121+0.01153 [39]     train-error:0.010069+0.001432     test-
error:0.048434+0.01162
```

```
[40]      train-error:0.009653+0.001387      test-
error:0.048435+0.01154
[41]      train-error:0.009236+0.001283      test-
error:0.048435+0.01179
[42]      train-error:0.008924+0.001173      test-
error:0.048748+0.01154
Stopping. Best iteration:
[37]      train-error:0.010625+0.001391      test-
error:0.048121+0.01162
```

Here, the best iteration has already occurred at number 37, and the confirmation of this is obtained five iterations down the line, thanks to the early_stopping_rounds = 5 option. Now that we've found the best iteration, we stop the process.

We will now look at how to add more iterations. This coding is for illustration purposes only. Using the option of nrounds = 10, and the earlier fitted spam_xgb, along with the options of data and label, we will ask the xgboost function to perform ten more iterations:

```
> # Continue training
> xgboost(xgb_model=spam_xgb,
+         data=spam_train$data,label=spam_train$label,
+         nrounds = 10)
[101]     train-error:0.000937
[102]     train-error:0.000937
[103]     train-error:0.000937
[104]     train-error:0.000937
[105]     train-error:0.000937
[106]     train-error:0.000937
[107]     train-error:0.000937
[108]     train-error:0.000937
[109]     train-error:0.000937
[110]     train-error:0.000937
##### xgb.Booster
raw: 136 Kb
call:
  xgb.train(params = params, data = dtrain, nrounds = nrounds,
    watchlist = watchlist, verbose = verbose, print_every_n = print_
every_n, early_stopping_rounds = early_stopping_rounds, maximize =
maximize, save_period = save_period, save_name = save_name, xgb_model
= xgb_model, callbacks = callbacks)
params (as set within xgb.train):
  silent = "1"
xgb.attributes:
  niter
callbacks:
  cb.print.evaluation(period = print_every_n)
  cb.evaluation.log()
  cb.save.model(save_period = save_period, save_name = save_name)
```

```
niter: 110
evaluation_log:
    iter train_error
       1    0.064062
       2    0.063437
---
     109    0.000937
     110    0.000937
```

The bold and large font of the iteration number is not the format thrown out by the R software. This change has been made to emphasize the fact that the number of iterations from the earlier fitted `spam_xgb` object will now continue from `101` and will go up to `110`. Adding additional iterations is easily achieved with the `xgboost` function.

The `xgb.plot.importance` function, working with the `xgb.importance` function, can be used to extract and display the most important variables as identified by the boosting method:

```
> # Variable Importance
> xgb.plot.importance(xgb.importance(names(spam_train$data),
+                                    spam_xgb)[1:10,])
```

The result is the following plot:

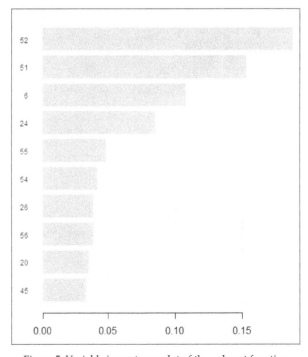

Figure 5: Variable importance plot of the xgboost function

We have now seen the power of the xgboost package. Next, we will outline the capabilities of the h2o package.

The h2o package

The R software .exe file size is 75 MB (version 3.4.1). The size of the h2o R package is 125 MB. This will probably indicate to you the importance of the h2o package. All the datasets used in this book are very limited in size, with the number of observations not exceeding 10,000. In most cases, the file size has been of a maximum of a few MB. However, the data science world works hard, and throws around files in GB, and in even higher formats. Thus, we need more capabilities, and the h2o package provides just that. We simply load the h2o package and have a peek:

```
> library(h2o)

-------------------------------------------------------------------

Your next step is to start H2O:
    > h2o.init()

For H2O package documentation, ask for help:
    > ??h2o

After starting H2O, you can use the Web UI at http://localhost:54321
For more information visit http://docs.h2o.ai

-------------------------------------------------------------------


Attaching package: 'h2o'

The following objects are masked from 'package:stats':

    cor, sd, var

The following objects are masked from 'package:base':

    %*%, %in%, &&, ||, apply, as.factor, as.numeric, colnames,
    colnames<-, ifelse, is.character, is.factor, is.numeric, log,
    log10, log1p, log2, round, signif, trunc

Warning message:
package 'h2o' was built under R version 3.4.4
> h2o.init()

H2O is not running yet, starting it now...
```

```
Note:  In case of errors look at the following log files:
    C:\Users\tprabhan\AppData\Local\Temp\Rtmpu6f0f0/h2o_TPRABHAN_
started_from_r.out
    C:\Users\tprabhan\AppData\Local\Temp\Rtmpu6f0f0/h2o_TPRABHAN_
started_from_r.err

java version "1.7.0_67"
Java(TM) SE Runtime Environment (build 1.7.0_67-b01)
Java HotSpot(TM) 64-Bit Server VM (build 24.65-b04, mixed mode)


Starting H2O JVM and connecting: .. Connection successful!

R is connected to the H2O cluster:
    H2O cluster uptime:         4 seconds 449 milliseconds
    H2O cluster version:        3.16.0.2
    H2O cluster version age:    7 months and 7 days !!!
    H2O cluster name:           H2O_started_from_R_TPRABHAN_saz680
    H2O cluster total nodes:    1
    H2O cluster total memory:   1.76 GB
    H2O cluster total cores:    4
    H2O cluster allowed cores:  4
    H2O cluster healthy:        TRUE
    H2O Connection ip:          localhost
    H2O Connection port:        54321
    H2O Connection proxy:       NA
    H2O Internal Security:      FALSE
    H2O API Extensions:         AutoML, Algos, Core V3, Core V4
    R Version:                  R version 3.4.0 (2017-04-21)

Warning message:
In h2o.clusterInfo() :
Your H2O cluster version is too old (7 months and 7 days)!
Please download and install the latest version from http://h2o.ai/
download/
```

Clusters and threads help in scaling up computations. For the more enthusiastic reader, the following sources will help in using the h2o package:

- http://blog.revolutionanalytics.com/2014/04/a-dive-into-h2o.
  html

- http://docs.h2o.ai/

- https://www.analyticsvidhya.com/blog/2016/05/h2o-data-table-
  build-models-large-data-sets/

Using the gbm, xgboost, and h2o packages, the reader can analyze complex and large datasets.

Summary

We began this chapter by briefly thinking about why boosting works. There are three perspectives that possibly explain the success of boosting, and these were covered before we looked deeper into this topic. The gbm package is very powerful, and it offers different options for tuning the gradient boosting algorithm, which deals with numerous data structures. We illustrated its capabilities with the shrinkage option and applied it to the count and survival data structures. The xgboost package is an even more efficient implementation of the gradient boosting method. It is faster and offers other flexibilities, too. We illustrated using the xgboost function with cross-validation, early stopping, and continuing further iterations as required. The h2o package/platform helps to implement the ensemble machine learning techniques on a bigger scale.

In the next chapter, we will look into the details of why ensembling works. In particular, we will see why putting multiple models together is often a useful practice, and we will also explore the scenarios that we can do this in.

7
The General Ensemble Technique

The previous four chapters have dealt with the ensembling techniques for decision trees. In each of the topics discussed in those chapters, the base learner was a decision tree and, consequently, we delved into the homogenous ensembling technique. In this chapter, we will demonstrate that the base learner can be any statistical or machine learning technique and their ensemble will lead to improved precision in predictions. An important requirement will be that the base learner should be better than a random guess. Through R programs, we will discuss and clarify the different possible cases in which ensembling will work. Voting is an important trait of the classifiers – we will state two different methods for this and illustrate them in the context of bagging and random forest ensemblers. The averaging technique is an ensembler for regression variables, which will follow the discussion of classification methods. The chapter will conclude with a detailed discussion of stacking methods, informally introduced in *Chapter 1*, *Introduction to Ensemble Techniques*. The topic flow unfolds as follows:

- Why does ensembling work?
- Ensembling by voting
- Ensembling by averaging
- Stack ensembles

Technical requirements

The libraries that will be used in this chapter are as follows:

- `rpart`
- `randomForest`

Why does ensembling work?

When using the bagging method, we combine the result of many decision trees and produce a single output/prediction by taking a majority count. Under a different sampling mechanism, the results had been combined to produce a single prediction for the random forests. Under a sequential error reduction method for decision trees, the boosting method also provides improved answers. Although we are dealing with uncertain data, which involves probabilities, we don't intend to have methodologies that give results out of a black box and behave without consistent solutions. A theory should explain the working and we need an assurance that the results will be consistent and there is no black magic about it. Arbitrary and uncertain answers are completely unwanted. In this section, we will look at how and why the ensembling solutions work, as well as scenarios where they will not work.

Ensembling methods have strong mathematical and statistical underpinnings that explain why they give the solutions that they do. We will consider the classification problem first. We will begin with a simplified setup and assume that we have T classifiers that are independent of each other, and that the accuracy associated with each of them is the same as $p, 0 \leq p \leq 1$. This is one of the simplest cases, and we will generalize the scenario later. Now, if we have T classifiers and each of them votes on observations such as +1 or -1, it begs the question, what will the overall accuracy be? Since the number of correct classifications of the T classifiers must outnumber the misclassifications, we would need at least $\left\lfloor \frac{T}{2}+1 \right\rfloor$ classifiers to vote the correct outcome. Here, $\lfloor \ \rfloor$ denotes the greatest integer that is less than the given fractional number. The majority classification is correct whenever $\left\lfloor \frac{T}{2}+1 \right\rfloor$ or a higher number of classifiers vote for the correct class.

To clarify, it is important to note that when we say a classifier has an accuracy p, we don't mean that the probability of the classifier marking the observation as +1 is p. Rather, what we mean here is that if the classifier makes 100 predictions, the predictions can be any combination of +1 and -1; 100*p predictions are correctly identified by the classifier. The accuracy is independent of the distribution of +1 and -1 in the population.

Under this setup, the probability of the number of classifiers marking a correct observation follows a binomial distribution with $n = T$ and a probability of p. Thus, the probability of the majority vote getting the correct prediction is as follows:

$$P_{\{Majority Vote\}} = \sum_{j=\left[\frac{T}{2}+1\right]}^{T} \binom{T}{j} p^{j} (1-p)^{T-j}$$

Since we have mentioned that the classifier must be better than a random guess, we will need the classifier accuracy to be in excess of 0.5. We will then increment the accuracy over multiple points and see how the increase in the number of classifiers impacts the probability of a majority vote:

```
> source("Utilities.R")
> windows(height=100,width=100)
> # Ensembling in Classification
> # Illustrating the ensemble accuracy with same accuracy for each
classifier
> # Different p's and T's with p > 0.5
> classifiers <- seq(9,45,2) # Number of classifiers
> accuracy <- seq(0.55,0.85,.05)
> plot(0,type='n',xlim=range(classifiers),ylim=c(0.6,1),
+       xlab="Number of Classifiers",ylab="Probability of Majority
Voting")
> for(i in 1:length(accuracy)){
+    Prob_MV <- NULL
+    for(j in 1:length(classifiers)){
+      Prob_MV[j] <- sum(dbinom(floor(classifiers[j]/2+1):classifiers
[j],
+        prob=accuracy[i],size=classifiers[j]))
+    }
+    points(classifiers,Prob_MV,col=i,"l")
+ }
> title("Classifiers with Accuracy Better Than Random Guess")
```

The `seq` function sets up an odd-numbered sequence of the number of classifiers in the `classifiers` R numeric vector. The accuracy percentage varies from `0.55` to `0.85` in the `accuracy` vector. To kick off the proceedings, we set up an empty `plot` of sorts, with appropriate x and y axis labels. Now, for each accuracy value, we will calculate the probability of the majority vote for range `floor(classif iers[j]/2+1):classifiers[j]`. The `floor(./2+1)` ensures that we select the correct starting point. For example, if the number of classifiers is nine, then the value of `floor(./2+1)` is 5. Furthermore, when we have nine classifiers, we need a minimum of five votes in favor of the event of interest. On the other hand, for an even number of classifiers (for example, eight) the value of `floor(./2+1)` is 5. The `dbinom` function calculates the probability of that specific value for the given size and probability. Over the range of `floor(classifiers[j]/2+1): classifiers[j]`, it gives the probability of the majority vote, or the accuracy of the majority vote. The output of the preceding code is presented in *Figure 1*. We can see from the result that as the number of classifiers increases (each with the same accuracy and better than the random guess), the accuracy of the majority voting also increases:

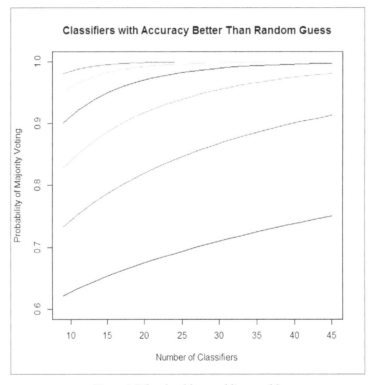

Figure 1: Why should ensembling work?

It would help us to see `Prob_MV` for one choice of the accuracy – for example, 0.65. We will run the loop with index j separately for `prob=0.65` and look at how the accuracy of the majority vote increases as the number of classifiers increases:

```
> Prob_MV <- NULL
> for(j in 1:length(classifiers)){
+    Prob_MV[j] <- sum(dbinom(floor(classifiers[j]/2+1):classifiers[j],
+                    prob=0.65,size=classifiers[j]))
+ }
> Prob_MV
 [1] 0.8282807 0.8513163 0.8705318 0.8867689 0.9006211 0.9125264
0.9228185
 [8] 0.9317586 0.9395551 0.9463770 0.9523633 0.9576292 0.9622714
0.9663716
[15] 0.9699991 0.9732133 0.9760651 0.9785984 0.9808513
```

Consequently, as the number of classifiers with equal accuracy increases, we can see that the accuracy of the majority vote also increases. Also, what is noteworthy here is that even though each of our classifiers had an accuracy of a mere `0.65`, the ensemble has way higher accuracy and almost becomes a perfect classifier. This is the main advantage of ensemble.

Will ensembling help any sort of classifier? If we have classifiers whose accuracy is worse than the random guess and hence is less than `0.5`, then we will search in the same way that we did with the previous case. For a host of a number of classifiers and accuracies less than `0.5`, we will compute the accuracy of the majority vote classifier:

```
> # When p < 0.5, ensemble accuracy goes to zero
> classifiers <- seq(6,50,2)
> accuracy <- seq(0.45,0.05,-0.05)
> plot(0,type='n',xlim=range(classifiers),ylim=c(0,0.3),
+      xlab="Number of Classifiers",ylab="Probability of Majority
Voting")
> for(i in 1:length(accuracy)){
+    Prob_MV <- NULL
+    for(j in 1:length(classifiers)){
+      Prob_MV[j] <- sum(dbinom(floor(classifiers[j]/2+1):classifiers
[j],
+                          prob=accuracy[i],size=classifiers[j]))
+    }
+    points(classifiers,Prob_MV,col=i,"l")
+    }
> title("Classifiers with Accuracy Worse Than Random Guess")
```

The result of the preceding R program is shown in *Figure 2*. Now, the first observation should be that it does not matter whether the accuracy is closer to 0.5 or to 0, the probability/accuracy of the majority vote classifier is on a decline and this adversely affects the performance. In every case, we see that the accuracy will eventually approach zero. The changes in the block of R code are the classifier sequence seq(6,50,2), and the accuracy levels decrease from 0.45 to 0.05 in seq(0.45,0.05,-0.05). Now, consider the case of accuracy being slightly less than 0.5. For example, let's keep it to 0.4999. Will we be lucky enough to see a performance improvement now?

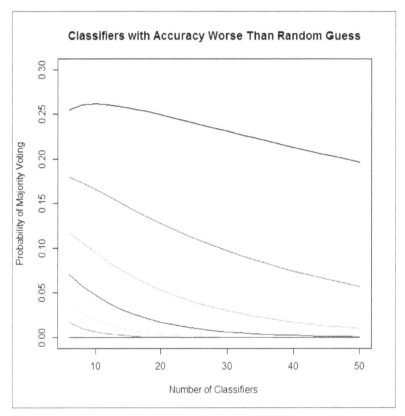

Figure 2: Ensemble is not alchemy!

```
> classifiers <- seq(10,200,10)
> Prob_MV <- NULL
> for(j in 1:length(classifiers)){
+    Prob_MV[j] <- sum(dbinom(floor(classifiers[j]/2+1):classifiers[j],
+                        prob=0.4999,size=classifiers[j]))
+ }
> Prob_MV
```

```
[1] 0.3767071 0.4115491 0.4273344 0.4368132 0.4433011 0.4480955
0.4518222
[8] 0.4548247 0.4573097 0.4594096 0.4612139 0.4627854 0.4641698
0.4654011
[15] 0.4665053 0.4675025 0.4684088 0.4692370 0.4699975 0.4706989
```

Again, it turns out that we can't match the accuracy of a single classifier. Consequently, we have the important and crucial condition that the classifier must be better than a random guess. What about the random guess itself? It is not at all difficult to pretend that we have a host of classifiers which are all random guesses. If the performance of the ensemble improves with the random guesses, we don't typically have to build any of the statistical or machine learning techniques. Given a set of random guesses, we can always improve the accuracy. Let's check this out.

There are two cases – an odd number of classifiers and an even number of classifiers – and we provide the program for both scenarios:

```
> accuracy <- 0.5
> classifiers <- seq(5,45,2)
> Prob_MV <- NULL
> for(j in 1:length(classifiers)){
+    Prob_MV[j] <- sum(dbinom(floor(classifiers[j]/2+1):classifiers[j],
+                     prob=accuracy,size=classifiers[j]))
+    }
> Prob_MV
 [1] 0.5 0.5 0.5 0.5 0.5 0.5 0.5 0.5 0.5 0.5 0.5 0.5 0.5 0.5 0.5 0.5
0.5 0.5
[19] 0.5 0.5 0.5
> classifiers <- seq(10,50,2)
> Prob_MV <- NULL
> for(j in 1:length(classifiers)){
+    Prob_MV[j] <- (sum(dbinom(floor(classifiers[j]/2):classifiers[j],
+                     prob=accuracy,size=classifiers[j]))+
+             sum(dbinom(floor(classifiers[j]/2+1):classifiers
[j],
+                     prob=accuracy,size=classifiers[j])))/2
+    }
> Prob_MV
 [1] 0.5 0.5 0.5 0.5 0.5 0.5 0.5 0.5 0.5 0.5 0.5 0.5 0.5 0.5 0.5 0.5
0.5 0.5
[19] 0.5 0.5 0.5
```

This is interesting! An ensemble of random guesses remains the same irrespective of the number of classifiers. Here, there is neither any improvement nor deterioration. Consequently, for ensembling purposes, we always need classifiers that are better than random guesses.

It is good to follow your intuition when it comes to understanding how ensembling works. We began with an oversimplified assumption that all models have the same accuracy, but such an assumption does not work well if we deal with models with varying accuracies. As a result, we need to consider cases in which we may have different accuracies for different classifiers. We will first consider a case where each classifier has an accuracy of higher than 0.5, or where each of them is better than a random guess. The approach to finding the accuracy of the majority vote is to evaluate the probabilities for each possible combination of the classifiers' outcomes. We consider the simpler case when the number of classifiers is an odd number.

Suppose we have T number of classifiers, and the accuracy of each classifier is $p^i, i = 1, 2, \ldots, T, 0.5 < p^i \leq 1$. Note that $\sum_{i=1}^{T} p_i > 1$, as these correspond to different measures.

The steps involved in evaluating the probability of a majority vote with unequal accuracies is given in the following steps:

- List all possible elementary events. If each classifier votes TRUE or FALSE for a given case, this means that it has two possible outcomes, and T number of classifiers. List the 2^T possible outcomes:
    - Example: If we have three classifiers, there would be eight possible cases, as follows:

Classifier 1	Classifier 2	Classifier 3
TRUE	TRUE	TRUE
FALSE	TRUE	TRUE
TRUE	FALSE	TRUE
FALSE	FALSE	TRUE
TRUE	TRUE	FALSE
FALSE	TRUE	FALSE
TRUE	FALSE	FALSE
FALSE	FALSE	FALSE

- Compute the probability of each possible event. Since each classifier has a different accuracy, the probabilities would then be different for each possible outcome:
    - ° Example: If the accuracies of the three classifiers (for TRUE) are 0.6, 0.7, and 0.8, then the probabilities of FALSE are, respectively, 0.4, 0.3, and 0.2, and the probabilities of the preceding table would be as follows:

Classifier 1	Classifier 2	Classifier 3
0.6	0.7	0.8
0.4	0.7	0.8
0.6	0.3	0.8
0.4	0.3	0.8
0.6	0.7	0.2
0.4	0.7	0.2
0.6	0.3	0.2
0.4	0.3	0.2

- In the next step, obtain the probability of the elementary event, which will be the product of the numbers in each column:

Classifier 1	Classifier 2	Classifier 3	Probability
0.6	0.7	0.8	0.336
0.4	0.7	0.8	0.224
0.6	0.3	0.8	0.144
0.4	0.3	0.8	0.096
0.6	0.7	0.2	0.084
0.4	0.7	0.2	0.056
0.6	0.3	0.2	0.036
0.4	0.3	0.2	0.024

- Find the events which have a majority count. In this case, this refers to a sum greater than or equal to 2:

Classifier 1	Classifier 2	Classifier 3	Vote Count
TRUE	TRUE	TRUE	3
FALSE	TRUE	TRUE	2
TRUE	FALSE	TRUE	2
FALSE	FALSE	TRUE	1
TRUE	TRUE	FALSE	2
FALSE	TRUE	FALSE	1
TRUE	FALSE	FALSE	1
FALSE	FALSE	FALSE	0

- The probability of the majority vote is then simply the sum of the probability in cases where the vote count is greater than or equal to 2. This is the sum of the entries in rows 1, 2, 3, and 5 of the Probability column, as 0.336 + 0.224 + 0.144 + 0.084 = 0.788.

We need to define a function here called Get_Prob, as follows:

```
> Get_Prob <- function(Logical,Probability){
+    return(t(ifelse(Logical,Probability,1-Probability)))
+ }
```

Given a logical vector and a vector of corresponding probabilities, the Get_Prob function will return a vector that consists of the probability that the logical condition is TRUE. If the logical value is FALSE, the complement (1 – probability) is returned.

The preceding steps are put in an R program, and are listed as follows:

```
> # Different accuracies T's illustration
> # For simplicity, we set the number of classifiers at odd number
> # Each p_i's greater than 0.5
> accuracy <- c(0.5,0.55,0.6,0.65,0.7,0.75,0.8,0.85,0.9)
> NT <- length(accuracy) # Number of classifiers
> APC <- expand.grid(rep(list(c(TRUE,FALSE)),NT)) # All possible
combinations
> head(APC)
   Var1   Var2   Var3 Var4 Var5 Var6 Var7 Var8 Var9
1  TRUE   TRUE   TRUE TRUE TRUE TRUE TRUE TRUE TRUE
2 FALSE   TRUE   TRUE TRUE TRUE TRUE TRUE TRUE TRUE
3  TRUE  FALSE   TRUE TRUE TRUE TRUE TRUE TRUE TRUE
4 FALSE  FALSE   TRUE TRUE TRUE TRUE TRUE TRUE TRUE
5  TRUE   TRUE  FALSE TRUE TRUE TRUE TRUE TRUE TRUE
```

```
6 FALSE   TRUE FALSE TRUE TRUE TRUE TRUE TRUE TRUE
> Elements_Prob <- t(apply(APC,1,Get_Prob,Probability=accuracy))
> head(Elements_Prob)
       [,1]  [,2]  [,3]  [,4]  [,5]  [,6]  [,7]  [,8]  [,9]
[1,]   0.5  0.55   0.6  0.65   0.7  0.75   0.8  0.85   0.9
[2,]   0.5  0.55   0.6  0.65   0.7  0.75   0.8  0.85   0.9
[3,]   0.5  0.45   0.6  0.65   0.7  0.75   0.8  0.85   0.9
[4,]   0.5  0.45   0.6  0.65   0.7  0.75   0.8  0.85   0.9
[5,]   0.5  0.55   0.4  0.65   0.7  0.75   0.8  0.85   0.9
[6,]   0.5  0.55   0.4  0.65   0.7  0.75   0.8  0.85   0.9
> Events_Prob <- apply(Elements_Prob,1,prod)
> Majority_Events <- (rowSums(APC)>NT/2)
> sum(Events_Prob*Majority_Events)
[1] 0.9112646
```

Given a numeric vector with accuracies, named `accuracy`, with an odd number of classifiers, we first find the number of classifiers in it with the `length` function and store it in `NT`. All possible combinations of `APC` are then generated using the `expand.grid` function, where the `rep` function will repeat the vector `(TRUE, FALSE)` `NT` number of times. Each element of the column of the `APC` object will then generate a column where the `TRUE` and `FALSE` condition will be replaced by the corresponding classifier's accuracy as well as the appropriate complement by using the `Get_Prob` function. Since we consider an odd number of classifiers, the majority vote is attended in cases when the number of `TRUE` in that elementary event is greater than 50 percent of the number of classifiers (that is, greater than `NT/2`). The rest of the computations are easier to follow. If the accuracy of the nine classifiers is 0.5, 0.55, 0.6, 0.65, 0.7, 0.75, 0.8, 0.85, and 0.9, then the computations show that the accuracy of the ensemble would be 0.9113, higher than the most accurate classifier here, which is 0.9. However, we must remember that each of the eight classifiers is less accurate than 0.9. Despite this, the ensemble accuracy is higher than the highest classifier we have on hand. To verify that the computations are working fine, we apply this approach to the example given on page 74 of Zhou (2012), and confirm the final majority vote probability at 0.933:

```
> accuracy <- c(0.7,0.7,0.7,0.9,0.9)
> NT <- length(accuracy) # Number of classifiers
> APC <- expand.grid(rep(list(c(TRUE,FALSE)),NT)) # All possible
combinations
> Elements_Prob <- t(apply(APC,1,Get_Prob,Probability=accuracy))
> Events_Prob <- apply(Elements_Prob,1,prod)
> Majority_Events <- (rowSums(APC)>NT/2)
> sum(Events_Prob*Majority_Events)
[1] 0.93268
```

What happens to the case when each classifier is worse than a random guess? We will simply turn out the accuracies of the nine classifier scenarios and repeat the program to get the following answer:

```
> # Each p_i's lesser than 0.5
> accuracy <- 1-c(0.5,0.55,0.6,0.65,0.7,0.75,0.8,0.85,0.9)
> NT <- length(accuracy) # Number of classifiers
> APC <- expand.grid(rep(list(c(TRUE,FALSE)),NT)) # All possible
combinations
> head(APC)
    Var1   Var2   Var3 Var4 Var5 Var6 Var7 Var8 Var9
1   TRUE   TRUE   TRUE TRUE TRUE TRUE TRUE TRUE TRUE
2  FALSE   TRUE   TRUE TRUE TRUE TRUE TRUE TRUE TRUE
3   TRUE  FALSE   TRUE TRUE TRUE TRUE TRUE TRUE TRUE
4  FALSE  FALSE   TRUE TRUE TRUE TRUE TRUE TRUE TRUE
5   TRUE   TRUE  FALSE TRUE TRUE TRUE TRUE TRUE TRUE
6  FALSE   TRUE  FALSE TRUE TRUE TRUE TRUE TRUE TRUE
> Elements_Prob <- t(apply(APC,1,Get_Prob,Probability=accuracy))
> head(Elements_Prob)
      [,1] [,2] [,3] [,4] [,5] [,6] [,7] [,8] [,9]
[1,]  0.5 0.45  0.4 0.35  0.3 0.25  0.2 0.15  0.1
[2,]  0.5 0.45  0.4 0.35  0.3 0.25  0.2 0.15  0.1
[3,]  0.5 0.55  0.4 0.35  0.3 0.25  0.2 0.15  0.1
[4,]  0.5 0.55  0.4 0.35  0.3 0.25  0.2 0.15  0.1
[5,]  0.5 0.45  0.6 0.35  0.3 0.25  0.2 0.15  0.1
[6,]  0.5 0.45  0.6 0.35  0.3 0.25  0.2 0.15  0.1
> Events_Prob <- apply(Elements_Prob,1,prod)
> Majority_Events <- (rowSums(APC)>NT/2)
> sum(Events_Prob*Majority_Events)
[1] 0.08873544
```

When each of the classifiers is worse than a random guess, the majority vote classifier gives horrible results in the case of ensembling. This leaves us with the final case. What if we have a mixture of classifiers of which some are better than the random guess classifier and some are worse than the random guess classifier? We will put the computing code block in a function known as `Random_Accuracy`. The accuracies in the classifiers then become randomly generated numbers in the unit interval. The function `Random_Accuracy` is then run over ten times to generate the following output:

```
> # Mixture of p_i's, some > 0.5, and some < 0.5
> Random_Accuracy <- function() {
+   accuracy <- runif(9)
+   NT <- length(accuracy)
+   APC <- expand.grid(rep(list(c(TRUE,FALSE)),NT))
```

```
+    Elements_Prob <- t(apply(APC,1,Get_Prob,Probability=accuracy))
+    Events_Prob <- apply(Elements_Prob,1,prod)
+    Majority_Events <- (rowSums(APC)>NT/2)
+    return(sum(Events_Prob*Majority_Events))
+  }
> Random_Accuracy()
[1]  0.3423631
> Random_Accuracy()
[1]  0.3927145
> Random_Accuracy()
[1]  0.5341844
> Random_Accuracy()
[1]  0.1624876
> Random_Accuracy()
[1]  0.4065803
> Random_Accuracy()
[1]  0.4687087
> Random_Accuracy()
[1]  0.7819835
> Random_Accuracy()
[1]  0.3124515
> Random_Accuracy()
[1]  0.6842173
> Random_Accuracy()
[1]  0.2531727
```

A mixed bag of results. As a result, if we need to get reasonable accuracy and performance from the ensembling method, it is imperative to ensure that each classifier is better than the random guess. A central assumption in our analysis thus far has been that the classifiers are independent of each other. This assumption is seldom true in practical settings, as the classifiers are built using the same dataset. However, this topic will be dealt with in the following chapter.

We will now move on to the problem of ensembling by voting.

Ensembling by voting

Ensembling by voting can be used efficiently for classification problems. We now have a set of classifiers, and we need to use them to predict the class of an unknown case. The combining of the predictions of the classifiers can proceed in multiple ways. The two options that we will consider are majority voting, and weighted voting.

Majority voting

Ideas related to voting will be illustrated through an ensemble based on the homogeneous base learners of decision trees, as used in the development of bagging and random forests. First, we will create 500 base learners using the randomForest function and repeat the program in the first block, as seen in *Chapter 4, Random Forests*. Ensembling has already been performed in that chapter, and we will elaborate on those steps here. First, the code block for setting up the random forest is given here:

```
> load("../Data/GC2.RData")
> set.seed(12345)
> Train_Test <- sample(c("Train","Test"),nrow(GC2),
+ replace = TRUE,prob = c(0.7,0.3))
> GC2_Train <- GC2[Train_Test=="Train",]
> GC2_TestX <- within(GC2[Train_Test=="Test",],rm(good_bad))
> GC2_TestY <- GC2[Train_Test=="Test","good_bad"]
> GC2_Formula <- as.formula("good_bad~.")
> # RANDOM FOREST ANALYSIS
> GC2_RF <- randomForest(GC2_Formula,data=GC2_Train,keep.inbag=TRUE,
+                        ntree=500)
```

Next, we will use the standard predict function to predict the class for the GC2_TestX data, and then, using the option of predict.all=TRUE, obtain the prediction for each tree generated in the random forest:

```
> # New data voting
> GC2_RF_Test_Margin <- predict(GC2_RF,newdata = GC2_TestX,
+                        type="class")
> GC2_RF_Test_Predict <- predict(GC2_RF,newdata=GC2_TestX,
+                        type="class",predict.all=TRUE
+                        )
```

The predicted GC2_RF_Test_Predict object will consist of further individual objects, which will have the predictions for each decision tree. We will first define a function called Row_Count_Max, which will return the prediction whose count is a maximum in the forest. The rudimentary voting method is then compared with the predict function's outcomes in the following code block:

```
> Row_Count_Max <- function(x) names(which.max(table(x)))
> # Majority Voting
> Voting_Predict <- apply(GC2_RF_Test_Predict$individual,1,
+ Row_Count_Max)
> head(Voting_Predict);tail(Voting_Predict)
      1      2      3      4      9     10
 "good"  "bad" "good"  "bad" "good"  "bad"
```

```
    974     980     983     984     988     996
  "bad"   "bad"  "good"  "good"  "good"  "good"
> all(Voting_Predict==GC2_RF_Test_Predict$aggregate)
[1] TRUE
> all(Voting_Predict==GC2_RF_Test_Margin)
[1] TRUE
> sum(Voting_Predict==GC2_TestY)/313
[1] 0.7795527
```

Consequently, we can see that the `predict` function implements the majority count technique. Next, we will quickly illustrate the ideas and thinking behind weighted voting.

Weighted voting

An implicit assumption in the use of simple voting is that all classifiers are equally accurate, or that all classifiers have equal voting power. Consider the simpler case in which we have five classifiers, three of them with an accuracy of 0.51 and the remaining two with an accuracy of 0.99. If the less accurate classifier votes an observation as a negative case (-1) and the two more accurate classifiers as a positive case (+1), then the simple voting method will call the observation (-1). With this voting pattern, the probability of the observation being -1 is $0.51^3 \times 0.01^2 = 0.00001$, while that of it being +1 is $0.49^3 \times 0.99^2 = 0.1153$. Thus, we can't pretend that all classifiers should have the same voting power. This is where we will make good use of the weighted voting method.

In this analysis, we will take the accuracy of the classifiers over the training dataset as the weights. We will treat $w_i, i = 1, \ldots, T$ as the weight associated with the classifier $h_i, i = 1, \ldots, T$. An important characteristic of the weights is that they should be non-negative and should add up to 1, that is, $w_i \geq 0, \sum_{i=1}^{T} w_i = 1$. We will normalize the accuracy of the classifiers to satisfy this constraint.

We will continue the analysis with the German Credit dataset. First, we will obtain the predictions for the 500 trees over the training dataset, and then obtain the accuracies:

```
> # Analyzing Accuracy of Trees of the Fitted Forest
> GC2_RF_Train_Predict <- predict(GC2_RF,newdata=GC2_Train[,-20],
+                                 type="class",predict.all=TRUE)
> head(GC2_RF_Train_Predict$individual[,c(1:5,496:500)])
    [,1]    [,2]    [,3]    [,4]    [,5]    [,6]    [,7]    [,8]    [,9]
[,10]
5  "bad"   "bad"   "bad"   "bad"  "good"   "bad"   "bad"   "bad"   "bad"
"bad"
```

```
6   "good" "good" "good" "good" "good" "good" "bad"  "bad"  "bad"
"good"
7   "good" "good" "good" "good" "good" "good" "good" "good" "good"
"good"
8   "good" "good" "good" "good" "good" "bad"  "good" "bad"  "good"
"good"
11  "bad"  "bad"  "bad"  "bad"  "bad"  "bad"  "bad"  "bad"  "bad"
"bad"
12  "good" "bad"  "bad"  "bad"  "bad"  "good" "bad"  "bad"  "bad"
"bad"
> RF_Tree_Train_Accuracy <- NULL
> for(i in 1:GC2_RF$ntree){
+    RF_Tree_Train_Accuracy[i] <- sum(GC2_RF_Train_
Predict$individual[,i]==
+                                  GC2_Train$good_bad)/nrow(GC2_
Train)
+ }
> headtail(sort(RF_Tree_Train_Accuracy),10)
 [1] 0.8340611 0.8369723 0.8384279 0.8398836 0.8398836 0.8413392
0.8413392
 [8] 0.8413392 0.8413392 0.8427948 0.8908297 0.8908297 0.8908297
0.8908297
[15] 0.8922853 0.8922853 0.8937409 0.8937409 0.8966521 0.8981077
```

What is the `headtail` function? It is available in the `Utilities.R` file. The analysis is repeated with the bagging ensemble as follows:

```
> # Bagging ANALYSIS
> GC2_Bagg <- randomForest(GC2_Formula,data=GC2_Train,keep.inbag=TRUE,
+                          mtry=ncol(GC2_TestX),ntree=500)
> GC2_Bagg_Test_Predict <- predict(GC2_Bagg,newdata=GC2_TestX,
+                               type="class",predict.all=TRUE)
> GC2_Bagg_Train_Predict <- predict(GC2_Bagg,newdata=GC2_Train[,-20],
+                               type="class",predict.all=TRUE)
> Bagg_Tree_Train_Accuracy <- NULL
> for(i in 1:GC2_Bagg$ntree){
+    Bagg_Tree_Train_Accuracy[i] <- sum(GC2_Bagg_Train_
Predict$individual[,i]==
+                                  GC2_Train$good_bad)/nrow(GC2_
Train)
+ }
> headtail(sort(Bagg_Tree_Train_Accuracy),10)
 [1] 0.8369723 0.8384279 0.8413392 0.8457060 0.8457060 0.8471616
0.8471616
 [8] 0.8471616 0.8471616 0.8486172 0.8966521 0.8966521 0.8966521
0.8966521
[15] 0.8966521 0.8981077 0.8995633 0.8995633 0.9024745 0.9097525
```

Next, we normalize the weights and calculate the weighted votes for the observations in the test samples, as shown in the following code:

```
> # Weighted Voting with Random Forest
> RF_Weights <- RF_Tree_Train_Accuracy/sum(RF_Tree_Train_Accuracy)
> Bagg_Weights <- Bagg_Tree_Train_Accuracy/sum(Bagg_Tree_Train_
Accuracy)
> RF_Weighted_Vote <- data.frame(matrix(0,nrow(GC2_TestX),ncol=3))
> names(RF_Weighted_Vote) <- c("Good_Weight","Bad_
Weight","Prediction")
> for(i in 1:nrow(RF_Weighted_Vote)){
+    RF_Weighted_Vote$Good_Weight[i] <-
+      sum((GC2_RF_Test_Predict$individual[i,]=="good")*RF_Weights)
+    RF_Weighted_Vote$Bad_Weight[i] <-
+      sum((GC2_RF_Test_Predict$individual[i,]=="bad")*RF_Weights)
+    RF_Weighted_Vote$Prediction[i] <- c("good","bad")[which.max(RF_
Weighted_Vote[i,1:2])]
+ }
> head(RF_Weighted_Vote,10)
   Good_Weight Bad_Weight Prediction
1    0.8301541 0.16984588       good
2    0.3260033 0.67399668        bad
3    0.8397035 0.16029651       good
4    0.4422527 0.55774733        bad
5    0.9420565 0.05794355       good
6    0.2378956 0.76210442        bad
7    0.4759756 0.52402435        bad
8    0.7443038 0.25569624       good
9    0.8120180 0.18798195       good
10   0.7799587 0.22004126       good
```

The weighted voting analysis is repeated for the `bagging` objects, as shown here:

```
> # Weighted Voting with Bagging
> Bagg_Weights <- Bagg_Tree_Train_Accuracy/sum(Bagg_Tree_Train_
Accuracy)
> Bagg_Weights <- Bagg_Tree_Train_Accuracy/sum(Bagg_Tree_Train_
Accuracy)
> Bagg_Weighted_Vote <- data.frame(matrix(0,nrow(GC2_TestX),ncol=3))
> names(Bagg_Weighted_Vote) <- c("Good_Weight","Bad_
Weight","Prediction")
> for(i in 1:nrow(Bagg_Weighted_Vote)){
+    Bagg_Weighted_Vote$Good_Weight[i] <-
+      sum((GC2_Bagg_Test_Predict$individual[i,]=="good")*Bagg_Weights)
+    Bagg_Weighted_Vote$Bad_Weight[i] <-
```

```
+      sum((GC2_Bagg_Test_Predict$individual[i,]=="bad")*Bagg_Weights)
+   Bagg_Weighted_Vote$Prediction[i] <- c("good","bad")[which.
max(Bagg_Weighted_Vote[i,1:2])]
+ }
> head(Bagg_Weighted_Vote,10)
   Good_Weight Bad_Weight Prediction
1    0.9279982 0.07200181       good
2    0.1634505 0.83654949        bad
3    0.8219618 0.17803818       good
4    0.4724477 0.52755226        bad
5    0.9619528 0.03804725       good
6    0.1698628 0.83013718        bad
7    0.4540574 0.54594265        bad
8    0.7883772 0.21162281       good
9    0.8301772 0.16982283       good
10   0.7585720 0.24142804       good
```

Now, with the voting mechanisms behind us, we turn our attention to regression problems.

Ensembling by averaging

Within the context of regression models, the predictions are the numeric values of the variables of interest. Combining the predictions of the output due to the various ensemblers is rather straightforward; because of the ensembling mechanism, we simply interpret the average of the predicted values across the ensemblers as the predicted value. Within the context of the classification problem, we can carry out simple averaging and weighted averaging. In the previous section, the ensemble had homogeneous base learners. However, in this section, we will deal with heterogeneous base learners.

We will now consider a regression problem that is dealt with in detail in *Chapter 8, Ensemble Diagnostics*. The problem is the prediction of housing prices based on over 60 explanatory variables. We have the dataset in training and testing partitions, and load them to kick off the proceedings:

```
> # Averaging for Regression Problems
> load("../Data/ht_imp_author.Rdata") # returns ht_imp object
> load("../Data/htest_imp_author.Rdata") # returns htest_imp
> names(ht_imp)[69] <- "SalePrice"
> dim(ht_imp)
[1] 1460    69
> dim(htest_imp)
[1] 1459    68
```

Consequently, we have many observations to build our models. The SalePrice is the variable of interest here. First, we create a formula and build a linear model; four regression trees with different depths; four neural networks with a different number of hidden neurons; and a support vector machine model in the following code block:

```
> hf <- as.formula("SalePrice~.")
> SP_lm <- lm(hf,data=ht_imp)
> SP_rpart2 <- rpart(hf,data=ht_imp,maxdepth=2)
> SP_rpart4 <- rpart(hf,data=ht_imp,maxdepth=4)
> SP_rpart6 <- rpart(hf,data=ht_imp,maxdepth=6)
> SP_rpart8 <- rpart(hf,data=ht_imp,maxdepth=8)
> SP_nn2 <- nnet(hf,data=ht_imp,size=2,linout=TRUE)
# weights:  267
initial  value 56996872361441.906250
final  value 9207911334609.976562
converged
> SP_nn3 <- nnet(hf,data=ht_imp,size=3,linout=TRUE)
# weights:  400
initial  value 56997125121706.257812
final  value 9207911334609.960938
converged
> SP_nn4 <- nnet(hf,data=ht_imp,size=4,linout=TRUE)
# weights:  533
initial  value 56996951452602.304687
iter  10 value 19328028546738.226562
iter  20 value 19324281941793.617187
final  value 9080312934601.205078
converged
> SP_nn5 <- nnet(hf,data=ht_imp,size=5,linout=TRUE)
# weights:  666
initial  value 56997435951836.507812
final  value 9196060713131.609375
converged
> SP_svm <- svm(hf,data=ht_imp)
```

We have the required setup here to consider the heterogeneous ensemble.

Simple averaging

We built ten models using the training dataset, and we will now make the predictions for these models on the training dataset using the `predict` function, as shown in the following:

```
> # Simple Averaging
> SP_lm_pred <- predict(SP_lm,newdata=htest_imp)
Warning message:
In predict.lm(SP_lm, newdata = htest_imp) :
  prediction from a rank-deficient fit may be misleading
> SP_rpart2_pred <- predict(SP_rpart2,newdata=htest_imp)
> SP_rpart4_pred <- predict(SP_rpart4,newdata=htest_imp)
> SP_rpart6_pred <- predict(SP_rpart6,newdata=htest_imp)
> SP_rpart8_pred <- predict(SP_rpart8,newdata=htest_imp)
> SP_nn2_pred <- predict(SP_nn2,newdata=htest_imp)
> SP_nn3_pred <- predict(SP_nn3,newdata=htest_imp)
> SP_nn4_pred <- predict(SP_nn4,newdata=htest_imp)
> SP_nn5_pred <- predict(SP_nn5,newdata=htest_imp)
> SP_svm_pred <- predict(SP_svm,newdata=htest_imp)
```

When it comes to classification problems, the predictions are either based on the class labels or the probability of the class of interest. Consequently, we don't come across *bad predictions* in terms of the magnitude of predictions, though we need to at least check if the predictions give a mixture of +1s or -1s. If the classifiers predict only +1 or -1, such classifiers can then be discarded from further analysis. For the regression problems, we need to see if the models can make reasonable predictions in terms of the magnitude, and we will simply obtain a plot of the magnitude of the predictions, as follows:

```
> windows(height=300,width=400)
> par(mfrow=c(2,5))
> plot.ts(SP_lm_pred,col=1)
> plot.ts(SP_rpart2_pred,col=2)
> plot.ts(SP_rpart4_pred,col=3)
> plot.ts(SP_rpart6_pred,col=4)
> plot.ts(SP_rpart8_pred,col=5)
> plot.ts(SP_nn2_pred,col=6)
> plot.ts(SP_nn3_pred,col=7)
> plot.ts(SP_nn4_pred,col=8)
> plot.ts(SP_nn5_pred,col=9)
> plot.ts(SP_svm_pred,col=10)
```

The result of the preceding code block is shown in the following figure:

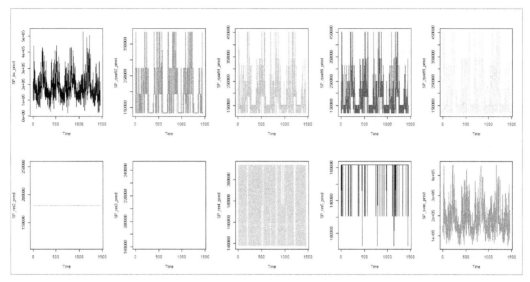

Figure 3: A simple plot of the predictions for the ten heterogeneous base learners

We can see that the predictions related to the neural network models with two or three hidden neurons produce no variation in the predictions. Consequently, we delete these two models from further analysis. The ensemble prediction is simply the average of the predictions across the remaining eight models:

```
> Avg_Ensemble_Prediction <- rowMeans(cbind(SP_lm_pred,SP_rpart2_pred,
+    SP_rpart4_pred,SP_rpart6_pred,
+             SP_rpart8_pred,SP_nn4_pred,SP_nn5_pred,SP_svm_pred))
> plot.ts(Avg_Ensemble_Prediction)
```

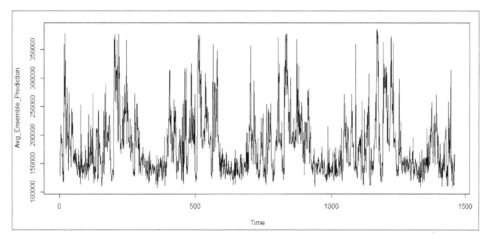

Figure 4: Ensemble predictions for the housing dataset

As with the extension of simple voting to weighted voting, we will now look at weighted averaging.

Weight averaging

In the case of classifiers, the weights were chosen from the accuracies of the classifiers for the training dataset. In this instance, we need unifying measures like this. A regressor model is preferred if it has less residual variance, and we will select the variance as a measure of accuracy. Suppose that the estimated residual variance for a weak base model i is $\hat{\sigma}_i^2, i = 1, 2, \ldots, T$. In the context of ensemble neural networks, Perrone and Cooper (1993) claim that the optimal weight for the ith weak base model can be obtained using the following equation:

$$w_i = \frac{\hat{\sigma}_i^2}{\sum_{i=1}^{T} \hat{\sigma}_i^2}, i = 1, 2, \ldots, T$$

Since the proportional constants do not matter, we will simply substitute $\hat{\sigma}_i^2$ with the mean of residual squares. In this direction, we will first obtain the $\hat{\sigma}_i^2$ up to a constant, by simply calculating `mean(residuals(model)^2)` for the eight models considered in the context of simple averaging, as shown:

```
> # Weighted Averaging
> SP_lm_sigma <- mean(residuals(SP_lm)^2)
> SP_rp2_sigma <- mean(residuals(SP_rpart2)^2)
> SP_rp4_sigma <- mean(residuals(SP_rpart4)^2)
> SP_rp6_sigma <- mean(residuals(SP_rpart6)^2)
> SP_rp8_sigma <- mean(residuals(SP_rpart8)^2)
> SP_nn4_sigma <- mean(residuals(SP_nn4)^2)
> SP_nn5_sigma <- mean(residuals(SP_nn5)^2)
> SP_svm_sigma <- mean(residuals(SP_svm)^2)
```

Next, we simply implement the formula of weights $w_i = \hat{\sigma}_i^2 \Big/ \sum_{i=1}^{T} \hat{\sigma}_i^2$ as follows:

```
> sigma_sum <- SP_lm_sigma + SP_rp2_sigma + SP_rp4_sigma +
+    SP_rp6_sigma + SP_rp8_sigma + SP_nn4_sigma +
+    SP_nn5_sigma + SP_svm_sigma
> sigma_sum
[1] 20727111061
> SP_lm_wts <- SP_lm_sigma/sigma_sum
> SP_rp2_wts <- SP_rp2_sigma/sigma_sum
> SP_rp4_wts <- SP_rp4_sigma/sigma_sum
> SP_rp6_wts <- SP_rp6_sigma/sigma_sum
> SP_rp8_wts <- SP_rp8_sigma/sigma_sum
> SP_nn4_wts <- SP_nn4_sigma/sigma_sum
> SP_nn5_wts <- SP_nn5_sigma/sigma_sum
> SP_svm_wts <- SP_svm_sigma/sigma_sum
```

The `rowMeans` and `cbind` functions simply give away the weighted averaging predictions:

```
> Weighted_Ensemble_Prediction <- rowMeans(cbind(SP_lm_wts*SP_lm_pred,
+                                       SP_rp2_wts*SP_rpart2_pred,
+                                       SP_rp4_wts*SP_rpart4_pred,
+                                       SP_rp6_wts*SP_rpart6_pred,
+                                       SP_rp8_wts*SP_rpart8_pred,
+                                       SP_nn4_wts*SP_nn4_pred,
+                                       SP_nn5_wts*SP_nn5_pred,
+                                       SP_svm_wts*SP_svm_pred))
> plot.ts(Weighted_Ensemble_Prediction)
```

The output for the preceding code is as follows:

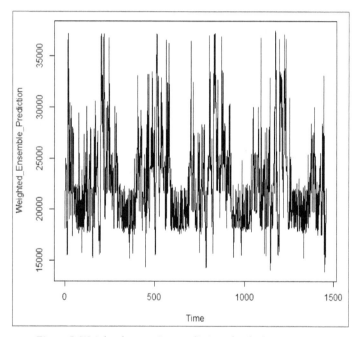

Figure 5: Weighted averaging predictions for the housing price

Stack ensembling

An introductory and motivational example of the stacked regression was provided in *Chapter 1, Introduction to Ensemble Techniques*. Here, we will continue the discussion of stacked ensembles for a regression problem which has not been previously developed.

With stacked ensembling, the outputs of several weak models are given as an input variable, along with the covariates used to build the earlier models, to build a stack model. The form of the stack model might be one of these, or it can be a different model. Here, we will simply use the eight regression models (used in previous sections) as weak models. The stacking regression model is selected as the gradient boosting model, and it will be given the original input variables and predictions of the new models, as follows:

```
> SP_lm_train <- predict(SP_lm,newdata=ht_imp)
Warning message:
In predict.lm(SP_lm, newdata = ht_imp) :
  prediction from a rank-deficient fit may be misleading
> SP_rpart2_train <- predict(SP_rpart2,newdata=ht_imp)
> SP_rpart4_train <- predict(SP_rpart4,newdata=ht_imp)
> SP_rpart6_train <- predict(SP_rpart6,newdata=ht_imp)
> SP_rpart8_train <- predict(SP_rpart8,newdata=ht_imp)
> SP_nn4_train <- predict(SP_nn4,newdata=ht_imp)
> SP_nn5_train <- predict(SP_nn5,newdata=ht_imp)
> SP_svm_train <- predict(SP_svm,newdata=ht_imp)
>
> ht_imp2 <- cbind(ht_imp[,-69],SP_lm_train,SP_rpart2_train,SP_rpart4_
train,
+                             SP_rpart6_train,SP_rpart8_train,SP_nn4_
train,SP_nn5_train,
+                             SP_svm_train,ht_imp[,69])
> names(ht_imp2)[77] <- "SalePrice"
> SP_gbm <- gbm(hf,data=ht_imp2,distribution = "gaussian",n.trees=200)
> headtail(predict(SP_gbm,n.trees=100),20)
 [1]  180260.6 177793.3 181836.9 177793.3 191927.7 177793.3 191927.7
182237.3
 [9]  177793.3 177793.3 177793.3 191927.7 177793.3 187520.7 177793.3
177793.3
[17]  177793.3 177793.3 177793.3 177793.3 177908.2 177793.3 191927.7
177793.3
[25]  177793.3 177793.3 177793.3 191927.7 177793.3 177793.3 177793.3
191927.7
[33]  177793.3 177793.3 177793.3 177793.3 179501.7 191927.7 177793.3
177793.3
```

This concludes our simple discussion of stacked ensemble regressions.

Summary

In this chapter, we looked at why ensemble works in the context of classification problems. A series of detailed programs illustrated the point that each classifier must be better than a random guess. We considered scenarios where all the classifiers have the same accuracy, different accuracy, and finally a scenario with completely arbitrary accuracies. Majority and weighted voting was illustrated within the context of the random forest and bagging methods. For the regression problem, we used a different choice of base learners and allowed them to be heterogeneous. Simple and weighted averaging methods were illustrated in relation to the housing sales price data. A simple illustration of stacked regression ultimately concluded the technical section of this chapter.

In the following chapter, we will look at ensembling diagnostics.

8
Ensemble Diagnostics

In earlier chapters, ensemble methods were found to be effective. In the previous chapter, we looked at scenarios in which ensemble methods increase the overall accuracy of a prediction. It has previously been assumed that different base learners are independent of each other. However, unless we have a very large sample and the base models are learners that use a distinct set of observations, such an assumption is very impractical. Even if we had a large enough sample to believe that the partitions are nonoverlapping, each base model is built on a different partition, and each partition carries with it the same information as any other partition. However, it is difficult to test validations such as this, so we need to employ various techniques in order to validate the independence of the base models on the same dataset. To do this, we will look at various different methods. A brief discussion of the need for ensemble diagnostics will kick off this chapter, and the importance of diversity in base models will be covered in the next section. For the classification problem, the classifiers can be compared with each other. We can then further evaluate the similarity and accuracy of the ensemble. Statistical tests that achieve this task will be introduced in the third section. Initially, a base learner will be compared with another one, and then we will look at all the models of the ensemble in a single step.

The topics that will be covered in this chapter are as follows:

- Ensemble diagnostics
- Ensemble diversity
- Pairwise comparison
- Interrater agreement

Technical requirements

We will be using the following libraries in the chapter:

- `rpart`

What is ensemble diagnostics?

The power of ensemble methods was demonstrated in the preceding chapters. An ensemble with decision trees forms a homogeneous ensemble, and this was the main topic of *Chapter 3, Bagging*, to *Chapter 6, Boosting Refinements*. In *Chapter 1, Introduction to Ensemble Techniques*, and *Chapter 7, The General Ensemble Technique*, we had a peek at stacked ensembles. A central assumption in an ensemble is that the models are independent of one another. However, this assumption is seldom true, and we know that the same data partition is used over and over again. This does not mean that ensembling is bad; we have every reason to use the ensembles while previewing the concerns in an ensemble application. Consequently, we need to see how close the base models are to each other and overall in their predictions. If the predictions are close to each other, then we might need those base models in the ensemble. Here, we will build logistic regression, Naïve Bayes, SVM, and a decision tree for the German credit dataset as the base models. The analysis and program is slightly repetitive here as it is carried over from earlier chapters:

```
> load("../Data/GC2.RData")
> table(GC2$good_bad)
 bad good
 300  700
> set.seed(12345)
> Train_Test <- sample(c("Train","Test"),nrow(GC2),replace =
+ TRUE,prob = c(0.7,0.3))
> head(Train_Test)
[1] "Test"  "Test"  "Test"  "Test"  "Train" "Train"
> GC2_Train <- GC2[Train_Test=="Train",]
> GC2_TestX <- within(GC2[Train_Test=="Test",],rm(good_bad))
> GC2_TestY <- GC2[Train_Test=="Test","good_bad"]
> GC2_TestY_numeric <- as.numeric(GC2_TestY)
> GC2_Formula <- as.formula("good_bad~.")
> p <- ncol(GC2_TestX)
> ntr <- nrow(GC2_Train)
> nte <- nrow(GC2_TestX)
> # Logistic Regression
> LR_fit <- glm(GC2_Formula,data=GC2_Train,family = binomial())
> LR_Predict_Train <- predict(LR_fit,newdata=GC2_Train,
+ type="response")
> LR_Predict_Train <- as.factor(ifelse(LR_Predict_Train>0.5,
+ "good","bad"))
> LR_Accuracy_Train <- sum(LR_Predict_Train==GC2_Train$good_bad)/
+ ntr
> LR_Accuracy_Train
[1] 0.78
> LR_Predict_Test <- predict(LR_fit,newdata=GC2_TestX,
+ type="response")
```

```
> LR_Predict_Test_Bin <- ifelse(LR_Predict_Test>0.5,2,1)
> LR_Accuracy_Test <- sum(LR_Predict_Test_Bin==
+ GC2_TestY_numeric)/nte
> LR_Accuracy_Test
[1] 0.757
> # Naive Bayes
> NB_fit <- naiveBayes(GC2_Formula,data=GC2_Train)
> NB_Predict_Train <- predict(NB_fit,newdata=GC2_Train)
> NB_Accuracy_Train <- sum(NB_Predict_Train==
+ GC2_Train$good_bad)/ntr
> NB_Accuracy_Train
[1] 0.767
> NB_Predict_Test <- predict(NB_fit,newdata=GC2_TestX)
> NB_Accuracy_Test <- sum(NB_Predict_Test==GC2_TestY)/nte
> NB_Accuracy_Test
[1] 0.808
> # Decision Tree
> CT_fit <- rpart(GC2_Formula,data=GC2_Train)
> CT_Predict_Train <- predict(CT_fit,newdata=GC2_Train,
+ type="class")
> CT_Accuracy_Train <- sum(CT_Predict_Train==
+ GC2_Train$good_bad)/ntr
> CT_Accuracy_Train
[1] 0.83
> CT_Predict_Test <- predict(CT_fit,newdata=GC2_TestX,
+ type="class")
> CT_Accuracy_Test <- sum(CT_Predict_Test==GC2_TestY)/nte
> CT_Accuracy_Test
[1] 0.706
> # Support Vector Machine
> SVM_fit <- svm(GC2_Formula,data=GC2_Train)
> SVM_Predict_Train <- predict(SVM_fit,newdata=GC2_Train,
+ type="class")
> SVM_Accuracy_Train <- sum(SVM_Predict_Train==
+ GC2_Train$good_bad)/ntr
> SVM_Accuracy_Train
[1] 0.77
> SVM_Predict_Test <- predict(SVM_fit,newdata=GC2_TestX,
+ type="class")
> SVM_Accuracy_Test <- sum(SVM_Predict_Test==GC2_TestY)/nte
> SVM_Accuracy_Test
[1] 0.754
```

In the next section, we will emphasize the need for diversity in ensembling.

Ensemble diversity

In an ensemble, we have many base models — say L number of them. For the classification problem, we have base models as classifiers. If we have a regression problem, we have the base models as learners. Since the diagnostics are performed on the training dataset only, we will drop the convention of train and valid partitions. For simplicity, during the rest of the discussion, we will assume that we have N observations. The L number of models implies that we have L predictions for each of the N observations, and thus the number of predictions is $L \times N$. It is in these predictions that we try to find the diversity of the ensemble. The diversity of the ensemble is identified depending on the type of problem we are dealing with. First, we will take the regression problem.

Numeric prediction

In the case of regression problems, the predicted values of the observations can be compared directly with their actual values. We can easily see which base models' predictions are closer to the actual value of the observation and which are far away from it. If all the predictions are closer to each other, the base models are not diverse. In this case, one of the predictions might suffice all the same. If the predictions exhibit some variance, combining them by using the average might provide stability. In the assessment of the diversity, it is also important to know how close the ensemble prediction is to the true observation value.

Let's consider a hypothetical scenario in which we have six observations, their actual values, three base learners, predictions by the learners, and the ensemble prediction. A sample dataset that will help you to understand the intricacies of ensemble diversity is given in the following table:

Observation Number	Actual	E1	E2	E3	EP
1	30	15	20	25	20
2	30	40	50	60	50
3	30	25	30	35	30
4	30	28	30	32	30
5	30	20	30	40	30
6	30	10	15	65	30

Table 1: Six observations, three base learners, and the ensemble

For ease of comparison, all the observations' true values are kept at 30 in *Table 1*. The ensemble predictions for the six observations/cases range from 10–65, while the ensemble prediction — the average of the base learner's prediction — ranges from 20–50. As a first step to understanding the diversity of the ensemble for specific observations and the associated predictions, we will visualize the data using the following program block:

```
> DN <- read.csv("../Data/Diverse_Numeric.csv")
> windows(height=100,width=100)
> plot(NULL,xlim=c(5,70),ylim=c(0,7),yaxt='n',xlab="X-values",ylab="")
> points(DN[1,2:6],rep(1,5),pch=c(19,1,1,1,0),cex=2)
> points(DN[2,2:6],rep(2,5),pch=c(19,1,1,1,0),cex=2)
> points(DN[3,2:6],rep(3,5),pch=c(19,1,1,1,0),cex=2)
> points(DN[4,2:6],rep(4,5),pch=c(19,1,1,1,0),cex=2)
> points(DN[5,2:6],rep(5,5),pch=c(19,1,1,1,0),cex=2)
> points(DN[6,2:6],rep(6,5),pch=c(19,1,1,1,0),cex=2)
> legend(x=45,y=7,c("Actual","Model","Ensemble"),pch=c(19,1,0))
> axis(2,at=1:6,labels=paste("Case",1:6),las=1)
```

The program's explanation is here. The first line of code imports the `Diverse_Numeric.csv` data from the code bundle folder. The `windows (X11)` function sets up a new graphical device in the Windows (Ubuntu) operating system. The `plot` function then sets up an empty plot and the axes' ranges specification is given by `xlim` and `ylim`. Each row of data from *Table 1* is embossed using the plot and the `points` function. Choosing `pch` needs further clarification. If we were to choose `pch` at, for example, `19`, `1`, and `0`, then this means that we are selecting a filled circle, a circle, and a square. The three shapes will denote the actual value, the model predictions, and the ensemble prediction respectively. The axis command helps us to get the labels in the right display. The result of the preceding R code block is the following plot:

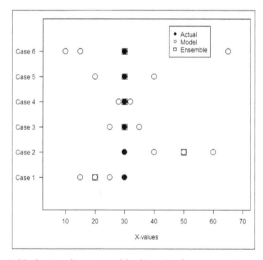

Figure 1: Understanding ensemble diversity for a regression problem

We have six observations, each labeled as a **Case**. Consider **Case 1** first. The filled circle for each observation is the actual value — **30**, in this case — and this is the same across the dataset. For this observation, the ensemble prediction is **20**. The empty square and the value predicted by the three base models of **15, 20**, and **25** are depicted in the blank circles. The ensemble forecast — the average of the base learner's prediction — is **20** and is denoted by a blank square. Now, the three values are less spread out, which is interpreted as indicating that the ensemble is less diverse for this observation. Consequently, this is an example of low diversity. The estimate of **20** is also far from the actual, and we can see that this is a poor estimate. Consequently, this is a *low diversity–poor estimate* case.

In the second case of *Table 1*, the three predictions are well spread out and have high diversity. However, the ensemble estimate of **50** is too far from the actual value of **30**, and we refer to this as a case of *high diversity–poor estimate*. **Case 3** and **Case 4** are thus seen as *low diversity–good estimate* since the ensemble prediction matches the actual value and the three ensemble predictions are close to each other. **Case 5** makes a fine balance between diversity and accuracy, and so we can label this as an example of *high diversity–good estimate*. The final case has good accuracy, though the diversity is too high to make the ensemble prediction any good. You can refer to Kuncheva (2014) for further details on the dilemma of diversity–accuracy of ensemble learners.

We will consider the diversity–accuracy problem for the classification problem next.

Class prediction

The previous section looked at the problem of diversity–accuracy for the regression problem. In the case of the classification problem, we can clearly mark whether or not the prediction of the classifier matches the actual output/label. Furthermore, we only have two potential predictions: 0 or 1. Consequently, we can compare how close two classifiers are with respect to each other over all observations. For instance, with two possible outcomes for classifier M_1 and two possible outcomes for M_2, we have four possible scenarios for a given observation $\mathbf{x}$:

- M_1 predicts the label as 1; M_2 predicts it as 1
- M_1 predicts the label as 1; M_2 predicts it as 0
- M_1 predicts the label as 0; M_2 predicts it as 1
- M_1 predicts the label as 0; M_2 predicts it as 0

In scenarios 1 and 4, the two classifiers *agree* with each other, and in 2 and 3, they *disagree*. If we have N observations, each observation that is predicted with the two models will fall into one of the four preceding scenarios. Before we consider the formal measures of agreement or disagreement of two or more models, we will consider two simpler cases in the forthcoming discussion.

There is a popular saying that if two people agree with each other all the time, one of them is not needed. This is similar to the way in which classifiers work. Similarly, say that a pair of geese are known to be very loyal; they stick with each other, facing problems together. Now, if we have two models that behave in the same way as these geese in all observations, then the diversity is lost for good. Consequently, in any given ensemble scenario, we need to eliminate the pair of geese and keep only one of them. Suppose then that we have a matrix of L predictions where the column corresponds to the classifier and the row to the N observations. In this case, we will define a function named GP, and an abbreviation for the geese pair, which will tell us which classifiers have a geese pair classifier agreeing with them across all observations:

```
> # Drop the Geese Pair
>GP<- function(Pred_Matrix) {
+    L<- ncol(Pred_Matrix) # Number of classifiers
+    N<- nrow(Pred_Matrix)
+    GP_Matrix <- matrix(TRUE,nrow=L,ncol=L)
+    for(i in 1:(L-1)){
+      for(j in (i+1):L){
+         GP_Matrix[i,j] <- ifelse(sum(Pred_Matrix[,i]==Pred_
Matrix[,j])==N,
+                                     TRUE,FALSE)
+         GP_Matrix[j,i] <- GP_Matrix[i,j]
+      }
+    }
+    return(GP_Matrix)
+ }
```

How does the geese pair GP function work? We give a matrix of predictions as the input to this function, with the columns for the classifiers and the rows for the observations. This function first creates a logical matrix of order $L \times L$ with default logical values as TRUE. Since a classifier will obviously agree with itself, we accept the default value. Furthermore, since a M_1 classifier agrees/disagrees with M_2 in the same way that M_1 agrees/disagrees with M_1, we make use of this fact to compute the lower matrix through a symmetrical relationship. In the two nested loops, we compare the predictions of a classifier with every other classifier. The ifelse function checks whether all the predictions of a classifier match with another classifier, and if the condition does not hold even for a single observation, we say that the two classifiers under consideration are not the geese pair, or that they disagree on at least one occasion:

Next, the GP function is applied to 500 classifiers that are set up for a classification problem. The CART_Dummy dataset is taken from the RSADBE package. The CART_DUMMY dataset and related problem description can be found in Chapter 9 of Tattar (2017). We adapt the code and the resulting output from the same source:

```
> data(CART_Dummy)
> CART_Dummy$Y <- as.factor(CART_Dummy$Y)
> attach(CART_Dummy)
> windows(height=100,width=200)
> par(mfrow=c(1,2))
> plot(c(0,12),c(0,10),type="n",xlab="X1",ylab="X2")
> points(X1[Y==0],X2[Y==0],pch=15,col="red")
> points(X1[Y==1],X2[Y==1],pch=19,col="green")
> title(main="A Difficult Classification Problem")
> plot(c(0,12),c(0,10),type="n",xlab="X1",ylab="X2")
> points(X1[Y==0],X2[Y==0],pch=15,col="red")
> points(X1[Y==1],X2[Y==1],pch=19,col="green")
> segments(x0=c(0,0,6,6),y0=c(3.75,6.25,2.25,5),
+           x1=c(6,6,12,12),y1=c(3.75,6.25,2.25,5),lwd=2)
> abline(v=6,lwd=2)
> title(main="Looks a Solvable Problem Under Partitions")
```

As can be seen from the program, we have three variables here: X1, X2, and Y. The variable denoted by Y is a binary variable—one class is denoted by green and another by red. Using the information provided by the X1 and X2 variables, the goal is to predict the class of Y. The red and green color points are intermingled, and so a single linear classifier won't suffice here to separate the reds from the greens. However, if we recursively partition the data space by X1 and X2, as shown on the right side of the resulting plots, as shown in *Figure 2*, the reds and greens look separable. The previous R code block results in the following diagram:

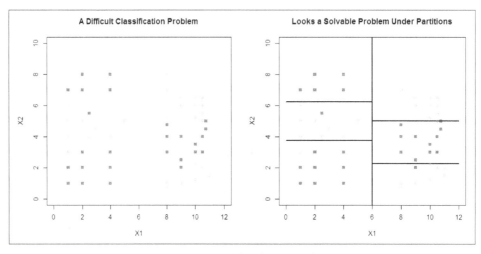

Figure 2: A typical classification problem

A random forest with 500 trees is set up for the CART_DUMMY dataset. The fixed seed ensures that the output here is reproducible on any execution. Using the fitted random forest, we next predict the output of all observations using the 500 trees. The options of type="class" and predict.all=TRUE are central to this code block. The GP function is then applied to the matrix of predictions for the 500 trees. Note that the diagonal elements of the GP matrix will always be TRUE. Consequently, if there is any classifier with which it has perfect agreement over all observations, the value of that cell will be TRUE. If the row sum then exceeds the count by 2, we have a geese classifier for that classifier. The following code captures the entire computation:

```
> CD <- CART_Dummy
> CD$Y <- as.factor(CD$Y)
> set.seed(1234567)
> CD_RF <- randomForest(Y~.,data=CD,ntree=500)
> CD_RF_Predict <- predict(CD_RF,newdata=CD,
+                          type="class",predict.all=TRUE)
> CD_RF_Predict_Matrix <- CD_RF_Predict$individual
> CD_GP <- GP(CD_RF_Predict_Matrix)
> CD_GP[1:8,1:8]
        [,1]  [,2]  [,3]  [,4]  [,5]  [,6]  [,7]  [,8]
[1,]   TRUE FALSE FALSE FALSE FALSE FALSE FALSE FALSE
[2,]  FALSE  TRUE FALSE FALSE FALSE FALSE FALSE FALSE
[3,]  FALSE FALSE  TRUE FALSE FALSE FALSE FALSE FALSE
[4,]  FALSE FALSE FALSE  TRUE FALSE FALSE FALSE FALSE
[5,]  FALSE FALSE FALSE FALSE  TRUE FALSE FALSE FALSE
[6,]  FALSE FALSE FALSE FALSE FALSE  TRUE FALSE FALSE
[7,]  FALSE FALSE FALSE FALSE FALSE FALSE  TRUE FALSE
[8,]  FALSE FALSE FALSE FALSE FALSE FALSE FALSE  TRUE
> rowSums(CD_ST)
  [1] 1 1 1 1 1 1 1 1 1 1 1 1 1 1 1 1 1 1 1 1 1 2 1 1 1 1 1 1 1 1 1 1 1
 1 1 1 1
 [38] 1 1 1 1 2 1 1 1 1 1 1 1 1 1 1 1 1 1 1 1 1 1 1 1 1 1 1 1 1 1 1 1 1
 1 1 1 1

 [149] 1 1 1 1 1 1 1 1 1 1 1 1 1 1 1 1 1 1 1 1 1 1 1 1 1 1 1 1 2 1 1 1 1
 1 1 1 1
 [186] 1 1 2 1 1 1 1 1 1 1 1 1 1 1 1 1 1 1 1 2 1 1 1 1 1 1 1 1 1 1 1 1 1
 1 1 1 2 1
 [223] 1 1 1 1 1 1 1 1 1 1 1 1 1 1 1 1 1 1 1 1 1 1 1 1 1 1 1 1 1 1 1 1 1
 1 2 1 1 1
 [260] 1 1 1 1 1 1 1 1 1 1 1 1 1 1 1 1 1 1 1 2 1 1 1 1 1 1 1 1 1 1 1 2 1
 1 1 1 1 1
 [297] 1 1 1 1 1 1 1 1 1 1 1 1 1 1 1 1 1 1 1 1 1 1 1 1 1 1 1 1 1 1 1 1 1
 1 1 1 1
```

```
[334] 1 1 1 1 1 1 1 1 1 1 1 1 1 1 1 1 1 1 1 1 1 1 1 1 1 1 1 1 1 1 2 1 2
1 1 1 1 1
[371] 1 1 1 1 1 1 1 1 1 1 1 1 1 1 2 1 1 1 1 1 1 1 1 1 1 1 1 1 1 1 1 1 1
1 1 1 1 1
[408] 1 1 1 1 1 1 1 1 1 1 1 1 1 1 1 1 1 2 1 1 1 1 1 1 1 1 1 1 1 1 1 1 1
1 1 2 1 1

[482] 1 1 1 1 1 1 1 1 1 1 1 1 1 1 1 1 1 1 1 1 1
```

The reader should note that the bold and larger font of 2 in the preceding output is not given by R. It has been modified by the software processing the text matter. Consequently, we have a lot of classifiers that have a geese classifier matching each of their own predictions. Using the which function, we first find all the classifier indexes that meet the criteria, and then, by applying the which function for the rows of the CD_GP matrix, we get the associated geese classifier:

```
> which(rowSums(CD_GP)>1)
 [1]   21   42 176 188 206 221 256 278 290 363 365 385 424 442
> which(CD_GP[21,]==TRUE)
[1]   21 188
> which(CD_GP[42,]==TRUE)
[1]   42 290
> which(CD_GP[176,]==TRUE)
[1] 176 363
> which(CD_GP[206,]==TRUE)
[1] 206 256
> which(CD_GP[221,]==TRUE)
[1] 221 278
> which(CD_GP[365,]==TRUE)
[1] 365 424
> which(CD_GP[385,]==TRUE)
[1] 385 442
```

As a result of running the preceding code, we are able to identify the geese classifier associated with the classifier. We can choose to remove any one member of the geese pair. In the next example, we will apply this method to the German credit data. The program tries to identify the geese classifier as follows:

```
> set.seed(12345)
> GC2_RF3 <- randomForest(GC2_Formula,data=GC2_Train,mtry=10,
+                         parms = list(split="information",
+                                     loss=matrix(c(0,1,1000,0),byrow
= TRUE,nrow=2)),
+                         ntree=1000)
> GC2_RF_Train_Predict <- predict(GC2_RF3,newdata=GC2_Train,
+                                 type="class",predict.all=TRUE)
```

```
> GC2_RF_Train_Predict_Matrix <- GC2_RF_Train_Predict$individual
> GC2_GP <- GP(GC2_RF_Train_Predict_Matrix)
> rowSums(GC2_GP)
  [1] 1 1 1 1 1 1 1 1 1 1 1 1 1 1 1 1 1 1 1 1 1 1 1 1 1 1 1 1 1 1 1 1 1 1 1
1 1 1 1
 [37] 1 1 1 1 1 1 1 1 1 1 1 1 1 1 1 1 1 1 1 1 1 1 1 1 1 1 1 1 1 1 1 1 1 1 1
1 1 1 1

[973] 1 1 1 1 1 1 1 1 1 1 1 1 1 1 1 1 1 1 1 1 1 1 1 1 1 1 1 1 1
> which(rowSums(GC2_GP)>1)
integer(0)
```

Since none of the classifiers have a corresponding geese classifier, we don't have to eliminate any of the trees.

In Kuncheva (2014), page 112, there is a useful metric known as *oracle output*. Next, we formally define the quantity. Remember that we have L number of classifiers and N number of observations. The original/actual values of the label are denoted by $Y_i, i = 1, 2, ..., N$. We will denote the ith predicted value using the classifier j by $\ddot{Y}_{ij}, i = 1, 2, ..., N, j = 1, 2, ..., L$.

Oracle output: The oracle output $O_{ij}, i = 1, 2, ..., N, j = 1, 2, ..., L$ is defined as **1** if the predicted value $\ddot{Y}_{ij}$ is equal to Y_i; otherwise it is defined as **0**. In mathematical terms, the oracle output is given using the following mathematical expression:

$$O_{ij} = \begin{cases} 1, & \text{if } \widehat{Y}_{ij} = Y_i, \\ 0, & \text{if } \widehat{Y}_{ij} \neq Y_i \end{cases}$$

So, what is the difference between the oracle output and the predictions? The predictions consist of the labels of the data, and the labels might be 1/0, GOOD/BAD, +1/-1, YES/NO, or some other binary pair of labels. Besides, in the case of a binary label, a prediction of 1 does not necessarily mean that the original value is 1; it might be 0 as well. The oracle output takes the value of 1 if 1 is predicted as 1, or if 0 is predicted as 0; otherwise, it takes the value of 0. A consequence of using the oracle output is that the proportion of 1s for a classifier will give us the accuracy of the classifier.

We will now create an R function named `Oracle`, which will give the oracle output when it is an input for the prediction matrix and the actual labels. After this, we will calculate the accuracy of the classifiers:

```
> # Oracle Output
> Oracle <- function(PM,Actual){
+   # PM = Prediction Matrix, Actual = the true Y's
```

```
+    OM <- matrix(0,nrow=nrow(PM),ncol=ncol(PM))
+    for(i in 1:ncol(OM)) {
+      OM[,i] <- as.numeric(PM[,i]==Actual)
+    }
+    return(OM)
+ }
> GC_Oracle <- Oracle(PM=GC2_RF_Train_Predict$individual,
+                      Actual=GC2_Train$good_bad)
> colSums(GC_Oracle)/nrow(GC_Oracle)
   [1] 0.872 0.884 0.859 0.869 0.866 0.878 0.888 0.872 0.869 0.875
 0.885 0.869
  [13] 0.881 0.866 0.879 0.856 0.870 0.869 0.857 0.870 0.878 0.868
 0.886 0.892
  [25] 0.881 0.863 0.866 0.856 0.886 0.876 0.873 0.879 0.875 0.885
 0.872 0.872

 [973] 0.860 0.873 0.869 0.888 0.863 0.879 0.882 0.865 0.891 0.863
 0.878 0.879
 [985] 0.878 0.869 0.856 0.872 0.889 0.881 0.868 0.881 0.884 0.854
 0.882 0.882
 [997] 0.862 0.884 0.873 0.885
```

The oracle matrix helps us in obtaining the accuracy of the classifiers. In the next section, we will discuss some measures that will help us in understanding how close the classifiers are to each other.

Pairwise measure

In this section, we will propose some measures of agreement between two classifiers. The intention is to fix the notions of agreement/disagreement for two classifiers and then take the concept to the overall classifiers of the ensemble in the next section. If M_1 and M_2 are classifier models with predictions $\ddot{Y}_{ij}, i = 1, 2, \ldots, N, j = 1, 2$, we can then obtain a table that gives us the following:

- M_1 predicts $\widehat{Y}_i, i = 1, 2, \ldots, N$ as 1; M_2 predicts it as 1
- M_1 predicts $\widehat{Y}_i$ as 1; M_2 predicts it as 0
- M_1 predicts $\widehat{Y}_i$ as 0; M_2 predicts it as 1
- M_1 predicts $\widehat{Y}_i$ as 0; M_2 predicts it as 0

The information across the N observations can be put in a tabular form, as follows:

	M1 predicts 1	**M1 predicts 0**
M2 predicts 1	n11	n10
M2 predicts 0	n01	n00

Table 2: Contingency table for two classifiers/raters

The diagonal elements of the preceding table show the agreement between the two models/classifiers, while the off-diagonal elements show the disagreement. The models are sometimes referred to as *raters*. The frequency table is also known as the **contingency table**. Using this setup, we will now discuss some useful measures of *agreement*. The comparisons are called pairwise measures as we take only a pair of classifiers into analysis.

Disagreement measure

The disagreement measure between two classifiers/rates is defined according to the following formula:

$$DM = \frac{n_{10} + n_{01}}{N}$$

We will now define a DM function that is given the predictions for the two classifiers. The function will first prepare the contingency table for the predictions. The calculation of the disagreement measure is then straightforward, and is given in the following code block:

```
> # Disagreement Measure
> DM <- function(prediction1,prediction2){
+    tp <- table(prediction1,prediction2)
+    Diss <- (tp[1,2]+tp[2,1])/length(prediction1)
+    return(Diss)
+ }
```

In the first section, we had the predictions for the German credit data based on the logistic regression model naïve Bayes, SVM, and a classification tree. Now we apply the DM function to these predictions and see how much these classifiers disagree with each other:

```
> DM(LR_Predict_Train,NB_Predict_Train)
[1] 0.121
> DM(LR_Predict_Train,CT_Predict_Train)
[1] 0.154
```

```
> DM(LR_Predict_Train,SVM_Predict_Train)
[1] 0.153
> DM(NB_Predict_Train,CT_Predict_Train)
[1] 0.179
> DM(NB_Predict_Train,SVM_Predict_Train)
[1] 0.154
> DM(CT_Predict_Train,SVM_Predict_Train)
[1] 0.167
```

Since we had four classifiers, there will be 3 + 2 + 1 = 6 pairwise comparisons. The naïve Bayes and classification tree have the maximum disagreement, and the least disagreement is between the logistic regression and the naïve Bayes classifiers. The DM measure can be used to easily obtain the disagreement of two models.

Yule's or Q-statistic

The Yule's coefficient is a measure of agreement, and when its value is nearly equal to zero, it will give the disagreement between the two raters. The Yule's measure is given using the following formula:

$$Q = \frac{n_{11}n_{00} - n_{10}n_{01}}{n_{11}n_{00} + n_{10}n_{01}}$$

The Q-statistic takes the value in the range of the correlation coefficient—that is, $-1 \leq Q \leq 1$. Consequently, if the Q values are closer to 1, this means that the two measures nearly always agree with each other, while the value closer to -1 means that the two models predict the opposite of each other. When the Q values are closer to 0, it means that there is a very weak association between the two raters. A Yule function is created and applied to the different model predictions in the following code block:

```
> # Q-statistic
> Yule <- function(prediction1,prediction2){
+    tp <- table(prediction1,prediction2)
+    Yu <- (tp[1,1]*tp[2,2]-tp[1,2]*tp[2,1])/(tp[1,1]*tp[2,2]+tp[1,2]*
tp[2,1])
+    return(Yu)
+ }
> Yule(LR_Predict_Train,NB_Predict_Train)
[1] 0.949
> Yule(LR_Predict_Train,CT_Predict_Train)
[1] 0.906
> Yule(LR_Predict_Train,SVM_Predict_Train)
[1] 0.98
```

```
> Yule(NB_Predict_Train,CT_Predict_Train)
[1] 0.865
> Yule(NB_Predict_Train,SVM_Predict_Train)
[1] 0.985
> Yule(CT_Predict_Train,SVM_Predict_Train)
[1] 0.912
```

The agreement between naïve Bayes predictions and the SVM predictions is highest. Note that if we take the complement of the disagreement measure and perform it easily using the following code, we get a measure of the following agreement:

```
> 1-DM(LR_Predict_Train,NB_Predict_Train)
[1] 0.879
> 1-DM(LR_Predict_Train,CT_Predict_Train)
[1] 0.846
> 1-DM(LR_Predict_Train,SVM_Predict_Train)
[1] 0.847
> 1-DM(NB_Predict_Train,CT_Predict_Train)
[1] 0.821
> 1-DM(NB_Predict_Train,SVM_Predict_Train)
[1] 0.846
> 1-DM(CT_Predict_Train,SVM_Predict_Train)
[1] 0.833
```

However, this analysis says that the highest agreement is between the logistic regression and naïve Bayes raters. Consequently, we note that the output and comparisons might lead to different conclusions. The correlation coefficient can also be computed for two raters; we will cover this next.

Correlation coefficient measure

The correlation coefficient between two numeric variables is very intuitive, and it is also a very useful measure of relationship when there is a linear relationship between them. If both variables are categorical in nature, then we can still obtain the correlation coefficient between them. For two raters, the correlation coefficient is calculated using the following formula:

$$\rho = \frac{n_{11}n_{00} - n_{01}n_{10}}{\sqrt{(n_{11} + n_{10})(n_{10} + n_{01})(n_{10} + n_{00})(n_{01} + n_{00})}}$$

We will define an `SS_Cor` function that will carry out the necessary computations and return the correlation coefficient:

```
> # Correlation coefficient
> # Sneath and Sokal, 1973
> SS_Cor <- function(prediction1, prediction2){
+   tp <- table(prediction1,prediction2)
+   a <- tp[1,1]; b <- tp[2,1]; c <- tp[1,2]; d <- tp[2,2]
+   SS <- (a*d-b*c)/sqrt(exp(log(a+b)+log(a+c)+log(c+d)+log(b+d)))
+   return(SS)
+ }
```

The correlation coefficient function is now applied to the predictions, as shown in the previous examples:

```
> SS_Cor(LR_Predict_Train,NB_Predict_Train)
[1] 0.69
> SS_Cor(LR_Predict_Train,CT_Predict_Train)
[1] 0.593
> SS_Cor(LR_Predict_Train,SVM_Predict_Train)
[1] 0.584
> SS_Cor(NB_Predict_Train,CT_Predict_Train)
[1] 0.531
> SS_Cor(NB_Predict_Train,SVM_Predict_Train)
[1] 0.587
> SS_Cor(CT_Predict_Train,SVM_Predict_Train)
[1] 0.493
```

The results show that the logistic and naïve Bayes predictions are in more agreement than any other combination. Correlation tests can be applied for inspecting whether the predictions of the classifiers are independent of each other.

Exercise: Apply the `chisq.test` to check for the independence of the predictions of the various classifiers here.

Cohen's statistic

The Cohen's statistic first appeared in 1960. It is based on the probability of the two raters agreeing with each other because of chance or coincidence. The probability of two raters agreeing with each other is demonstrated as follows:

$$\theta_1 = \frac{n_{11} + n_{00}}{N}$$

However, the probability of agreeing randomly or because of chance is found as follows:

$$\theta_2 = \frac{\left(n_{11} + n_{10}\right)\left(n_{11} + n_{01}\right) + \left(n_{01} + n_{00}\right)\left(n_{10} + n_{00}\right)}{N^2}$$

Using the definition of θ_1 and θ_2, the Cohen's statistic is defined by the following:

$$\kappa = \frac{\theta_1 - \theta_2}{1 - \theta_2}$$

The Cohen's kappa can take negative values as well. If its value is 1, this means that the raters agree with each other completely. The value of 0 means that the agreement is only by chance, and a negative value means that the agreement is less than the expected number by chance. First, the R function Kappa is created in the following code:

```
> # Kappa-statistic
> # Cohen's Statistic
> Kappa <- function(prediction1, prediction2){
+    tp <- table(prediction1,prediction2)
+    a <- tp[1,1]; b <- tp[2,1]; c <- tp[1,2]; d <- tp[2,2]
+    n <- length(prediction1)
+    theta1 <- (a+d)/n
+    theta2 <- (((a+b)*(a+c))+((c+d)*(b+d)))/n^2
+    kappa <- (theta1-theta2)/(1-theta2)
+    return(kappa)
+ }
```

The coding part is a clear implementation of the formulas, and the choice of a, b, c, d, theta1, and theta2 has been made to make the code easy to interpret and follow. Next, we apply the predictions to the German training dataset:

```
> Kappa(LR_Predict_Train,NB_Predict_Train)
[1] 0.69
> Kappa(LR_Predict_Train,CT_Predict_Train)
[1] 0.592
> Kappa(LR_Predict_Train,SVM_Predict_Train)
[1] 0.524
> Kappa(NB_Predict_Train,CT_Predict_Train)
[1] 0.53
> Kappa(NB_Predict_Train,SVM_Predict_Train)
[1] 0.525
> Kappa(CT_Predict_Train,SVM_Predict_Train)
[1] 0.453
```

Again, the agreement between the logistic and naïve Bayes predictions is the highest. We now move to the final disagreement measure.

Double-fault measure

In tennis, a double fault refers to when the serve fails. The server has two opportunities to get the right serve, and if they do not, the point is conceded to the opponent. The double fault measure occurs when both classifiers get the wrong prediction:

$$DF = \frac{\sum_{i=1}^{N} I\left(\widehat{Y}_{i1} \neq Y_i, \widehat{Y}_{i2} \neq Y_i\right)}{N}$$

Clearly, we need the DF to be as low as possible and close to 0. This function is easy to interpret, and so this will be left as an exercise for the reader to follow. The R function for the double fault measure and its application is given in then following code:

```
> # Double-fault Measure
> Double_Fault <- function(prediction1,prediction2,actual){
+    DF <- sum((prediction1!=actual)*(prediction2!=actual))/
+          length(actual)
+    return(DF)
+ }
> Double_Fault(LR_Predict_Train,NB_Predict_Train,
+ GC2_Train$good_bad)
[1] 0.166
> Double_Fault(LR_Predict_Train,CT_Predict_Train,
+ GC2_Train$good_bad)
[1] 0.118
> Double_Fault(LR_Predict_Train,SVM_Predict_Train,
+ GC2_Train$good_bad)
[1] 0.148
> Double_Fault(NB_Predict_Train,CT_Predict_Train,
+ GC2_Train$good_bad)
[1] 0.709
> Double_Fault(NB_Predict_Train,SVM_Predict_Train,
+ GC2_Train$good_bad)
[1] 0.154
> Double_Fault(CT_Predict_Train,SVM_Predict_Train,
+ GC2_Train$good_bad)
[1] 0.116
```

The reader should identify the best agreement by using the double fault measure.

Exercise: In the case of multilabels (more than two categories), the extension of the metrics discussed in this section becomes cumbersome. Instead, one can use the oracle matrix and repeat these metrics. The reader should apply these measures to the oracle output.

The methods discussed thus far apply to only one classifier pair. In the next section, we will measure the diversity of all classifiers of an ensemble.

Interrating agreement

A simple extension of the measures discussed in the previous section on the ensemble classifiers is to compute the measures for all possible pairs of the ensemble and then simply average over all those values. This task constitutes the next exercise.

Exercise: For all possible combinations of ensemble pairs, calculate the disagreement measure, Yule's statistic, correlation coefficient, Cohen's kappa, and the double-fault measure. After doing this, obtain the average of the comparisons and report them as the ensemble diversity.

Here, we will propose alternative measures of diversity and kick-start the discussion with the entropy measure. In all discussions in this section, we will use the oracle outputs.

Entropy measure

You may recall that we denote the oracle outputs according to $O_{ij}, i = 1, 2, \ldots, N, j = 1, 2, \ldots, L$. For a particular instance, the ensemble is most diverse if the number of classifiers misclassifying it is $[L/2]$. This means that $[L/2]$ of the O_{ij}s are 0s, and the rest of the $L - [L/2]$, O_{ij}s are 1s. The *entropy measure for the ensemble* is then defined by the following:

$$E = \frac{2}{N(L-1)} \sum_{i=1}^{N} \min \left\{ \sum_{j=1}^{L} O_{ij}, L - \sum_{j=1}^{L} O_{ij} \right\}$$

The value of the entropy measure E is in the unit interval. If the E value is closer to 0, this means that there is no diversity in the ensemble, while a value close to 1 means that the diversity is at the highest possible level. Given the oracle matrix, we can easily calculate the entropy measure as follows:

```
> # Entropy Measure
> # Page 250 of Kuncheva (2014)
> Entropy_Measure <- function(OM){
+    # OM = Oracle Matrix
```

```
+    N <- nrow(OM); L <- ncol(OM)
+    E <- 0
+    for(i in 1:N){
+      E <- E+min(sum(OM[i,]),L-sum(OM[i,]))
+    }
+    E <- 2*E/(N*(L-1))
+    return(E)
+ }
> Entropy_Measure(GC_Oracle)
[1] 0.255
```

By applying the `Entropy_Measure` on the ensemble for the German credit data, we can see that the entropy measure value is `0.255`. The random forest ensemble exhibits diversity as the entropy measure is not closer to 0. However, it is also far away from 1, which implies diversity. However, there are no critical values or tests to interpret whether the diversity is too low, or even too high, for that matter.

Kohavi-Wolpert measure

The Kohavi–Wolpert measure is based on the variance of the prediction as 1s or 0s. It is based on a decomposition formula for the error rate of a classifier. For the binary problem, or when using oracle input, the variance is the same as the Gini index. This is given according to the following formula:

$$Var(x) = \frac{1}{2}\left(1 - P(1|x)^2 - P(0|x)^2\right)$$

The Kohavi-Wolpert measure is the average of the variance across all observations. By using the prediction probability given by the oracle matrix, or as a side product of the fitted objects, we can obtain the variance and then average it across the observations. An R function is now created and applied to some of the predictions obtained for the German credit data, as follows:

```
> # Kohavi-Wolpert variance
> # Using the predicted probability
> KW <- function(Prob){
+    N <- nrow(Prob)
+    kw <- mean(1-Prob[,1]^2-Prob[,2]^2)/2
+    return(kw)
+ }
> GC2_RF_Train_Predict_Prob <- predict(GC2_RF3,newdata=GC2_Train,
+                                  type="prob",predict.all=TRUE)
```

```
> GC2_RF_Train_Prob <- GC2_RF_Train_Predict_Prob$aggregate
> KW(GC2_RF_Train_Prob)
[1]  0.104
```

The Kohavi–Wolpert measure can also be obtained using the oracle output. We define a mathematical entity that will count the number of classifiers that correctly classify the observation as follows:

$$l(x_1) = \sum_{j=1}^{L} O_{ij}, i = 1, \ldots, N$$

The probability of being correctly predicted is as follows:

$$P(Y_i = 1 \mid \mathbf{x}) = \frac{l(\mathbf{x}_i)}{L}, P(Y_i = 0 \mid \mathbf{x}) = \frac{L - l(\mathbf{x}_i)}{L}$$

Using these probabilities, the variance can be obtained as follows:

$$Var(x) = \frac{1}{2}\left(1 - P(Y_i = 1 \mid \mathbf{x})^2 - P(Y_i = 0 \mid \mathbf{x})^2\right)$$

This method is implemented in the following code using the KW_OM function:

```
> # Using the Oracle matrix
> KW_OM<- function(OM){
+    # OM is the oracle matrix
+    N <- nrow(OM); L <- ncol(OM)
+    kw <- 0
+    for(i in 1:N){
+      lz <- sum(OM[i,])
+      kw <- kw + lz*(L-lz)
+    }
+    kw <- kw/(N*L^2)
+    return(kw)
+ }
> KW_OM(GC_Oracle)
[1]  0.104
```

From this, we can see that the two methods give us the same result. It is also clear that we don't have a great deal of diversity following the construction of the random forests.

Disagreement measure for ensemble

The disagreement measure between two classifiers can be defined using the following:

$$D_{jj'} = \frac{1}{N}\sum_{i=1}^{N}\left(O_{ij} - O_{ij'}\right)^2$$

The disagreement measure of the ensemble is given by the following:

$$D = \frac{1}{L(L-1)}\sum_{j'=1}^{L}\sum_{j=1, j\neq j'}^{L} D_{jj'}$$

The Kohavi–Wolpert and disagreement measure are related as follows:

$$KW = \frac{L-1}{2L}D$$

The next R code block delivers the implementation of the Kohavi–Wolper measure using the oracle outputs as follows:

```
> # Disagreement Measure OVerall on Oracle Matrix
> DMO <- function(OM){
+    # OM is the oracle matrix
+    N <- nrow(OM); L <- ncol(OM)
+    dmo <- 0
+    for(i in 1:L){
+      for(j in c(c(1:L)[c(1:L)!=i])){
+        dmo <- dmo + sum((OM[,i]-OM[,j])^2)/N
+      }
+    }
+    dmo <- dmo/(L*(L-1))
+    return(dmo)
+ }
> DM_GC <- DMO(OM=GC_Oracle)
> DM_GC
[1] 0.208
> KW(GC_Oracle)
[1] 0.104
> DM_GC*999/2000
[1] 0.104
```

Again, we don't see much diversity displayed across the ensemble. We will now move on to looking at the final measure of an ensemble's diversity.

Measurement of interrater agreement

In the introductory discussion of oracle output, we showed how it can be easily used to obtain the accuracy of a classifier. The average of the classifier accuracy is defined as the average individual classification accuracy, and it is denoted by $\overline{p}$. The measurement of the interrater agreement is defined by the following:

$$\kappa_1 = 1 - \frac{\frac{1}{L}\sum_{i=1}^{N} l(\mathbf{x_i})(L - l(\mathbf{x_i}))}{N(L-1)\overline{p}(1-\overline{p})}$$

This measure is related to the Kohavi–Wolpert measure as follows:

$$\kappa_1 = 1 - \frac{L}{(L-1)\overline{p}(1-\overline{p})} KW = 1 - \frac{1}{2\overline{p}(1-\overline{p})} D$$

The implementation of the preceding relation can be understood with the help of the following code block:

```
> Avg_Ensemble_Acc <- function(Oracle){
+    return(mean(colSums(GC_Oracle)/nrow(GC_Oracle)))
+ }
> Avg_Ensemble_Acc(GC_Oracle)
[1] 0.872
> Kappa <- function(Oracle){
+    pbar <- Avg_Ensemble_Acc(Oracle)
+    AvgL <- 0
+    N <- nrow(Oracle); L <- ncol(Oracle)
+    for(i in 1:N){
+       lz <- sum(Oracle[i,])
+      AvgL <- AvgL + lz*(L-lz)
+    }
+    Avgl <- AvgL/L
+    kappa <- 1-Avgl/(N*(L-1)*pbar*(1-pbar))
+    return(kappa)
+ }
> Kappa(GC_Oracle)
[1] 0.0657
> 1-DM_GC/(2*Avg_Ensemble_Acc(GC_Oracle)*(1-
+ Avg_Ensemble_Acc(GC_Oracle)))
[1] 0.0657
```

This concludes our discussion of the agreement in an ensemble.

Summary

Ensemble methods have been found to be very effective for classification, regression, and other related problems. Any statistical and machine learning method must always be followed up with appropriate diagnostics. The assumption that all base models are independent of each other is central to the success of an ensembling method. However, this independence condition is rarely satisfied, especially because the base models are built on the same dataset. We kicked off the chapter with the simplest measure: the geese pair method. With this, we essentially searched for the models that agree with each other at all times. If such models are present in the ensemble, it is safer to remove one of them. With a large dataset and a high number of variables, it is indeed possible that there won't be any base models that speak the same language as another. However, we still need to check whether they are equal. With this in mind, we first proposed measures that compare only two base models at a time. Different measures can lead to conflicting conclusions. However, this is generally not a problem. The concept of pairwise comparison was then extended to entire ensemble base models. While we found that our base models were not too diverse, it is also important to note here that most of the values are a safe distance away from the boundary value of 0. When we are performing the diagnostics on an ensemble and find that the values are equal to zero, it is then clear that the base models are not offering any kind of diversity. In the next chapter, we will look at the specialized topic of regression data.

9
Ensembling Regression Models

Chapters 3, *Bagging*, to Chapters 8, *Ensemble Diagnostics*, were devoted to learning different types of ensembling methods. The discussion was largely based on the classification problem. If the regressand/output of the supervised learning problem is a numeric variable, then we have a regression problem, which will be addressed here. The housing price problem is selected for demonstration purposes throughout the chapter, and the dataset is chosen from a Kaggle competition: `https://www.kaggle.com/c/house-prices-advanced-regression-techniques/`. The data consists of numerous variables, including as many as 79 independent variables, with the price of the house as the output/dependent variable. The dataset needs some pre-processing as some variables have missing dates, some variables have lots of levels, with a few of them only occurring very rarely, and some variables have missing data in more than 20% of observations.

The pre-processing techniques will be succeeded by variable reduction methods and then we will fit important regression models: linear regression, neural network, and regression trees. An ensemble extension of the regression tree will first be provided, and then we will apply the bagging and random forest methods. Various boosting methods will be used to improve the prediction. Stacked ensemble methods will be applied in the concluding section.

In this chapter, we will cover the following:

- Data pre-processing and visualization
- Variable reduction techniques
- Regression models

- Bagging and Random Forests for the regression data
- Boosting regression models
- Stacked ensemble methods for regression data

Technical requirements

We will need the following R packages for this chapter:

- `adabag`
- `caret`
- `caretEnsemble`
- `ClustofVar`
- `FactoMinR`
- `gbm`
- `ipred`
- `missForest`
- `nnet`
- `NeuralNetTools`
- `plyr`
- `rpart`
- `RSADBE`

Pre-processing the housing data

The dataset was selected from `www.kaggle.com` and the title of the project is **House Prices: Advanced Regression Techniques**. The main files we will be using are `test.csv` and `train.csv`, and the files are available in the companion bundle package. A description of the variables can be found in the `data_description.txt` file. Further details, of course, can be obtained at `https://www.kaggle.com/c/house-prices-advanced-regression-techniques/`. The train dataset contains 1460 observations, while the test dataset contains 1459 observations. The price of the property is known only in the train dataset and are not available for those in the test dataset. We will use the train dataset for model development only. The datasets are first loaded into an R session and a beginning inspection is done using the `read.csv`, `dim`, `names`, and `str` functions:

```
> housing_train <- read.csv("../Data/Housing/train.csv",
+                           row.names = 1,na.strings = "NA",
+                           stringsAsFactors = TRUE)
```

```
> housing_test <- read.csv("../Data/Housing/test.csv",
+                          row.names = 1,na.strings = "NA",
+                          stringsAsFactors = TRUE)
> dim(housing_train)
[1] 1460    80
> dim(housing_test)
[1] 1459    79
> names(housing_train)
 [1] "MSSubClass"   "MSZoning"     "LotFrontage"  "LotArea"
 [5] "Street"       "Alley"        "LotShape"     "LandContour"
 [9] "Utilities"    "LotConfig"    "LandSlope"    "Neighborhood"


[69] "X3SsnPorch"   "ScreenPorch"  "PoolArea"     "PoolQC"
[73] "Fence"        "MiscFeature"  "MiscVal"      "MoSold"
[77] "YrSold"       "SaleType"     "SaleCondition" "SalePrice"
> str(housing_train)
'data.frame':    1460 obs. of  80 variables:
 $ MSSubClass  : int  60 20 60 70 60 50 20 60 50 190 ...
 $ MSZoning    : Factor w/ 5 levels "C (all)","FV",..: 4 4 4 4 4 4
4 5 4 ...
 $ LotFrontage : int  65 80 68 60 84 85 75 NA 51 50 ...
 $ LotArea     : int  8450 9600 11250 9550 14260 14115 10084 10382
6120 7420 ...
 $ Street      : Factor w/ 2 levels "Grvl","Pave": 2 2 2 2 2 2 2 2
2 ...
 $ Alley       : Factor w/ 2 levels "Grvl","Pave": NA NA NA NA NA NA
NA NA NA NA ...


 $ MiscFeature : Factor w/ 4 levels "Gar2","Othr",..: NA NA NA NA NA
3 NA 3 NA NA ...
 $ MiscVal     : int  0 0 0 0 0 700 0 350 0 0 ...
 $ MoSold      : int  2 5 9 2 12 10 8 11 4 1 ...
 $ YrSold      : int  2008 2007 2008 2006 2008 2009 2007 2009 2008
2008 ...
 $ SaleType    : Factor w/ 9 levels "COD","Con","ConLD",..: 9 9 9 9 9
9 9 9 9 ...
 $ SaleCondition: Factor w/ 6 levels "Abnorml","AdjLand",..: 5 5 5 1 5
5 5 5 1 5 ...
 $ SalePrice   : int  208500 181500 223500 140000 250000 143000
307000 200000 129900 118000 ...
```

In this snippet, the `read.csv` function enabled importing the data from the comma-separated values file. The size of the imported data frame is evaluated using the `dim` function, while `names` gives us the variable names as stored in the original file. The `str` function gives a quick preview of the variable types and also gives a few of the observations.

The dimensions of the data frames give the number of variables and the number of observations. The details of all the variables can be found in the `data_description.txt` file. It can be seen that what we have on hand is a comprehensive dataset. Now, we ran the option of `na.strings = "NA"` in the `read.csv` import function, and quite naturally, this implied that we have missing data. When we have missing data in both the training and test data partitions, the author recommends combining the covariates in the partitions and then examining them further. The covariates are first combined and then we find the number of missing observations for each of the variables:

```
> housing <- rbind(housing_train[,1:79],housing_test)
> dim(housing)
[1] 2919    79
> sort(sapply(housing,function(x) sum(is.na(x))),dec=TRUE)
       PoolQC    MiscFeature         Alley          Fence    FireplaceQu
         2909           2814          2721           2348           1420
  LotFrontage    GarageYrBlt   GarageFinish     GarageQual     GarageCond
          486            159           159            159            159
   GarageType       BsmtCond   BsmtExposure       BsmtQual    BsmtFinType2
          157             82            82             81             80
 BsmtFinType1     MasVnrType     MasVnrArea       MSZoning      Utilities
           79             24            23              4              2
 BsmtFullBath   BsmtHalfBath     Functional     Exterior1st    Exterior2nd
            2              2             2              1              1
    BsmtFinSF1     BsmtFinSF2      BsmtUnfSF    TotalBsmtSF     Electrical
            1              1             1              1              1
  KitchenQual     GarageCars     GarageArea       SaleType     MSSubClass
            1              1             1              1              0
      LotArea         Street       LotShape    LandContour      LotConfig
            0              0             0              0              0

   OpenPorchSF   EnclosedPorch     X3SsnPorch    ScreenPorch       PoolArea
            0              0             0              0              0
      MiscVal         MoSold         YrSold  SaleCondition
            0              0             0              0
```

The `rbind` function combines the data in the training and testing datasets. The `is.na(x)` code inspects the absence of the values for every element of x, and the `sum` applied tells us the number of missing observations for the variable. The function is then applied for every variable of `housing` using the `sapply` function. The count of missing observations for the variables is sorted in descending order using the `sort` function with the argument `dec=TRUE`, and hence it enables us to find the variables with the most missing numbers in the beginning.

The reader might be wondering about the rationale behind the collation of the observations. The intuitive reasoning behind the collation is that while some variables might have missing data, more in the training data than in the test data, or the other way around, it is important that the overall missing percentage does not exceed a certain threshold of the observations. Although we have missing data imputation techniques, using them when the missing data percentage is too high might cause us to miss out on the important patterns of the features. Consequently, we arbitrarily make a choice of restricting the variables if more than 10% of the values are missing. If the missing percentage of any variable exceeds 10%, we will avoid analyzing that variable further. First, we identify the variables that exceed 10%, and then we remove them from the master data frame. The following R code block gives us the desired result:

```
> miss_variables <- names(which(sapply(housing,
+           function(x) sum(is.na(x)))>0.1*nrow(housing_train)))
> miss_variables
 [1] "LotFrontage"  "Alley"        "FireplaceQu"  "GarageType"
 [5] "GarageYrBlt"  "GarageFinish" "GarageQual"   "GarageCond"
 [9] "PoolQC"       "Fence"        "MiscFeature"
> length(miss_variables)
[1] 11
> housing[,miss_variables] <- NULL
> dim(housing)
[1] 2919   68
```

The variables that have more than 10% missing observations are first identified and then stored in the `miss_variables` character vector, and we have 11 variables that meet this criterion. Such variables are eliminated with the `NULL` assignment for them.

Next, we find the number of levels (distinct) of factor variables. We define a function, `find_df`, which will find the number of levels of a factor variable. For numeric and integer variables, it will return 1. The purpose of this exercise will become clear soon enough. The `find_df` function is created in the next block:

```
> find_df <- function(x){
+    if(class(x)=="numeric") mdf <- 1
+    if(class(x)=="integer") mdf <- 1
```

```
+    if(class(x) =="factor") mdf <- length(levels(x))
+    if(class(x) =="character") mdf <- length(unique(x))
+    return(mdf)
+ }
> sapply(housing,find_df)
   MSSubClass      MSZoning       LotArea        Street      LotShape
            1             4             1             2             3
  LandContour     Utilities     LotConfig     LandSlope  Neighborhood
            2             3             4             2            25
   Condition1    Condition2      BldgType    HouseStyle   OverallQual
            3             2             3             4             1


    X3SsnPorch   ScreenPorch      PoolArea       MiscVal        MoSold
            1             1             1             1             1
       YrSold      SaleType SaleCondition
            1             4             4
> dim(housing)
[1] 2919   68
```

We need to inspect 67 variables, following the elimination of 11 variables with more than 10% missing observations. Some of these might not be factor variables. The find_df function shows that, for factor variables, the number of levels varies from 2-25. A quick problem now arises for the Condition2 and Exterior1st variables:

```
> round(table(housing$Condition2)/nrow(housing),2)
 Artery  Feedr   Norm   PosA   PosN   RRAe   RRAn   RRNn
   0.00   0.00   0.99   0.00   0.00   0.00   0.00   0.00
> round(table(housing$Exterior1st)/nrow(housing),2)
AsbShng AsphShn BrkComm BrkFace  CBlock CemntBd HdBoard ImStucc
MetalSd
   0.02    0.00    0.00    0.03    0.00    0.04    0.15    0.00
   0.15
Plywood   Stone  Stucco VinylSd Wd Sdng WdShing
   0.08    0.00    0.01    0.35    0.14    0.02
```

In many practical problems, it appears that there will be **factor variables** that have some levels that occur very infrequently. Now, if we have new levels in the test/validation partition, it is not possible to make predictions. From a statistical perspective, we have a technical problem: losing too many **degrees of freedom**. A rudimentary approach is pursued here, and we will simply put together all the observations in the Others umbrella. A Truncate_Factor function is created, and this has two arguments: x and alpha. The x object is the variable to be given to the function, and alpha is the specified fraction below which any variable frequency would be pooled to obtain Others.

If there are certain levels of a factor that are new in the test dataset, no analytical method will be able to incorporate the influence. Thus, in cases where we have too many infrequent levels, the chances of some levels not being included in the training dataset will be high and the prediction will not yield the output for the test observations.

The `Truncate_Factor` function is now created:

```
> Truncate_Factor <- function(x,alpha){
+    xc <- as.character(x); n <- length(x)
+    if(length(unique(x))<=20) {
+      critical <- n*alpha
+        xc[xc %in% names(which((prop.table(table(xc)))<alpha))] <-
"Others"
+    }
+    xc <- as.factor(xc)
+    return(xc)
+ }
> for(i in 1:ncol(housing)){
+    if(any(class(housing[,i]) == c('character','factor')))
+      housing[,i] = Truncate_Factor(housing[,i],0.05)
+ }
> table(housing$Condition2)/nrow(housing)
  Norm Others
  0.99   0.01
> table(housing$Exterior1st)/nrow(housing)
HdBoard MetalSd  Others Plywood VinylSd Wd Sdng
  0.151   0.154   0.126   0.076   0.351   0.141
```

We can now see that the `Others` level is more frequent and if we randomly create partitions, it is very likely that the problem of unknown levels will not occur.

You may recollect that we have eliminated the variables that have excessive missing observations thus far. This does not mean that we are free of missing data, as can be quickly noticed:

```
> sum(is.na(housing))
[1] 474
> prod(dim(housing))
[1] 198492
```

The 474 values can't be ignored. Missing data imputation is an important way of filling the missing values. Although the EM algorithm is a popular method to achieve that, we will apply the Random Forests technique to simulate the missing observations. The missForest package was introduced in *Chapter 4, Random Forests*, and an example was used to simulate the missing values. We will apply this function to the housing data frame. Since the default number of variables chosen in this function is mtry=5 and we have 68 variables in housing, the number of variables chosen for splitting a node is changed to about p/3 and hence the option of mtry=20 is seen in the next R block. On a machine with 8 GB of RAM, the next single-line code takes several hours to run. Next, we will apply the missForest function, save the imputed object for future reference, and create the test and training dataset with imputed values:

```
> housing_impute <- missForest(housing,maxiter = 10,ntree=500,mtry=20)
  missForest iteration 1 in progress...done!
  missForest iteration 2 in progress...done!
  missForest iteration 3 in progress...done!
  missForest iteration 4 in progress...done!
  missForest iteration 5 in progress...done!
  missForest iteration 6 in progress...done!
  missForest iteration 7 in progress...done!
There were 14 warnings (use warnings() to see them)
> save(housing_impute,file=
+ '../Data/Housing/housing_covariates_impute.Rdata')
> ht_imp <- cbind(housing_impute$ximp[1:nrow(housing_train),],
+ housing_train$SalePrice)
> save(ht_imp,file='../Data/Housing/ht_imp.Rdata')
> htest_imp <- housing_impute$ximp[(nrow(housing_train)+1):nrow(
+ housing),]
> save(htest_imp,file='../Data/Housing/htest_imp.Rdata')
```

The reader should certainly run the missForest code line on their local machine. However, to save time, the reader can also skip the line and then load the ht_imp and htest_imp objects from the code bundle. The next section will show a way of visualizing a large dataset and two data reduction methods.

Visualization and variable reduction

In the previous section, the housing data underwent a lot of analytical pre-processing, and we are now ready to further analyze this. First, we begin with visualization. Since we have a lot of variables, the visualization on the R visual device is slightly difficult. As seen in earlier chapters, to visualize the random forests and other large, complex structures, we will initiate a PDF device and store the graphs in it. In the housing dataset, the main variable is the housing price and so we will first name the output variable `SalePrice`. We need to visualize the data in a way that facilitates the relationship between the numerous variables and the `SalePrice`. The independent variables can be either numeric or categorical. If the variables are numeric, a scatterplot will indicate the kind of relationship between the variable and the `SalePrice` regressand. If the independent variable is categorical/factor, we will visualize the boxplot at each level of the factor. The `pdf`, `plot`, and `boxplot` functions will help in generating the required plots:

```
> load("../Data/Housing/ht_imp_author.Rdata")
> names(ht_imp)[69] <- "SalePrice"
> SP <- ht_imp$SalePrice
> pdf("../Output/Visualizing_Housing_Data.pdf")
> for(i in 1:68){
+    if(class(ht_imp[,i])=="numeric") {
+      plot(ht_imp[,i],SP,xlab=names(ht_imp)[i],ylab="Sales Price")
+      title(paste("Scatter plot of Sales Price against ",
+ names(ht_imp)[i]))
+    }
+    if(class(ht_imp[,i])=="factor") {
+      boxplot(SP~ht_imp[,i],xlab=names(ht_imp)[i],ylab=
+ "Sales Price",notch=TRUE)
+      title(paste("Boxplot of Salesprice by ",names(ht_imp)[i]))
+    }
+ }
> dev.off()
null device
          1
```

The `ht_imp` object is loaded from the `ht_imp_author.Rdata` file. Note that, if you run the `missForest` function on your own and work on that file, then the results will be different from `ht_imp_author.Rdata`. The `pdf` function is known to initiate a file of the same name, as seen many times earlier. For the numeric variable, the `if` condition is checked and a scatter plot is displayed with the `xlab` taking the actual name of the variable as a name for the label along the *x* axis. The `title` function slaps the output of the `paste` function, and the `paste` function ensures that we have a suitable title for the generated plot. Similar conditions are tested for the factor variables. We will now look at some of the interesting plots. The first plot of `SalePrice` with `MSSubClass` (see the `Visualizing_Housing_Data.pdf` file) is the following:

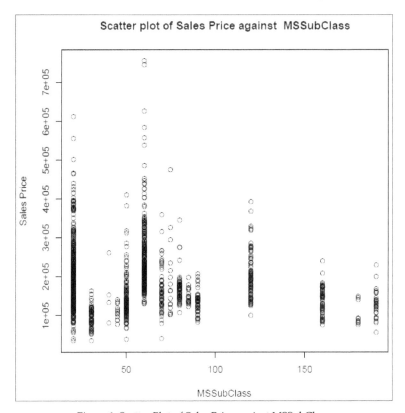

Figure 1: Scatter Plot of Sales Price against MSSubClass

 Note here that although we specified the `MSSubClass` variable as a numeric variable, the scatterplot does not give the same impression. Here, the values of the `MSSubClass` variable are cluttered around a specific point and then the scale jumps to the next value.

In short, it does not appear to be a continuous variable and this can be easily verified using the following:

```
> table(ht_imp$MSSubClass)
  20   30   40   45   50   60   70   75   80   85   90  120  160  180  190
 536   69    4   12  144  299   60   16   58   20   52   87   63   10   30
```

Exercise: The reader should convert the `MSSubClass` variable to a factor and then apply `Truncate_Factor` to reduce the noise. Identify other numeric variables exhibiting this property in the `Visualizing_Housing_Data.pdf` file.

Let's now look at the boxplot for the `MSZoning` factor variable:

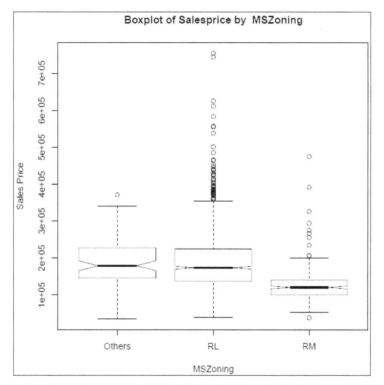

Figure 2: Box plots of Sales Price at Three Levels of MSZoning

The points beyond the whiskers indicate the presence of outliers. However, with complex problems, the interpretation is also likely to go awfully wrong. The notches are a useful trick in the display of boxplots. If the notches do not overlap for two levels of variables, it means that the levels are significant and the information is therefore useful, as seen in the display of the boxplot of `SalePrice` against the `MSZoning` levels.

The next display of the scatterplot of `SalePrice` against `LotArea` is taken up:

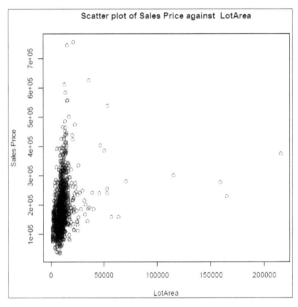

Figure 3: Scatter Plot of Sales Price against Lot Area

Clearly, the scatterplot shows that there is no meaningful relationship between the two variables `SalePrice` and `LotArea`. A different type of display is seen between `SalePrice` and `TotalBsmtSF` in the following figure:

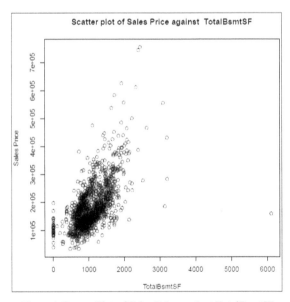

Figure 4: Scatter Plot of Sales Price against TotalBsmtSF

We can clearly see an outlier in the `TotalBsmtSF` value at the extreme right of the figure. There is also a cluttering of values at 0 with `TotalBsmtSF`, which might be controlled by some other variable. Alternatively, it may be discovered that there is a zero-inflation of the variable and it therefore could be a mixture variable. Similarly, all other plots can be interpreted. The correlation between the `SalePrice` and other numeric variables is obtained next:

```
> cor(ht_imp[sapply(ht_imp,is.numeric)])[,1]
    MSSubClass         LotArea     OverallQual     OverallCond       YearBuilt
        1.0000         -0.1398          0.0326         -0.0593          0.0279
   YearRemodAdd       MasVnrArea      BsmtFinSF1      BsmtFinSF2       BsmtUnfSF
        0.0406          0.0206         -0.0698         -0.0656         -0.1408
    TotalBsmtSF        X1stFlrSF       X2ndFlrSF    LowQualFinSF       GrLivArea
       -0.2385         -0.2518          0.3079          0.0465          0.0749
   BsmtFullBath     BsmtHalfBath        FullBath        HalfBath     BedroomAbvGr
        0.0035         -0.0023          0.1316          0.1774         -0.0234
   KitchenAbvGr     TotRmsAbvGrd      Fireplaces      GarageCars      GarageArea
        0.2817          0.0404         -0.0456         -0.0401         -0.0987
     WoodDeckSF      OpenPorchSF   EnclosedPorch      X3SsnPorch     ScreenPorch
       -0.0126         -0.0061         -0.0120         -0.0438         -0.0260
       PoolArea          MiscVal          MoSold          YrSold       SalePrice
        0.0083         -0.0077         -0.0136         -0.0214         -0.0843
```

Exercise: Interpret all the relationships in the `Visualizing_Housing_Data.pdf` file and sort the correlations by their absolute value in the preceding R code.

We made use of the variable of interest for the visualization, and in turn this led to useful insights. As previously stated, *p = 68* is a lot of covariates/independent variables. With big data, the complexity will increase in the north direction, and it is known that for many practical applications we have thousands of independent variables. While most visualization techniques are insightful, a shortcoming is that we seldom get insights into higher order relationships. For instance, when it comes to three or more variables, a relationship is seldom richly brought out in graphical displays. It is then important to deploy methods that will reduce the number of variables without being at the expense of information. The two methods of data reduction to be discussed here are **principal component analysis** and **variable clustering**.

Principal Component Analysis (PCA) is a method drawn from the larger pool of **multivariate statistics**. This is useful in data reduction as, given the original number of variables, it tries to give a new set of variables that covers most of the variance of the original data in as few new variables as possible. A brief explanation of PCA is given here.

Suppose we have a random vector of observations $X = (X_1, X_2, ..., X_p)$. Given the random vector X, PCA finds a new vector of *principal components* $Y = (Y_1, Y_2, ..., Y_p)$ such that each Yi is a linear combination of $(X_1, X_2, ..., X_p)$. Furthermore, the principal components are such that the variance of $Y1$ is higher than the variance of $Y2$ and both are uncorrelated; the variance of $Y2$ is higher than the variance of $Y3$ and $Y1$; $Y2$ and $Y3$ are uncorrelated, and so forth. This relates to $Var(Y_1) \geq Var(Y_2) \geq \cdots \geq Var(Y_p)$, none of which are correlated with each other. The principal components are set up so that most of the variance of $(X_1, X_2, ..., X_p)$ is accumulated in the first few principal components (see Chapter 15 of Tattar, et al. (2016) for more information on this). As a result, we can achieve a lot of data reduction. However, the fundamental premise of PCA is that $X = (X_1, X_2, ..., X_p)$ is a vector of continuous random variables. In our dataset, we also have factor variables. Consequently, we can't use PCA for our purposes. A crude method is to ignore the factor variables and simply run the data reduction on the continuous variables. Instead, we would use factor analysis for mixed data, and the software functions to carry this out are available in the FactoMineR package.

Since data reduction only needs to be performed on the covariates and we do not have longitudinal data, the data reduction is applied on the entire set of observations available, and not only on the training dataset. The rationale for carrying out the data reduction on the entire dataset is the same as for truncating the number of levels of a factor variable. The housing_impute data frame is available in housing_covariates_impute.Rdata. We will first load it and then apply the FAMD function to carry out the factor analysis for mixed data:

```
> load("../Data/Housing/housing_covariates_impute.Rdata")
> housing_covariates <- housing_impute$ximp
> housing_cov_famd <- FAMD(housing_covariates,ncp=68,graph=FALSE)
> colnames(housing_cov_famd$eig) <- c("Component","Variance",
+     "Cumulative")
> housing_cov_famd$eig
           Component       Variance Cumulative
comp 1   12.2267562274 9.3334017003  9.33340170
comp 2    5.4502085801 4.1604645650 13.49386627
comp 3    4.5547218487 3.4768869074 16.97075317
comp 4    4.0710151565 3.1076451576 20.07839833
comp 5    3.1669428163 2.4175136002 22.49591193
comp 6    2.8331129142 2.1626816139 24.65859354
comp 7    2.6471571767 2.0207306692 26.67932421
comp 8    2.1871762983 1.6696002277 28.34892444
comp 9    2.1563067109 1.6460356572 29.99496010
comp 10   2.0083000432 1.5330534681 31.52801357


comp 66   0.7691341212 0.5871252834 80.58667899
```

```
comp 67   0.7648033308 0.5838193365 81.17049833
comp 68   0.7559712365 0.5770772798 81.74757561
> windows(height=100,width=200)
> pareto.chart(housing_cov_famd$eig[,2])
```

In the FAMD function, the ncp option is set as equal to 68, since that is the number of variables we have. We would also like to look at how the principal components respond to the dataset. If the graph=TRUE option is selected, the function will display the related graphs. The colnames of housing_cov_famd$eig is changed as the default names don't do justice to the output it generates. We can see from the Eigen value analysis that the overall 68 components do not complete with the entire variation available in the data. Furthermore, even for the 50% of variance explained by the components, we need to pick 26 of them. As a consequence, the data reduction here does not seem to be productive. However, this does not mean that performance will be poor in the next set of analyses. When applying the pareto.chart function from the quality control package qcc, on frequency data gives a Pareto chart. As demonstrated by the percentages, it is clear that if we need 90% of the variance in the original variables to be explained by the principal components, then we will need nearly 60 principal components. Consequently, the number of variables reduced is only 8 and the interpretation is also an additional complexity. This is not good news. However, we will still save the data of principal components:

```
> save(housing_cov_famd,file='../Data/Housing/Housing_FAMD.Rdata')
> Housing_FAMD_Data <- housing_cov_famd$ind$coord
> save(Housing_FAMD_Data,file='../Data/Housing/
+ Housing_FAMD_Data.Rdata')
```

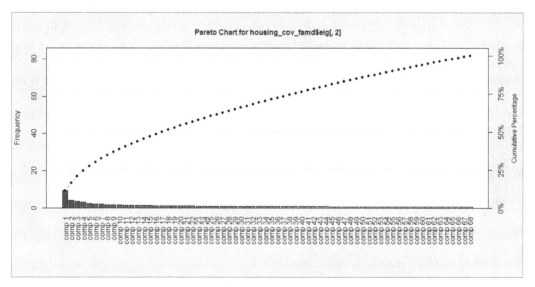

Figure 5: Pareto Chart for Contribution of Principal Components

Exercise: Explore the use of the PCAmix function from the R package PCAmix to reduce the number of variables through principal component analysis.

Variable clustering

Variables can be grouped together as we do with observations. To achieve this, we will use the kmeansvar function from the ClustOfVar package. The variable clustering package needs to be specified as the quantitative (numeric) variable separately, and the qualitative (factor) variables also need to be specified separately. In addition, we need to specify how many variable clusters we need. The init option helps in its specification here. The is.numeric and is.factor functions are used to identify the numeric and factor variables and the variable clusters are set up:

```
> Housing_VarClust <- kmeansvar(
+       X.quanti = housing_covariates[sapply(housing_covariates,
+                        is.numeric)],
+       X.quali = housing_covariates[sapply(housing_covariates,
+                        is.factor)],init=4)
Error: Some categorical variables have same names of categories,
            rename categories or use the option rename.level=TRUE to
rename it automatically
```

Oops! It is an error. It is important to recollect that all infrequent levels of factor variables have been labeled as Others. It might be the case that there are other levels that have the same name across variables, which is a very common label choice in survey data, including options such as Very Dissatisfied < Dissatisfied < OK < Good < Excellent. This choice of variable levels can be the same across multiple questions. However, we need the names of the levels to be distinct across all variables. A manual renaming of labels will be futile and an excessive waste of time. Consequently, we will approach the problem with a set of names that will be unique across the variables, namely the variable names themselves. The variable names will be concatenated with the variable levels and thus we will have distinct factor levels throughout. Using the paste0 function and mapvalues from the plyr package, we will carry out the level renaming manipulation first and then apply kmeansvar again:

```
> hc2 <- housing_covariates
> for(i in 1:ncol(hc2)){
+   if(class(hc2[,i])=="factor") {
+     hc2[,i] <- mapvalues(hc2[,i],from=levels(hc2[,i]),
+     to=paste0(names(hc2)[i],"_",levels(hc2[,i])))
+   }
+ }
> Housing_VarClust <- kmeansvar(
+         X.quanti = hc2[sapply(hc2,is.numeric)],
```

```
+           X.quali = hc2[sapply(hc2,is.factor)], init=4)
> Housing_VarClust$cluster
    MSSubClass         LotArea     OverallQual     OverallCond       YearBuilt
             2               1               1               4               4
  YearRemodAdd      MasVnrArea      BsmtFinSF1      BsmtFinSF2       BsmtUnfSF
             4               3               1               2               4

      BsmtCond    BsmtExposure    BsmtFinType1    BsmtFinType2         Heating
             3               1               4               2               3
     HeatingQC      CentralAir      Electrical     KitchenQual      Functional
             4               1               4               4               4
    PavedDrive        SaleType   SaleCondition
             1               4               4
> summary(Housing_VarClust)

Call:
kmeansvar(X.quanti = hc2[sapply(hc2, is.numeric)], X.quali =
hc2[sapply(hc2,      is.factor)], init = 4)

number of iterations:  2

Data:
   number of observations:  2919
   number of  variables:  68
       number of numerical variables:  34
       number of categorical variables:  34
   number of clusters:  4

Cluster  1 :
          squared loading correlation
X1stFlrSF             0.6059          0.778
TotalBsmtSF           0.5913          0.769
OverallQual           0.5676          0.753

PoolArea              0.0166          0.129
MiscVal               0.0059          0.077
MoSold                0.0024          0.049


Cluster  2 :
          squared loading correlation
X2ndFlrSF             0.8584         -0.927
HouseStyle            0.7734             NA
TotRmsAbvGrd          0.5185         -0.720

BsmtFinType2          0.0490             NA
```

```
BsmtFinSF2                0.0408        0.202
X3SsnPorch                0.0039        0.063


Cluster  3 :
          squared loading correlation
MasVnrType            0.83189              NA
MasVnrArea            0.82585          -0.909
Heating              0.03532              NA
BsmtCond             0.02681              NA
Utilities            0.00763              NA
YrSold               0.00084           0.029


Cluster  4 :
            squared loading correlation
Neighborhood          0.7955              NA
YearBuilt             0.7314          -0.855
BsmtQual              0.6792              NA

BsmtHalfBath          0.0087           0.093
Street                0.0041              NA
Condition2            0.0015              NA


Gain in cohesion (in %):  11.56
```

The important question is that although we have marked the variables in groups, how do we use them? The answer is provided in the coefficients of the variables within each group. To display the coefficients, run $coef in adjunct to the clustvar object Housing_VarClust:

```
> Housing_VarClust$coef
$cluster1
                        [,1]
const              -7.1e+00
LotArea             2.1e-05
OverallQual         2.2e-01

CentralAir_N       -5.3e-01
CentralAir_Y        3.8e-02
PavedDrive_N       -5.2e-01
PavedDrive_Others  -2.8e-01
PavedDrive_Y        5.0e-02

$cluster2
                        [,1]
```

```
const                       3.79789
MSSubClass                 -0.00472
BsmtFinSF2                  0.00066

HouseStyle_1.5Fin          -0.11967
HouseStyle_1Story           0.41892
HouseStyle_2Story          -0.69610
HouseStyle_Others           0.10816
BsmtFinType2_Others  0.33286
BsmtFinType2_Unf           -0.04491

$cluster3
                               [,1]
const                      -33.1748
MasVnrArea                  -0.0039
YrSold                       0.0167

BsmtCond_TA                 -0.0365
Heating_GasA                -0.0179
Heating_Others               1.1425

$cluster4
                               [,1]
const                      45.30644
OverallCond                 0.09221
YearBuilt                   -0.01009

SaleCondition_Normal        0.03647
SaleCondition_Others        0.20598
SaleCondition_Partial -0.58877
```

Now, for the observations in the data, the corresponding variables are multiplied by the coefficients of the variable clusters to obtain a single vector for that variable cluster. Consequently, we will then have reduced the 68 variables to 4 variables.

Exercise: Obtain the cluster variables for the `housing_covariates` data frame using the coefficients displayed previously.

The data pre-processing for the housing problem is now complete. In the next section, we will build the base learners for the regression data.

Regression models

Sir Francis Galton invented the simple linear regression model near the end of the nineteenth century. The example used looked at how a parent's height influences the height of their child. This study used data and laid the basis of regression analysis. The correlation between the height of parents and children is well known, and using data on 928 pairs of height measurements, a linear regression was developed by Galton. In an equivalent form, however, the method might have been in informal use before Galton officially invented it. The simple linear regression model consists of a single input (independent) variable and the output is also a single output.

In this supervised learning method, the target variable/output/dependent variable is a continuous variable, and it can also take values in intervals, including non-negative and real numbers. The input/independent variable has no restrictions and as such it can be numeric, categorical, or in any other form we used earlier for the classification problem. Interestingly though, linear regression models started much earlier than classification regression models such as logistic regression models. Machine learning problems are more often conceptualized based on the classification problem, and the ensemble methods, especially boosting, have been developed by using classification as the motive. The primary reason for this is that the error improvisation gives a nice intuition, and the secondary reason might be due to famous machine learning examples such as digit recognition, spam classification, and so on.

The simple linear regression extension is the multiple linear regression where we allow more than one independent variable. We will drop the convention of simple and multiple regression altogether and adhere simply to regression. As a base learner, the linear regression model is introduced first. Interesting datasets will be used to kick-start the linear regression model.

Linear regression model

In more formal terms, let $X_1, X_2, ..., X_p$ be a set of p independent variables, and Y be the variable of interest. We need to understand the regressand Y in terms of the regressors $X_1, X_2, ..., X_p$. The linear regression model is given by:

$$Y = \beta_0 + \beta_1 X_1 + \beta_2 X_2 + \cdots + \beta_p X_p + \in$$

The relationship between Y and the regressors is in linear form; β_0 is the intercept term; $\beta_1, \beta_2, \ldots, \beta_p$ are the regression coefficients; and $\in$ is the error term. It needs to be mentioned that the linearity is in terms of the regression coefficients. It is also important to note that the regressors can come in any form and can sometimes be taken as other forms, including log, exponential, and quadratic. The error term $\in$ is often assumed to follow the normal distribution with unknown variance and zero mean. More details about the linear regression model can be found in Draper and Smith (1999), Chatterjee and Hadi (2012), and Montgomery, et al. (2005). For information on the implementation of this technique using R software, see Chapter 12 of Tattar, et al. (2016) or Chapter 6 of Tattar (2017).

First, we will explain the core notions of the linear regression model using the Galton dataset. The data is loaded from the RSADBE package and, using the lm function, we can build the model:

```
> data(galton)
> cor(galton)
       child parent
child   1.00   0.46
parent  0.46   1.00
> plot(galton)
> head(galton)
   child parent
1     62     70
2     62     68
3     62     66
4     62     64
5     62     64
6     62     68
> cp_lm <- lm(child~parent,data=galton)
> summary(cp_lm)
Call:
lm(formula = child ~ parent, data = galton)

Residuals:
    Min      1Q  Median      3Q     Max
 -7.805  -1.366   0.049   1.634   5.926

Coefficients:
             Estimate Std. Error t value Pr(>|t|)
(Intercept)  23.9415     2.8109    8.52   <2e-16 ***
parent        0.6463     0.0411   15.71   <2e-16 ***
---
```

```
Signif. codes:  0 '***' 0.001 '**' 0.01 '*' 0.05 '.' 0.1 ' ' 1

Residual standard error: 2.2 on 926 degrees of freedom
Multiple R-squared:  0.21,    Adjusted R-squared:  0.21
F-statistic:  247 on 1 and 926 DF,  p-value: <2e-16
```

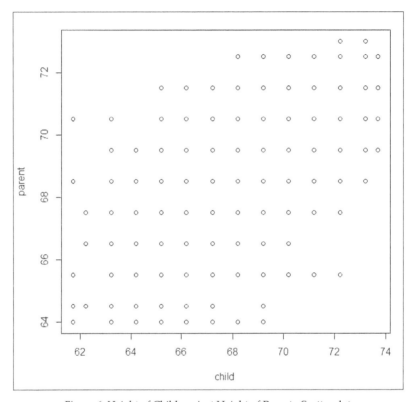

Figure 6: Height of Child against Height of Parent - Scatterplot

What does this code block tell us? First, we will load the galton data from the RSADBE package and then look at the `cor` correlation between the height of parent and child. The correlation is `0.46`, which seems to be a strong, positive correlation. The plot scatterplot indicates the positive correlation too, and consequently we proceed to build the linear regression model of the height of the child as a function of the height of the parent. It is advisable to look at the p-value associated with the model first, which in this case is given in the last line of `summary(cp_lm)` as `<2e-16`. The smaller p-value means that we reject the null hypothesis of the model being insignificant, and hence the current fitted model is useful. The p-values associated with the intercept and variable term are both `<2e-16`, and that again means that the terms are significant. The regression coefficient of `0.6463` implies that if a parent is an inch taller, the child's height would increase by a magnitude of the regression coefficient.

The value of `Multiple R-squared` (technically simple R-squared) and `Adjusted R-squared` are both `0.21`, which is expected as we have a single variable in the model. The interpretation of R-squared is that if we multiply it by 100 (so 21%, in this case), the resulting number is the percentage of variation in the data (height of the child) as explained by the fitted value. The higher the value of this metric, the better the model is. In this example, it means that the height of the parent explains only about 21% of the variation of the child's height. This means that we need to consider other variables. In this case, one starting point might be to consider the height of both parents. The multiple R-square value will keep on increasing if you add more variables, and hence it is preferable to use the more robust adjusted R-square value. Is it possible to obtain a perfect R-square, for example 1, or 100%?

A dataset named `Mantel` is available online in the bundle package, and we will build a linear regression model to check for its R-square. To do this, we import the dataset and run the `lm` function over it:

```
> Mantel <- read.csv("../Data/Mantel.csv")
> Mantel
   Y   X1   X2   X3
1  5    1 1004  6.0
2  6  200  806  7.3
3  8  -50 1058 11.0
4  9  909  100 13.0
5 11  506  505 13.1
> Mantel_lm <- lm(Y~.,data=Mantel)
> summary(Mantel_lm)

Call:
lm(formula = Y ~ ., data = Mantel)

Residuals:
         1         2         3         4         5
-2.49e-13  2.92e-13  3.73e-14 -3.89e-14 -4.14e-14

Coefficients:
             Estimate Std. Error  t value Pr(>|t|)
(Intercept) -1.00e+03   2.73e-10 -3.67e+12 1.7e-13 ***
X1           1.00e+00   2.73e-13  3.67e+12 1.7e-13 ***
X2           1.00e+00   2.73e-13  3.67e+12 1.7e-13 ***
X3           1.33e-14   2.16e-13  6.00e-02    0.96
---
Signif. codes:  0 '***' 0.001 '**' 0.01 '*' 0.05 '.' 0.1 ' ' 1

Residual standard error: 3.9e-13 on 1 degrees of freedom
Multiple R-squared:     1,    Adjusted R-squared:      1
F-statistic: 4.99e+25 on 3 and 1 DF,  p-value: 1.04e-13
```

Here, we can see that the R-square is perfect. Let's have some fun before we embark on the serious task of analyzing the housing price data.

For the `galton` dataset, we will add a new variable called `frankenstein`, and this variable will be the residuals from the fitted model `cp_lm`. A new dataset will be created, which will augment the `galton` dataset with the residuals; the linear model will then be fitted using the `lm` function and its R-square will be checked:

```
> d2 <- cbind(galton,residuals(cp_lm))
> names(d2)
[1] "child"            "parent"              "residuals(cp_lm)"
> names(d2) <- c("child","parent","frankenstein")
> cpf_lm <- lm(child~.,d2)
> summary(cpf_lm)
Call:
lm(formula = child ~ ., data = d2)
Residuals:
      Min        1Q     Median        3Q        Max
-2.60e-15 -7.40e-16 -3.00e-16  2.10e-16  1.02e-13
Coefficients:
              Estimate Std. Error  t value Pr(>|t|)
(Intercept)   2.39e+01   5.74e-15 4.17e+15   <2e-16 ***
parent        6.46e-01   8.40e-17 7.69e+15   <2e-16 ***
frankenstein 1.00e+00   6.71e-17 1.49e+16   <2e-16 ***
---
Signif. codes:  0 '***' 0.001 '**' 0.01 '*' 0.05 '.' 0.1 ' ' 1
Residual standard error: 4.6e-15 on 925 degrees of freedom
Multiple R-squared:     1,     Adjusted R-squared:     1
F-statistic: 1.41e+32 on 2 and 925 DF,  p-value: <2e-16
Warning message:
In summary.lm(cpf_lm) : essentially perfect fit: summary may be
unreliable
```

Don't ignore the warning function. You may recall that such a warning function was not displayed for the `Mantel` dataset. This is because this warning can be eliminated by adding a little noise to the `frankenstein` variable, consequently making him more monstrous:

```
> d2$frankenstein <- jitter(d2$frankenstein)
> summary(lm(child~.,d2))
Call:
lm(formula = child ~ ., data = d2)
Residuals:
      Min        1Q     Median        3Q        Max
-0.004072 -0.002052  0.000009  0.001962  0.004121
```

```
Coefficients:
             Estimate Std. Error t value Pr(>|t|)
(Intercept)  2.39e+01  2.92e-03     8210   <2e-16 ***
parent       6.46e-01  4.27e-05    15143   <2e-16 ***
frankenstein 1.00e+00  3.41e-05    29331   <2e-16 ***
---
Signif. codes:  0 '***' 0.001 '**' 0.01 '*' 0.05 '.' 0.1 ' ' 1
Residual standard error: 0.0023 on 925 degrees of freedom
Multiple R-squared:      1,     Adjusted R-squared:      1
F-statistic: 5.45e+08 on 2 and 925 DF,  p-value: <2e-16
```

We have thus mastered the art of obtaining a perfect R-square. Playtime is over now; let's move on to the housing dataset. We previously saved the housing dataset for the train and test blocks as the `ht_imp.Rdata` and `htest_imp.Rdata` files. The author's filename version has been modified by renaming the filenames as `_author` to make things clearer. We then separate the training block into training and testing ones. Then, we use the `load` function to import the data, partition it with the `sample` function, and then use the `lm` function to build the regression model:

```
> load("../Data/Housing/ht_imp_author.Rdata")
> load("../Data/Housing/htest_imp_author.Rdata")
> ls()
[1] "ht_imp"     "htest_imp"
> Y <- "SalePrice"
> X <- names(ht_imp)[-69]
> set.seed(12345)
> BV <- sample(c("Build","Validate"),nrow(ht_imp),replace = TRUE,
+              prob=c(0.7,0.3))
> HT_Build <- ht_imp[BV=="Build",]
> HT_Validate <- ht_imp[BV=="Validate",]
> HT_Formula <- as.formula("SalePrice~.")
> HT_LM_01 <- lm(HT_Formula,data=HT_Build)
> summary(HT_LM_01)

Call:
lm(formula = HT_Formula, data = HT_Build)

Residuals:
    Min      1Q  Median      3Q     Max
-268498  -12222    -409   11351  240990

Coefficients: (2 not defined because of singularities)
                   Estimate Std. Error t value Pr(>|t|)
(Intercept)        -2.87e+03   1.53e+06    0.00  0.99850
MSSubClass         -1.52e+02   7.95e+01   -1.91  0.05583 .
```

```
MSZoningRL              8.55e+03    6.27e+03    1.36   0.17317
MSZoningRM              1.20e+04    7.50e+03    1.60   0.11011
LotArea                 4.90e-01    1.21e-01    4.04   5.8e-05  ***
StreetPave              2.81e+04    1.70e+04    1.65   0.09979  .
LotShapeOthers         -3.59e+03    6.12e+03   -0.59   0.55733
LotShapeReg             1.25e+03    2.40e+03    0.52   0.60111
LandContourOthers      -1.22e+04    3.99e+03   -3.05   0.00236  **
UtilitiesOthers        -5.76e+04    3.25e+04   -1.77   0.07637  .
LotConfigCulDSac        1.21e+04    4.96e+03    2.44   0.01477  *
LotConfigInside        -1.62e+03    2.58e+03   -0.63   0.52972
LotConfigOthers        -1.28e+04    5.57e+03   -2.30   0.02144  *


EnclosedPorch           6.95e+00    1.91e+01    0.36   0.71628
X3SsnPorch              3.81e+01    3.87e+01    0.98   0.32497
ScreenPorch             3.78e+01    2.01e+01    1.88   0.05988  .
PoolArea                5.13e+01    2.60e+01    1.98   0.04842  *
MiscVal                 5.13e-02    6.57e+00    0.01   0.99377
MoSold                 -4.38e+02    3.67e+02   -1.19   0.23313
YrSold                 -1.01e+02    7.53e+02   -0.13   0.89376
SaleTypeOthers         -4.88e+04    2.19e+04   -2.23   0.02598  *
SaleTypeWD             -5.10e+04    2.20e+04   -2.32   0.02061  *
SaleConditionNormal     1.93e+03    4.31e+03    0.45   0.65421
SaleConditionOthers     1.87e+03    7.42e+03    0.25   0.80168
SaleConditionPartial   -3.21e+04    2.21e+04   -1.45   0.14641
---
Signif. codes:  0 '***' 0.001 '**' 0.01 '*' 0.05 '.' 0.1 ' ' 1

Residual standard error: 28400 on 861 degrees of freedom
Multiple R-squared:  0.884,   Adjusted R-squared:  0.867
F-statistic: 51.1 on 129 and 861 DF,  p-value: <2e-16
```

The accuracy assessment of the fitted linear model will be carried out after fitting three more base learners. The adjusted R-square value is about 87%. However, we have 68 variables, and we can see from the p-value of the previous summary that a lot of variables don't have p-values less than either 0.05 or 0.1. Consequently, we need to get rid of the insignificant variables. The step function can be slapped on many fitted regression models to eliminate the insignificant variables while retaining most of the model characteristics.

Running the step function in the R session leads to a huge display of output in the console. The initial output is lost to the space restrictions. Consequently, the author ran the script with the option of **Compile Report from R Script in RStudio**, chose the option of MS Word as the report output format, and saved that file. An abbreviated version of the results from that file is given here:

```
## Start:  AIC=20446.87
## SalePrice ~ MSSubClass + MSZoning + LotArea + Street + LotShape +
##      LandContour + Utilities + LotConfig + LandSlope + Neighborhood
+
##      Condition1 + Condition2 + BldgType + HouseStyle + OverallQual +
##      OverallCond + YearBuilt + YearRemodAdd + RoofStyle + RoofMatl +
##      Exterior1st + Exterior2nd + MasVnrType + MasVnrArea + ExterQual
+
##      ExterCond + Foundation + BsmtQual + BsmtCond + BsmtExposure +
##      BsmtFinType1 + BsmtFinSF1 + BsmtFinType2 + BsmtFinSF2 +
BsmtUnfSF +
##      TotalBsmtSF + Heating + HeatingQC + CentralAir + Electrical +
##      X1stFlrSF + X2ndFlrSF + LowQualFinSF + GrLivArea + BsmtFullBath
+
##      BsmtHalfBath + FullBath + HalfBath + BedroomAbvGr +
KitchenAbvGr +
##      KitchenQual + TotRmsAbvGrd + Functional + Fireplaces +
GarageCars +
##      GarageArea + PavedDrive + WoodDeckSF + OpenPorchSF +
EnclosedPorch +
##      X3SsnPorch + ScreenPorch + PoolArea + MiscVal + MoSold +
##      YrSold + SaleType + SaleCondition
##
##
## Step:  AIC=20446.87
## SalePrice ~ MSSubClass + MSZoning + LotArea + Street + LotShape +
##      LandContour + Utilities + LotConfig + LandSlope + Neighborhood
+
##      Condition1 + Condition2 + BldgType + HouseStyle + OverallQual +
##      OverallCond + YearBuilt + YearRemodAdd + RoofStyle + RoofMatl +
##      Exterior1st + Exterior2nd + MasVnrType + MasVnrArea + ExterQual
+
##      ExterCond + Foundation + BsmtQual + BsmtCond + BsmtExposure +
##      BsmtFinType1 + BsmtFinSF1 + BsmtFinType2 + BsmtFinSF2 +
BsmtUnfSF +
##      TotalBsmtSF + Heating + HeatingQC + CentralAir + Electrical +
##      X1stFlrSF + X2ndFlrSF + LowQualFinSF + BsmtFullBath +
BsmtHalfBath +
```

```
##      FullBath + HalfBath + BedroomAbvGr + KitchenAbvGr + KitchenQual
+
##      TotRmsAbvGrd + Functional + Fireplaces + GarageCars +
GarageArea +
##      PavedDrive + WoodDeckSF + OpenPorchSF + EnclosedPorch +
X3SsnPorch +
##      ScreenPorch + PoolArea + MiscVal + MoSold + YrSold + SaleType +
##      SaleCondition
##
##
## Step:  AIC=20446.87
## SalePrice ~ MSSubClass + MSZoning + LotArea + Street + LotShape +
##      LandContour + Utilities + LotConfig + LandSlope + Neighborhood
+
##      Condition1 + Condition2 + BldgType + HouseStyle + OverallQual +
##      OverallCond + YearBuilt + YearRemodAdd + RoofStyle + RoofMatl +
##      Exterior1st + Exterior2nd + MasVnrType + MasVnrArea + ExterQual
+
##      ExterCond + Foundation + BsmtQual + BsmtCond + BsmtExposure +
##      BsmtFinType1 + BsmtFinSF1 + BsmtFinType2 + BsmtFinSF2 +
BsmtUnfSF +
##      Heating + HeatingQC + CentralAir + Electrical + X1stFlrSF +
##      X2ndFlrSF + LowQualFinSF + BsmtFullBath + BsmtHalfBath +
##      FullBath + HalfBath + BedroomAbvGr + KitchenAbvGr + KitchenQual
+
##      TotRmsAbvGrd + Functional + Fireplaces + GarageCars +
GarageArea +
##      PavedDrive + WoodDeckSF + OpenPorchSF + EnclosedPorch +
X3SsnPorch +
##      ScreenPorch + PoolArea + MiscVal + MoSold + YrSold + SaleType +
##      SaleCondition
##
##                 Df  Sum of Sq        RSS    AIC
## - Exterior2nd    5 2.6926e+09 6.9890e+11 20441
## - HeatingQC      3 8.4960e+08 6.9706e+11 20442
## - MasVnrType     3 9.3578e+08 6.9714e+11 20442
## - OverallQual    1 3.2987e+10 7.2919e+11 20491
## - X2ndFlrSF      1 3.9790e+10 7.3600e+11 20500
## - Neighborhood  24 1.6770e+11 8.6391e+11 20613
##
## Step:  AIC=20440.69
## SalePrice ~ MSSubClass + MSZoning + LotArea + Street + LotShape +
##      LandContour + Utilities + LotConfig + LandSlope + Neighborhood
+
##      Condition1 + Condition2 + BldgType + HouseStyle + OverallQual +
```

```
##       OverallCond + YearBuilt + YearRemodAdd + RoofStyle + RoofMatl +
##       Exterior1st + MasVnrType + MasVnrArea + ExterQual + ExterCond +
##       Foundation + BsmtQual + BsmtCond + BsmtExposure + BsmtFinType1
+
##       BsmtFinSF1 + BsmtFinType2 + BsmtFinSF2 + BsmtUnfSF + Heating +
##       HeatingQC + CentralAir + Electrical + X1stFlrSF + X2ndFlrSF +
##       LowQualFinSF + BsmtFullBath + BsmtHalfBath + FullBath +
HalfBath +
##       BedroomAbvGr + KitchenAbvGr + KitchenQual + TotRmsAbvGrd +
##       Functional + Fireplaces + GarageCars + GarageArea + PavedDrive
+
##       WoodDeckSF + OpenPorchSF + EnclosedPorch + X3SsnPorch +
ScreenPorch +
##       PoolArea + MiscVal + MoSold + YrSold + SaleType + SaleCondition


## Step:  AIC=20386.81
## SalePrice ~ MSSubClass + LotArea + Street + LandContour + Utilities
+
##       LotConfig + LandSlope + Neighborhood + Condition1 + Condition2
+
##       BldgType + HouseStyle + OverallQual + OverallCond + YearBuilt +
##       RoofStyle + RoofMatl + Exterior1st + BsmtQual + BsmtCond +
##       BsmtExposure + BsmtFinType1 + BsmtFinSF1 + BsmtFinType2 +
##       X1stFlrSF + X2ndFlrSF + LowQualFinSF + BsmtFullBath + FullBath
+
##       HalfBath + KitchenAbvGr + KitchenQual + TotRmsAbvGrd +
Functional +
##       Fireplaces + GarageCars + WoodDeckSF + ScreenPorch + PoolArea +
##       MoSold + SaleType
##
##                   Df  Sum of Sq        RSS   AIC
## <none>                          7.1467e+11 20387
## - KitchenAbvGr  1 1.4477e+09 7.1612e+11 20387
## - MoSold        1 1.6301e+09 7.1630e+11 20387
## - BldgType      2 3.1228e+09 7.1779e+11 20387
## - Utilities     1 1.7130e+09 7.1639e+11 20387
## - BsmtCond      1 1.7554e+09 7.1643e+11 20387
## - BsmtFinType2  1 1.8708e+09 7.1654e+11 20387
## - YearBuilt     1 2.0543e+09 7.1673e+11 20388
## - Street        1 2.1163e+09 7.1679e+11 20388
## - LowQualFinSF  1 2.1785e+09 7.1685e+11 20388
## - ScreenPorch   1 2.2387e+09 7.1691e+11 20388
## - MSSubClass    1 2.2823e+09 7.1695e+11 20388
```

```
## - LandSlope       1 2.5566e+09 7.1723e+11 20388
## - PoolArea        1 2.6036e+09 7.1728e+11 20388
## - Exterior1st     5 9.1221e+09 7.2379e+11 20389
## - Functional      1 3.4117e+09 7.1808e+11 20390
## - Condition1      2 4.9604e+09 7.1963e+11 20390
## - BsmtFinSF1      1 3.9442e+09 7.1862e+11 20390
## - Condition2      1 4.0659e+09 7.1874e+11 20390
## - RoofStyle       2 6.1817e+09 7.2085e+11 20391
## - HalfBath        1 5.3010e+09 7.1997e+11 20392
## - FullBath        1 5.4987e+09 7.2017e+11 20392
## - Fireplaces      1 6.0438e+09 7.2072e+11 20393
## - TotRmsAbvGrd    1 7.0166e+09 7.2169e+11 20395
## - LandContour     1 7.7036e+09 7.2238e+11 20395
## - WoodDeckSF      1 8.8947e+09 7.2357e+11 20397
## - LotConfig       3 1.2015e+10 7.2669e+11 20397
## - RoofMatl        1 9.0967e+09 7.2377e+11 20397
## - BsmtFullBath    1 9.4178e+09 7.2409e+11 20398
## - HouseStyle      3 1.2940e+10 7.2761e+11 20399
## - BsmtFinType1    5 1.7704e+10 7.3238e+11 20401
## - SaleType        2 1.5305e+10 7.2998e+11 20404
## - LotArea         1 1.4293e+10 7.2897e+11 20404
## - OverallCond     1 1.8131e+10 7.3280e+11 20410
## - BsmtQual        3 2.3916e+10 7.3859e+11 20413
## - X1stFlrSF       1 2.1106e+10 7.3578e+11 20414
## - BsmtExposure    3 2.8182e+10 7.4285e+11 20419
## - GarageCars      1 2.6886e+10 7.4156e+11 20421
## - KitchenQual     3 3.1267e+10 7.4594e+11 20423
## - OverallQual     1 3.7361e+10 7.5203e+11 20435
## - X2ndFlrSF       1 4.3546e+10 7.5822e+11 20443
## - Neighborhood   24 1.8921e+11 9.0389e+11 20572
```

The `model` is summarized as follows:

```
> summary(HT_LM_Final)

Call:
lm(formula = SalePrice ~ MSSubClass + LotArea + Street + LandContour +
    Utilities + LotConfig + LandSlope + Neighborhood + Condition1 +
    Condition2 + BldgType + HouseStyle + OverallQual + OverallCond +
    YearBuilt + RoofStyle + RoofMatl + Exterior1st + BsmtQual +
    BsmtCond + BsmtExposure + BsmtFinType1 + BsmtFinSF1 + BsmtFinType2
+
    X1stFlrSF + X2ndFlrSF + LowQualFinSF + BsmtFullBath + FullBath +
    HalfBath + KitchenAbvGr + KitchenQual + TotRmsAbvGrd + Functional
+
```

```
        Fireplaces + GarageCars + WoodDeckSF + ScreenPorch + PoolArea +
        MoSold + SaleType, data = HT_Build)

Residuals:
     Min       1Q    Median       3Q      Max
  -272899   -11717      -42    11228   235349

Coefficients:
                      Estimate Std. Error t value Pr(>|t|)
  (Intercept)        -2.64e+05   1.78e+05   -1.48  0.13894
  MSSubClass         -1.27e+02   7.46e+01   -1.70  0.08965 .
  LotArea             4.75e-01   1.12e-01    4.25  2.3e-05 ***

  MoSold             -4.99e+02   3.48e+02   -1.44  0.15136
  SaleTypeOthers     -1.69e+04   5.85e+03   -2.89  0.00396 **
  SaleTypeWD         -1.76e+04   4.00e+03   -4.40  1.2e-05 ***
  ---
  Signif. codes:  0 '***' 0.001 '**' 0.01 '*' 0.05 '.' 0.1 ' ' 1

  Residual standard error: 28100 on 904 degrees of freedom
  Multiple R-squared:  0.881,   Adjusted R-squared:  0.87
  F-statistic: 78.1 on 86 and 904 DF,  p-value: <2e-16
```

The small module covering the `step` function is available in the `Housing_Step_LM.R` file and the output generated by using R Markdown is saved in the file named `Housing_Step_LM.docx`. The output of the `step` function runs over forty-three pages, but we don't have to inspect the variables left out at each step. It suffices to say that a lot of insignificant variables have been eliminated without losing the traits of the model. The accuracy assessment of the validated partition will be seen later. Next, we will extend the linear regression model to the nonlinear model and work out the neural networks.

Exercise: Build linear regression models using the principal component and variable cluster variables. Does the accuracy – the R-square – with the set of relevant variables improve the linear regression model?

Neural networks

The neural network architecture was introduced in the *Statistical/machine learning models* section of *Chapter 1, Introduction to Ensemble Techniques*. Neural networks are capable of handling nonlinear relationships, the choice of the number of hidden neurons, the choice of transfer functions, and the learning rate (or decay rate) provides a great flexibility in building useful regression models. Haykin (2009) and Ripley (1996) provide two detailed explanations of the theory of neural networks.

We have looked at the use of neural networks for classification problems and have also seen the stack ensemble models in action. For the regression model, we need to tell the nnet function that the output/dependent variable is a continuous variable through the linout=TRUE option. Here, we will build a neural network with five hidden neurons, size=5, and run the function for a maximum of 100 iterations, maxit=100:

```
> HT_NN <- nnet(HT_Formula,data=HT_Build,linout=TRUE,maxit=100,size=5)
# weights:  666
initial  value 38535430702344.617187
final  value 5951814083616.587891
converged
> summary(HT_NN)
a 131-5-1 network with 666 weights
options were - linear output units
    b->h1    i1->h1    i2->h1    i3->h1    i4->h1    i5->h1    i6->h1    i7-
>h1
-1.0e-02  6.5e-01 -8.0e-02  4.6e-01  5.0e-02 -4.0e-02  3.9e-01  1.3e-
01
   i8->h1    i9->h1   i10->h1   i11->h1   i12->h1   i13->h1   i14->h1   i15-
>h1
 2.1e-01  4.6e-01  1.9e-01  5.2e-01 -6.6e-01  3.2e-01 -3.0e-02  2.2e-
01
  i16->h1   i17->h1   i18->h1   i19->h1   i20->h1   i21->h1   i22->h1   i23-
>h1
-2.5e-01 -1.2e-01  3.3e-01 -2.8e-01 -4.6e-01 -3.8e-01 -4.1e-01 -3.2e-
01


-4.0e-01 -2.9e-01 -5.1e-01 -2.6e-01  2.5e-01 -6.0e-01  1.0e-02  1.5e-
01
i120->h5 i121->h5 i122->h5 i123->h5 i124->h5 i125->h5 i126->h5 i127-
>h5
 3.7e-01 -2.0e-01  2.0e-01  1.0e-02 -3.3e-01 -2.4e-01 -1.9e-01  7.0e-
01
i128->h5 i129->h5 i130->h5 i131->h5
-1.3e-01 -3.4e-01 -6.9e-01 -6.6e-01
    b->o     h1->o     h2->o     h3->o     h4->o     h5->o
 6.3e+04  6.3e+04  6.3e+04 -9.1e+04  4.7e-01 -8.4e+03
```

Note that the neural network architecture is not very useful. However, sometimes we are asked to display what we have built. Thus, we will use the `plotnet` function from the `NeuralNetTools` package to generate the network. Since there are too many variables (68 in this case), we save the plot to the `Housing_NN.pdf` PDF file and the reader can open it and zoom into the plot to inspect it:

```
> pdf("../Output/Housing_NN.pdf",height = 25, width=60)
> plotnet(HT_NN) # very chaotic network
> dev.off()
RStudioGD
        2
```

The prediction of the neural network will be performed shortly.

Exercise 1: Build neural networks with different decay options; the default is 0. Vary the decay value in the range of 0-0.2, with increments of 0.01, 0.05, and so on.

Exercise 2: Improve the neural network fit using `reltol` values, decay values, and a combination of these variables.

Regression tree

The regression tree forms the third base learner for the housing dataset and provides the decision tree structure for the regression problems. The advantages of the decision tree naturally get carried over to the regression tree. As seen in *Chapter 3, Bagging*, the options for many decision trees are also available for the regression tree.

We will use the `rpart` function from the `rpart` library with the default settings to build the regression tree. Using the plot and text functions, we set up the regression tree:

```
> HT_rtree <- rpart(HT_Formula,data=HT_Build)
> windows(height=100,width=100)
> plot(HT_rtree,uniform = TRUE); text(HT_rtree)
> HT_rtree$variable.importance
 OverallQual Neighborhood    YearBuilt    ExterQual   KitchenQual
      3.2e+12      2.0e+12      1.7e+12      1.7e+12       1.4e+12
   Foundation    GarageCars     GrLivArea   GarageArea     X1stFlrSF
      1.3e+12      8.0e+11      6.9e+11      6.1e+11       3.8e+11
    X2ndFlrSF    TotalBsmtSF  TotRmsAbvGrd     BsmtQual    MasVnrArea
      3.8e+11      3.2e+11      2.7e+11      2.7e+11       1.8e+11
     FullBath      HalfBath    HouseStyle   BsmtFinSF1  YearRemodAdd
      1.7e+11      1.3e+11      1.2e+11      1.1e+11       5.3e+10
```

```
    MSZoning BsmtFinType1 BedroomAbvGr  Exterior1st BsmtFullBath
    4.6e+10       4.4e+10       4.0e+10       2.4e+10       1.1e+10
    LotArea
    5.7e+09
```

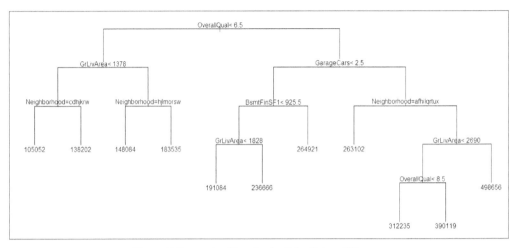

Figure 7: Regression Tree for the Sales Price of Houses

Which variables are important here? The answer to this is provided by the variable importance metric. We extract the variable importance from `HT_rtree` and the variable with the highest bar length is the most important of all the variables. We will now use the `barplot` function for the `HT_rtree`:

```
> barplot(HT_rtree$variable.importance,las=2,yaxt="n")
```

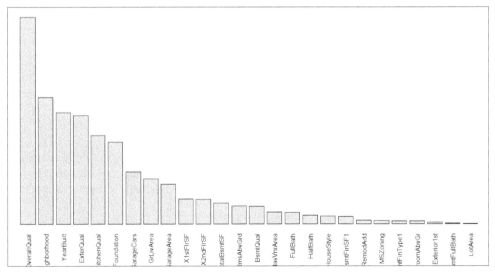

Figure 8: Variable Importance of the Regression Tree of Housing Model

Exercise: Explore the pruning options for a regression tree.

Next, we will look at the performance of the three base learners for the validation dataset.

Prediction for regression models

We separated the housing training dataset into two sections: train and validate. Now we will use the built models and check how well they are performing. We will do this by looking at the MAPE metric : |Actual-Predicted|/Actual. Using the predict function with the newdata option, the predictions are first obtained, and then the MAPE is calculated for the observations in the validated section of the data:

```
> HT_LM_01_val_hat <- predict(HT_LM_01,newdata = HT_Validate[,-69])
Warning message:
In predict.lm(HT_LM_01, newdata = HT_Validate[, -69]) :
  prediction from a rank-deficient fit may be misleading
> mean(abs(HT_LM_01_val_hat - HT_Validate$SalePrice)/HT_
Validate$SalePrice)
[1] 0.11
> HT_LM_Final_val_hat <- predict(HT_LM_Final,newdata = HT_
Validate[,-69])
> mean(abs(HT_LM_Final_val_hat - HT_Validate$SalePrice)/HT_
Validate$SalePrice)
[1] 0.11
> HT_NN_val_hat <- predict(HT_NN,newdata = HT_Validate[,-69])
> mean(abs(HT_NN_val_hat - HT_Validate$SalePrice)/HT_
Validate$SalePrice)
[1] 0.37
> HT_rtree_val_hat <- predict(HT_rtree,newdata = HT_Validate[,-69])
> mean(abs(HT_rtree_val_hat - HT_Validate$SalePrice)/HT_
Validate$SalePrice)
[1] 0.17
```

The linear regression model HT_LM_01 and the most efficient linear model (by AIC) HT_LM_Final both give the same accuracy (up to two digits) and the MAPE is 0.11 for these two models. The neural network model HT_NN (with five hidden neurons) results in a MAPE of 0.37, which is a bad result. This again reinforces the well-known fact that complexity does not necessarily mean accuracy. The accuracy of the regression tree HT_rtree is 0.17.

The predicted prices are visualized in the following program:

```
> windows(height = 100,width = 100)
> plot(HT_Validate$SalePrice,HT_LM_01_val_hat,col="blue",
+      xlab="Sales Price",ylab="Predicted Value")
> points(HT_Validate$SalePrice,HT_LM_Final_val_hat,col="green")
> points(HT_Validate$SalePrice,HT_NN_val_hat,col="red")
> points(HT_Validate$SalePrice,HT_rtree_val_hat,col="yellow")
> legend(x=6e+05,y=4e+05,lty=3,
+        legend=c("Linear","Best Linear","Neural Network","Regression
Tree"),
+        col=c("blue","green","red","yellow"))
```

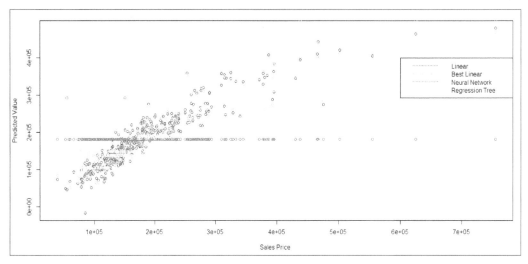

Figure 9: Predicting Housing Sales Prices

Now we have set up the base learners, it is time to build the ensembles out of them. We will now build ensemble models based on the homogeneous base learner of the decision tree.

Bagging and Random Forests

Chapter 3, Bagging, and *Chapter 4, Random Forests*, demonstrate how to improve the stability and accuracy of the basic decision tree. In this section, we will primarily use the decision tree as base learners and create an ensemble of trees in the same way that we did in *Chapter 3, Bagging*, and *Chapter 4, Random Forests*.

The `split` function is the primary difference between bagging and random forest algorithms for classification and regression trees. Thus, unsurprisingly, we can continue to use the same functions and packages for the regression problem as the counterparts that were used in the classification problem. We will first use the `bagging` function from the `ipred` package to set up the bagging algorithm for the housing data:

```
> housing_bagging <- bagging(formula = HT_Formula,data=ht_
imp,nbagg=500,
+                                 coob=TRUE,keepX=TRUE)
> housing_bagging$err
[1] 35820
```

The trees in the bagging object can be saved to a PDF file in the same way as in *Chapter 3, Bagging*:

```
> pdf("../Output/Housing_Bagging.pdf")
> for(i in 1:500){
+    temp <- housing_bagging$mtrees[[i]]
+    plot(temp$btree)
+    text(temp$btree,use.n=TRUE)
+ }
> dev.off()
RStudioGD
        2
```

Since variable importance is not given directly by the `ipred` package, and it is always an important measure to know which variables are important, we run a similar loop and program to what was used in *Chapter 3, Bagging*, to get the variable importance plot:

```
> VI <- data.frame(matrix(0,nrow=500,ncol=ncol(ht_imp)-1))
> vnames <- names(ht_imp)[-69]
> names(VI) <- vnames
> for(i in 1:500){
+    VI[i,] <- as.numeric(housing_bagging$mtrees[[i]]$btree$variable.
importance[vnames])
```

```
+ }
> Bagging_VI <- colMeans(VI,na.rm = TRUE)
> Bagging_VI <- sort(Bagging_VI,dec=TRUE)
> barplot(Bagging_VI,las=2,yaxt="n")
> title("Variable Importance of Bagging")
```

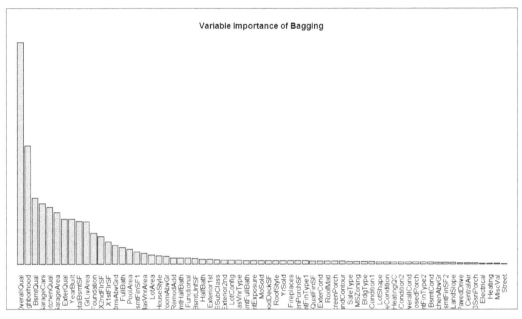

Figure 10: Variable Importance Plot of the Bagging Algorithm for the Housing Data

Exercise: Compare *Figure 10* with *Figure 8* to decide whether we have an overfitting problem in the regression tree.

Did bagging improve the prediction performance? This is the important criterion that we need to evaluate. Using the `predict` function with the `newdata` option, we again calculate the MAPE as follows:

```
> HT_bagging_val_hat <- predict(housing_bagging,newdata = HT_
Validate[,-69])
> mean(abs(HT_bagging_val_hat - HT_Validate$SalePrice)/HT_
Validate$SalePrice)
[1] 0.13
```

The simple regression tree had a MAPE of 17%, and now it is down to 13%. This leads us into the next exercise.

Exercise: Use some of the pruning options with `rpart.control` to improve the performance of bagging.

The next step following bagging is the random forest. We will use the `randomForest` function from the package of the same name. Here, we explore 500 trees for this forest. For the regression data, the default setting for the number of covariates to be randomly sampled for splitting a node is `mtry = p/3`, where p is the number of covariates. We will use the default choice. The `randomForest` function is used to set up the tree ensemble and then `plot_rf`, defined in *Chapter 4, Random Forests,* is used to save the trees of the forest to a PDF file:

```
> housing_RF <- randomForest(formula=HT_Formula,data=ht_imp,ntree=500,
+                            replace=TRUE,importance=TRUE)
> pdf("../Output/Housing_RF.pdf",height=100,width=500)
Error in pdf("../Output/Housing_RF.pdf", height = 100, width = 500) :
  cannot open file '../Output/Housing_RF.pdf'
> plot_RF(housing_RF)
[1]  1
[1]  2
[1]  3

[1]  498
[1]  499
[1]  500
> dev.off()
null device
          1
> windows(height=100,width=200)
> varImpPlot(housing_RF2)
```

The variable importance plot for the random forest is given next:

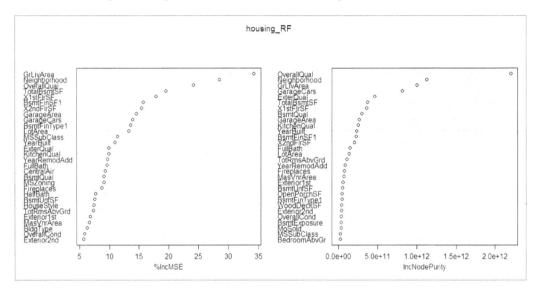

Figure 11: Variable Importance of the Random Forest for the Housing Data

Exercise: Find the difference between the two variable importance plots %IncMSE and IncNodePurity. Also, compare the variable importance plot of the random forest with the bagging plot and comment on this.

How accurate is our forest? Using the `predict` function, we will get our answer:

```
> HT_RF_val_hat <- predict(housing_RF,newdata = HT_Validate[,-69])
> mean(abs(HT_RF_val_hat - HT_Validate$SalePrice)/HT_
Validate$SalePrice)
[1] 0.038
```

This is simply brilliant stuff, and the random forest has significantly improved the accuracy by drastically reducing the MAPE from 0.17 to 0.038. This is the outright winner of all the models built thus far.

Exercise: In spite of the increased accuracy, try to build forests based on pruned trees and calculate the accuracy.

Let's see how boosting changes the performance of the trees next.

Boosting regression models

Chapter 5, Boosting, introduced the boosting method for trees when we had a categorical variable of interest. The adaptation of boosting to the regression problem requires lot of computational changes. For more information, refer to papers by Zemel and Pitassi (2001), `http://papers.nips.cc/paper/1797-a-gradient-based-boosting-algorithm-for-regression-problems.pdf` , or Ridgeway, et al. (1999), `http://dimacs.rutgers.edu/Research/MMS/PAPERS/BNBR.pdf`.

The `gbm` function from the `gbm` library will be used to boost the weak learners generated by using random forests. We generate a thousand trees, `n.trees=1e3`, and use the `shrinkage` factor of `0.05`, and then boost the regression trees using the gradient boosting algorithm for regression data:

```
> housing_gbm <- gbm(formula=HT_Formula,data=HT_Build,distribution =
"gaussian",
+                    n.trees=1e3,shrinkage = 0.05,keep.data=TRUE,
+                    interaction.depth=1,
+                    cv.folds=3,n.cores = 1)
> summary(housing_gbm)
                        var    rel.inf
OverallQual     OverallQual 29.22608012
GrLivArea          GrLivArea 18.85043432
Neighborhood    Neighborhood 13.79949556

PoolArea           PoolArea  0.00000000
MiscVal             MiscVal  0.00000000
YrSold               YrSold  0.00000000
```

This summary gives the variable importance in descending order. The performance of the boosting can be looked into using the `gbm.perf` function and since our goal was always to generate a technique that performs well on new data, the out-of-bag curve is also laid over as follows:

```
> windows(height=100,width=200)
> par(mfrow=c(1,2))
> gbm.perf(housing_gbm,method="OOB",plot.it=TRUE,
+                         oobag.curve = TRUE,overlay=TRUE)
[1] 135
```

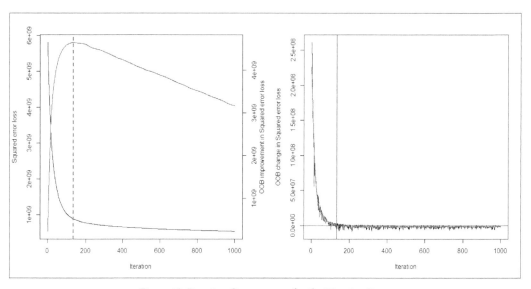

Figure 12: Boosting Convergence for the Housing Data

The boosting method has converged at iteration **137**. Next, we look at the performance of the boosting procedure on the validated data:

```
> HT_gbm_val_hat <- predict(housing_gbm,newdata = HT_Validate[,-69])
Using 475 trees...
> mean(abs(HT_gbm_val_hat - HT_Validate$SalePrice)/HT_
Validate$SalePrice)
[1] 0.11
```

The MAPE has decreased from 17% to 11%. However, the random forest continues to be the most accurate model thus far.

Stacking methods for regression models

Linear regression models, neural networks, and regression trees are the three methods that will be stacked here. We will require the `caret` and `caretEnsemble` packages to do this task. The stacked ensemble methods have been introduced in detail in *Chapter 7, The General Ensemble Technique*. First, we specify the control parameters for the training task, specify the list of algorithms, and create the stacked ensemble:

```
> control <- trainControl(method="repeatedcv", number=10, repeats=3,
+                         savePredictions=TRUE, classProbs=TRUE)
> algorithmList <- c('lm', 'rpart')
> set.seed(12345)
> Emodels <- caretList(HT_Formula, data=HT_Build, trControl=control,
+                   methodList=algorithmList,
+                   tuneList=list(
+                       nnet=caretModelSpec(method='nnet',
trace=FALSE,
+                                           linout=TRUE)
+
+                           )
+                           )
There were 37 warnings (use warnings() to see them)
```

The neural network is specified through `caretModelSpec`. `Emodels` needs to be resampled for further analysis:

```
> Enresults <- resamples(Emodels)
> summary(Enresults)

Call:
summary.resamples(object = Enresults)

Models: nnet, lm, rpart
Number of resamples: 30

MAE
        Min. 1st Qu. Median  Mean 3rd Qu.   Max. NA's
nnet  30462   43466  47098 47879   53335 58286    0
lm    16153   18878  20348 20138   21337 23865    0
rpart 30369   33946  35688 35921   37354 42437    0

RMSE
        Min. 1st Qu. Median  Mean 3rd Qu.   Max. NA's
nnet  42598   66632  70197 69272   73089 85971    0
lm    22508   26137  29192 34347   39803 66875    0
```

```
rpart 38721    46508   50528 50980    55705 65337    0

Rsquared
        Min. 1st Qu. Median Mean 3rd Qu. Max. NA's
nnet  0.0064    0.16   0.32 0.31    0.44 0.74    4
lm    0.4628    0.77   0.85 0.81    0.88 0.92    0
rpart 0.4805    0.55   0.57 0.58    0.61 0.69    0

> dotplot(Enresults)
```

The `dotplot` is displayed next:

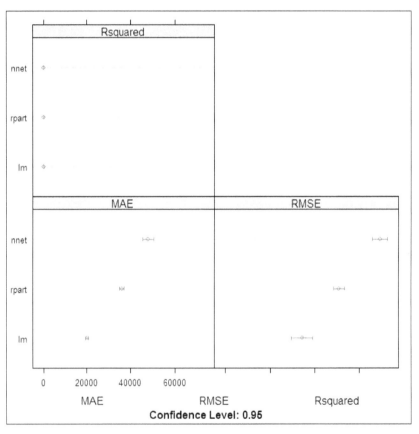

Figure 13: R-square, MAE, and RMSE for Housing Data

We can see from *Figure 13* that the R-square is similar for the three models, although MAE and RMSE are significantly different across the three models. The model correlations can be found using the `modelCor` function:

```
> modelCor(Enresults)
        nnet     lm rpart
nnet    1.000  0.033 -0.44
lm      0.033  1.000  0.29
rpart  -0.441  0.288  1.00
```

We now apply the ensemble method to the validation data:

```
> HT_Validate_Predictions <- rowMeans(predict(Emodels,newdata = HT_
Validate))
Warning message:
In predict.lm(modelFit, newdata) :
  prediction from a rank-deficient fit may be misleading
> mean(abs(HT_Validate_Predictions - HT_Validate$SalePrice)/HT_
Validate$SalePrice)
[1] 0.16
```

Note that the results from the neural network are default and we did not specify the size of the hidden layers. The MAPE of 16% is not desirable and we are better off using the random forest ensemble.

Exercise: Perform the stacked ensemble methods on the principal components and variable cluster data.

Summary

In this chapter, we extended most of the models and methods learned earlier in the book. The chapter began with a detailed example of housing data, and we carried out the visualization and pre-processing. The principal component method helps in reducing data, and the variable clustering method also helps with the same task. Linear regression models, neural networks, and the regression tree were then introduced as methods that will serve as base learners. Bagging, boosting, and random forest algorithms are some methods that helped to improve the models. These methods are based on homogeneous ensemble methods. This chapter then closed with the stacking ensemble method for the three heterogeneous base learners.

A different data structure of censored observations will be the topic of the next chapter. Such data is referred to as survival data, and it commonly appears in the study of clinical trials.

10
Ensembling Survival Models

The primary biliary cirrhosis data was introduced in first two chapters using the jackknife method. Observations in clinical trials are usually subject to censoring, and the jackknife method helps to complete incomplete observations through the idea of pseudo values. Since pseudo values are likely to be dependent on each other, the generalized estimating equation framework made it possible to estimate the impact of twelve covariates at the time of interest. The idea of pseudo values and the generalized estimating equation framework makes it easy for practitioners to interpret the results. However, this method might not be useful if the number of censored observations is exceptionally high. Furthermore, it is also preferable to have statistical methods that preserve the incompleteness of the observations and yet make good use of them. The general (linear) regression framework with time as the dependent variable and the error term following appropriate lifetime distribution can be set up in the usual regression framework. However, it turns out to be unreliable, and in many cases, it is known to be unstable, or the convergence simply does not take place. In *Regression Models and Life-Tables* (`http://www.stat.cmu.edu/~ryantibs/journalclub/cox_1972.pdf`), Cox (1972) achieved a breakthrough in the regression modeling of the survival data when he proposed the proportional hazards model. So, what is a hazards model?

This chapter will open with core survival analysis concepts such as hazard rate, cumulative hazard function, and survival function. A few parametric lifetime models are also discussed and visualized through R programs. For the given data, we will then study how to carry out inference for the lifetime distribution through nonparametric methods. An estimation of the survival function and cumulative hazard function is then illustrated for the time to event of interest for the pbc dataset. Hypothesis testing through the use of the logrank test is demonstrated for different segments of the pbc data. Regression models will begin with a simple illustration of the parametric regression model, using exponential distribution as an example. It is known that the parametric models are not very useful for clinical trials data. This leads to an important variant in the Cox proportional hazards regression model, which is a **semiparametric** model in the sense that the baseline hazard rate is left completely unspecified and the impact of covariates is modeled through an exponential linear term on the hazard rate.

Survival trees are an important variant of the decision tree applicable to the survival data. The split criteria are based on the **logrank** test. Naturally, we will be interested in ensemble methods for the survival data, and hence we develop the survival random forests in the concluding section.

We will cover the following topics in this chapter:

- Essential concepts of survival analysis, such as hazard rate, cumulative hazard function, and survival function
- The Nelson-Aalen and Kaplan Meier estimators as respective estimators of the cumulative hazard function and the survival function
- Logrank tests for the comparison of survival curves
- Parametric and semiparametric methods analyzing the impact of independent covariates on the hazard rate
- Survival tree based on logrank test
- Random forests as ensemble methods for the survival data

Core concepts of survival analysis

Survival analysis deals with censored data, and it is very common that parametric models are unsuitable for explaining the lifetimes observed in clinical trials.

Let T denote the survival time, or the time to the event of interest, and we will naturally have $T \geq 0$, which is a continuous random variable. Suppose that the lifetime cumulative distribution is F and the associated density function is f. We define important concepts as required for further analysis. We will explore the concept of *survival function* next.

Suppose that T is the continuous random variable of a lifetime and that the associated cumulative distribution function is F. The survival function at time t is the probability the observation is still alive at the time, and it is defined by the following:

$$S(t) = P(T > t) = 1 - F(t) = 1 - P(T \leq t)$$

The survival function can take different forms. Let's go through some examples for each of the distributions to get a clearer picture of the difference in survival functions.

Exponential Distribution: Suppose that the lifetime distribution of an electronic component follows exponential distribution with rate $\lambda > 0$. Then, its density function is as follows:

$$f(t) = \frac{1}{\lambda} \exp\left\{-\frac{t}{\lambda}\right\}, t \geq 0$$

The cumulative distribution function is as follows:

$$F(t) = 1 - \exp\left\{-\frac{t}{\lambda}\right\}$$

The mean and variance of the exponential distribution are, respectively, λ and λ^2. The survival function of the exponential distribution is as follows:

$$S(t) = 1 - \left(1 - \exp\left\{-\frac{t}{\lambda}\right\}\right) = \exp\left\{-\frac{t}{\lambda}\right\}, t \geq 0$$

The mean of exponential distribution is $E(X) = \lambda$. The exponential distribution is driven by a single parameter and it also enjoys an elegant property, which is known as a memoryless property (see Chapter 6, Tattar, et al. (2016)).

Gamma Distribution: We say that the lifetime random variable follows a gamma distribution with rate $\lambda, \lambda > 0$ and shape $\alpha, \alpha > 0$, if its probability density function f is of the following form:

$$f(t \mid \alpha, \lambda) = \frac{t^{\alpha-1}}{\Gamma(\alpha)\lambda^\alpha} \exp\left\{-\frac{t}{\lambda}\right\}, t \geq 0$$

The mean and variance of gamma distribution are, respectively, $\alpha\lambda$ and $\alpha\lambda^2$. A closed form of the cumulative distribution functions, and hence the survival function, does not exist.

Weibull Distribution: A lifetime random variable is said to follow a Weibull distribution with rate $\lambda, \lambda > 0$ and shape $\alpha, \alpha > 0$, if its probability density function f is of the following form:

$$f(t \mid \alpha, \lambda) = \frac{\alpha}{\lambda} \left(\frac{t}{\lambda} \right)^{\alpha - 1} \exp\left\{ -\left(\frac{t}{\lambda} \right)^{\alpha} \right\}, t \geq 0$$

The cumulative distribution function of the Weibull distribution is demonstrated as follows:

$$F(t \mid \alpha, \lambda) = 1 - \exp\left\{ -\left(\frac{t}{\lambda} \right)^{\alpha} \right\}$$

The survival function is as follows:

$$S(t \mid \alpha, \lambda) = \exp\left\{ -\left(\frac{t}{\lambda} \right)^{\alpha} \right\}$$

Next, we will define the concept of hazard rate, which is also known as the instantaneous failure rate.

Let T denote the lifetime random variable and F denote the associated cumulative distribution function, then the hazard rate at time t is defined as follows:

$$h(t) = \lim_{s \downarrow 0} \frac{P(t \leq T < t + s)}{s}$$

$$= \lim_{s \downarrow 0} \frac{F(t + s) - F(t)}{s}$$

$$= \lim_{s \downarrow 0} \frac{S(t) - S(t + s)}{s}$$

The problem of estimating the hazard rate is as difficult as that of the density function, and hence the cumulative function concept will be useful.

Let T denote the lifetime random variable and $h(t)$ be the associated hazard rate, then the cumulative hazard function is defined using the following:

$$H(t) = \int_0^t h(s) \, ds$$

The following relationship exists between these three quantities:

$$S(t) = \exp\{-H(t)\}$$

$$h(t) = \frac{f(t)}{S(t)}$$

The expected value is related to the survival function as follows:

$$E(T) = \int_0^\infty S(u)\,du$$

In the next R program, we will visualize the three survival quantities for the three probability distributions. First, we will set up a graphical device for nine plots with the par and mfrow functions. The program is explained for the exponential distribution. Consider the time period 0-100 and create a numeric object Time in the program. We will begin with the computation of the values of the density functions using the dexp function for the Time object. This means that dexp(Time) will calculate the value of the density function *f(t)* for each point between 0–100. Since the survival function is related to the cumulative distribution by $S(t) = 1 - F(t)$ and pexp gives us the values of *F* at the time point *t*, the survival function for the exponential distribution is computed as *1-pexp()*. The hazard rate, density function, and survival function are related by $h(t) = f(t) / S(t)$ and can be easily obtained. The cumulative hazard function is obtained by using the values of the survival function and the relationship as follows:

$$H(t) = -\log S(t)$$

The program is then repeated for the gamma and Weibull distribution with changes in the appropriate specification of the parameters, as shown in the following code:

```
> par(mfrow=c(3,3))
> Time <- seq(0,100,1)
> lambda <- 1/20
> expdens <- dexp(Time,rate=lambda)
> expsurv <- 1-pexp(Time,rate=lambda)
> exphaz <- expdens/expsurv
> expcumhaz <- -log(expsurv)
> plot(Time,exphaz,"l",xlab="Time",ylab="Hazard Rate",ylim=c(0,0.1))
> plot(Time,expcumhaz,"l",xlab="Time",ylab="Cumulative Hazard
Function")
> mtext("Exponential Distribution")
> plot(Time,expsurv,"l",xlab="Time",ylab="Survival Function")
>
> # Gamma Distribution
> lambda <- 1/10; k <- 2
> gammadens <- dgamma(Time,rate=lambda,shape=k)
```

```
> gammasurv <- 1-pgamma(Time,rate=lambda,shape=k)
> gammahaz <- gammadens/gammasurv
> gammacumhaz <- -log(gammasurv)
> plot(Time,gammahaz,"l",xlab="Time",ylab="Hazard Rate")
> plot(Time,gammacumhaz,"l",xlab="Time",ylab="Cumulative Hazard
Function")
> mtext("Gamma Distribution")
> plot(Time,gammasurv,"l",xlab="Time",ylab="Survival Function")
>
> # Weibull Distribution
> lambda <- 25; k <- 2
> Weibulldens <- dweibull(Time,scale=lambda,shape=k)
> Weibullsurv <- 1-pweibull(Time,scale=lambda,shape=k)
> Weibullhaz <- Weibulldens/Weibullsurv
> Weibullcumhaz <- -log(Weibullsurv)
> plot(Time,Weibullhaz,"l",xlab="Time",ylab="Hazard Rate")
> plot(Time,Weibullcumhaz,"l",xlab="Time",ylab="Cumulative Hazard
Function")
> mtext("Weibull Distribution")
> plot(Time,Weibullsurv,"l",xlab="Time",ylab="Survival Function")
```

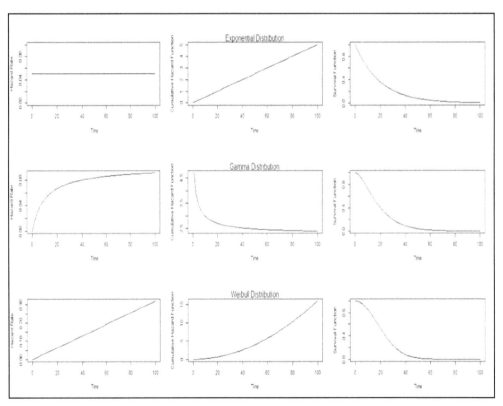

Figure 1: Hazard rate, Cumulative hazard function, and Survival function for Exponential, Gamma, and Weibull distributions

Repeat the preceding program for different parameter values and prepare a summary of your observations for the change in the hazard function, cumulative hazard function, and the survival function. Summarize your observations separately for the three distributions of exponential, gamma, and Weibull.

Now, we need to see how well the model fits to the pbc dataset. Here, we will fit the exponential, gamma, and Weibull distributions to the lifetimes of interest in the pbc dataset. Note that, since we have censored data, the incomplete observations can't simply be thrown away, as 257 out of 418 are incomplete observations. Though we can't go into the mathematics of the maximum likelihood estimation for survival data, it is important to note here that the contribution of a complete observation to the likelihood is *f(t)* and if it is incomplete/censored, it is *S(t)*. Consequently, it is important for the software to know which observation is complete and which is incomplete. Here we will use the Surv function from the survival package to specify this, and then use the flexsurvreg function from the flexsurv package to fit an appropriate lifetime distribution. The option of dist helps set up the appropriate distributions, as can be seen in the following program:

```
> pbc <- survival::pbc
> Surv(pbc$time,pbc$status==2)
   [1]   400  4500+ 1012  1925  1504+ 2503  1832+ 2466  2400    51  3762
  [12]   304  3577+ 1217  3584  3672+  769   131  4232+ 1356  3445+  673

 [397] 1328+ 1375+ 1260+ 1223+  935   943+ 1141+ 1092+ 1150+  703
1129+
[408] 1086+ 1067+ 1072+ 1119+ 1097+  989+  681  1103+ 1055+  691+
976+
> pbc_exp <- flexsurvreg(Surv(time,status==2)~1,data=pbc,dist="expone
ntial")
> pbc_exp
Call:
flexsurvreg(formula = Surv(time, status == 2) ~ 1, data = pbc,
    dist = "exponential")

Estimates:
      est       L95%      U95%       se
rate  2.01e-04  1.72e-04  2.34e-04  1.58e-05

N = 418,  Events: 161,  Censored: 257
Total time at risk: 801633
Log-likelihood = -1531.593, df = 1
AIC = 3065.187

> windows(height=100,width=100)
```

```
> plot(pbc_exp,ylim=c(0,1),col="black")
> pbc_gamma <- flexsurvreg(Surv(time,status==2)~1,data=pbc,dist="gam
ma")
> pbc_gamma
Call:
flexsurvreg(formula = Surv(time, status == 2) ~ 1, data = pbc,
    dist = "gamma")

Estimates:
        est       L95%       U95%        se
shape  1.10e+00  9.21e-01  1.30e+00  9.68e-02
rate   2.33e-04  1.70e-04  3.21e-04  3.78e-05

N = 418,  Events: 161,  Censored: 257
Total time at risk: 801633
Log-likelihood = -1531.074, df = 2
AIC = 3066.147

> plot(pbc_gamma,col="blue",add=TRUE)
> pbc_Weibull <- flexsurvreg(Surv(time,status==2)~1,data=pbc,dist="we
ibull")
> pbc_Weibull
Call:
flexsurvreg(formula = Surv(time, status == 2) ~ 1, data = pbc,
    dist = "weibull")

Estimates:
        est       L95%       U95%        se
shape  1.08e+00  9.42e-01  1.24e+00  7.48e-02
scale  4.71e+03  3.96e+03  5.59e+03  4.13e+02

N = 418,  Events: 161,  Censored: 257
Total time at risk: 801633
Log-likelihood = -1531.017, df = 2
AIC = 3066.035

> plot(pbc_Weibull,col="orange",add=TRUE)
> legend(3000,1,c("Exponential","Gamma","Weibull"),
+         col=c("black","blue","orange"),merge=TRUE,lty=2)
```

The resulting diagram is given here:

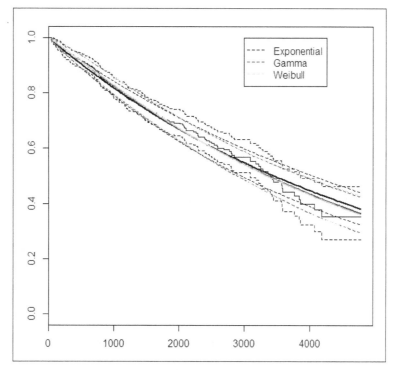

Figure 2: Fitting exponential, gamma, and Weibull distributions for censored data

The AIC value for the fitted exponential model is 3065.187, for the fitted gamma model it is 3066.147, and for Weibull it is 3066.035. The lower the criteria, the better. Consequently, the exponential is the best fit according to the AIC criteria. This is then followed by the Weibull and gamma distributions. The exponential distribution with a single parameter is a better fit here than the more complex models of gamma and Weibull.

Some explanation of the R program is in order now. The `pbc` dataset is loaded with `survival::pbc` since the R package `randomForestSRC` also has a dataset with the same name and it is a slightly different version. Consequently, the `survival::pbc` code ensures that we continue to load the `pbc` dataset as we did in earlier instances. The event of interest for us is indicated by `status==2` and `Surv(pbc$time,pbc$status==2)`, which creates a survival object that has complete observations mentioned in the numeric object. If the `status` is anything other than `2`, the observation is censored and this is indicated by the number followed by the + sign. The `Surv(time,status==2)~1` code creates the necessary formula, which is useful for applying survival functions. The `dist="exponential"` option ensures that exponential distribution is fitted on the survival data. When the fitted model `pbc_exp` is run on the console, we get a summary of the fitted model and it returns the estimates of the parameters of the model, the 95% confidence interval, and the standard error of the parameter's estimate. We also get the count of complete and censored observations, the total time at risk for all patients, the likelihood function value, and the AIC. Note how the degrees of freedom vary across the three fitted distributions.

The parametric models detailed here give an idea of the survival concepts. When we don't have enough evidence to construct a parametric model, we resort to nonparametric and semiparametric models for carrying out the statistical inference. In the following section, we will continue our analysis of the `pbc` data.

Nonparametric inference

Survival data is subject to censoring and we need to introduce a new quantity to capture this information. Suppose that we have a n IID random sample of lifetime random variables in $T_1, T_2, \ldots, T_n$, and we know that the event of interest might have occurred or that it will occur sometime in the future. The additional information is captured by the Kronecker indicator variable, $i = 1, 2, \ldots, n$:

$$\delta_i = \begin{cases} 1, & \text{if the } i^{th} \text{ observation is a complete} \\ 0, & \text{if the } i^{th} \text{ observation is incomplete} \end{cases}$$

Thus, we have n pairs of random observations in the *Ts* and δ s, $(T_i, \delta_i), i = 1, \ldots n$. To obtain the estimates of the cumulative hazard function and the survival function, we will need an additional notation. Let $t_1, t_2, \ldots, t_D$ denote the unique times of Ts at which the event of interest is observed. Next, we denote $n_1, n_2, \ldots, n_D$ to represent the number of observations that are at risk just before times $t_1, t_2, \ldots, t_D$ and $d_1, d_2, \ldots, d_D$ the number of events that occur at that time. Using these quantities, we now propose to estimate the cumulative hazard function using the following:

$$\hat{\Lambda}(t) = \sum_{j:t_j \leq t} \frac{d_j}{n_j}$$

The estimator $\hat{\Lambda}(t)$ is the famous Nelson-Aalen estimator. The Nelson-Aalen estimator enjoys statistical properties including the fact that (i) it is the nonparametric maximum likelihood estimator for the cumulative hazard function, and (ii) it follows an asymptotically normal distribution. An estimator of the survival function is given by the following:

$$\hat{S}(t) = \prod_{j:t_j \leq t} \left(1 - \frac{d_j}{n_j}\right)$$

The estimator $\hat{S}(t)$ is the well-known Kaplan-Meier estimator. The properties of the Nelson-Aalen estimator get carried over to the Kaplan-Meier estimator by an application of the functional-delta theorem. It should be noted that the Kaplan-Meier estimator is again the nonparametric maximum likelihood estimator and asymptotically, it follows the normal distribution. We will now look at how to obtain the estimates for a given dataset using R software.

We have already created the survival object using the `Surv(pbc$time, pbc$status==2)` code. Now, applying the `survfit` function on the survival object, we set up the Kaplan-Meier estimator in the `pbc_sf` survfit object:

```
> pbc_sf <- survfit(Surv(time,status==2)~1,pbc)
> pbc_sf
Call: survfit(formula = Surv(time, status == 2) ~ 1, data = pbc)
      n   events  median 0.95LCL 0.95UCL
    418     161    3395    3090    3853
```

The output shows that we have `418` observations. Out of these, `161` experience the event of interest. We would like to obtain the survival function at different time points of interest. The median survival time is shown as `3395` and the confidence interval for this point estimate is `3090` and `3853`. However, if you find the median of the overall times, the median time for complete observations, and for censored observations, none of that will come closer to the displayed value of `3395`. A quick code reveals the results as follows:

```
> median(pbc$time)
[1] 1730
> median(pbc$time[pbc$status==2])
[1] 1083
> median(pbc$time[pbc$status!=2])
[1] 2157
```

You may ask yourself, Why is there so much of a difference between the estimated median survival time and these medians? The answer will become clear soon enough.

The `summary` function will be used to obtain that answer. For the ten deciles of the observed time, inclusive of censored times, we will obtain the Kaplan-Meier estimates and the associated 95% confidence interval, which is based on the variance estimate, which in turn is based on Greenwood's formula:

```
> summary(pbc_sf,times=as.numeric(quantile(pbc$time,seq(0,1,0.1))))
Call: survfit(formula = Surv(time, status == 2) ~ 1, data = pbc)
```

time	n.risk	n.event	survival	std.err	lower 95% CI	upper 95% CI
41	418	2	0.995	0.00338	0.989	1.000
607	376	39	0.902	0.01455	0.874	0.931
975	334	31	0.827	0.01860	0.791	0.864
1218	292	19	0.778	0.02061	0.738	0.819
1435	251	8	0.755	0.02155	0.714	0.798
1730	209	13	0.713	0.02323	0.669	0.760
2107	167	12	0.668	0.02514	0.621	0.719
2465	126	9	0.628	0.02702	0.577	0.683
2852	84	10	0.569	0.03032	0.512	0.632
3524	42	10	0.478	0.03680	0.411	0.556
4795	1	8	0.353	0.04876	0.270	0.463

We have now obtained the Kaplan-Meier estimates at each of the decile time points, the standard error, and the confidence interval at each of the points. Using the `plot` function, we will now visualize the fitted Kaplan-Meier estimator for the `pbc` dataset:

```
> plot(pbc_sf,xlab="Time",ylab="Survival Function Confidence Bands")
```

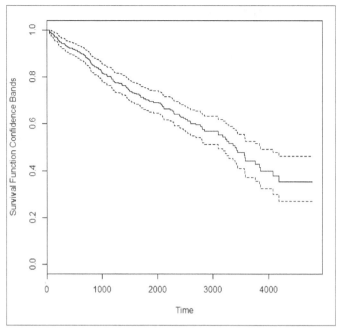

Figure 3: Kaplan-Meier estimator for the PBC dataset

Now, if you look at the time at which the survival time becomes nearly 0.5, the earlier answer of median survival time being 3395 becomes clear enough. Next, we look at the cumulative hazard function.

To obtain the cumulative hazard function, we will apply the `coxph` function on the survival object and use the `basehaz` function to get the baseline cumulative hazard function, as shown in the following code:

```
> pbc_na <- basehaz(coxph(Surv(time,status==2)~1,pbc))
> pbc_na
        hazard time
1   0.004790426    41
2   0.007194272    43
3   0.009603911    51
4   0.012019370    71

396 1.030767970  4509
397 1.030767970  4523
398 1.030767970  4556
399 1.030767970  4795
```

We will use the following code to create a visual display of the Nelson-Aalen estimator:

```
> plot(pbc_na$time,pbc_na$hazard,"l",xlab="Time",ylab="Cumulative
Hazard Function")
```

The following graph illustrates the Nelson-Aalen estimator:

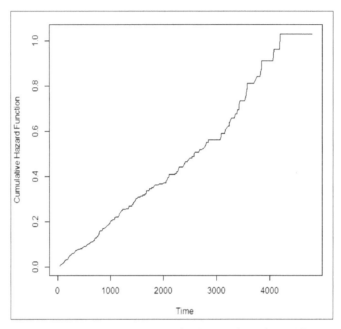

Figure 4: The Nelson-Aalen estimator for the cumulative hazard function

Note that one might be tempted to use the $\Lambda(t) = -\log S(t)$ relationship to obtain the Kaplan-Meier estimator, or vice versa. Let us check it out using the following code:

```
> str(exp(-pbc_na$hazard))
 num [1:399] 0.995 0.993 0.99 0.988 0.986 ...
> str(summary(pbc_sf,times=pbc_na$time)$surv)
 num [1:399] 0.995 0.993 0.99 0.988 0.986 ...
```

Everything seems to be right here, so let's check it in its entirety:

```
> round(exp(-pbc_na$hazard),4)==round(summary(pbc_sf,
+ times=pbc_na$time)$surv,4)
  [1]   TRUE   TRUE   TRUE FALSE FALSE   TRUE   TRUE   TRUE   TRUE   TRUE
TRUE
 [12]   TRUE   TRUE FALSE FALSE FALSE FALSE FALSE   TRUE   TRUE   TRUE
FALSE
 [23] FALSE FALSE FALSE FALSE FALSE FALSE FALSE FALSE   TRUE FALSE
FALSE
```

```
   [34] FALSE FALSE FALSE FALSE FALSE FALSE FALSE FALSE FALSE FALSE
 FALSE

 [375] FALSE FALSE FALSE FALSE FALSE FALSE FALSE FALSE FALSE FALSE
 FALSE
 [386] FALSE FALSE FALSE FALSE FALSE FALSE FALSE FALSE FALSE FALSE
 FALSE
 [397] FALSE FALSE FALSE
```

After a certain length of time, the estimates will differ vastly, and hence we compute these two quantities separately. Next, we will look at how to carry out statistical tests to compare the equality of survival curves.

As noted previously, we are feeding a formula to the survfit function. It appeared as an extra specification '~1' in the Surv formula. As the formula is essential for further analysis of survival data, we can now make good use of this framework. If we replace 1 with a categorical variable such as sex, then we will then obtain survival curves for each level of the categorical variable. For the pbc data, we will plot the survival curves. The Kaplan-Meier estimates for males and females separately.

```
>plot(survfit(Surv(time,status==2)~sex,pbc),conf.
int=TRUE,xlab="Time",+        ylab="Survival Probability",
col=c("red","blue"))
```

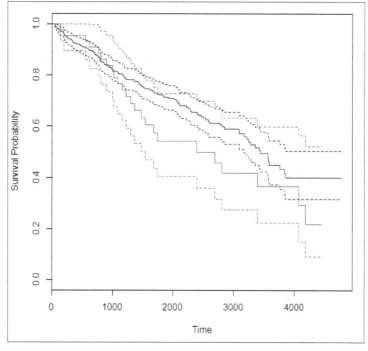

Figure 5: Gender-wise comparison of the survival curves for the PBC data

The survival curves (indicated by the blue and red continuous lines) clearly show differences and we need to evaluate whether the observed difference is statistically significant. To that end, we apply the `survdiff` function and check if the difference is significant, as shown in the following code:

```
> survdiff(Surv(time,status==2)~sex,pbc)
Call:
survdiff(formula = Surv(time, status == 2) ~ sex, data = pbc)

          N Observed Expected (O-E)^2/E (O-E)^2/V
sex=m   44       24     17.3     2.640      2.98
sex=f  374      137    143.7     0.317      2.98
 Chisq= 3  on 1 degrees of freedom, p= 0.0845
```

The p-value is `0.0845`, and hence if the chosen significance is 95%, we conclude that the difference is insignificant.

A note to the reader: the significance level is pre-determined. If you have fixed it at 95% before carrying out the analysis and then look at the p-value and find that it is between 0.05 and 0.10, don't change the level. Stick to what was agreed on earlier.

In the analysis thus far, we have looked at parametric and nonparametric methods, and now we need to develop a larger framework. The impact of covariates needs to be evaluated clearly, and we will explore this topic in the following section.

Regression models – parametric and Cox proportional hazards models

You may recall that the survival data consists of complete as well as censored observations, and we saw that the lifetimes look like 400, 4500+, 1012, 1925, 1504+, … for the `pbc` dataset. Although the lifetimes are continuous random variables, a regression model of the form $T = f(\mathbf{x}, \boldsymbol{\beta}) + \epsilon$ will not be appropriate here. In fact, there were many attempts to correct and improvise on models of this form in the 1970s, and most often the results were detrimental. We will define a generic **hazards regression model** as follows:

$$\lambda\big((t,\delta)\,|\,\mathbf{x},\boldsymbol{\beta}\big) = f\big(\lambda_0(t),\boldsymbol{\beta}'\mathbf{x}\big)$$

Here, t is the lifetime, δ is the lifetime indicator, $\mathbf{x}$ is the covariate vector, $\boldsymbol{\beta}$ is the vector of regression coefficients, and λ_0 is the baseline hazard rate. A relative risks model that is of specific interest is the following:

$$\lambda\big((t,\delta)\,|\,\mathbf{x},\boldsymbol{\beta}\big) = \lambda_0(t)\exp\big(\boldsymbol{\beta}'\mathbf{x}\big)$$

We will focus solely on this class of model. First, the parametric hazards regression is considered. This means that we will specify the hazard rate $\lambda_0(t)$ through a parametric model, for example, through exponential distribution. But what does this mean? It means that the baseline hazard function is of the following form:

$$\lambda_0(t) = \mu, \mu \, is \, unknown$$

Consequently, the hazards regression model is as follows:

$$\lambda\big((t,\delta)\,|\,\mathbf{x}, \boldsymbol{\beta}\big) = \mu \exp\big(\boldsymbol{\beta}'\mathbf{x}\big)$$

The estimation problem is then to find μ and $\boldsymbol{\beta}$. The R function `survreg` from the `flexsurv` package will be useful to fit the parametric hazards regression model. It is demonstrated as continuity on the `pbc` dataset. The `survival` formula will be extended to include all the covariates in the model, as shown in the following code:

```
> pbc_Exp <- survreg(Surv(time,status==2)~trt + age + sex + ascites
+                       hepato + spiders + edema + bili + chol +
albumin
+                       copper + alk.phos + ast + trig + platelet +
+                       protime + stage,
+                     dist="exponential", pbc)
> pbc_Exp_summary <- summary(pbc_Exp)
> pbc_Exp_summary
Call:
survreg(formula = Surv(time, status == 2) ~ trt + age + sex +
    ascites + hepato + spiders + edema + bili + chol + albumin +
    copper + alk.phos + ast + trig + platelet + protime + stage,
    data = pbc, dist = "exponential")
                 Value Std. Error       z        p
(Intercept)   1.33e+01    1.90e+00   7.006 2.46e-12
trt           6.36e-02    2.08e-01   0.305 7.60e-01
age          -2.81e-02    1.13e-02  -2.486 1.29e-02
sexf          3.42e-01    3.00e-01   1.140 2.54e-01
ascites      -1.01e-01    3.70e-01  -0.273 7.85e-01
hepato       -7.76e-02    2.43e-01  -0.320 7.49e-01
spiders      -1.21e-01    2.36e-01  -0.513 6.08e-01
edema        -8.06e-01    3.78e-01  -2.130 3.32e-02
bili         -4.80e-02    2.49e-02  -1.929 5.37e-02
chol         -4.64e-04    4.35e-04  -1.067 2.86e-01
albumin       4.09e-01    2.87e-01   1.427 1.54e-01
copper       -1.63e-03    1.11e-03  -1.466 1.43e-01
alk.phos     -4.51e-05    3.81e-05  -1.182 2.37e-01
ast          -3.68e-03    1.92e-03  -1.917 5.52e-02
```

```
trig         1.70e-04   1.37e-03  0.124 9.01e-01
platelet    -2.02e-04   1.16e-03 -0.174 8.62e-01
protime     -2.53e-01   9.78e-02 -2.589 9.61e-03
stage       -3.66e-01   1.66e-01 -2.204 2.75e-02
Scale fixed at 1

Exponential distribution
Loglik(model)= -984.1   Loglik(intercept only)= -1054.6
Chisq= 141.17 on 17 degrees of freedom, p= 0
Number of Newton-Raphson Iterations: 5
n=276 (142 observations deleted due to missingness)
```

Here, the convergence occurs after five iterations. The p-value is nearly equal to zero, which implies that the fitted model is significant. However, not all the p-values associated with the covariates indicate significance. We will use the following code to find it:

```
> round(pbc_Exp_summary$table[,4],4)
(Intercept)        trt         age        sexf       ascites
hepato
     0.0000     0.7601      0.0129      0.2541       0.7846
0.7491
     spiders      edema        bili        chol       albumin
copper
     0.6083     0.0332      0.0537      0.2859       0.1536
0.1426
   alk.phos         ast        trig     platelet       protime
stage
     0.2372     0.0552      0.9010      0.8621       0.0096
0.0275
> AIC(pbc_exp)
[1] 3065.187
```

The AIC value is also very high, and we try to see if this can be improved on. Hence, we slap the `step` function on the fitted exponential hazards regression model and eliminate the covariates that are insignificant, as shown in the following code:

```
> pbc_Exp_eff <- step(pbc_Exp)
Start:  AIC=2004.12
Surv(time, status == 2) ~ trt + age + sex + ascites + hepato +
    spiders + edema + bili + chol + albumin + copper + alk.phos +
    ast + trig + platelet + protime + stage

            Df    AIC
- ascites    1 2002.2
- trt        1 2002.2
```

```
- hepato     1 2002.2
- spiders    1 2002.4
- chol       1 2003.2
- sex        1 2003.4
- alk.phos   1 2003.4
- albumin    1 2004.1
<none>         2004.1
- ast        1 2005.5
- bili       1 2005.5
- edema      1 2006.5
- stage      1 2007.2
- protime    1 2008.0
- age        1 2008.3
- trig       1 2020.4
- copper     1 2020.7
- platelet   1 2021.8


Step:  AIC=2002.19
Surv(time, status == 2) ~ trt + age + sex + hepato + spiders +
    edema + bili + chol + albumin + copper + alk.phos + ast +
    trig + platelet + protime + stage


Step:  AIC=1994.61
Surv(time, status == 2) ~ age + edema + bili + albumin + copper +
    ast + trig + platelet + protime + stage


           Df    AIC
<none>         1994.6
- albumin    1 1995.5
- edema      1 1996.3
- ast        1 1996.9
- bili       1 1998.8
- protime    1 1999.2
- stage      1 1999.7
- age        1 2000.9
- platelet   1 2012.1
- copper     1 2014.9
- trig       1 2198.7
There were 50 or more warnings (use warnings() to see the first 50)
> pbc_Exp_eff_summary <- summary(pbc_Exp_eff)
> round(pbc_Exp_eff_summary$table[,4],4)
(Intercept)         age        edema        bili      albumin
copper
```

```
      0.0000         0.0037         0.0507         0.0077         0.0849
   0.0170
         ast           trig       platelet        protime          stage
      0.0281         0.9489         0.7521         0.0055         0.0100
> AIC(pbc_Exp_eff)
[1] 1994.607
```

We see here that all the covariates in the current model are significant, except the `trig` and `platelet` variables. The AIC value has also decreased drastically.

Parametric models are often not acceptable in life sciences. A flexible framework for $\lambda((t,\delta)\,|\,x,\boldsymbol{\beta})$ is the famous Cox proportional hazards model. It is a semi-parametric regression model in that the baseline hazard function $\lambda_0(t)$ is completely unspecified. Cox (1972) proposed this model, which is one of the most important models in statistics. The only requirement of the baseline hazard function $\lambda_0(t)$ is that it must be non-negative and the associated probability distribution with it must be a *proper* probability distribution. In this model, the regression coefficient vector $\boldsymbol{\beta}$ is estimated by treating the baseline hazard function as a nuisance factor. Its inference is based on the important notion of partial likelihood function; see Cox (1975) for complete details. Here, we will only specify the form of the Cox proportional hazards model and refer the interested reader to Kalbfleisch and Prentice (2002):

$$\lambda\big((t,\delta)\,|\,\mathbf{x},\boldsymbol{\beta}\big)=\lambda_0(t)\exp\big(\boldsymbol{\beta}'\mathbf{x}\big)$$

We will use the `coxph` function from the `survival` package to fit the proportional hazards regression model. For some technical reason, we will have to omit all rows from the `pbc` dataset which have missing values, and the remaining steps parallel the fitting of the exponential hazards regression model:

```
> pbc2 <- na.omit(pbc)
> pbc_coxph <- coxph(Surv(time,status==2)~trt + age + sex + ascites
+                    hepato + spiders + edema + bili + chol +
albumin
+                    copper + alk.phos + ast + trig + platelet +
+                    protime + stage,                    pbc2)
> pbc_coxph_summary <- summary(pbc_coxph)
> pbc_coxph_summary
Call:
coxph(formula = Surv(time, status == 2) ~ trt + age + sex + ascites +
    hepato + spiders + edema + bili + chol + albumin + copper +
    alk.phos + ast + trig + platelet + protime + stage, data = pbc2)

  n= 276, number of events= 111
```

```
              coef  exp(coef)   se(coef)        z Pr(>|z|)
trt      -1.242e-01  8.832e-01  2.147e-01  -0.579  0.56290
age       2.890e-02  1.029e+00  1.164e-02   2.482  0.01305 *
sexf     -3.656e-01  6.938e-01  3.113e-01  -1.174  0.24022
ascites   8.833e-02  1.092e+00  3.872e-01   0.228  0.81955
hepato    2.552e-02  1.026e+00  2.510e-01   0.102  0.91900
spiders   1.012e-01  1.107e+00  2.435e-01   0.416  0.67760
edema     1.011e+00  2.749e+00  3.941e-01   2.566  0.01029 *
bili      8.001e-02  1.083e+00  2.550e-02   3.138  0.00170 **
chol      4.918e-04  1.000e+00  4.442e-04   1.107  0.26829
albumin  -7.408e-01  4.767e-01  3.078e-01  -2.407  0.01608 *
copper    2.490e-03  1.002e+00  1.170e-03   2.128  0.03337 *
alk.phos  1.048e-06  1.000e+00  3.969e-05   0.026  0.97893
ast       4.070e-03  1.004e+00  1.958e-03   2.078  0.03767 *
trig     -9.758e-04  9.990e-01  1.333e-03  -0.732  0.46414
platelet  9.019e-04  1.001e+00  1.184e-03   0.762  0.44629
protime   2.324e-01  1.262e+00  1.061e-01   2.190  0.02850 *
stage     4.545e-01  1.575e+00  1.754e-01   2.591  0.00958 **
---
Signif. codes:  0 '***' 0.001 '**' 0.01 '*' 0.05 '.' 0.1 ' ' 1

          exp(coef) exp(-coef) lower .95 upper .95
trt          0.8832     1.1323    0.5798    1.3453
age          1.0293     0.9715    1.0061    1.0531
sexf         0.6938     1.4414    0.3769    1.2771
ascites      1.0924     0.9155    0.5114    2.3332
hepato       1.0259     0.9748    0.6273    1.6777
spiders      1.1066     0.9037    0.6865    1.7835
edema        2.7487     0.3638    1.2697    5.9505
bili         1.0833     0.9231    1.0305    1.1388
chol         1.0005     0.9995    0.9996    1.0014
albumin      0.4767     2.0977    0.2608    0.8714
copper       1.0025     0.9975    1.0002    1.0048
alk.phos     1.0000     1.0000    0.9999    1.0001
ast          1.0041     0.9959    1.0002    1.0079
trig         0.9990     1.0010    0.9964    1.0016
platelet     1.0009     0.9991    0.9986    1.0032
protime      1.2617     0.7926    1.0247    1.5534
stage        1.5754     0.6348    1.1170    2.2219

Concordance= 0.849  (se = 0.031 )
Rsquare= 0.455    (max possible= 0.981 )
Likelihood ratio test= 167.7  on 17 df,   p=0
Wald test             = 174.1  on 17 df,   p=0
```

```
Score (logrank) test = 283.7  on 17 df,   p=0

> round(pbc_coxph_summary$coefficients[,5],4)
     trt      age     sexf  ascites    hepato  spiders     edema
bili
  0.5629   0.0131   0.2402   0.8195   0.9190   0.6776   0.0103
0.0017
    chol  albumin   copper alk.phos      ast     trig platelet
protime
  0.2683   0.0161   0.0334   0.9789   0.0377   0.4641   0.4463
0.0285
   stage
  0.0096
> AIC(pbc_coxph)
[1] 966.6642
```

Since we find that a lot of variables are insignificant, we will attempt to improve on it by using the step function and then calculating the improved AIC value, as shown in the following code:

```
> pbc_coxph_eff <- step(pbc_coxph)
Start:  AIC=966.66
Surv(time, status == 2) ~ trt + age + sex + ascites + hepato +
    spiders + edema + bili + chol + albumin + copper + alk.phos +
    ast + trig + platelet + protime + stage
          Df    AIC
- alk.phos  1 964.66
- hepato    1 964.67
- ascites   1 964.72
- spiders   1 964.84
- trt       1 965.00
- trig      1 965.22
- platelet  1 965.24
- chol      1 965.82
- sex       1 965.99
<none>        966.66
- ast       1 968.69
- copper    1 968.85
- protime   1 968.99
- albumin   1 970.35
- age       1 970.84
- edema     1 971.00
- stage     1 971.83
- bili      1 973.34


Step:  AIC=952.58
```

```
Surv(time, status == 2) ~ age + edema + bili + albumin + copper +
    ast + protime + stage


          Df    AIC
<none>        952.58
- protime  1 955.06
- ast      1 955.79
- edema    1 955.95
- albumin  1 957.27
- copper   1 958.18
- age      1 959.97
- stage    1 960.11
- bili     1 966.57
> pbc_coxph_eff_summary <- summary(pbc_coxph_eff)
> pbc_coxph_eff_summary
Call:
coxph(formula = Surv(time, status == 2) ~ age + edema + bili +
    albumin + copper + ast + protime + stage, data = pbc2)
  n= 276, number of events= 111
               coef  exp(coef)   se(coef)      z Pr(>|z|)
age       0.0313836  1.0318812  0.0102036  3.076  0.00210 **
edema     0.8217952  2.2745795  0.3471465  2.367  0.01792 *
bili      0.0851214  1.0888492  0.0193352  4.402 1.07e-05 ***
albumin  -0.7185954  0.4874364  0.2724486 -2.638  0.00835 **
copper    0.0028535  1.0028576  0.0009832  2.902  0.00370 **
ast       0.0043769  1.0043865  0.0018067  2.423  0.01541 *
protime   0.2275175  1.2554794  0.1013729  2.244  0.02481 *
stage     0.4327939  1.5415584  0.1456307  2.972  0.00296 **
---
Signif. codes:  0 '***' 0.001 '**' 0.01 '*' 0.05 '.' 0.1 ' ' 1


        exp(coef) exp(-coef) lower .95 upper .95
age        1.0319     0.9691    1.0114    1.0527
edema      2.2746     0.4396    1.1519    4.4915
bili       1.0888     0.9184    1.0484    1.1309
albumin    0.4874     2.0515    0.2858    0.8314
copper     1.0029     0.9972    1.0009    1.0048
ast        1.0044     0.9956    1.0008    1.0079
protime    1.2555     0.7965    1.0292    1.5314
stage      1.5416     0.6487    1.1588    2.0508

Concordance= 0.845  (se = 0.031 )
Rsquare= 0.448   (max possible= 0.981 )
Likelihood ratio test= 163.8  on 8 df,    p=0
```

```
Wald test              = 176.1  on 8 df,    p=0
Score (logrank) test = 257.5  on 8 df,    p=0
> round(pbc_coxph_eff_summary$coefficients[,5],4)
   age    edema    bili albumin   copper     ast protime    stage
 0.0021  0.0179  0.0000  0.0084   0.0037  0.0154  0.0248   0.0030
> AIC(pbc_coxph_eff)
[1]  952.5814
```

We can now see that almost all the variables in the `pbc_coxph_eff` model are significant. The AIC value has also decreased from its earlier value.

In most survival data analyses, the purpose is to find the effective covariates and their impact on the hazard rate. Accuracy measures, such as AUC with classification problems, do not exist in the context of survival data. On similar (though important) lines, the prediction of the lifetime for a given choice of covariates might not again be of importance. In *Chapter 2, Bootstrapping*, we looked at the application of pseudo values and the jackknife methods that provided ease of interpretation. We will look at a different approach in the following section.

Survival tree

The parametric hazards regression model is sometimes seen as a restrictive class of models by practitioners, and the Cox proportional hazards regression is sometimes preferred over its parametric counterpart. Compared with the parametric models, the interpretation is sometimes lost, and the regular practitioner finds it difficult to connect with the hazards regression model. Of course, an alternative is to build a survival tree over the pseudo observations. Such an attempt can be seen in Tattar's (2016) unpublished paper. Gordon and Olshen (1985) made the first attempt to build a survival tree and many scientists have continued constructing it. LeBlanc and Crowley (1992) are among the most important contributors to set up a survival tree. Zhang and Singer (2010) have also given a systematic development of related methods, and chapters 7-10 of their book deal with survival trees. The basic premise remains the same, and we need good splitting criteria in order to create the survival tree.

LeBlanc and Crowley proposed the splitting criteria based on the node deviance measure between a saturated model log-likelihood and the maximum log-likelihood, and then the unknown full likelihood is approximated by replacing the baseline cumulative hazard function as estimated by the Nelson-Aalen estimator. As suggested by Hamad et al. (2011), note that the advantage of this method is that any software that can carry out the implementation of Poisson trees would be able to create the survival tree. This approach has been exploited in the `rpart` R package created by Therneau and Atkinson (2017). The terminal nodes of the survival tree can be summarized by the Kaplan-Meier survival function for the observations belonging in the node.

We will now set up the survival tree for the `pbc` dataset using the `rpart` library:

```
> pbc_stree <- rpart(Surv(time,status==2)~trt + age + sex + ascites +
+                    hepato + spiders + edema + bili + chol +
albumin +
+                    copper + alk.phos + ast + trig + platelet +
+                    protime + stage,
+                pbc)
> pbc_stree
n= 418

node), split, n, deviance, yval
      * denotes terminal node

  1) root 418 555.680700 1.0000000
    2) bili< 2.25 269 232.626500 0.4872828
      4) age< 51.24162 133   76.376990 0.2395736
        8) alk.phos< 1776 103   30.340440 0.1036750 *
        9) alk.phos>=1776 30   33.092480 0.6135695 *
      5) age>=51.24162 136 136.800300 0.7744285
       10) protime< 10.85 98   80.889260 0.5121123 *
       11) protime>=10.85 38   43.381670 1.4335430
         22) age< 65.38125 26   24.045820 0.9480269
           44) bili< 0.75 8    5.188547 0.3149747 *
           45) bili>=0.75 18   12.549130 1.3803650 *
         23) age>=65.38125 12    8.392462 3.2681510 *
    3) bili>=2.25 149 206.521900 2.6972690
      6) protime< 11.25 94   98.798830 1.7717830
       12) stage< 3.5 57   56.734150 1.2620350
         24) age< 43.5332 25   16.656000 0.6044998 *
         25) age>=43.5332 32   32.986760 1.7985470 *
       13) stage>=3.5 37   32.946240 2.8313470 *
      7) protime>=11.25 55   76.597760 5.1836880
       14) ascites< 0.5 41   52.276360 4.1601690
         28) age< 42.68172 7    6.829564 1.4344660 *
         29) age>=42.68172 34   37.566600 5.1138380 *
       15) ascites>=0.5 14   17.013010 7.9062910 *
```

A text display of the survival tree is displayed by running `pbc_stree` at the console. The asterisk (*) at the end of the `yval` for a node indicates censorship.

We will now look at the `cptable` and variable importance associated with the survival tree, as shown in the following program:

```
> pbc_stree$cptable
           CP nsplit rel error    xerror        xstd
1  0.20971086      0 1.0000000 1.0026398 0.04761402
2  0.05601298      1 0.7902891 0.8179390 0.04469359
3  0.03500063      2 0.7342762 0.8198147 0.04731189
4  0.02329408      3 0.6992755 0.8247148 0.04876085
5  0.02254786      4 0.6759815 0.8325230 0.05132829
6  0.01969366      5 0.6534336 0.8363125 0.05160507
7  0.01640950      6 0.6337399 0.8373375 0.05268262
8  0.01366665      7 0.6173304 0.8336743 0.05406099
9  0.01276163      9 0.5899971 0.8209714 0.05587843
10 0.01135209     10 0.5772355 0.8248827 0.05612403
11 0.01000000     11 0.5658834 0.8255873 0.05599763
> pbc_stree$variable.importance
       bili     protime         age     albumin       edema       stage
 138.007841   70.867308   54.548224   32.239919   25.576170   15.231256
    ascites    alk.phos    platelet         sex      copper         ast
  14.094208   13.440866   10.017966    2.452776    2.114888    1.691910
```

The variable importance shows that the `bili` variable is the most important, followed by `protime` and `age`. We conclude this section with a visual depiction of the survival tree, using the following code:

```
> windows(height=100,width=60)
> plot(pbc_stree,uniform = TRUE)
> text(pbc_stree,use.n=TRUE)
```

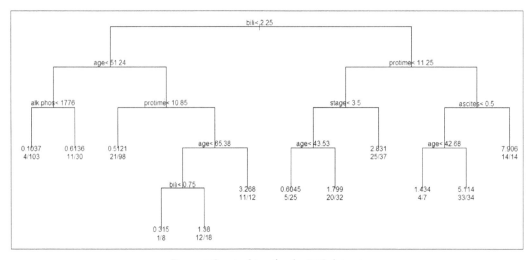

Figure 6: Survival tree for the PBC dataset

As with the problem of overfitting with a single tree, we need to look at an important alternative method of ensembles of survival trees.

Ensemble survival models

The random forest package `randomForestSRC` will continue to be useful for creating the random forests associated with the survival data. In fact, the `s` of `SRC` in the package name stands for survival! The usage of the `rfsrc` function remains the same as in previous chapters, and we will now give it a `Surv` object, as shown in the following code:

```
> pbc_rf <- rfsrc(Surv(time,status==2)~trt + age + sex + ascites +
+                 hepato + spiders + edema + bili + chol + albumin+
+                 copper + alk.phos + ast +trig + platelet + protime+
+                 stage, ntree=500, tree.err = TRUE, pbc)
```

We will find some of the basic settings that have gone into setting up this random forest:

```
> pbc_rf$splitrule
[1] "logrankCR"
> pbc_rf$nodesize
[1] 6
> pbc_rf$mtry
[1] 5
```

Thus, the splitting criteria is based on the log-rank test, the minimum number of observations in a terminal node is six, and the number of variables considered at random for each split is five.

Next, we will find the variable importance for both events and apply the function `var.select` as we have done in earlier chapters. We will then show a part of the iteration run using the following code:

```
> vimp(pbc_rf)$importance
              event.1       event.2
trt        0.0013257796 0.0002109143
age        0.0348848966 0.0166352983
sex        0.0007755091 0.0004011303
ascites    0.0008513276 0.0107212361
hepato     0.0050666763 0.0015445001
spiders   -0.0001136547 0.0003552415
edema      0.0006227470 0.0147982184
bili       0.0696654202 0.0709713627
chol       0.0002483833 0.0107024051
```

```
albumin  -0.0106392917 0.0115188264
copper    0.0185417386 0.0255099568
alk.phos  0.0041407841 0.0022297323
ast       0.0029317937 0.0063469825
trig     -0.0040190463 0.0014371745
platelet  0.0021021396 0.0002388797
protime   0.0057968358 0.0133710339
stage    -0.0023944666 0.0042808034
> var.select(pbc_rf, method = "vh.vimp", nrep = 50)
-------------------- Iteration: 1   --------------------
 selecting variables using Variable Hunting (VIMP) ...
 PE: 38.8889     dim: 2
-------------------- Iteration: 2   --------------------
 selecting variables using Variable Hunting (VIMP) ...
 PE: 23.6842     dim: 2
-------------------- Iteration: 3   --------------------
 selecting variables using Variable Hunting (VIMP) ...
 PE: 50.6667     dim: 1




-------------------- Iteration: 48   --------------------
 selecting variables using Variable Hunting (VIMP) ...
 PE: 38.3562     dim: 2
-------------------- Iteration: 49   --------------------
 selecting variables using Variable Hunting (VIMP) ...
 PE: 19.4737     dim: 2
-------------------- Iteration: 50   --------------------
 selecting variables using Variable Hunting (VIMP) ...
 PE: 55.914      dim: 2
fitting forests to final selected variables ...


-----------------------------------------------------------
family             : surv-CR
var. selection     : Variable Hunting (VIMP)
conservativeness   : medium
dimension          : 17
sample size        : 276
K-fold             : 5
no. reps           : 50
nstep              : 1
ntree              : 500
nsplit             : 10
mvars              : 4
nodesize           : 2
```

```
refitted forest     : TRUE
model size          : 2.16 +/- 0.6809
PE (K-fold)         : 43.3402 +/- 17.7472


Top variables:
        rel.freq
bili         28
hepato       24
ast          24
-------------------------------------------------------------
```

Next, the error rate plot as the number of trees increases will be depicted using the following code:

```
> plot(pbc_rf,plots.one.page = TRUE)
```

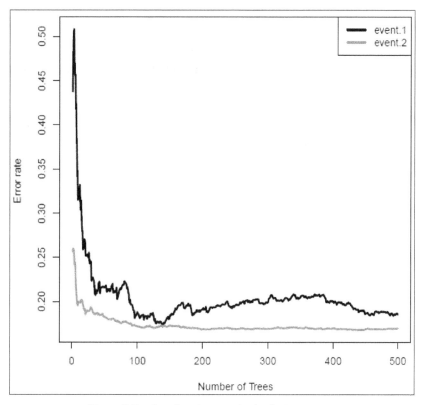

Figure 7: Random forest error rates for the two events

Consequently, we have now seen the construction and setup of random forests for the survival data.

Summary

Survival data is different to typical regression data, and the incomplete observations pose a challenge. Since the data structure is completely different, we need specialized techniques to handle the incomplete observations and to that end, we introduced core survival concepts, such as hazard rate and survival function. We then introduced parametric lifetime models, which gives us a brief peek at how the lifetime distribution should look. We even fitted these lifetime distributions into the pbc dataset.

We also learned that the parametric setup might be very restrictive, and hence considered the nonparametric methods of the estimation of survival quantities. We also demonstrated the utility of the Nelson-Aalen estimator, the Kaplan-Meier survival function, and the log-rank test. The parametric hazards regression model was backed with the Cox proportional hazards regression model and applied to the pbc dataset. The logrank test can also help in the splitting criteria, and it has also been seen as the criteria for the random forest. Survival trees were demonstrated in the earlier section.

In the next chapter, we will look at another kind of data structure: time series data. The reader does not need to be familiar with time series analysis in order to follow the ensemble methods applied in it.

11
Ensembling Time Series Models

All of the models developed in this book so far have dealt with situations that arise when observations are independent of each other. The example of overseas visitors explains a time series in which the observations are dependent on the previously observed data. In a brief discussion of this example, it was established that it is necessary to develop time series models. Since the time series is sequential in nature, the time stamp may be displayed in nanoseconds, seconds, minutes, hours, days, or months.

This chapter will open with a quick review of the important concepts of time series in autocorrelation and partial autocorrelation functions, as well as fitted model assessment measures. Much like the classification and regression models, a host of methods are available for analyzing time series data. An important class of time series models in seasonal decomposition includes LOESS (STL), exponential smoothing state space models (ets), Box-Jenkins (ARIMA) models, and autoregressive neural network models. These will be discussed and illustrated in the following section. The ensembling of time series models will be illustrated in the final section of the chapter.

The main areas that will be covered in this chapter include the following:

- Time series datasets
- Time series visualization
- Core concepts
- Time series models
- Bagging time series
- Ensembling time series models

Technical requirements

In this chapter, we will be using the following R libraries:

- `forecast`
- `forecastHybrid`

Time series datasets

Time series data is structurally different from the data discussed up until now. A glimpse of time series data was seen in *Overseas Visitor* in *section 1* of *Chapter 1, Introduction to Ensemble Techniques*, and the bootstrapping of the time series models was briefly touched on in *Chapter 2, Bootstrapping*. The complexity that arises in the analysis of time series data is that the observations are not independent and, consequently, we need to specify the dependence. Box et al. (2015) is the benchmark book for the statistical analysis of time series, and its first edition was published in 1970. The class of models invented and popularized in Box and Jenkins is the popular autoregressive integrated moving average, famously abbreviated as ARIMA. This is also often known as the Box-Jenkins model.

Table 1 summarizes twenty-one time series datasets. The Length column gives the number of observations/data points of the series, while the **Frequency** column gives the periodicity of the time series, and the remaining six columns are simply the summaries obtained by applying the summary function to a numeric object. The first column, of course, gives the names of the datasets as they are available in R, and hence we have not changed the cases, upper or lower. The numbers of observations in the datasets range from 19 to 7980.

But what does frequency or periodicity mean? In a dataset which includes periodicity, the associated time index gets repeated. For instance, we might have yearly, quarterly, monthly, or weekly data, and thus, in the middle two cases, the frequency will be **4** and **12** respectively. The frequency need not be an integer and can also be a fractional value. For example, carcinogenesis tests will have values in nanoseconds. The summary of the time series data is simply the result of applying the summary function to a numeric dataset. Consequently, we implicitly assume that time series data is numeric. The variation as seen in the summaries also shows that different datasets will require different handling. A quick introduction to a time series application can be found in Chapter 10 of Tattar et al. (2017).

A description of the datasets used in this chapter can be found in the following table:

Dataset	Length	Frequency	Minimum	Q1	Median	Mean	Q3	Maximum
AirPassengers	144	12	104.00	180.00	265.50	280.30	360.50	622.00
BJsales	150	1	198.60	212.58	220.65	229.98	254.68	263.30
JohnsonJohnson	84	4	0.44	1.25	3.51	4.80	7.13	16.20
LakeHuron	98	1	575.96	578.14	579.12	579.00	579.88	581.86
Nile	100	1	456.00	798.50	893.50	919.35	1032.50	1370.00
UKgas	108	4	84.80	153.30	220.90	337.63	469.90	1163.90
UKDriverDeaths	192	12	1057.00	1461.75	1631.00	1670.31	1850.75	2654.00
USAccDeaths	72	12	6892.00	8089.00	8728.50	8788.79	9323.25	11317.00
WWWusage	100	1	83.00	99.00	138.50	137.08	167.50	228.00
airmiles	24	1	412.00	1580.00	6431.00	10527.83	17531.50	30514.00
austres	89	4	13067.30	14110.10	15184.20	15273.45	16398.90	17661.50
co2	468	12	313.18	323.53	335.17	337.05	350.26	366.84
discoveries	100	1	0.00	2.00	3.00	3.10	4.00	12.00
lynx	114	1	39.00	348.25	771.00	1538.02	2566.75	6991.00
nhtemp	60	1	47.90	50.58	51.20	51.16	51.90	54.60
nottem	240	12	31.30	41.55	47.35	49.04	57.00	66.50
presidents	120	4	23.00	46.00	59.00	56.31	69.00	87.00
treering	7980	1	0.00	0.84	1.03	1.00	1.20	1.91
gas	476	12	1646.00	2674.75	16787.50	21415.27	38628.50	66600.00
uspop	19	0.1	3.93	15.00	50.20	69.77	114.25	203.20
sunspots	2820	12	0.00	15.70	42.00	51.27	74.93	253.80

Table 1: Time Series Datasets in R

AirPassengers

The AirPassengers dataset contains the monthly totals of international airline passengers from 1949 to 1960. The monthly count numbers are in thousands. Over twelve years, the monthly data accumulated 144 observations. Since we have multiple observations across the years for the months, the seasonality aspect of the travelers count can be captured from the data. This was popularized in Box et al. (2015).

co2

The co2 time series data is related to atmospheric concentrations of carbon dioxide. The concentration is expressed in parts per million (ppm), and this dataset is reported in the preliminary 1997 SIO manometric mole fraction scale. This time series was captured on a monthly basis for the period of 1959–97. On the help page of co2, it is noted that the missing values for the months of February, March, and April, 1964 are obtained by linearly interpolating between the values for January and May of 1964.

uspop

The US census population (in millions), uspop, was recorded by the decennial census between 1790 and 1970. This was made available in a small time series dataset and, accordingly, it only consists of 19 data points. Seasonality is not captured in this dataset.

gas

The gas time series data contains Australian monthly gas production. The data available here is for the period of 1956–95. Consequently, we have 476 observations here. This dataset is drawn from the forecast package.

Car Sales

The car sales data is adapted from Abraham and Ledolter (1983). For more information, refer to Table 2.7, page 68 of the book. The sales and advertising data is available for a period of 36 months. Here, we have additional information on the amount spent on advertisements each week. This is the first instance of additional variables availability, and it calls for specialized treatment, which we will explore further later in the chapter. The data is available in the Car_Sales.csv file and this is available in the code bundle.

austres

The austres time series dataset consists of a quarterly number of Australian residents for the period March 1971 to March 1994.

WWWusage

The WWWusage time series dataset consists of the number of users connected to the internet through a server. The data is collected at a time interval of one minute. The time series values are collected for 100 observations.

Visualization gives invaluable insights and we will plot some of the time series next.

Time series visualization

The main characteristic of time series data is that the observations are taken at regular intervals. A plot of the time series values (the y axis) against the time itself (x axis) is of great importance and gives away many structural insights. A time series plot is not merely a scatterplot with time as the x axis. The time is non-decreasing and hence it has more importance and meaning in a time series plot than the mere x axis in a scatterplot. For instance, lines can connect the points of a time series plot that will indicate the path of the time series, and such a connection would be meaningless in the scatterplot, which would be all over the place. The path will generally indicate the trend and as such, shows in which direction the series will go next. Changes in time series are easily depicted in the plot. We will now visualize the different time series.

The plot.ts function is central to the scheme of visualization here. An external graphical device of appropriate size is first invoked with the windows function. The X11 function can be used in Ubuntu/Linux. Next, we run the plot.ts function on the AirPassengers dataset:

```
> windows(height=100,width=150)
> plot.ts(AirPassengers)
```

The following plot shows an increase in the number of monthly passengers across the years, on average:

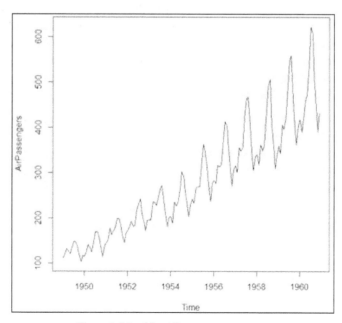

Figure 1: Monthly airline passenger count

We can see here that a pattern seems to be repeating itself after a cycle of 12 months, which indicates a seasonal trend across the months. It would be nice to obtain a plot where we select the first year and look at the plot across the months, then move to the next year and impose the next year's monthly data and visualize it, and so on until the entire data is displayed. A `plotts` function is created which achieves a plot of this description, and its structure is given in *Figure 3*:

```
plotts <- function(ts){
  tf <- frequency(ts)
  if(tf<=1) plot.ts(ts) else
    {
      beginy <- start(ts)[1]; endy <- end(ts)[1]
      plot(x=NULL,y=NULL,ylim=range(ts),xlim=c(1,tf),
           ylab="Time Series",xlab="Time","l",col=1)
      points(start(ts)[2]:tf,window(ts,start=start(ts),end=c(beginy,tf)),
             col=beginy,"l")
      for(i in (beginy+1):(endy-1)){
        points(1:tf,window(ts,start=c(i,1),end=c(i,tf)),col=i,"l")
      }
      points(1:end(ts)[2],window(ts,start=c(endy,1),end=end(ts)),
             col=endy,"l")
    }
}
```

Figure 2: The time series frequency plot function

The `plotts` function is now applied on the `AirPassengers` data. The function is available in the `Utilities.R` file of the companion chapter code bundle, and it is invoked in the beginning of the `C11.R` file using the `source` command. The data has 12 years of data, and thus we will have 12 curves on the resulting time series plots. The `legend` of the plot will require more than the usual area, and hence we plot it on the right-hand side of the graph. The required manipulations are accomplished with the `par`, `mar`, and `legend` functions as follows:

```
> par(mar=c(5.1, 4.1, 4.1, 8.1), xpd=TRUE)
> plotts(AirPassengers)
> legend("topright", inset=c(-0.2,0), "-",
+        legend=c(start(AirPassengers)[1]:end(AirPassengers)[1]),
+        col=start(AirPassengers)[1]:end(AirPassengers)[1],lty=2)
```

We can now clearly see the seasonal impact in the following figure:

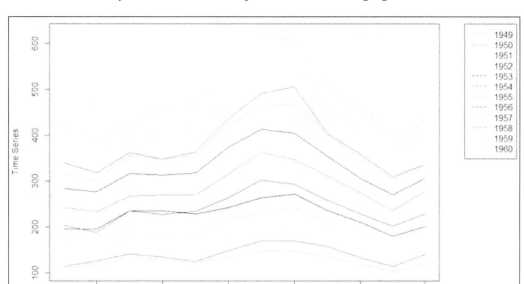

Figure 3: Seasonal plot for the AirPassengers dataset

The monthly passenger count visit hits a low in the months of February and November. The monthly passenger count increases steadily from February to July, remains at a similar level for August, and then decreases steeply until November. A slight increase can be seen for the months of December and January. Consequently, the seasonal plots give more insights, and they should be used complementarily with the `plot.ts` function. Hyndman's forecast package contains a function named `seasonalplot` which accomplishes the same result as the `plotts` function defined here.

The Australian residents dataset `austres` is covered next. The `plotts` function and legend will be used to enhance the display:

```
>plot.ts(austres)
>windows(height=100,width=150)
>par(mar=c(5.1, 4.1, 4.1, 8.1), xpd=TRUE)
>plotts(austres)
>legend("topright", inset=c(-0.2,0), "-",
+        legend=c(start(austres)[1]:end(austres)[1]),
+        col=start(austres)[1]:end(austres)[1],lty=2)
```

The following plot is a quarterly time series of the number of Australian residents:

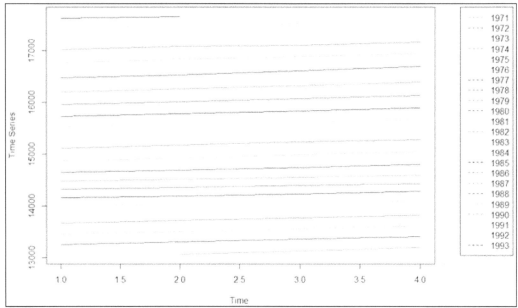

Figure 4: Quarterly time series of the number of Australian residents

What is the difference between the seasonal plots of *Figure 4* and *Figure 5*? Of course, we are looking for differences other than the trivial monthly and quarterly periodicity. In *Figure 5*, we can see that, although there is an increase in the quarterly number of monthly residents, it is hardly a seasonal factor; it appears to be more of a trend factor than a seasonal one. Thus, the seasonal contribution appears less in comparison with the AirPassengers dataset.

The time series plot for the carbon dioxide concentrations is visualized next. We use the plot.ts function on the co2 dataset:

```
>plot.ts(co2)
```

The result of running the `plot.ts` function is the next output:

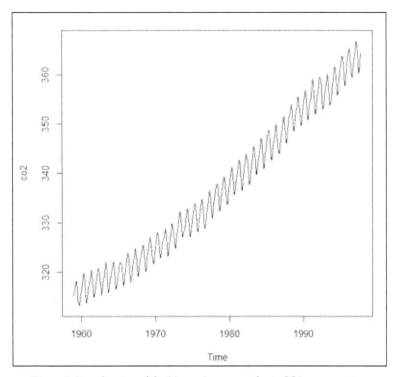

Figure 5: Visualization of the Mauna Loa atmospheric CO2 concentration

A seasonal impact is easily seen in the time series plot of the carbon dioxide concentrations. A seasonal plot might provide more insight, and we will use the `plotts` function next:

```
>windows(height=100,width=150)
>par(mar=c(5.1, 4.1, 4.1, 8.1), xpd=TRUE)
>plotts(co2)
>legend("topright",inset=c(-0.2,0),
+          "-",
+          legend=c(c(start(co2)[1]:(start(co2)[1]+3)),". . . ",
+                 c((end(co2)[1]-3):end(co2)[1])),
+          col=c(c(start(co2)[1]:(start(co2)[1]+3)),NULL,
+              c((end(co2)[1]-3):end(co2)[1])),lty=2)
```

The `plotts` and `legend` functions have been used in the same way as previously. The result of the program is shown in *Figure 7*, and we can clearly see the seasonal impact in the time series display:

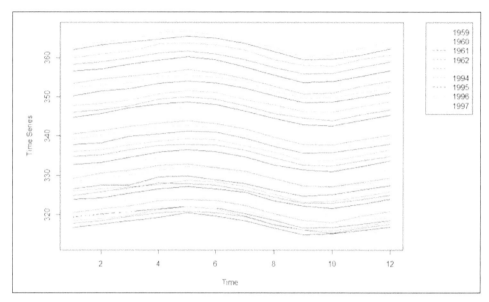

Figure 6: Seasonal plot of the Mauna Loa Atmospheric CO2 concentration

Exercise: Use the `seasonalplot` function from the `forecast` package and replicate the seasonal plots. What is the difference here, if any?

The seasonality is an important aspect of the time series. It is important to identify it early so that an appropriate model is chosen for analysis of the time series. We will visualize three more time series datasets, `UKDriverDeaths`, `gas`, and `uspop`:

```
>windows(height=100,width=300)
>par(mfrow=c(1,3))
>plot.ts(UKDriverDeaths,main="UK Driver Deaths")
>plot.ts(gas,main="Australian monthly gas production")
>plot.ts(uspop,main="Populations Recorded by the US Census")
```

The three displays in *Figure 7* are unlike any seen thus far. It seems unlikely that the models that fit well earlier will perform similarly here. We see a lot of variability for the `UKDriverDeaths` and `gas` datasets. For `UKDriverDeaths`, it appears that there was a decline in fatalities after the year 1983. For the gas dataset, we can see that there was a regular seasonal impact until the year 1970, and following that year, the `gas` productivity shot up drastically. It might be an indication of some technological breakthrough or some other phenomenological changes. The variability also increases, and barely appears constant across the time horizon. The `uspop` shows an exponential growth.

Exercise: Visually inspect if there is a seasonal impact for the UKDriverDeaths and gas datasets:

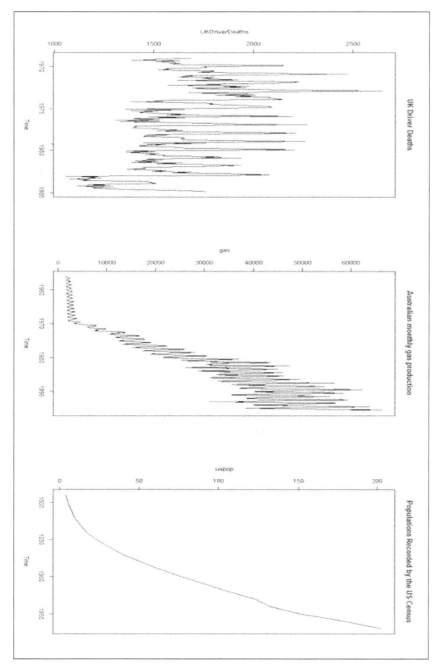

Figure 7: Three time series plots: UKDriverDeaths, gas, and uspop

Core concepts and metrics

The visualization of the time series data has conveyed a similar story in all the examples, from *Figure 1* to *Figure 7*. The trend and seasonality of the observations imply that the future values of the time series are dependent on the current values, and thus we can't assume that the observations are independent of each other. But what does this mean? To reiterate the point, consider the simpler uspop (US population) dataset, the third-right panel display of *Figure 7*. Here, we don't have a seasonal influence. Now, consider the census year 1900. The population at the next census is certainly not less than in the year 1890, and it is not well beyond the same number of the same year. A similar narrative holds for most time series; for example, if we are recording the maximum temperature of the day. Here, if today's maximum temperature is 42°C, the next day's maximum temperature is highly influenced by this number and it is almost completely ruled out that the next day's maximum temperature will be either 55°C or 25°C. Although it is easily seen that the observations are dependent on each other, the formal specification is also a challenge in itself. Let us formally introduce a time series.

We will denote a time series by $\{Y_t\}_{t=1}^{\infty}$ that is observed at times $t = 1,2,3,\ldots$. An alternative notation for a time series observed up to time T is $Y_t, 1 \leq t \leq T$. A time series may be conceptualized as a stochastic process Y observed at times t =1, 2, 3, ….

Associated with the time series process $\{Y_t\}_{t=1}^{\infty}$ is the error process $\{\in_t\}_{t=1}^{\infty}$. The error process is generally assumed to be a white noise process with zero mean and some constant variance. The error process is often referred to as the innovation process. Note that the time series Y_t might depend on the past values of the process in $Y_{t-1}, Y_{t-2}, \ldots$, as well as the values of error $\in_t$ and the past values of the error process $\in_{t-1}, \in_{t-2}, \ldots$. The value Y_{t-1} is also referred to as the first lag value of Y_t, Y_{t-2} the second lag value of Y_t, and so on. Now, if the observations are dependent on each other, the specification of the relationship between them is the biggest challenge. Of course, we can't go into detail here. However, if we believe that the first-order lagged terms are dependent, there must be a relationship here, and we can obtain a scatterplot with the observations Y_t on the y-axis and the first-order lagged terms on the x-axis. The first-order lagged scatterplot for the AirPassengers dataset is obtained as follows:

```
>plot(AirPassengers[1:143],AirPassengers[2:144],
+       xlab="Previous Observation",
+       ylab="Current Observation")
```

The use of indexing changes the class of time series objects to a numeric object:

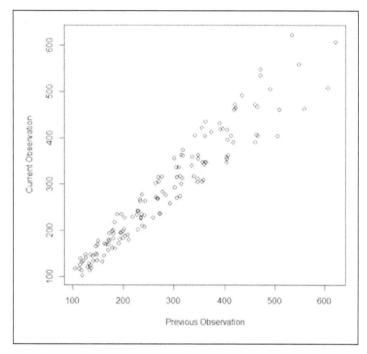

Figure 8: Lag plot of the AirPassengers dataset

In the preceding graphical display, we can clearly see that there is (almost) a linear relationship between the lagged observations, and thus a model might be of the form $Y_t = \beta_0 + \beta_1 Y_{t-1} + \epsilon_t$. Can the scatterplot help in determining the order of the dependency? Hardly! We will obtain a plot of the WWWusage dataset next and look at the lagged plots:

```
>windows(height=200,width=200)
>par(mfrow=c(2,2))
>plot.ts(WWWusage)
>plot(WWWusage[1:99],WWWusage[2:100],
+       xlab="Previous Observation",
+       ylab="Current Observation",main="Lag-1 Plot"
+       )
>plot(WWWusage[1:98],WWWusage[3:100],
+       xlab="Previous Observation",
+       ylab="Current Observation",main="Lag-2 Plot"
+       )
>plot(WWWusage[1:97],WWWusage[4:100],
+       xlab="Previous Observation",
+       ylab="Current Observation",main="Lag-3 Plot"
+       )
```

Following are the lagged plots for WWWUsage:

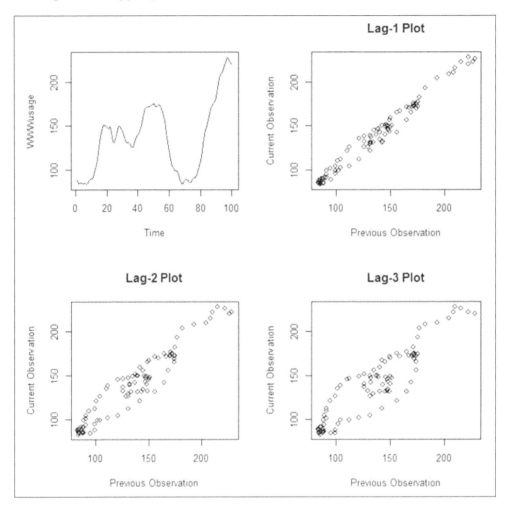

Figure 9: Lagged plots for WWWUsage

The first lagged plot might give the impression that the observations are correlated. However, the higher-order lagged plots barely make any sense, and going back to the first-order lagged plot creates more confusion. As a consequence, we need a more formal method of obtaining insights on the order of lags.

The two measures that are useful for understanding the nature of dependency in time series data are **auto-correlation function (ACF)** and **partial auto-correlation function (PACF)**. As the name suggests, ACF is the correlation of a time series with its own lagged values. The PACF's partial nomenclature accounts for removing the impact of intermediate variables from the lagged one. In simple terms, the PACF for lag 3 will include only the first Y_t; third lagged variables Y_{t-3} and the Y_{t-1}, Y_{t-2} variables are not allowed to influence the PACF. The lag-k ACF is defined as the correlation between the random variable Y_t and the k-th lagged variable Y_{t-k}:

$$\rho_k = \frac{E\left(Y_t - \mu\right)\left(Y_{t-k} - \mu\right)}{\sigma^2}$$

Where σ^2 is the variance of the time series. The partial autocorrelation function PACF between Yt and its k-th lag $Yt-k$ is the partial correlation of the time series when controlling the values at shorter lags $Y_{t-1}, Y_{t-2}, ..., Y_{t-k+1}$. It is not possible to go into the mathematical details of the PACF concept; the reader may refer to Box et al. (2015) for more information. The sample ACF formula, based on n observations, is given using the following:

$$\hat{\rho}_k = \frac{\sum_{t=k+1}^{n}\left(Y_t - \bar{Y}\right)\left(Y_{t-k} - \bar{Y}\right)}{\sum_{t=1}^{n}\left(Y_t - \bar{Y}\right)^2}, k = 0, 1, 2, ...$$

For an explicit formula of the PACF, we refer the reader to the document available on the web at http://mondi.web.elte.hu/spssdoku/algoritmusok/acf_pacf.pdf.

In spite of the intimidating formula, we have an easy getaway by simply using the acf and pacf functions on two datasets, austres and uspop:

```
>jpeg("ACF_PACF_Plots.jpeg")
>par(mfrow=c(2,2))
>acf(austres,main="ACF of Austres Data")
>pacf(austres,main="PACF of Austres Data")
>acf(uspop,main="ACF of US Population")
>pacf(uspop,main="PACF of US Population")
>dev.off()
RStudioGD
        2
```

We will keep the interpretation of ACF and PACF plots simpler. The important guideline in ACF and PACF plots are the horizontal blue lines. Any lagged ACF and PACF plots beyond the two lines are significant, and those within the limits are insignificant:

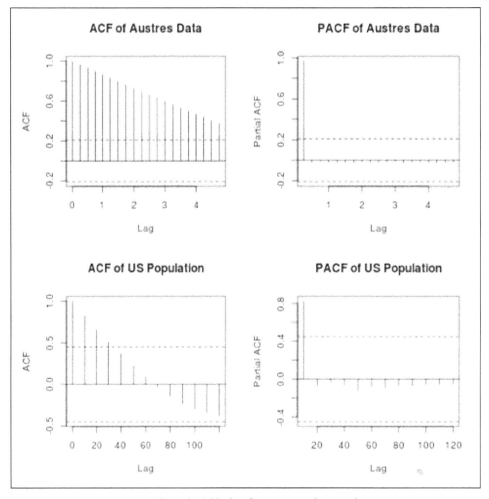

Figure 10: ACF and PACF plots for austres and uspop datasets

We can see from *Figure 10* for the `austres` time series that we need to extend the ACF plot to include more lags. This is because all plotted lags are beyond the horizontal blue lines. For the `uspop` time series, the first time series, the first four lags are significant and the rest are within the horizontal blue lines. The PACF plots can be interpreted in a similar way.

The ACF and PACF plots play an important role in the identification of the ARMA models. Even if the plots reveal information about the lag for the case of AR, it can be used to specify the number of previous values of the time series as part of the input vector for a neural network adapted for the time series data.

In many practical problems, we have additional variables, and we might refer to these as covariate time series or exogenous variables. Let us denote the covariate time series by $\{X_t\}_{t=1}^{\infty}$, where X_t might be a scalar or vector time series. We adopt the convention that only the current and past values of $X_t, t = t, t-1, t-2, \ldots$, will influence Y_t and that the future values of $X_t, t = t, t+1, t+2, \ldots$ will not impact Y_t in any manner. That is, only the lagged values of the covariates will have influence, as opposed to their lead values. In the `Car Sales` dataset, the sales are the time series of interest, and it is the advertising aspect that we believe impacts the sales; sales can't possibly explain the advertisement amount! The `ccf` function is used to obtain the cross-correlation coefficients as follows:

```
>CarSales <- read.csv("../Data/Car_Sales.csv")
>summary(CarSales)
      Sales          Advertising
 Min.    :12.0    Min.    : 1.0
 1st Qu.:20.3    1st Qu.:15.8
 Median :24.2    Median :23.0
 Mean    :24.3    Mean    :28.5
 3rd Qu.:28.6    3rd Qu.:41.0
 Max.    :36.5    Max.    :65.0
>jpeg("CCF_Car_Sales_Advertising.jpeg")
>ccf(x=CarSales$Advertising,y=CarSales$Sales,
+      main="Cross Correlation Between Sales and Advertising")
>dev.off()
RStudioGD
        2
```

The following figure shows the cross correlation between sales and advertising:

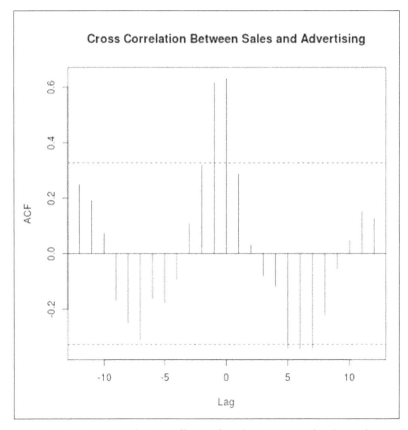

Figure 11: Cross-correlation coefficients for advertising spend and car sales

Should we look at the positive lag values or the negative lag values? Note that the ccf plot is not symmetrical, and hence we can't be absolved for ignoring the signs of the lag values. On running ?ccf at the R terminal, we get The lag k value returned by ccf(x, y) from the help file, which estimates the correlation between x[t+k] and y[t]. Consequently, the positive lags are the lead-ins, while the negative lags are of interest to us. In this example, only the previous lags of X_t, (that is, X_t and X_{t-1}) are significant.

We close this section with a brief discussion of the accuracy measurements. As with earlier learning problems, we will have a slew of models available for us. This is the main topic of discussion in the next section, and we need to define certain assessment metrics accordingly. Let $\{Y_t\}_{t=1}^{\infty}$ denote the time series and, as a consequence of using a certain model, the fitted values will be $\{\widehat{Y}_t\}_{t=1}^{\infty}$. We can access the accuracy of the models through various methods; some of the accuracy measurements include the following:

$$Mean\ Error : ME = \frac{1}{T}\sum_{t=1}^{T} r_t = \frac{1}{T}\sum_{t=1}^{T}\left(Y_t - \widehat{Y}_t\right)$$

$$Root\ Mean\ Square\ Error : RMSE = \left(\frac{1}{T}\sum_{t=1}^{T} r_t^2\right)^{1/2} = \left(\frac{1}{T}\sum_{t=1}^{T}\left(Y_t - \widehat{Y}_t\right)^2\right)^{1/2}$$

$$Mean\ Absolute\ Error : MAE = \frac{1}{T}\sum_{t=1}^{T}|r_t| = \frac{1}{T}\sum_{t=1}^{T}|Y_t - \widehat{Y}_t|$$

$$Mean\ Percentage\ Error : MPE = 100 \times \frac{1}{T}\sum_{t=1}^{T}\frac{r_t}{Y_t} = 100 \times \frac{1}{T}\sum_{t=1}^{T}\frac{Y_t - \widehat{Y}_t}{Y_t}$$

$$Mean\ Absolute\ Percentage\ Error : MAPE = 100 \times \frac{1}{T}\sum_{t=1}^{T}|\frac{r_t}{Y_t}| = 100 \times \frac{1}{T}\sum_{t=1}^{T}|\frac{Y_t - \widehat{Y}_t}{Y_t}|$$

For the moment, we will not concern ourselves with the model. Instead, we will use it as a main tool to extract fitted values and help in obtaining the defined metrics. Using the `subset` function, we will define the training dataset and fit a model using the `auto.arima` function from the `forecast` package. Using the `accuracy` and `forecast` functions, we will then obtain the different accuracies:

```
>co2_sub <- subset(co2,start=1,end=443)
>co2_arima <- auto.arima(co2_sub)
>accuracy(forecast(co2_arima,h=25),x=co2[444:468])
                ME    RMSE   MAE      MPE     MAPE   MASE   ACF1
Training set  0.0185 0.283  0.225   0.00541 0.0672 0.211  0.0119
Test set     -0.0332 0.349  0.270  -0.00912 0.0742 0.252   NA
```

The `forecast` function is a very important one. Given a fitted time series, it will provide predictions for the future periods as requested, and the accuracy function computes the required accuracy for the seven different criteria. The mean error criteria is often useless, and for near unbiased models, its numerical value will be in the vicinity of 0. The metrics RMSE, MAE, MPE, and MAPE are often useful, and the lower their values, the better the model fit is. Furthermore, the training set error and test set error must be comparable. If they are very different from one other, then the model is not useful for forecasts. In the following section, we will review a class of useful time series models.

Essential time series models

We have encountered a set of models for the different regression models thus far. Time series data brings additional complexity, and hence we have even more models to choose from (or rather, ensemble from). A quick review of the important models is provided here. Most of the models discussed here deal with univariate time series $\{Y_t\}_{t=1}^{\infty}$, and we need even more specialized models and methods to incorporate $\{X_t\}_{t=1}^{\infty}$. We will begin with the simplest possible time series model and then move up to the neural network implementations.

Naïve forecasting

Suppose that we have the data $\{Y_t\}_{t=1}^{T}$, and we need forecasts for the next h time points $Y_{T+1}, Y_{T+2}, \ldots, Y_{T+h}$. The naïve forecast model does not require any modeling exercises or computations, it simply returns the current value as future predictions, and thus $\hat{Y}_{T+1} = Y_T, \hat{Y}_{T+2} = Y_T, \ldots, \hat{Y}_{T+h} = Y_T$. It's that simple. Even for this simple task, we will use the naïve function from the forecast package and ask it to provide the forecast for the next 25 observations with h=25:

```
>co2_naive <- naive(co2_sub,h=25,level=c(90,95))
>summary(co2_naive)

Forecast method: Naive method

Model Information:
Call: naive(y = co2_sub, h = 25, level = c(90, 95))

Residual sd: 1.1998

Error measures:
              ME RMSE  MAE   MPE   MAPE  MASE   ACF1
Training set 0.1  1.2 1.07 0.029 0.319 0.852 0.705

Forecasts:
          Point Forecast Lo 90 Hi 90 Lo 95 Hi 95
Dec 1995             360   358   362   357   362
Jan 1996             360   357   362   356   363
Feb 1996             360   356   363   356   364

Oct 1997             360   350   369   348   371
Nov 1997             360   350   369   348   371
Dec 1997             360   350   370   348   371
```

As anticipated, the forecast values remain the same throughout the period. They can be visualized easily, and the accuracies can also be easily computed as follows:

```
>plot(co2_naive) # Output suppressed
>accuracy(forecast(co2_naive,h=25),x=co2[444:468])
                 ME RMSE  MAE   MPE  MAPE MASE  ACF1
Training set 0.10 1.20 1.07 0.029 0.319 1.00 0.705
Test set     3.54 4.09 3.55 0.972 0.974 3.32   NA
```

The natural question that arises is whether the naïve forecasts are any good. An answer to this can be provided in other ways. Complex and sophisticated models will always claim to have advantages and merits. The models might indeed have advantages, but the reference and benchmarking should be clear. The naïve forecasts provide this important benchmark. Note that, for the training period, the accuracy values are different for the naïve forecasts, and it is important that the proposed models are at least better than the metrics of the naïve forecasts. This is the main purpose of the naïve forecasts.

Seasonal, trend, and loess fitting

Season, trend, and loess are the three technical words that are combined to form the stl model. Earlier, we saw in the visual displays of the time series that some of them depict seasonal effects, some show a trend, some show a combination of both seasonal and trend, and some are simply irregular time series. The displays thus indicate the presence or absence of the specific nature of the underlying phenomenon. In this section, we will look at how to make use of the seasonal and trend part of the time series. The third component of the stl model in loess is not explained at all. Loess is a nonparametric regression technique, and stands for local polynomial regression, which generalizes the weighted least squares criteria to a p-th order polynomial. The loess method also consists of a vital component known as kernel. Kernel is a smoothing method, but we will not go into too much detail about this.

Cleveland et al. (1990) proposed a seasonal-trend decomposition based on the loess, and the full details of the procedure can be obtained from the following source: `http://www.scb.se/contentassets/ca21efb41fee47d293bbee5bf7be7fb3/stl-a-seasonal-trend-decomposition-procedure-based-on-loess.pdf`. This paper is readable, intuitive, and insightful, and the reader should truly follow it. The stl model is a filtering method that decomposes a seasonal time series in three parts: trend, seasonal, and remainder. Let $\{Y_t\}_{t=1}^{T}$ be the time series, and we denote trend, seasonal, and remainder parts by $\{T_t\}_{t=1}^{T}$, $\{S_t\}_{t=1}^{T}$, and $\{R_t\}_{t=1}^{T}$; then we will have the following:

$$Y_t = T_t + S_t + R_t, t = 1, 2, \ldots, T.$$

Refer to Cleveland et al.'s paper for complete details.

Using the `stl` function from the `stats` package, we decompose the `AirPassengers` data as follows:

```
>AP_stl <- stl(AirPassengers,s.window=frequency(AirPassengers))
>summary(AP_stl)
 Call:
 stl(x = AirPassengers, s.window = frequency(AirPassengers))

 Time.series components:
    seasonal            trend          remainder
 Min.   :-73.3    Min.   :123    Min.   :-36.2
 1st Qu.:-25.1    1st Qu.:183    1st Qu.: -6.4
 Median : -5.5    Median :260    Median :  0.3
 Mean   :  0.1    Mean   :280    Mean   : -0.2
 3rd Qu.: 20.4    3rd Qu.:375    3rd Qu.:  5.9
 Max.   : 94.8    Max.   :497    Max.   : 48.6
 IQR:
     STL.seasonal STL.trend STL.remainder data
      46               192          12             180
   %  25.2            106.4         6.8            100.0

 Weights: all == 1

 Other components: List of 5
 $ win  : Named num [1:3] 12 21 13
 $ deg  : Named int [1:3] 0 1 1
 $ jump : Named num [1:3] 2 3 2
 $ inner: int 2
 $ outer: int 0
>jpeg("STL_Decompose_AirPassengers.jpeg")
>plot(AP_stl)
>dev.off()
windows
      2
>accuracy(forecast(AP_stl))
                 ME RMSE  MAE    MPE MAPE  MASE      ACF1
Training set 0.00498 11.2 8.29 -0.129 3.29 0.259 0.000898
```

By executing the preceding code, the following graph plot is obtained:

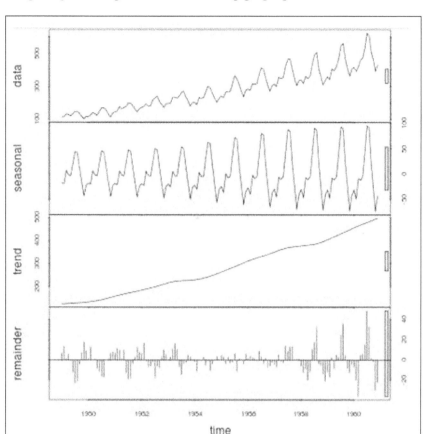

Figure 12: STL decompose of AirPassengers

It is important to specify the seasonality through the `s.window` option in the `stl` function. From the seasonal plot, we can see that each component increases with time. However, we get a clear picture of the different components of the passenger count over time. Though the seasonal part increases in magnitude, the pattern remains the same throughout the period. The trend shows a linear increase, which indicates the direction in which the series is headed. It is clear that seasonality plays an important role in this context.

Exercise: It has been previously remarked that seasonality does not appear to be a useful factor in the analysis of the `austres` dataset. Use the `stl` decomposition and check whether the observation holds true.

A more parametric model will be considered next, in the form of an exponential smoothing model.

Exponential smoothing state space model

The basic exponential smoothing model can be clearly defined. Denote the smoothing factor by $\alpha, 0 < \alpha < 1$, and initialize $S_1 = Y_1$. The basic exponential smoothing model is defined as follows:

$$S_t = \alpha Y_t + (1 - \alpha) S_{t-1} + \in_t$$

The details of the exponential models can be found at `https://labs.omniti.com/people/jesus/papers/holtwinters.pdf`. A more general model form is the **exponential smoothing state space model**. Here, a model is specified on three fronts, as in the stl model: the error component, the trend component, and the third is the seasonal component. In the `ets` function of the forecast package, the component can have **additive** effect denoted by **A**, it can have a **multiplicative** effect, denoted by M, or it might be asked to be automatically selected (Z), and this specification is possible for each of the components. The effect can be specified to be neither additive nor multiplicative with the letter N. A model in the `ets` function is thus specified with the first letter for error component, the second letter for the trend component, and the third letter for the seasonal component. Consequently, the notation `model="ZZZ"` means that each of the three components is selected automatically. `model="AMZ"` means that the error component is additive, the trend is multiplicative, the seasonal component is automatically chosen, and so on. Hyndman et al. (2008) provides a comprehensive account of the details of exponential smoothing methods. Next, we will use the `ets` function from the `forecast` package to fit the exponential smoothing model:

```
>uspop_sub <- subset(uspop,start=1,end=15)
>USpop_ets <- ets(uspop_sub)
>summary(USpop_ets)
ETS(A,A,N)

Call:
 ets(y = uspop_sub)

  Smoothing parameters:
    alpha = 0.8922
    beta  = 0.8922

  Initial states:
    l = 2.3837
    b = 1.7232

  sigma:  1.68

  AIC AICc  BIC
66.2 72.8 69.7

Training set error measures:
              ME RMSE MAE  MPE MAPE    MASE  ACF1
Training set 1.11 1.68 1.4 3.26  4.6 0.0318 -0.28
```

The `ets` function has fit an additive error for the error and trend component, while choosing not to add any of it for the seasonal factor. This makes sense because there is no seasonal component for the `uspop` dataset. Using this fitted model, we will `forecast` the US population for the period of 1940–70, calculate the accuracies for the training and test dataset with the `accuracy` function, and also compare with the `naive` forecasts:

```
>forecast(USpop_ets,h=4)
     Point Forecast Lo 80 Hi 80 Lo 95 Hi 95
1940            139    137    141    136    142
1950            156    151    160    149    162
1960            172    165    180    161    183
1970            189    178    200    173    205
>plot(forecast(USpop_ets,h=4))
>accuracy(forecast(USpop_ets,h=4),x=uspop[16:19])
                ME RMSE   MAE   MPE MAPE   MASE   ACF1
Training set 1.11 1.68  1.40 3.259 4.60  0.165  -0.28
Test set     2.33 9.02  8.26 0.578 4.86  0.973     NA
>accuracy(forecast(naive(uspop_sub),h=4),x=uspop[16:19])
                ME  RMSE    MAE  MPE MAPE MASE   ACF1
Training set  8.49  9.97   8.49 21.7 21.7 1.00  0.778
Test set     43.58 51.35  43.58 24.2 24.2 5.13     NA
```

Following is a plot depicting exponential smoothing for US population data:

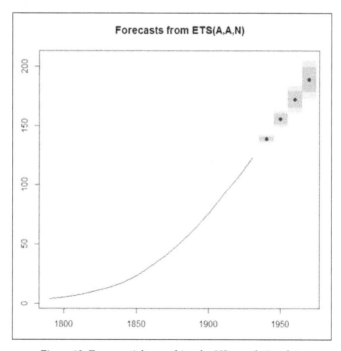

Figure 13: Exponential smoothing for US population data

The accuracy comparison is performed with the naïve forecasts, and we find that there is a significant improvement with the `ets` forecasts. Consequently, the `ets` forecasts are useful, and we can use them for future predictions.

Next, we will move on to the popular Box-Jenkins/ARIMA models.

Auto-regressive Integrated Moving Average (ARIMA) models

Box and Jenkins' approach to time series with the ARIMA models changed the way analysis and forecasts of time series data is performed. The ARIMA model is a special case of the more general linear process model, and for the time series $\{Y_t\}_{t=1}^{\infty}$ with the innovation process $\{\epsilon_t\}_{t=1}^{\infty}$, it is given as follows:

$$Y_t = \epsilon_t + \psi_1 \epsilon_{t-1} + \psi_2 \epsilon_{t-2} + \cdots$$

Here, $\psi_1, \psi_2, \ldots$ are the coefficients of the linear process. Note that there is no restriction on the lagged values of the innovation process and we indeed mean that there are infinite terms in this linear process model. In the popular autoregressive AR(p) model, p is the order of the AR model. This is given using the following:

$$Y_t = \phi_1 Y_{t-1} + \phi_2 Y_{t-2} + \cdots + \phi_p Y_{t-p} + \epsilon_t$$

The AR model can be shown to be a particular case of the linear process model. When the time series is expressed in terms of the innovation process, another useful model is the moving average MA(q) model of order q:

$$Y_t = \epsilon_t - \theta_1 \epsilon_{t-1} - \theta_2 \epsilon_{t-2} - \cdots - \theta_q \epsilon_{t-q}$$

A time series might depend on past errors as well as past values, and such a structural dependency is captured in an autoregressive moving average ARMA(p,q) model of order (p,q):

$$Y_t = \phi_1 Y_{t-1} + \phi_2 Y_{t-2} + \cdots + \phi_p Y_{t-p} + \epsilon_t - \theta_1 \epsilon_{t-1} - \theta_2 \epsilon_{t-2} - \cdots - \theta_q \epsilon_{t-q}$$

The order of p and q can be decided by the rule of thumb related through ACF and PACF in *Table 2*:

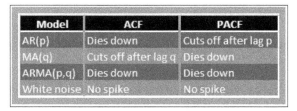

Model	ACF	PACF
AR(p)	Dies down	Cuts off after lag p
MA(q)	Cuts off after lag q	Dies down
ARMA(p,q)	Dies down	Dies down
White noise	No spike	No spike

Table 2: ACF and PACF for ARMA models

The ARMA models work well with stationary time series data, and here stationary loosely means that the variability of the series is constant throughout. It is a restrictive assumption, and for many time series phenomena, it does not hold true. In many practical scenarios, it has been that stationary can be obtained by differencing the series $\{Y_t\}_{t=1}^{\infty}$, that is, we can consider the difference $\{Y_t - Y_{t-1}\}_{t=2}^{\infty}$. The difference $Y_t - Y_{t-1}$ is a first-order difference, and sometimes, one may require higher order difference. In most practical scenarios, differencing up to order 4 has been known to bring stationarity. The order of differencing is generally denoted by the letter d, and applying ARMA models on the difference is referred to as an autoregressive integrated moving average model, or ARIMA model. A succinct abbreviation is ARIMA(p,d,q).

We have come across the seasonal component too often in this chapter, and it is accommodated in ARIMA through seasonal ARIMA models. The motivated reader can go through Chapter 10 of Tattar et al. (2017) for more details. We will simply add here that we have further notation in capital letters (P, D, Q) for the seasonal parameters, along with the frequency term. We are now in a position to understand the fitted model at the end of the previous section. The co2_arima accuracy had been accessed, and we will now look at the summary:

```
>summary(co2_arima)
Series: co2_sub
ARIMA(2,1,2)(1,1,2)[12]

Coefficients:
         ar1     ar2     ma1     ma2     sar1    sma1    sma2
        0.033   0.250  -0.369  -0.246  -0.828   0.014  -0.750
s.e.    0.341   0.122   0.342   0.197   0.230   0.210   0.173
```

```
sigma^2 estimated as 0.0837:  log likelihood=-73.4
AIC=163   AICc=163   BIC=195


Training set error measures:
                  ME   RMSE   MAE     MPE   MAPE  MASE    ACF1
Training set 0.0185 0.283 0.225 0.00541 0.0672 0.179 0.0119
```

The best fit ARIMA model order is (2,1,2)(1,1,2)[12], which means that the seasonal frequency is at 12 (something we already knew), and that the seasonal order (P,D,Q) is (1,1,2) and the ARIMA order (p,d,q) is (2,1,2). It is this differencing order that achieves stationarity. The forecasts are obtained and then visualized:

```
>jpeg("CO2_Forecasts.jpeg")
>plot(forecast(co2_arima,h=25))
```

The following figure shows the output:

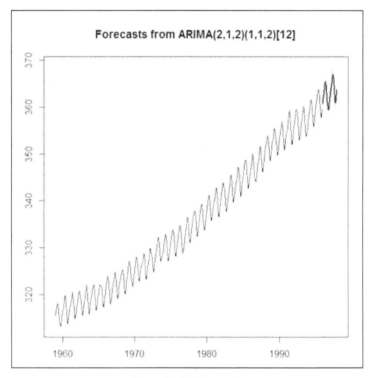

Figure 14: CO2 forecast

Consequently, we have fitted the ARIMA models for the carbon dioxide concentration levels.

Next, we will look at the nonlinear neural network time series models.

Auto-regressive neural networks

Neural networks have previously been seen in action for classification as well as regression problems. Since the time series are dependent observations, we need to tweak the architecture of neural networks to incorporate the dependency. The tweaking is to allow the lagged values of the time series as the members of the input layer. The rest of the architecture follows the same structure as the usual neural network. The nnetar function in the `forecast` stands for neural network autoregressive, and the `p=` option allows the lagged values of the time series, which we apply to the `gas` problem:

```
>gas_sub <- subset(gas,start=1,end=450)
>gas_nnetar <- nnetar(gas_sub,p=25,P=12,size=10,repeats=10)
>plot(forecast(gas_nnetar,h=26))
>accuracy(forecast(gas_nnetar,h=26),x=gas[451:476])
                ME  RMSE   MAE    MPE  MAPE  MASE     ACF1
Training set     2   318   237 -0.127  1.78 0.148  -0.0879
Test set      5033  6590  5234 10.566 10.94 3.276       NA
```

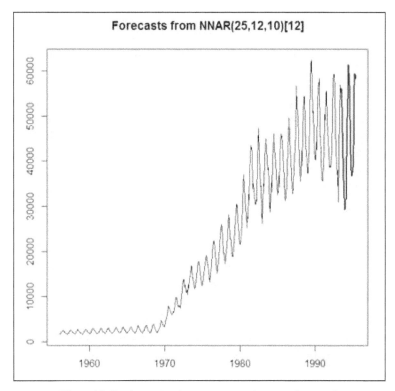

Figure 15: Gas forecast using auto-regressive neural network

We have now seen the autoregressive neural network in action.

Messing it all up

We began the chapter with a brief introduction of seven datasets and a mention of 21 datasets in *Table 1*. The data visualization provides moderate insight, and the accuracy metrics are useful in analyzing the usefulness of the models. A series of models have been introduced in this section up to now, and now we will mess it all up. A get_Accuracy function, which will fit six different time series models, is defined. The **LM**, which stands for **linear model**, has not been explained; neither has the TBATS model. The linear model is very simple, in that the time index is taken as a covariate. In general, if a time series has T observations, the covariate vector simply consists of the values 1, 2, 3, ..., T. We expect the linear model to perform poorly. The TBATS model won't be explained in further detail here and so it is recommended to do some extra reading in order to get more information on this. The get_Accuracy model fits each of the six models to the 21 datasets, names the model, and enlists its performance over the entire dataset. The following program gets the desired results:

```
>get_Accuracy<- function(ts){
+    tsname <- deparse(substitute(ts))
+    Acc_Mat <- data.frame(TSName = rep(tsname,6),Models=c(
+                "ETS","STL","LM","ARIMA","NNETAR","TBATS"),
+                 ME=numeric(6),RMSE=numeric(6),MAE=numeric(6),
+                 MPE=numeric(6), MAPE=numeric(6),MASE=numeric(6))
+    for(i in 1:nrow(Acc_Mat)){
+      Acc_Mat[1,3:8] <- accuracy(ets(ts)$fitted,ts)[1:6]
+      if(frequency(ts)>1) Acc_Mat[2,3:8] <- accuracy(ts-stl(ts,
+            frequency(ts))$time.series[,3],ts)[1:6] else
+        Acc_Mat[2,3:8] <- NA
+      Acc_Mat[3,3:8] <- accuracy(fitted(lm(ts~I(1:length(ts)))),ts)
[1:6]
+      Acc_Mat[4,3:8] <- accuracy(auto.arima(ts)$fitted,ts)[1:6]
+      Acc_Mat[5,3:8] <- accuracy(fitted(nnetar(ts)),ts)[1:6]
+      Acc_Mat[6,3:8] <- accuracy(fitted(tbats(ts)),ts)[1:6]
+    }
+    Acc_Mat
+ }
> TSDF <- data.frame(TSName=character(0),Models=character(0),
+ Accuracy=numeric(0))
> TSDF <- rbind(TSDF,get_Accuracy(AirPassengers))
> TSDF <- rbind(TSDF,get_Accuracy(BJsales))
> TSDF <- rbind(TSDF,get_Accuracy(JohnsonJohnson))
> TSDF <- rbind(TSDF,get_Accuracy(LakeHuron))
> TSDF <- rbind(TSDF,get_Accuracy(Nile))
> TSDF <- rbind(TSDF,get_Accuracy(UKgas))
> TSDF <- rbind(TSDF,get_Accuracy(UKDriverDeaths))
```

```
> TSDF <- rbind(TSDF,get_Accuracy(USAccDeaths))
> TSDF <- rbind(TSDF,get_Accuracy(WWWusage))
> TSDF <- rbind(TSDF,get_Accuracy(airmiles))
> TSDF <- rbind(TSDF,get_Accuracy(austres))
> TSDF <- rbind(TSDF,get_Accuracy(co2))
> TSDF <- rbind(TSDF,get_Accuracy(discoveries))
> TSDF <- rbind(TSDF,get_Accuracy(lynx))
> TSDF <- rbind(TSDF,get_Accuracy(nhtemp))
> TSDF <- rbind(TSDF,get_Accuracy(nottem))
> TSDF <- rbind(TSDF,get_Accuracy(presidents))
In addition: Warning message:
In ets(ts) :
  Missing values encountered. Using longest contiguous portion of time
series
> TSDF <- rbind(TSDF,get_Accuracy(treering))
> TSDF <- rbind(TSDF,get_Accuracy(gas))
> TSDF <- rbind(TSDF,get_Accuracy(uspop))
> TSDF <- rbind(TSDF,get_Accuracy(sunspots))
> write.csv(TSDF,"../Output/TS_All_Dataset_Accuracies.csv",row.
names=F)
```

The output of the preceding code block is the following table:

TSName	Model	ME	RMSE	MAE	MPE	MAPE	MASE
AirPassengers	ETS	1.5807	10.6683	7.7281	0.4426	2.8502	0.0164
AirPassengers	STL	-0.1613	11.9379	8.5595	-0.0662	3.4242	0.5515
AirPassengers	LM	0.0000	45.7362	34.4055	-1.2910	12.3190	0.7282
AirPassengers	ARIMA	1.3423	10.8462	7.8675	0.4207	2.8005	-0.0012
AirPassengers	NNETAR	-0.0118	14.3765	11.4899	-0.2964	4.2425	0.5567
AirPassengers	TBATS	0.4655	10.6614	7.7206	0.2468	2.8519	0.0215
BJsales	ETS	0.1466	1.3272	1.0418	0.0657	0.4587	-0.0110
BJsales	STL	NA	NA	NA	NA	NA	NA
BJsales	LM	0.0000	9.1504	7.1133	-0.1563	3.1686	0.9872
BJsales	ARIMA	0.1458	1.3281	1.0447	0.0651	0.4601	-0.0262
BJsales	NNETAR	-0.0001	1.4111	1.0849	-0.0040	0.4798	0.2888
BJsales	TBATS	0.1622	1.3566	1.0666	0.0732	0.4712	-0.0113
JohnsonJohnson	ETS	0.0495	0.4274	0.2850	1.0917	7.0339	-0.2948
JohnsonJohnson	STL	-0.0088	0.1653	0.1080	-0.5953	2.8056	-0.4155
JohnsonJohnson	LM	0.0000	1.6508	1.3287	22.6663	66.3896	0.6207
JohnsonJohnson	ARIMA	0.0677	0.4074	0.2676	2.0526	6.5007	0.0101
JohnsonJohnson	NNETAR	0.0003	0.3501	0.2293	-0.6856	5.8778	-0.0347

TSName	Model	ME	RMSE	MAE	MPE	MAPE	MASE
JohnsonJohnson	TBATS	0.0099	0.4996	0.3115	0.9550	7.5277	-0.1084
sunspots	ETS	-0.0153	15.9356	11.2451	#NAME?	Inf	0.0615
sunspots	STL	0.0219	12.2612	8.7973	NA	Inf	0.18
sunspots	LM	0	42.9054	34.1212	#NAME?	Inf	0.9196
sunspots	ARIMA	-0.0267	15.6006	11.0258	NA	Inf	-0.0106
sunspots	NNETAR	-0.0672	10.3105	7.6878	NA	Inf	0.0108
sunspots	TBATS	-0.0514	15.5788	11.0119	NA	Inf	-0.0013

Table 3: Accuracy for six models across 21 datasets

The overall message is the same as what was obtained in the introductory chapter for the classification problem. Since it is not always possible for us to carry out the inspection of the results all the time, it is desirable to combine the results of multiple models to put across a unified story of greater accuracy. We begin this task with the simple idea of bagging the exponential time series models.

Bagging and time series

In this section, we will only illustrate the bagging technique for the ETS model. The main purpose of bagging is to stabilize the predictions or forecasts. Here, we will base the bagging on the Box-Cox and Loess-based decomposition. Using 500 such bootstrap samples, the bagging model for ETS will be obtained:

```
>uspop_bagg_ets <- baggedETS(uspop_sub,bootstrapped_series =
+                            bld.mbb.bootstrap(uspop_sub, 500))
>forecast(uspop_bagg_ets,h=4);subset(uspop,start=16,end=19)
    Point Forecast Lo 100 Hi 100
1940            141    136    145
1950            158    150    165
1960            175    164    184
1970            193    178    204
Time Series:
Start = 1940
End = 1970
Frequency = 0.1
[1] 132 151 179 203
>plot(forecast(uspop_bagg_ets,h=4))
```

Is there an advantage to using the bagging method? We can quickly check this using the confidence intervals:

```
>forecast(uspop_bagg_ets,h=4)
     Point Forecast Lo 100 Hi 100
1940            141    136    145
1950            158    150    165
1960            175    164    184
1970            193    178    204
>forecast(USpop_ets,h=4,level=99.99)
     Point Forecast Lo 99.99 Hi 99.99
1940            139      133      146
1950            156      142      169
1960            172      150      194
1970            189      157      221
```

The confidence intervals of the bagged ETS are clearly shorter, and hence reflect the decrease in the variance, which is the main purpose of bagging:

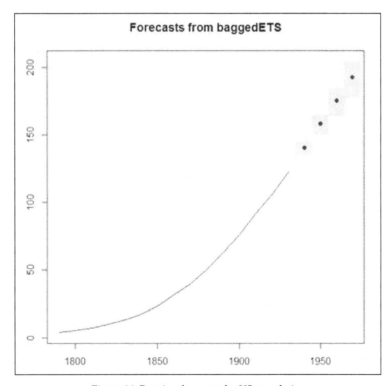

Figure 16: Bagging forecasts for US population

The accuracy comparison is also easily performed here:

```
>accuracy(forecast(USpop_ets,h=4),x=uspop[16:19])
                ME RMSE  MAE   MPE MAPE  MASE  ACF1
Training set 1.11 1.68 1.40 3.259 4.60 0.165 -0.28
Test set     2.33 9.02 8.26 0.578 4.86 0.973    NA
>accuracy(forecast(uspop_bagg_ets,h=4),x=subset(uspop,start=16,e
nd=19))
                ME RMSE  MAE    MPE MAPE   MASE  ACF1 Theil's U
Training set  1.137 1.44 1.24  2.226 4.48 0.0283 0.563        NA
Test set     -0.359 7.87 7.48 -0.995 4.63 0.1700 0.296     0.299
```

The advantage of ensembling homogeneous base learners is clearly seen here. Next, we move to the heterogeneous base learners and their ensemble.

Ensemble time series models

The `forecastHybrid` R package gives a platform to ensemble heterogeneous time series models. The main function that enables this task is the `hybridModel` function. The core function provides the option referred to as `models`. It takes as input a string of up to six characters, and the characters are representatives of the models: a for the `auto.arima` model, e for `ets`, f for `thetam`, n denoting `nnetar`, s for `stlm`, and finally, t represents `tbats`. Consequently, if we give a character string of `ae` to `models`, it will combine results from the ARIMA and ets models. This is illustrated on the CO_2 dataset for different combinations of the time series models:

```
>accuracy(forecast(co2_arima,h=25),x=co2[444:468])
                  ME  RMSE   MAE     MPE   MAPE  MASE   ACF1
Training set  0.0185 0.283 0.225  0.00541 0.0672 0.211 0.0119
Test set     -0.0332 0.349 0.270 -0.00912 0.0742 0.252    NA
>AP_Ensemble_02 <- hybridModel(co2_sub,models="ae")
Fitting the auto.arima model
Fitting the ets model
>accuracy(AP_Ensemble_02,h=25,x=co2[444:468])
             ME  RMSE   MAE     MPE   MAPE   ACF1 Theil's U
Test set 0.0258 0.271 0.219 0.00755 0.0653 0.00289     0.226
>AP_Ensemble_03 <- hybridModel(co2_sub,models="aen")
Fitting the auto.arima model
Fitting the ets model
Fitting the nnetar model
>accuracy(AP_Ensemble_03,h=25,x=co2[444:468])
            ME  RMSE   MAE    MPE  MAPE  ACF1 Theil's U
Test set 0.017 0.304 0.245 0.0049 0.073 0.282      0.25
```

```
>AP_Ensemble_04 <- hybridModel(co2_sub,models="aens")
Fitting the auto.arima model
Fitting the ets model
Fitting the nnetar model
Fitting the stlm model
>accuracy(AP_Ensemble_04,h=25,x=co2[444:468])
             ME   RMSE    MAE     MPE   MAPE  ACF1 Theil's U
Test set 0.0165  0.275  0.221 0.00478  0.066 0.209     0.226
>AP_Ensemble_05 <- hybridModel(co2_sub,models="aenst")
Fitting the auto.arima model
Fitting the ets model
Fitting the nnetar model
Fitting the stlm model
Fitting the tbats model
>accuracy(AP_Ensemble_05,h=25,x=co2[444:468])
             ME   RMSE    MAE     MPE   MAPE  ACF1 Theil's U
Test set 0.0123  0.267  0.216 0.00348 0.0645 0.153      0.22
```

Though the discussion of the ensemble is very brief here, time series literature has only recently begun to adapt to ensembling techniques.

Exercise: The options of `weights` and `errorMethod` are crucial to put different time series models together. Explore these options for the different datasets introduced and discussed in the chapter.

Summary

Time series data poses new challenges and complexities. The chapter began with an introduction to important and popular datasets. We looked at different time series and their intricacies. Visualization of time series provides great insight, and the time series plots, along with the seasonal plot, are complementarily used for clear ideas and niche implementations. Accuracy metrics are different for the time series, and we looked at more than a handful of these. The concepts of ACF and PACF are vital in model identification, and seasonal components are also important to the modeling of time series. We also saw that different models express different datasets, and the degree of variation is something similar to the usual regression problems. The bagging of time series (ets only) reduces the variance of the forecasts. Combining heterogeneous base learners was discussed in the concluding section. The next chapter is the concluding chapter. We will summarize the main takeaways from the first eleven chapters and outline some shortcomings and further scope.

12
What's Next?

Throughout this book, we have learned about ensemble learning and explored its applications in many scenarios. In the introductory chapter, we looked at different examples, datasets, and models, and found that there is no single model or technique that performs better than the others. This means that our guard should always be up when dealing with this matter, and hence the analyst has to proceed with extreme caution. The approach of selecting the best model from among the various models means that we reject all of the models whose performance is slightly less than that of the others, and hence a lot of resources are wasted in pursuit of the *best* model.

In *Chapter 7, The General Ensemble Technique*, we saw that if we have multiple classifiers with each classifier being better than a random guess, majority voting of the classifiers gives improved performance. We also saw that with a fairly good number of classifiers, the overall accuracy of the majority voting is higher than the most accurate classifier. Though majority voting works on the oversimplified assumption that the classifiers are independent classifiers, the basis and importance of *ensemble learning* is realized and the prospect looks brighter as we are assured of an ensemble classifier with the highest accuracy. The classifiers or models of the ensemble are called the *base classifiers/learners/models*. If all the base models belong to the same family of models, or if the family is a logistic model, a neural network, a decision tree, or an SVM, then we will classify these as a homogeneous ensemble. If the base models belong to two or more families of models, then the ensemble is referred to as a heterogeneous ensemble.

A fundamental aspect of ensemble learning lies in *resampling techniques*. The jackknife and bootstrap methods were introduced in *Chapter 2, Bootstrapping,* and these two methods were illustrated for different classes of models. The jackknife method uses pseudovalues, and we witnessed its application in a few complex scenarios. The pseudovalues are underutilized in the machine learning domain, and they might be useful in scenarios in which the relationship or a parameter of interest is quite complex and a more flexible approach may be possible. The concept of pseudovalues can also be used in ensemble diagnostics, and a *pseudoaccuracy* measure can be created that will give the impact of the classifier in the ensemble additional accuracy. Efron and Tibshirani (1990) discuss the different methods available for obtaining bootstrap samples. In the resamples that we obtained in the steps for bagging and random forest, we follow the simple bootstrap samples of drawing observations with replacement. Accessing the different sampling methods that are driven from existing bootstrap literature is a potential area of work for the future.

Bagging, random forest, and boosting are the homogeneous ensembles that have the decision tree as their base learner. The decision tree discussed in this book can be referred to as the frequentist method or the classical method. A Bayesian implementation of the decision tree is available in a technique known as the **Bayesian additive regression tree**. The R implementation of this method is available in the BART package, located at `https://cran.r-project.org/web/packages/BART/index.html`. The theoretical foundations of BART are available at `https://arxiv.org/pdf/0806.3286.pdf`. The extension of homogeneous ensembles based on BART needs to be undertaken in a comprehensive way. In particular, bagging and random forests need to be extended with BART as a base learner.

Ensemble models for heterogeneous base models are set up using the stack ensembling method. For classification problems, we can expect weighted voting to be more useful than simple majority voting. Similarly, the weighted prediction of the models is expected to perform better than simple averaging. The statistical tests proposed to test the similarity of base models are all *classical* tests. Bayesian measures of agreement are expected to give us further guidelines, and the author of this book is now aware of such assessments being performed in the context of ensemble diversity. You can read Broemeling (2009) for more information on this at `https://www.crcpress.com/Bayesian-Methods-for-Measures-of-Agreement/Broemeling/p/book/9781420083415`. Furthermore, when it comes to large datasets, the option of generating an independent set of models needs to be systematically developed.

Time series data is of a different structure, and the dependency of the observations means that we can't directly apply the ensemble methods without the appropriate tweaking. *Chapter 11, Ensembling Time Series Models*, looks at this topic in more detail. Random forests have been developed for time series data very recently. An implementation of the random forests can be seen at `https://petolau.github.io/Ensemble-of-trees-for-forecasting-time-series/`, and if you are interested, you can refer to this link for more information.

High-dimensional data analysis is another more recent topic that is not covered in this book. Chapter 12 of Buhlmann and van de Geer (2011) (see `https://www.springer.com/in/book/9783642201912`) gives useful pointers in this area. For boosting data, the treatise of Schapire and Freund (2012) (at `https://mitpress.mit.edu/books/boosting`) is a real treasure. Zhou (2012) (found at `https://www.crcpress.com/Ensemble-Methods-Foundations-and-Algorithms/Zhou/p/book/9781439830031`) is also a very important book on ensemble methods, and this book benefits from its insights. Kuncheva (2004-14) (found at `https://onlinelibrary.wiley.com/doi/book/10.1002/9781118914564`) is probably the first book to detail ensemble methods, and it contains a lot of other details regarding ensemble diagnostics. Dixit (2017) (found at `https://www.packtpub.com/big-data-and-business-intelligence/ensemble-machine-learning`) is another recent title on ensemble methods, and the methods are illustrated in the book using Python software.

Finally, the reader should always keep continuous track of recent developments. For R implementation, the best place for resources is `https://cran.r-project.org/web/views/MachineLearning.html`.

Next, we will look at a list of important journals. A lot of developments and discussions are taking place in these journals on the subject of machine learning, and therefore ensemble learning too. These journals are as follows:

- Journal of Machine Learning Research (`http://www.jmlr.org/`)
- IEEE Transactions on Pattern Analysis and Machine Intelligence (`https://ieeexplore.ieee.org/xpl/RecentIssue.jsp?punumber=34`)
- Pattern Recognition Letters (`https://www.journals.elsevier.com/pattern-recognition-letters`)
- Machine Learning(`https://www.springer.com/computer/ai/journal/10994`)
- Neurocomputing (`https://www.journals.elsevier.com/neurocomputing`)
- And last, but not least (though this is not a journal), `https://www.packtpub.com/tech/Machine-Learning`

If you found this book useful, we should meet again in the next edition!

Bibliography

References

Abraham, B. and Ledolter, J. (https://onlinelibrary.wiley.com/doi/book/10.1002/9780470316610), 1983. *Statistical methods for forecasting*. J. Wiley

Andersen, P.K., Klein, J.P. and Rosthøj, S., (https://doi.org/10.1093/biomet/90.1.15) 2003. Generalised linear models for correlated pseudo-observations, with applications to multi-state models. *Biometrika, 90*(1), pp.15-27.

Berk, R.A., (https://www.springer.com/in/book/9783319440477) 2016. *Statistical learning from a regression perspective, Second Edition*. New York: Springer.

Bou-Hamad, I., Larocque, D. and Ben-Ameur, H., (https://projecteuclid.org/euclid.ssu/1315833185) 2011. A review of survival trees. *Statistics Surveys, 5*, pp.44-71.

Box, G.E., Jenkins, G.M., Reinsel, G.C. and Ljung, G.M., (https://onlinelibrary.wiley.com/doi/book/10.1002/9781118619193)2015. *Time series analysis: forecasting and control*. John Wiley & Sons.

Breiman, L., (https://link.springer.com/article/10.1007/BF00058655) 1996. Bagging predictors. *Machine learning, 24*(2), pp.123-140.

Breiman, L., Friedman, J.H., Olshen, R.A. and Stone, C.J., (https://www.taylorfrancis.com/books/9781351460491) 1984. *Classification and regression trees*. Routledge.

Broemeling, L.D., (https://www.crcpress.com/Bayesian-Methods-for-Measures-of-Agreement/Broemeling/p/book/9781420083415)2009. *Bayesian methods for measures of agreement*. Chapman and Hall/CRC.

Bühlmann, P. and Van De Geer, S., (https://www.springer.com/in/book/9783642201912) 2011. *Statistics for high-dimensional data: methods, theory and applications.* Springer Science & Business Media.

Chatterjee, S. and Hadi, A.S., (https://www.wiley.com/en-us/Regression+Analysis+by+Example%2C+5th+Edition-p-9780470905845) 2012. Regression Analysis by Example, Fifth edition. John Wiley & Sons.

Ciaburro, G., (https://www.packtpub.com/big-data-and-business-intelligence/regression-analysis-r) 2018. Regression Analysis with R, Packt Publishing Ltd.

Cleveland, R.B., Cleveland, W.S., McRae, J.E. and Terpenning, I., (http://www.nniiem.ru/file/news/2016/stl-statistical-model.pdf) 1990. STL: A Seasonal-Trend Decomposition. *Journal of Official Statistics*, 6(1), pp.3-73.

Cox, D.R., (https://eclass.uoa.gr/modules/document/file.php/MATH394/Papers/%5BCox(1972)%5D Regression Models and Life Tables.pdf) 1972. Regression models and life-tables. *Journal of the Royal Statistical Society*. Series B (Methodological), **34**, pp. 187-220

Cox, D.R., (https://academic.oup.com/biomet/article-abstract/62/2/269/337051) 1975. Partial likelihood. *Biometrika*, 62(2), pp.269-276.

Dixit, A., (https://www.packtpub.com/big-data-and-business-intelligence/ensemble-machine-learning)2017. *Ensemble Machine Learning: A beginner's guide that combines powerful machine learning algorithms to build optimized models.* Packt Publishing Ltd.

Draper, N.R. and Smith, H., (https://onlinelibrary.wiley.com/doi/book/10.1002/9781118625590)1999/2014. *Applied regression analysis*, (Vol. 326). John Wiley & Sons.

Efron, B. (https://projecteuclid.org/download/pdf_1/euclid.aos/1176344552) 1979. Bootstrap methods (https://link.springer.com/chapter/10.1007/978-1-4612-4380-9_41): another look at the jackknife, *The Annals of Statistics*, 7, 1-26.

Efron, B. and Hastie, T., 2016. (https://web.stanford.edu/~hastie/CASI_files/PDF/casi.pdf) *Computer age statistical inference* (Vol. 5). Cambridge University Press.

Efron, B. and Tibshirani, R.J., (https://www.crcpress.com/An-Introduction-to-the-Bootstrap/Efron-Tibshirani/p/book/9780412042317) 1994. *An introduction to the bootstrap.* CRC press.

Friedman, J.H., Hastie, T. and Tibshirani, R. (https://projecteuclid.org/download/pdf_1/euclid.aos/1016218223)2001. Greedy function approximation: A gradient boosting machine. *Annals of Statistics*, 29(5):1189–1232.

Gordon, L. and Olshen, R.A., (https://europepmc.org/abstract/med/4042086)1985. Tree-structured survival analysis. Cancer treatment reports, 69(10), pp.1065-1069.

Hastie, T., Tibshirani, R., and Friedman, J. (https://www.springer.com/in/book/9780387848570) ,2009., *The Elements of Statistical Learning, Second Edition*, Springer.

Haykin, S.S, 2009. (https://www.pearson.com/us/higher-education/program/Haykin-Neural-Networks-and-Learning-Machines-3rd-Edition/PGM320370.html) *Neural networks and learning machines* (Vol. 3). Upper Saddle River, NJ, USA:: Pearson.

Kalbfleisch, J.D. and Prentice, R.L. (https://onlinelibrary.wiley.com/doi/abs/10.2307/3315078), 2002. *The statistical analysis of failure time data*. John Wiley & Sons.

Kuncheva, L.I., (https://www.wiley.com/en-us/Combining+Pattern+Classifiers%3A+Methods+and+Algorithms%2C+2nd+Edition-p-9781118315231) 2014. *Combining pattern classifiers: methods and algorithms*. Second Edition. John Wiley & Sons.

LeBlanc, M. and Crowley, J., (https://www.jstor.org/stable/2532300)1992. Relative risk trees for censored survival data. *Biometrics*, pp.411-425.

Lee, S.S. and Elder, J.F., (http://citeseerx.ist.psu.edu/viewdoc/download;jsessionid=6B151AAB29C69A4D4C35C8C4BBFC67F5?doi=10.1.1.34.1753&rep=rep1&type=pdf) 1997. Bundling heterogeneous classifiers with advisor perceptrons. *White Paper*.

Mardia, K. , Kent, J., and Bibby, J.M.., (https://www.elsevier.com/books/multivariate-analysis/mardia/978-0-08-057047-1) 1979. *Multivariate analysis*. Academic Press.

Montgomery, D.C., Peck, E.A. and Vining, G.G., (https://www.wiley.com/en-us/Introduction+to+Linear+Regression+Analysis%2C+5th+Edition-p-9781118627365) 2012. *Introduction to linear regression analysis* (Vol. 821). John Wiley & Sons.

Perrone, M.P., and Cooper, L.N., (https://www.worldscientific.com/doi/abs/10.1142/9789812795885_0025)1993. When Networks Disagree: Ensemble Methods for Hybrid Neural Networks. In Mammone, R.J. (Ed.), *Neural Networks for Speech and Image Processing*. Chapman Hall.

Ripley, B.D., (http://admin.cambridge.org/fk/academic/subjects/statistics-probability/computational-statistics-machine-learning-and-information-sc/pattern-recognition-and-neural-networks)2007. *Pattern recognition and neural networks*. Cambridge university press.

Quenouille, M.H., (https://www.cambridge.org/core/journals/mathematical-proceedings-of-the-cambridge-philosophical-society/article/approximate-tests-of-correlation-in-timeseries-3/F6D24B2A8574F1716E44BE788696F9C7) 1949, July. Approximate tests of correlation in time-series 3. In *Mathematical Proceedings of the Cambridge Philosophical Society* (Vol. 45, No. 3, pp. 483-484). Cambridge University Press.

Quinlan, J. R. (1993), (https://www.elsevier.com/books/c45/quinlan/978-0-08-050058-4) *C4.5: Programs for Machine Learning*, Morgan Kaufmann.

Ridgeway, G., Madigan, D. and Richardson, T., (http://dimacs.rutgers.edu/archive/Research/MMS/PAPERS/BNBR.pdf) 1999, January. Boosting methodology for regression problems. In *AISTATS*.

Schapire, R.E. and Freund, Y., (http://dimacs.rutgers.edu/archive/Research/MMS/PAPERS/BNBR.pdf) 2012. *Boosting: Foundations and algorithms*. MIT press.

Seni, G. and Elder, J.F., (https://www.morganclaypool.com/doi/abs/10.2200/S00240ED1V01Y200912DMK002)2010. Ensemble methods in data mining: improving accuracy through combining predictions. *Synthesis Lectures on Data Mining and Knowledge Discovery*, 2(1), pp.1-126.

Tattar, P.N., Ramaiah, S. and Manjunath, B.G., (https://onlinelibrary.wiley.com/doi/book/10.1002/9781119152743) 2016. *A Course in Statistics with R*. John Wiley & Sons.

Tattar, P.N., 2017. (https://www.packtpub.com/big-data-and-business-intelligence/statistical-application-development-r-and-python-second-edition) *Statistical Application Development with R and Python*. Packt Publishing Ltd.

Tattar, P., Ojeda, T., Murphy, S.P., Bengfort, B. and Dasgupta, A., (https://www.packtpub.com/big-data-and-business-intelligence/practical-data-science-cookbook-second-edition) 2017. *Practical Data Science Cookbook*. Packt Publishing Ltd.

Zhang, H. and Singer, B.H., (https://www.springer.com/in/book/9781441968234)2010. *Recursive partitioning and applications*. Springer Science & Business Media.

Zemel, R.S. and Pitassi, T., (http://papers.nips.cc/paper/1797-a-gradient-based-boosting-algorithm-for-regression-problems.pdf)2001. A gradient-based boosting algorithm for regression problems. In *Advances in neural information processing systems* (pp. 696-702).

Zhou, Z.H., (https://www.crcpress.com/Ensemble-Methods-Foundations-and-Algorithms/Zhou/p/book/9781439830031)2012. *Ensemble methods: foundations and algorithms*. Chapman and Hall/CRC.

R package references

Prabhanjan Tattar (2015). ACSWR: A Companion Package for the Book "A Course in Statistics with R". R package version 1.0.

https://CRAN.R-project.org/package=ACSWR

Alfaro, E., Gamez, M. Garcia, N.(2013). adabag: An R Package for Classification with Boosting and Bagging. Journal of Statistical Software, 54(2), 1-35. URL http://www.jstatsoft.org/v54/i02/.

Angelo Canty and Brian Ripley (2017). boot: Bootstrap R (S-Plus) Functions. R package version 1.3-19.

John Fox and Sanford Weisberg (2011). An {R} Companion to Applied Regression, Second Edition. Thousand Oaks CA: Sage. URL:

http://socserv.socsci.mcmaster.ca/jfox/Books/Companion car

Max Kuhn. Contributions from Jed Wing, Steve Weston, Andre Williams, Chris Keefer, Allan Engelhardt, Tony Cooper, Zachary Mayer, Brenton Kenkel, the R Core Team, Michael Benesty, Reynald Lescarbeau, Andrew Ziem, Luca Scrucca, Yuan Tang, Can Candan and Tyler Hunt. (2017). caret: Classification and Regression Training. R package version 6.0-77. https://CRAN.R-project.org/package=caret

Zachary A. Deane-Mayer and Jared E. Knowles (2016). `caretEnsemble`:
Ensembles of Caret Models. R package version 2.0.0.
`https://CRAN.R-project.org/package=caretEnsemble`

Venables, W. N. & Ripley, B. D. (2002) Modern Applied Statistics
with S. Fourth Edition. Springer, New York. ISBN 0-387-95457-0 `class`

Marie Chavent, Vanessa Kuentz, Benoit Liquet and Jerome Saracco
(2017). `ClustOfVar`: Clustering of Variables. R package version 1.1.
`https://CRAN.R-project.org/package=ClustOfVar`

David Meyer, Evgenia Dimitriadou, Kurt Hornik, Andreas Weingessel
and Friedrich Leisch (2017). `e1071`: Misc Functions of the Department
of Statistics, Probability Theory Group (Formerly: E1071), TU Wien.
R package version 1.6-8. `https://CRAN.R-project.org/package=e1071`

Alboukadel Kassambara and Fabian Mundt (2017). `factoextra`: Extract
and Visualize the Results of Multivariate Data Analyses. R package
version 1.0.5. `https://CRAN.R-project.org/package=factoextra`

Sebastien Le, Julie Josse, Francois Husson (2008). `FactoMineR`: An R
Package for Multivariate Analysis. Journal of Statistical Software,
25(1), 1-18. 10.18637/jss.v025.i01

Alina Beygelzimer, Sham Kakadet, John Langford, Sunil Arya, David
Mount and Shengqiao Li (2013). FNN: Fast Nearest Neighbor Search
Algorithms and Applications. R package version 1.1.
`https://CRAN.R-project.org/package=FNN`

Hyndman RJ (2017). `_forecast`: Forecasting functions for time series
and linear models_. R package version 8.2, <URL:
`http://pkg.robjhyndman.com/forecast`>.

David Shaub and Peter Ellis (2018). forecastHybrid: Convenient Functions for Ensemble Time Series Forecasts. R package version 2.0.10. `https://CRAN.R-project.org/package=forecastHybrid`

Greg Ridgeway with contributions from others (2017). `gbm`: Generalized Boosted Regression Models. R package version 2.1.3. `https://CRAN.R-project.org/package=gbm`

Vincent J Carey. Ported to R by Thomas Lumley and Brian Ripley. Note that maintainers are not available to give advice on using a package they did not author. (2015). `gee`: Generalized Estimation Equation Solver. R package version 4.13-19. `https://CRAN.R-project.org/package=gee`

The H2O.ai team (2017). `h2o`: R Interface for H2O. R package version 3.16.0.2. `https://CRAN.R-project.org/package=h2o`

Andrea Peters and Torsten Hothorn (2017). `ipred`: Improved Predictors. R package version 0.9-6. `https://CRAN.R-project.org/package=ipred`

Alexandros Karatzoglou, Alex Smola, Kurt Hornik, Achim Zeileis (2004). `kernlab` - An S4 Package for Kernel Methods in R. Journal of Statistical Software 11(9), 1-20. URL `http://www.jstatsoft.org/v11/i09/`

Friedrich Leisch & Evgenia Dimitriadou (2010). `mlbench`: Machine Learning Benchmark Problems. R package version 2.1-1.

Daniel J. Stekhoven (2013). `missForest`: Nonparametric Missing Value Imputation using Random Forest. R package version 1.4.

Alan Genz, Frank Bretz, Tetsuhisa Miwa, Xuefei Mi, Friedrich Leisch,

Fabian Scheipl, Torsten Hothorn (2017). `mvtnorm`: Multivariate Normal

and t Distributions. R package version 1.0-6. URL

`http://CRAN.R-project.org/package=mvtnorm`

Beck M (2016). `_NeuralNetTools`: Visualization and Analysis Tools for

Neural Networks_. R package version 1.5.0, <URL:

`https://CRAN.R-project.org/package=NeuralNetTools>`.

Venables, W. N. & Ripley, B. D. (2002) Modern Applied Statistics

with S. Fourth Edition. Springer, New York. ISBN 0-387-95457-0 `nnet`

Michael P. Fay, Pamela A. Shaw (2010). Exact and Asymptotic Weighted

Logrank Tests for Interval Censored Data: The interval R Package.

Journal of Statistical Software, 36(2), 1-34. URL

`http://www.jstatsoft.org/v36/i02/.perm`

Hadley Wickham (2011). The Split-Apply-Combine Strategy for Data

Analysis. Journal of Statistical Software, 40(1), 1-29. URL

`http://www.jstatsoft.org/v40/i01/.plyr`

Xavier Robin, Natacha Turck, Alexandre Hainard, Natalia Tiberti,

Frédérique Lisacek, Jean-Charles Sanchez and Markus Müller (2011).

`pROC`: an open-source package for R and S+ to analyze and compare ROC

curves. BMC Bioinformatics, 12, p. 77. DOI: 10.1186/1471-2105-12-77

`http://www.biomedcentral.com/1471-2105/12/77/`

Maja Pohar Perme and Mette Gerster (2017). `pseudo`: Computes

Pseudo-Observations for Modeling. R package version 1.4.3.

`https://CRAN.R-project.org/package=pseudo`

A. Liaw and M. Wiener (2002). Classification and Regression by

`randomForest`. R News 2(3), 18--22.

Aleksandra Paluszynska and Przemyslaw Biecek (2017).

  `randomForestExplainer`: Explaining and Visualizing Random Forests in

  Terms of Variable Importance. R package version 0.9.

  `https://CRAN.R-project.org/package=randomForestExplainer`

Terry Therneau, Beth Atkinson and Brian Ripley (2017). `rpart`:

  Recursive Partitioning and Regression Trees. R package version

  4.1-11. `https://CRAN.R-project.org/package=rpart`

Prabhanjan Tattar (2013). RSADBE: Data related to the book "R

  Statistical Application Development by Example". R package version

  1.0. `https://CRAN.R-project.org/package=RSADBE`

Therneau T (2015). _A Package for Survival Analysis in S_. version

  2.38, <URL: `https://CRAN.R-project.org/package=survival`>. `survival`

Terry M. Therneau and Patricia M. Grambsch (2000). _Modeling Survival

  Data: Extending the Cox Model_. Springer, New York. ISBN

  0-387-98784-3.

Tianqi Chen, Tong He, Michael Benesty, Vadim Khotilovich and Yuan

  Tang (2018). `xgboost`: Extreme Gradient Boosting. R package version

  0.6.4.1. `https://CRAN.R-project.org/package=xgboost`

Other Books You May Enjoy

If you enjoyed this book, you may be interested in these other books by Packt:

Machine Learning with R - Second Edition

Brett Lantz

ISBN: 9781784393908

- Harness the power of R to build common machine learning algorithms with real-world data science applications
- Get to grips with R techniques to clean and prepare your data for analysis, and visualize your results
- Discover the different types of machine learning models and learn which is best to meet your data needs and solve your analysis problems
- Classify your data with Bayesian and nearest neighbor methods

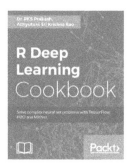

R Deep Learning Cookbook

Dr. PKS Prakash, Achyutuni Sri Krishna Rao

ISBN: 9781787121089

- Build deep learning models in different application areas using TensorFlow, H2O, and MXnet
- Analyzing a Deep boltzmann machine
- Setting up and Analysing Deep belief networks
- Building supervised model using various machine learning algorithms
- Set up variants of basic convolution function
- Represent data using Autoencoders
- Explore generative models available in Deep Learning

Leave a review - let other readers know what you think

Please share your thoughts on this book with others by leaving a review on the site that you bought it from. If you purchased the book from Amazon, please leave us an honest review on this book's Amazon page. This is vital so that other potential readers can see and use your unbiased opinion to make purchasing decisions, we can understand what our customers think about our products, and our authors can see your feedback on the title that they have worked with Packt to create. It will only take a few minutes of your time, but is valuable to other potential customers, our authors, and Packt. Thank you!

Index

A

adabag packages
  using 142-144
AdaBoost algorithm 122
adaptive boosting algorithm
  about 124-134, 150
  working 150-154
additive effect 322
advantages, extreme gradient boosting
     implementation
  cross platform 163
  cross-validation 163
  missing values 163
  parallel computing 163
  pruning 163
  regularization 163
  saving and reloading 163
Akaike Information Criteria (AIC) 1
amyotrophic lateral sclerosis (ALS) 141
area under curve (AUC) 30
auto-correlation function (ACF) 313
Auto-regressive Integrated Moving
     Average (ARIMA) models 324, 325

B

bagging
  about 76-85
  comparing, with boosting 145, 146
  comparing, with random forests 145, 146
  for regression data 259-261
  technique, describing 330-332
BART package
  reference 336
Bayesian Information Criteria (BIC) 1

board stiffness dataset 14
boot package 59-62
Bootstrap
  about 45, 46
  eigen values 55-59
  parametric bootstrap 52-55
  rule of thumb 59
  standard error of correlation
     coefficient 47-51
bootstrap hypothesis testing
     problems 62-64

C

Chi-square Automatic Interaction
     Detector (CHAID) 94
chi-square test 32-34
Classification and Regression
     Trees (CART)
  about 94
  advantages 94
  drawbacks 94
classification trees 72-76
class prediction 204-209
Cohen's statistic 214, 215
complementary statistical tests
  about 30
  chi-square test 32-34
  McNemar test 32-34
  permutation test 30, 31
  ROC test 34, 35
complexity parameter (Cp) 74
contingency table 211
correlation coefficient measure 213, 214
Cox proportional hazards models 288-292

D

E

F

G

H

I

Kohavi-Wolpert measure 218, 219
measurement 221
Iris dataset 8
iterative reweighted least squares
(IRLS) algorithm 16

J

jackknife technique
about 38, 39
for mean and variance 39-42
pseudovalues method for survival data 42
Journal of Machine Learning Research
reference 337

K

Kaplan-Meier estimator 279
k-NN bagging 88-90
k-NN classifier 86-88
Kohavi-Wolpert measure 218, 219

L

linear regression model 242-253
logistic regression model
about 15, 16
for hypothyroid classification 16, 17
logrank test 270

M

Machine Learning
reference 337
McNemar test 32-34
memoryless property 271
metrics 310, 311
missForest function
reference 115
missing data
handling, random forests used 115-118
modeling dilemma 26
model selection 1
multishapes dataset 12, 13
multivariate statistics 235

N

Naïve Bayes classifier
about 20
for hypothyroid classification 20
Nelson-Aalen estimator 279
neural networks
about 17, 18, 253-255
for hypothyroid classification 19
neurocomputing
reference 337
nonparametric inference 278-284
number prediction 202-204

O

Overseas Visitors dataset
about 10, 11
reference 10

P

pairwise measure
about 210, 211
Cohen's statistic 214, 215
correlation coefficient measure 213, 214
disagreement measure 211, 212
double-fault measure 216
Q-statistic 212, 213
Yule's coefficient 212
partial auto-correlation function (PACF)
about 313-317
reference 313
partial likelihood function 288
Pattern Recognition Letters
reference 337
permutation test 30
Pima Indians Diabetes dataset 8
Primary Biliary Cirrhosis dataset 12
Principal Component Analysis (PCA) 235
proximity plots
using 105, 106
pruning 72-76

Q

Q-statistic 212, 213

W

waveform datasets 6
Weibull distribution 272-278

X

xgboost package
  about 163-169
  reference 163

Y

Yule's coefficient 212